Ambassadors at Sea

HENRY E.

CATTO

JR.

Ambassadors at Sea

✳

THE HIGH AND LOW
ADVENTURES
OF A DIPLOMAT

University of Texas Press, Austin

Requests for permission to reproduce material from this work should be sent to Permissions, University of Texas Press, Box 7819, Austin, TX 78713-7819.

∞ The paper used in this publication meets the minimum requirements of American National Standard for Information Sciences—Permanence of Paper for Printed Library Materials, ANSI z39.48-1984.

LIBRARY OF CONGRESS CATALOGING-IN-PUBLICATION DATA

Catto, Henry E., Jr. 1930–
Ambassadors at sea : the high and low adventures of a diplomat /
Henry E. Catto, Jr. — 1st University of Texas Press ed.
p.   cm.
Includes index. ISBN 0-292-71212-X (alk. paper)
1. Catto, Henry E., 1930– . 2. Diplomats—United States—Biography.
3. United States—Foreign relations—1945–1989. 4. United States—Foreign relations—1989– 5. United States Information Agency—Biography. I. Title.
E840.8.C38A3   1998
327.73′0092—dc21
[B]   98-23612

TO JESSICA, OF COURSE.

Contents

Preface

MY GRANDFATHER, John Innes Nichol Catto, was born in Ceylon (now Sri Lanka) on his father's coffee plantation, near the highland city of Kandi. When Alexander, his father, died young, his mother gathered up her brood and returned to Aberdeenshire, whence the family sprang.

They lived on a farm (which I was to visit many years later), and Grandfather attended an excellent school in Aberdeen. In 1886, then grown, he moved to Texas and worked for the Texas Land and Mortgage Company. He married a Tennessee girl named Lizzie Paxton Gray, who bore him four sons and two daughters, and they lived happily ever after. He never became an American citizen.

That's it. No record remains of what must have been a fascinating life. No letters, no diaries, no idea of his fears and failures, triumphs and tragedies.

I have often brooded on the pity of it all. What a pleasure it would have been if he had left some sort of record—a memoir, a diary. It would in this Age of Roots have given my parents, me, and my offspring a taste of where we came from and who we are.

Thinking about this grandfather whom I knew so briefly and reflecting, with some surprise, on my own varied life led me to the vow that I would write a memoir of my own for the benefit of future generations and also for myself. I've often said I don't know what I think until I write it down, and while I've been no Samuel Pepys, I have kept a good record of what I've done. Furthermore, I have proved that guilt has its uses.

In 1969, when my wife, Jessica, our four children, and I moved from San Antonio to Washington, D.C., my mother and father were crushed. They loved having their only son, his lively wife, and their four grandchildren nearby. Guilt-stricken and trying to lighten their sadness, I assured Mother that we would be gone only two years and that I would tape our activities every week and send her the tapes.

As it turned out, my first promise proved, well, inaccurate. We didn't return permanently for twenty-four years. I did better with the promise of tapes. Over the years, they piled up in a big box in Mother's room, and just a year or so before she died in 1980, she and Dad asked Hazel Johnson, a retired colleague from our family firm, to transcribe the lot.

It was a huge job, but Hazel soldiered on — and on. When she finished, Mother and Dad presented me with four volumes totaling more than two thousand pages, chockablock with names, dates, and events long forgotten. These pages, supplemented by other tapes, sporadic diaries, engagement books, and the memories of family and friends enabled me to put together what follows.

Acknowledgments

SO LITTLE space, so much to acknowledge. A great chunk of thanks goes to Hazel Johnson, who transcribed a small mountain of tapes, as well as to Kay Evans of Washington, D.C., and Trinity University professor and Graham Greene biographer Norman Sherry. Kay, the first to read the manuscript, offered the advice of a veteran editor and encouraged me to persevere. From Norman I learned to rewrite, and then rewrite again and again. Kate Medina, editor and mountaineer, also gave her suggestions and warm encouragement and introduced me to Carl Brandt, a book agent of wide contacts and pervasive humor. Jane Geniesse, biographer and author, inspired me. Don Carlton of the Center for American History at the University of Texas urged me on and provided introductions at the University of Texas Press, where Shannon Davies kept me primed and moving. As I spent my days scrawling on a yellow pad on my lap, the late Marty Hollinger of San Antonio turned the scrawl into proper manuscript form, along the way providing the kind of support only a long-time friend can give. And when Marty died, another friend, Tina Sagris of Portsmouth, New Hampshire, took up the unenviable task. Patti Mullins labored long and well putting together lists of friends who might be interested in the book. There are others, family and friends, too numerous to mention, who helped along the way with advice and counsel. To them all, my eternal gratitude.

Ambassadors at Sea

Part 1

Life Before Forty

Rocky Mountain High

AUGUST 2, 1990, was to be a memorable day. As I staggered out of bed at our small ranch in Woody Creek, Colorado, and cocked an eye at the early-morning sky, I was relieved: blue as far as I could see. The Rocky Mountains had never looked prettier. The reason for my concern lay in the fact that the president of the United States, George Bush, was due to arrive at our ranch just before noon. Countless hours of planning over the previous two years had gone into this day, and I wanted it to go smoothly, with perfect weather to complement the careful preparation. At 5:00 P.M. the day before, Margaret Thatcher, prime minister of the United Kingdom, had arrived at nearby Sardy Field in Aspen. My wife, Jessica, and I had met her and her husband, Denis, at the airport. Although exhausted from jet lag and hours of flying, Mrs. Thatcher looked perfect: crisp black and white suit, faultless skin, beautiful face, not a hair out of place. No arrival ceremonies had been scheduled. Mrs. Thatcher was to ride with me in the limo provided by the ever watchful Secret Service; Denis and Jessica were to go in a rather less deluxe transport, but after a quick look at his proposed wheels, Denis hopped in the limo with his wife and me, leaving Jessica and our friend Bob Cunningham to return alone. Just as we were pulling away, the mayor of Aspen, Bill Stirling, loped up to the car, tardy and breathless, to present a scroll of welcome. The prime minister accepted it through the window, and we were off, bearing our distinguished visitors to our guest house (coincidentally but appropriately named Parliament House).

This excitement in normally tranquil Woody Creek had its roots in a discussion in late 1988 of how to celebrate the fortieth anniversary of the founding of the unique Aspen Institute, of which I was vice chairman. Albert Schweitzer had helped launch the institute in 1950; we wanted figures of similar stature to come and speak to us, simultaneously providing enlightenment and, we hoped, a bit of favorable national attention for the institute.

Early on I had plumped for Mrs. Thatcher, who combined being famous, bright, and articulate with being a woman, a balance that we desired. Jessica, also on the planning committee, felt we should have an American as well and suggested our longtime friend George Bush, who was then president-elect. In one of those coincidences that add sparkle to life, in December 1988 George asked me to be ambassador to Great Britain, making access to the Iron Lady considerably easier. Over the succeeding months, Jessica chipped away at the National Security Council (NSC) chairman, Brent Scowcroft, about pinning down the president, while I, in London, broached the matter with Mrs. Thatcher's brilliant assistant, Charles Powell. In the end, both agreed: Aspen and Woody Creek, its nearby neighbor, would host the president and the prime minister for two days in August.

My early-morning reverie disappeared at about 7:00 A.M. when the phone jarred me back to earth. The White House operator announced General Brent Scowcroft, and I learned some startling news: overnight, Kuwait had been swallowed up by its neighbor Iraq. "Will you cancel the trip?" I asked. "No," Brent replied, "we'll come and make the speech, but we can't spend the night. We'll leave in the early evening."

At 11:40 A.M., the president's small jet (*Air Force One*, his main transportation, was far too big for Aspen's runway) set down and out leaped George, concerned by the previous night's events but ebullient as always. We hopped in the presidential limo, flown out from Washington, as it is for all of the president's travel. As we pulled away, Mayor Stirling appeared once again outside the car, jogging along, waving a welcome, which he delivered with apologies for his tardiness. Chief of Staff John Sununu, General Scowcroft, British ambassador Sir Antony Acland, and others completed the motorcade, and we sped off to Woody Creek.

Back at the ranch, it was no place like home. The Secret Service had arrived several days before, creating a sterile area within which our guests would be safe. Jessica, aware from experience during presidential visits to London, had warned the Secret Service that murder would be the fate of any agent who hassled our family or neighbors, but even so, security was tight. Secret Service vans lined the dusty road to the house, providing communications, provisions, and a headquarters. They had given all of us "bomb reports," to be filled out after any bombing that might occur. We found it a bit ludicrous, as did Mrs. Thatcher's two Scotland Yard officers, who privately poked fun at the expensive and elaborate precautions of their American counterparts. Having never lost a protectee, they could afford to condescend.

The White House Press Corps, numbering perhaps fifty, had arrived before the president and were lined up behind barricades in our garden, ready to extract a comment if they could as the president walked by. (Jessica had warned them not to trample the flowers; they didn't.) Jessica and Mrs. Thatcher waited at the house to welcome George, and shortly thereafter the principals, advisers Brent Scowcroft and Charles Powell, Chief of Staff John Sununu, Ambassador Acland, and I settled ourselves in the living room. The Woody Creek Summit had begun.

The president began the proceedings with a rundown of recent events: the United States was working on a joint statement with the Soviets, condemning the invasion; Jordan's King Hussein had assured Bush that the crisis was abating and was humiliated that his prediction proved wrong; a boycott of Iraq was being organized; Kuwaiti assets in U.S. banks had been frozen.

Mrs. Thatcher, never at a loss for words or reluctant to give advice, said, "This is no time to go wobbly, George," a highly unlikely prospect, since George was not the wobbly type. If Iraq prevailed, she continued, no small state would be safe and Iraqi control of Middle East oil would be unacceptable: "He has to be stopped and we must use all means possible." She, too, had frozen Kuwaiti assets to keep them out of Iraqi hands, and she discussed cutting the Iraqi oil pipelines into Turkey and Saudi Arabia.

The president and the prime minister were seated in twin chairs, a small table between them, the Elk Mountain range providing the distant backdrop. Mrs. Thatcher sat, as always, bolt upright, spine straight as a queen's, an expression of concern on her face. I noted with surprise how often she flattered George. "The Turks," she said at one point, "don't take the big view like you do."

The two had not always had an easy relationship. At their first meeting as equals, a Camp David visit not long after Bush became president (and I, ambassador to the United Kingdom), Mrs. Thatcher had talked without letup, as was her custom. George put up with it, but I sensed he was not amused. At an early opportunity back in London, I confided to Charles Powell, her principal adviser, that perhaps more give-and-take might be in order. Whether because of my suggestion or her (or Powell's) intuition, at their next meeting her lectures stopped and the two of them began to get along famously.

The president, as usual, sprawled in his chair, his lanky frame periodically rearranging itself as necessary to make points. He feared the Israelis might hit Iraq with nuclear weapons, thus uniting the shattered "Arab Nation," always more rhetoric than reality. But, he added, "Israel was right and we were wrong" about Saddam and his intentions. He mused on the problems of an invasion of Saudi Arabia, saying such an event would mean a quick Western military reaction. From time to time, he left the room to take calls, one from the Saudi king.

The talk shifted to other subjects, but the rest of us—Scowcroft, Sununu, Acland, Powell, and I—held our peace; it was a Thatcher-Bush dialogue. Gorbachev's cooperation, the near-bankruptcy of the Soviet Norodny Bank, the Vietnamese "boat people" being held in Hong Kong (Mrs. Thatcher warned that she would send them back by force if necessary, a position that was anathema to the president), difficulties presented by Pakistan's nuclear program—all these topics were touched on.

After an hour it was time for the leaders to face the press. There was some speculation on possible questions. "Suppose," someone interjected, "they ask if our soft approach to Iraq has been a failure." Cocking his eyes toward the speaker, Bush said, "At this point, I wouldn't say it's been an outstanding success." We adjourned to the garden and the eager Fourth Estate, which they both handled with ease.

The day went swiftly. Bush made a good speech at the Aspen Institute (the next day Mrs. Thatcher made a brilliant one, perhaps the best I had ever heard). He sneaked away to our mountain pond for an hour of solitary fishing, catching and releasing one rainbow trout. (The leader of his Secret Service protective team told Jessica, "Thank heaven he caught one. When he doesn't, he blames us for scaring the fish away.") He greeted our dinner guests and danced with Jenny Acland, the ambassador's wife, to the music of a Western band that Jessica had found for the event. By 7:30 P.M., it was time for the presidential party to leave. As the big car carried us toward the airport, I pointed out our neighbor Melanie Griffith and her friend Jill St. John, standing outside Melanie's house to see the president pass. Melanie was holding her (and Don Johnson's) new baby. George asked the driver to stop so he could say hello. Fifteen minutes later he was gone, winging back to Washington to begin building the Grand

Coalition that would free Kuwait and bring George Bush the greatest triumph of his career.

At this point I stop and wonder: what must the reader think of the narrator? It is early to know, I admit. Clearly, he has a good job, ambassador to the Court of St. James's. He knows major figures on the world stage and seems at ease with them. He is a player, albeit a minor one, in great events. Married to a strong woman, he lives in a beautiful place. Can one then conclude that he was to the manor (or manner) born? That he is a gifted, mature politician? If you do, like, man — as my offspring might say — are you ever be wrong! Here's how it happened.

Beginnings

THE MANOR to which I was born was typical of a Dallas suburb in 1930. It belonged to Maurine Halsell Catto and Henry Edward Catto. The Depression was beginning to bite, and the Cattos were not rich — far from it. Dad managed a stockbrokerage office, Mother looked after their only child, me. If not wealthy, they were well educated. He had gone to New York University, probably because she went to Barnard College, also in New York City.

The market sank, business slowed, and in 1936 Dad took a bold step. He accepted an offer from his brother Jack to come to San Antonio and join not a stockbrokerage but an insurance brokerage firm. Jack, one of Dad's five siblings, had moved to San Antonio years before and was well settled. He had married a beautiful and wealthy widow, Roxana Gage Negley, an owner of the 500,000-acre Gage Ranch in West Texas, and as helping Roxana with the ranch consumed more time, he needed help with his insurance business.

In San Antonio, Dad worked hard and the business prospered. Under Mother's watchful, loving, and sheltering eye, I grew. I went to the local military school, where I was promptly assigned to the awkward squad, a unit that tried with modest success to turn those like me with two left feet into budding Prussians. Every summer we spent at the ranch with Jack, Roxana, their four young — Alfred, Julie, Joan, and Roxana — and Roxana's sister's family, who provided me with some of the give-and-take that an only child lacked. My cousins accepted me as part of the gang; they taught me to ride and swim, teased me, allowed me to sneak cigarettes with them, and generally kept me from being hopelessly spoiled. I nevertheless felt the outsider, skinny, athletically untalented, and a bit the poor relation.

Upon graduation from the Texas Military Institute, I went to Williams College in Massachusetts, knowing little about it save that Dad's closest friend had gone there. Pledged to a good fraternity, freed from the paternal thumbs, and as a Texan a bit of an oddity, I prospered. Ties to family, however, remained strong. I wrote home every other day and Mother reciprocated; Dad came up for the fraternity's fathers' day, an unexpected and most welcome surprise. Dates were mostly Texans gone east, though as the years passed, the girls of nearby Bennington College became increasingly appealing (reported to be free spirits and free lovers, but not one of them saw fit to leap into my bed). Academically a slow starter and never a "big man on campus," by senior year I had nonetheless decent grades, many friends, and an inordinate pride of college.

After a two-month graduation-present trip to Europe with two fraternity brothers, I returned to San Antonio and Dad's business, very "Ivy League" in outlook and dress, very highbrow, voguishly liberal politically, and a bit of a snob. Invited to join the "right" clubs, I relished being the escort of the young debutantes, throwing down more whiskey and sodas than was wise in the process. Still, I began to bring new accounts to the firm and to follow my parents in doing civic good works.

A friend once commented that I had the thinnest arms he had ever seen. Stung, I began to sneak off to a gym, a primitive and rather smelly second-story walk-up not far from our office. To my surprise, I stuck with it, with gratifying results. Another friend, seeing me in a bathing suit for the first time in a year, said, "My God, Henry, what's happened to you? Have you lost weight?" I glowed inwardly with pleasure. Encouraged, I took up tennis and later became a dedicated runner and an enthusiastic skier.

Though my parents lived very comfortable lives, their Depression-induced caution combined with my inertia to keep me living at home. As my twenty-fifth year rolled around, though comfortably settled, I began to take dating seriously: it was time to get married. (Hints about the joys of grandparenthood came from Mother with increasing frequency.) In November 1956, I became engaged to a girl I had dated for more than a year. The following day (after we had told parents and friends), she called it off. I was crestfallen and embarrassed, but no amount of further wooing could change her mind: I was again footloose and fiancée free.

Then, a friend's bad luck became my good: Robert Tobin, struck by acute appendicitis, asked me to look after his date for San Antonio's Fiesta. Her name was Jessica Hobby, she was from Houston, and she was gorgeous; blond with sparkling blue eyes, an hourglass figure, and an impish sense of fun. We cut official parties to play chess, we danced like dervishes, we had a glorious time. I was smitten.

Weekend commutes between San Antonio and Houston became commonplace for Jessica and me, though I was intimidated by her family. Her father, William P. Hobby, had been governor of Texas and publisher of the *Houston Post*. Her mother, Oveta Culp Hobby, had been wartime head of the Women's Army Corps (I am the only man I know whose mother-in-law was a colonel) and Eisenhower's secretary of health, education, and welfare (the second woman ever to serve in a Cabinet post). The governor, 77, was relaxed and charming; Mrs. Hobby, 52, was beautiful and articulate, telling stories of her extraordinary life in a modulated voice from which all trace of her Texas upbringing had been eradicated. I was awed by her, and she viewed this candidate for son-in-law with at best a raised eyebrow. On the other hand, the governor (to Jessica's annoyance and my delight) would bid me Sunday night farewell with "Come back again soon!" Mother and Dad viewed Jessica with affection. As for me? I was deeply in love.

On November 2, 1957, romantic fool that I am, I proposed: "Marriage is like an icy pool: you hold your nose and jump in. How about it?" A week later (a long week), Jessica called me and said yes. I was ecstatic. The wedding, set for February 15, was large and formal, with an army of attendants. A stroke had disabled the governor, but he recovered sufficiently to give away the bride, the most beautiful sight I had ever seen. After a trip to Acapulco, where we both managed to fall ill, we settled in San Antonio, in a small house that Jessica's talent for interior design made beautiful. Mrs. Hobby offered me a job with the *Houston Post* at a princely salary. Though flattered, I nonetheless declined; San Antonio and the family firm of Catto and Catto suited us nicely.

By early summer, Jessica began to feel unwell. We feared a stomach ulcer. Dr. Horace Sweet, an old family friend, laughed at that idea: "You're pregnant," he said. Heather was born in April 1959, followed by John, William, and Elizabeth, all within six years. Jessica proved to be a fine mother and managed at the same time to become the art critic for the *San Antonio Express*.

While Jessica spent more or less six years pregnant, I did my insurance work and continued volunteer activities. A principal interest was the United Way. I worked my prospects enthusiastically but lunchtime report meetings were gut-wrenching when I had to stand up and report progress, for I dreaded public speaking. The YMCA and the Symphony Society took time. I headed a committee of volunteers who, disturbed by the plight of thousands of young black soldiers and airmen in the heavily military but segregated city, attempted with remarkable success a year before the Civil Rights Act of 1964 to persuade local hotels, restaurants, movie theaters, and bowling alleys to admit black patrons. And somewhere in my mind there formed an inchoate urge to become involved in politics.

Party of Choice

TEXAS IN the 1940s and 1950s was solidly Democratic. The state usually voted for the Democrats in national elections, and Republicans did not even run in local races. Political wars were internecine: conservative Democrats fought liberal Democrats in the political equivalent of mud wrestling. Frequently conservatives would sit on their hands when liberals won control of the national or state party. In 1952, for example, when Dwight Eisenhower won the Republican presidential nomination, conservative Democratic governor Allen Shivers bolted to Ike and helped him carry the state. That did not, however, mean that Shivers became a Republican. He and his fellow Tories continued to run under the sign of the donkey, to the dismay and disgust of the liberals.

In 1954 I had run for Democratic precinct chairman and had won. Enthralled by Adlai Stevenson's eloquence, I had voted for him in 1952, and did so again in 1956, albeit with much less enthusiasm.

By the late 1950s, I became interested in a new political phenomenon. Republican activists throughout the state had concluded that one-party dominance of political life was unhealthy and had begun to contest local elections. A Republican actually won a congressional seat in Dallas in 1954. San Antonio Republicans came alive by 1960 and planned a serious effort in state legislative races. I decided to join the movement and run, along with four other young business and professional men. In those days, ideological moorings were loose and one could find a comfortable niche in either party.

Jessica was surprised that I had become a Republican, and she was made very uncomfortable by some of the extreme right-wingers who had become active in the party, but she worked hard for me. Her Democratic father's reaction went further. Told I was going to run, he approved. When told I was running as a Republican, he asked if I had lost my mind. In Texas it just wasn't done that way.

Still, I persevered and picked the race I thought would hold the most promise. The Democrats had nominated as legislative candidate an un-educated but shrewd professional gambler named Virgil E. "Red" Berry. In his sixties, Red was a longtime local character. In his earlier days, he had twice been indicted, but never convicted, for murder. He earned a handsome living by operating an illegal gaming house in a vast estate on San Antonio's east side. By running, he hoped to accomplish two things: gain respectability for himself and return legal pari-mutuel betting to Texas.

To me, it looked like a natural. I was young, had a beautiful wife and two small children (Heather had arrived in April 1959 and John in August 1960). Our name was well known, thanks to the family insurance firm's advertising over the years. How could an earnest chap like me lose? Members of the religious community flocked to my side, opposed as they were to gambling. I assiduously courted black voters, for I was a firm be-liever in civil rights. And I worked hard.

The campaigning theory of the day held that downtown offices were good places to seek votes. I would start at the top of a building and walk down, boldly going into every office, handing out cards and urging a vote for Catto. It was pleasant and the reception was gratifying. But after I had covered the better buildings, I found myself left only with older, less respectable targets — housing loan offices, plaintiffs attorneys, and such.

One day I reached the bottom of the barrel, a seedy building of some twelve stories. Undaunted, I started as usual at the top and plowed through each office. At one point I entered a chiropractor's office. There was no one in the reception room, but having been trained never to be deterred, I boldly opened an inside door. Again there was no one. Taking a deep breath, I marched through a third door into an innermost room.

It was dimly lit, but I could see it was occupied. "Hi," I said. "I'm Henry Catto, running for the legislature." To my horror, I realized there was a naked woman on a table. The doctor was doing an adjustment— or something—to the woman. The occupant growled, "Get out of here, son," an instruction I did not need, as I bolted for the door, strewing my handout cards behind me.

The race got a lot of publicity. Red and I even had a television debate, which became heated as he dubbed me "fat cat Catto" and I reminded viewers of his checkered past. My confidence proved unfounded, for on election day, I was clobbered, 54 percent to 46 percent. I wrote Red a congratulatory note; he replied in longhand, "If your pretty wife would have ran she would have win." He went on to become state senator and to lay the groundwork for the "return of the ponies," as he put it.

The following year I ran again for the legislature in a special election to fill vacancies in both Congress and the Texas House of Representatives. My teammate, congressional candidate and attorney John Goode, and I ran hard. Former president Eisenhower came to town to help, but we both lost. The old habit of voting the straight Democratic ticket was just too strong.

In spite of this evidence that the people of San Antonio did not want me to serve them, my interest in politics remained keen. I heard that a young oilman had been elected head of the Houston Republican Party, and inasmuch as I was toying with the idea of running for the same post in San Antonio, I called the Houston tyro and asked if we might have lunch. His name was George Bush, and he readily agreed. We ate at the Petroleum Club, high above downtown Houston, and I liked him at once. Although I did not run for county chairman, we became friends and allies in the endless ideological wars that have frequently wracked the Texas Republican Party.

George's wife, Barbara, and Jessica became friends as well. We liked Barbara's intense loyalty and her habit of pulling no punches, and George's wacky, laid-back humor we found impossible to resist. One day the Bushes came to Sunday lunch at our house north of San Antonio (we had by then built a place on a seven-acre tract on a bluff overlooking the distant city). After lunch we took a walk, with son Will, then four, coming along. Tiring of George's shoulders, whereon he had wheedled a ride, he ran about in search of adventure. Suddenly he chirped, "George, what is that?" To my horror, I saw he was pointing at a used condom, left over from earlier days, before our property was inhabited. I was at a loss for words, but quick-minded George replied, "Oh, Will, that is an ancient Indian balloon. We'd better leave it where it is." The adults roared with laughter, while Will, satisfied, scampered on.

The 1961 election to the Senate of obscure college professor John Tower to succeed Lyndon Johnson (who had become President Kennedy's vice president) gave Republicans a huge boost. I had worked on Tower's campaign, but it wasn't easy. Although he had a rich speaking voice, John developed "presence" only after he became senator. A graduate of the London School of Economics, he was given to pin-striped suits and bowler hats, and he wore a bushy mustache that his party advisers nearly had to throw him to shave. I felt that if Republicans were to succeed, they should court the black vote and I offered to shepherd John's campaigning on San Antonio's east side, where most blacks lived. Though not at all a bigot, he was dubious, fearing damage in segregationist East Texas. Finally he agreed, though he added a caveat: "Let's go there at night so I won't be so obvious."

In the 1964 senatorial election, George Bush ran against the liberal-populist incumbent, Ralph Yarborough. Though Mexican Americans later became open to Republican courting, in those days they were solidly Democratic, and Republicans harbored a justified fear that some might be tempted to cast more than one vote, given financial blandishment. A law of the time prohibited the use of any language but English at polling places. Knowing a good bit of Spanish, I volunteered for duty as a poll watcher on election day at a precinct deep in the heart of the Spanish-speaking barrio (neighborhood). It was tedious duty until one Mexican American woman official began to give instructions in Spanish, a clear violation of the law. I cautioned her several times, provoking ever greater annoyance on her part. Finally, angered beyond control, she flung a glass of orange soda pop in the face of her arrogant gringo tormentor. As I dried myself, a deputy of the vigorously partisan Democratic sheriff happened to come by. The woman, in machine-gun-rapid Spanish, told the deputy how badly behaved I was, and he arrested me forthwith, driving me to the county courthouse.

By the time we arrived, batteries of Republican lawyers, led by party elder John Goode, waited. The sheriff, fearing that his man might have gone too far, sent me on my way and I was spared durance vile.

Jessica and I went to the 1964 Republican convention in San Francisco and saw the fault line that rent the party at its starkest: Governor Nelson Rockefeller, fighting Senator Barry Goldwater for the nomination, was greeted by waves of boos when he arrived to speak. Both of us were disgusted. That event and the Goldwater acceptance speech led us to abandon the nominee in November and quietly vote for Lyndon B. Johnson. (In later life I regretted my apostasy and Goldwater became one of my heroes.)

In 1967 we began to get Potomac fever. Through Jessica's family, we had met President and Mrs. Johnson and during the run-up to Hemisfair, the San Antonio world's fair that opened in 1968, we saw them often. At Johnson's request, Jessica was put in charge of the care and feeding of the press corps when they came to Texas with the president. We and Jessica's family gave a pre-wedding party for Lynda Johnson and Chuck Robb in Houston, and we went to the wedding. On one trip, we spent a night at the White House and flew home with LBJ in *Air Force One*. It was heady stuff.

During the mid-1960s a variety of outside activities took up my time. I invested with considerable success in real estate. I wrote a column for the monthly Republican newspaper, gossip mostly but gratifying to the ego. I began polishing my Spanish, looking toward I knew not what. I began seeing a psychiatrist in hopes of getting guidance on ultimate goals in life and help in being an effective person. Rereading notes of those meetings leaves me today with the sad conviction that change in personality or character is woefully difficult: the foolish things I did then (such as fantasizing how I would waste a bully with a well-turned phrase) I still do today, though perhaps with less intensity.

At home, life seemed serene enough. The children suffered the usual illnesses, and sometimes we suffered right along with them. One morning in 1964 I woke up, looked at Jessica, and asked, "What is wrong with your face? It looks swollen." She groggily looked at me and said, "So does yours." We both had the mumps, caught from one of the young.

We bought a small ranch in the nearby Hill Country of Central Texas and enjoyed times there and at my parents' lake home, where Dad taught the elder two of our young to fish and water-ski. But beneath all this tranquillity, I ached for recognition, to stand out from the crowd, to prove myself. Jessica, too, seemed ready for new horizons.

Boarding the Train

SIRHAN SIRHAN, in a chaotic act long before chaos theory existed, affected our lives profoundly. Until he murdered Bobby Kennedy in June 1968, the prospects for the Republicans did not seem bright. With one heinous step, Sirhan made Richard Nixon's star rise and, as it turned out, mine along with it.

One of my classmates at Williams was a bright and amusing person named Tom Evans. A lawyer, he worked for the same firm in New York that Richard Nixon later joined, and Nixon took to him. As the campaign began to take form, he played an increasingly prominent role, and when I learned that, I called and told him I would like to help. With the nomination safely Nixon's, Tom asked me to serve as finance chairman of Citizens for Nixon-Agnew and spend as much time as I could in Washington. I accepted, and in September I began to commute to the nation's capital.

Citizens for Nixon-Agnew was an arm of the campaign that organized professional, ethnic, and other groups for endorsements and helped to raise money from them. I put up $10,000 to get things rolling and went to work. We were headquartered in the Willard Hotel, once elegant but by then vacant, and the staff was mostly young, hardworking, and ambitious. There I met a number of people who were to become friends in future incarnations, among them Lamar Alexander, who later became governor of Tennessee and secretary of education in the Bush administration; John Warner, who would one day marry actress Elizabeth Taylor and be elected senator from Virginia; Dick Scaife, publisher and supporter of conservative causes; and Bill Fitzgerald, later Bush's ambassador to Ireland, and his warm and aristocratic wife, Annelise.

There was great camaraderie, a scent of victory, and occasionally, a sense of humor. Each of the elevators had Nixon posters pasted on the wall, so as we moved about the building we would see the image of the leader and be inspired. One such bore the legend "Nixon's the One." Some wag scribbled on one of them, "Agnew's one, too."

When Nixon did win, I let Tom know I would like to join the administration that was being formed. My interest lay in Latin America, thanks to my Spanish and the proximity of my native Texas to Mexico. A sage once said that all ambition should be rooted in reality, but I had not learned that, so my first choice of job was assistant secretary of state for Latin America, which proved laughably out of reach. As a fallback, I put down ambassador to the Organization of American States, the OAS.

My awareness of the OAS stemmed from a visit LBJ had organized for the OAS ambassadors to his ranch in 1967, in support of Hemisfair, the San Antonio–based world's fair. Jessica and I were very much involved and had as our special charge during the visit the United States ambassador to the OAS, Sol Linowitz and his wife, Toni. The Linowitzes were among the most attractive people we had ever met. Under Sol's tutelage, I learned a bit about the OAS and determined that being the U.S. representative would be an exciting challenge.

On March 9 I went to Washington for an interview with Wilmot Hastings, an aide to Deputy Secretary of State Elliot Richardson, and two weeks later I met Richardson himself. It was my first job interview with someone other than my father; I was nervous, but I need not have been. Richardson, wry and laconic, put me at ease, and I felt it was a successful meeting. Shortly thereafter I got a call from a personnel officer named David Lissy and was offered not the top job but the number two position, deputy U.S. representative, with the personal rank of ambassador and a salary of $36,000 a year. My goal had been to board the train, and I leapt on — even though it was the caboose. I did not regret it.

Twenty-three Rabbits and an Elephant

IN JULY we moved to Washington. We had rented the spacious District of Columbia house of former Lyndon Johnson aide Doug Cater and his wife, Libby, for the summer, while waiting for the house we had bought in Bethesda, a Maryland suburb, to be vacated.

My qualifications for the job I was about to assume were minimal. Several years before, as I mentioned, I had resumed the study of Spanish in my spare time. My purpose in doing so had in part to do with the forthcoming Hemisfair '68. Jessica and I were both very involved, she as a member of the executive committee and I as a director. President Johnson was a strong supporter of the fair, and with his encouragement, many

Latin American countries had come aboard. I thought a thorough un-derstanding of Spanish would be useful and that down the line, if some-thing else came up, I would be prepared.

The early days at my new post were dizzying. The United States mis-sion to the Organization of American States was housed on the fifth floor of the Department of State. The OAS itself was several blocks away, in the old Pan American Union Building, built in 1906 and possibly the most beautiful building in Washington. Not only did I have to learn how the State Department worked but I also needed to meet the vast, impene-trable bureaucracy of the OAS, along with the ambassadors and staffs of the member states. The OAS resembled the United Nations but oper-ated as a regional rather than a global organization. Tasks included mat-ters political, cultural, educational, and developmental. A secretary gen-eral orchestrated activities (in my day, a handsome, vigorous Ecuadoran named Galo Plaza), while a council consisting of the representatives of the member countries made the decisions. The United States footed two-thirds of the bill but, at least in my time, suffered from Latin resentment of our wealth and power. Galo Plaza once described the OAS relationship with the United States as twenty-three rabbits in a barrel with an ele-phant. No matter how carefully the elephant moved, a rabbit was likely to be hurt when it did.

My boss was to be Ambassador John Jova, who made the learning process easier and more fun. A career foreign service officer, subtle of mind, quick of wit, and an old hand at the bureaucratic game, he had been ambassador to Honduras when he was chosen to become OAS ambas-sador. I recall walking through the endless corridors of the State Depart-ment with him one day. Our destination, on the opposite side of the build-ing, was on the same floor as our offices, the fifth. Rather than stay on five, however, he guided me up a floor. I asked why. He replied, "Chance meetings can be important, and the people who might be useful to run into have offices on the sixth floor!"

Shortly after my arrival at State I was sworn in as a foreign service re-serve officer, but getting the promised rank of ambassador proved difficult. "Bestowing rank of" was a presidential prerogative, and no Senate con-firmation was required (though today all ambassadorial appointments go to the Senate). This custom sorely nettled Senator J. William Fulbright of Arkansas, chairman of the Foreign Relations Committee, and each time a president used the privilege, Fulbright rumbled menacingly. Apparently, there was fear at the White House that if I were given the rank via this shortcut, other fish then frying before Fulbright would be endangered. Weeks passed with no anointing forthcoming, and I was alarmed and annoyed. Chivvying the department produced no results, so I called Congressman George Bush (he had been elected to represent a Houston district in 1966) and asked him to check.

George's inquiries were met with excuses; dealing with the White House is like swimming through a pot of glue. He was told that the president's letter granting rank had been lost, that Henry Kissinger, head of the National Security Council, had accidentally taken it on a trip (a biographer had described Henry's briefcase as a "black hole"). State Department officials began to get cold feet, and Assistant Secretary for Latin America Charles Meyer suggested that I forget about the whole thing. Then, inexplicably, a letter from the president did indeed arrive, and I was Ambassador Catto. It proved not only gratifying to the ego but also highly useful in dealing with Latin American diplomats, and if Senator Fulbright fulminated, I was blissfully unaware of it.

Office routine varied, and the learning process included meetings with congressmen, briefings at other agencies, and understanding how the State Department worked. Ambassador Jova was a great help, as was a young officer named Leslie Scott, assigned to work with me. Les became a close friend and kept me from pitfalls to which political appointees are subject. One day he suggested we go to the Pentagon for a briefing and I agreed with alacrity.

As I came to know twelve years later, the Pentagon, just across the Potomac from Washington, consists of a warren of corridors, rings, and layers. But as a few days' acquaintance shows, complexity gives way to logic once the architectural code is broken, and finding any office becomes easy. Getting into any office is another matter altogether. Les and I started at the heavily controlled National Military Command Center, escorted by a two-star general named Givens. The briefing took place in a large room with every imaginable kind of screen to show maps and military dispositions. We sat in comfortable, overstuffed chairs, our places marked with signs showing who was to sit where.

The military is a master of protocol and of making people feel important, the theory being that you never know who can turn out to be useful later. (The military services run rings around the Department of State and other agencies when it comes to congressional liaison.)

The most interesting facet of the visit turned out to be the famous "hot line" between Moscow and Washington. In those days it was a teletype machine. Operators at both ends made sure it worked by sending hourly messages back and forth. One from Moscow arrived during our visit: "If you think the world is flat, just notice that the bow of a ship sailing away disappears before the stern." Right. We replied with a few sentences on Indian history. I asked if our people knew their counterparts. "Not really," the young communicator said. "We don't send personal messages, but we do know, because of the structure of Russian grammar, that one of their operators is a woman and that all are civilians. We do feel a certain community with them because they are the only people in the world that know the importance of our job." Up to that time, the hot line had been used only once, during the 1967 Arab-Israeli war, when some twenty messages passed between LBJ and Soviet leader Aleksei Kosygin.

In many countries of Latin America, the military provides an escalator to the top of the social heap. Aware of this, our military paid court to comrades to the south through an institution called the Inter-American Defense Board. A relic of World War II, when we feared Nazi penetration of Latin America, the board brought senior officials to Washington from all the hemisphere countries. In detailed courses, they studied sociology, economics, and, of course, military science and formed bonds with our people, which became useful later on. Les and I visited the board in October and enjoyed lunch at the Army-Navy Club in downtown Washington, courtesy of two generals and two admirals.

While I learned the ropes, I took more Spanish from the Foreign Service Institute. The main concern at the office, meanwhile, was settling the brutal, brief "Soccer War" between Honduras and El Salvador. Although a soccer game between teams from the two countries caused tensions to boil over, the war that broke out in the summer of 1969 and took some five hundred lives was really a demographic conflict. The border between the two countries, never well defined, allowed relatively free passage for Salvadorans to cross to seek work in the neighboring country. Honduras, large and relatively empty, proved a magnet for enterprising Salvadorans, whose tiny country was the most densely populated in Spanish America. Hondurans resented the competition for jobs and land, and discrimination ensued. The 1969 eruption of hostilities lasted only five days; while Salvadoran troops invaded, the superior Honduras air force blew up a refinery and otherwise tried, largely in vain, to cripple the enemy's robust economy.

The real tragedy lay in the disruption of the Central American Common Market. For a number of years, the five Central American countries (Nicaragua, Costa Rica, and Guatemala being the other three) had opened their markets to one another's goods, and the resultant prosperity promised real economic progress. The war ended the market and stunted the prosperity. The OAS, like all the king's horses and men, tried to put things together again, but without success. The best that could be claimed was that the Salvadoran invasion ceased (as much from want of gasoline as from international pressure), withdrawal took place, and endless negotiations about the border began. To this day, the memory of the war vexes relations between the two countries.

All the American states save Cuba belonged to the OAS. (Cuba had been expelled when Fidel Castro's communism became clear. He was not amused. Seldom given to understatement, he said about the organization: ". . . filthy rotten bilge with no honor . . . a court of bandits . . . causes fits of vomiting in my country.") The most important of the three OAS councils was the political, which met frequently in numbingly wordy debate. John Jova covered that beat, while I was assigned to the educational and cultural council. Its meetings were less frequent but no less characterized by garrulity. Key issues included educational projects, technology transfer, and cultural exchange. Contention inevitably centered on why the United States did not do more to help, and why we didn't pay more than the agreed two-thirds of the budget. We, of course, tried to cut our percentage (it was eventually reduced to 50 percent) and tried always to guide our often volatile colleagues into realistic channels, hoping to avoid overlap with UN and other development efforts.

I recall one meeting at which I proposed a development project for the United States, my idea being to show that our country was not perfect and could benefit from Latin help. My colleagues, unsure that I was serious, quickly turned to other matters; money was supposed to flow from north to south, not vice versa.

Foreign aid always sparked controversy. U.S. politicians loved to blast it; recipients felt grudging and resentful at taking it; and administering it created great problems and bureaucratic mayhem. In the 1960s and earlier, aid was frequently "tied"—that is, recipients had to spend the money with U.S. firms. This arrangement sometimes meant that the developing country (political correctness changed "underdeveloped" to "developing") was unable to buy at the best world prices, and loud were the cries when that happened.

In October 1969 President Nixon made a speech on Latin American – U.S. relations, and with much fanfare he untied aid. But there was a joker: products made in, say, Brazil, had to be at least 90 percent manufactured there. Thus, for example, a Volkswagen truck essentially made in Germany but then shipped to Brazil for final assembly didn't count; if Brazil wanted to use aid funds for a truck, it would have to buy a U.S. truck. When this mode became clear, the Latins reacted bitterly, complaining that Nixon had a "credibility gap." As the recipient of a good bit of Latin resentment, I brought this matter up at Assistant Secretary of State Charles Meyer's staff meeting, but the AID representative — surprisingly, I thought — was not concerned. Later I came to understand the predicament of the Agency for International Development (AID). AID people had learned from bitter experience that the only way to get their bills passed in Congress was to present them as a sort of subsidy for American business and a jobs program for labor. Untying aid thus became bureaucratically untenable.

Another irritant between north and south arose when Ecuador, whose seas are rich in fish, claimed the right to territorial waters of not just the traditional three miles but two hundred miles. Ecuadoran Navy boats (loaned to Ecuador by the U.S. Navy) began to stop U.S. fishing boats, fine them $50,000 per incident, and force them to buy $150,000 licenses. The fine money, incidentally, went to the Ecuadoran Navy; thus there was plenty of incentive for zealous searches of foreign fishing boats.

Members of Congress were outraged and demanded that the U.S. Navy escort U.S. fishing vessels, and then let's see who arrests whom. Congressmen seemed to overlook the possible consequences of such a policy.

First, U.S. investment in Ecuador, always hostage to the threat of nationalization, was substantial. The Ecuadoran government, typically shaky, found itself particularly subject to coup threats from its leftist sector. (The United States, of course, assiduously avoided any actions likely to lead to new communist governments in the hemisphere; the Cold War affected every facet of American foreign policy.) Ecuador had considerable oil, much of it produced by U.S. companies, which meant pressure from American petroleum interests to walk softly. Finally, although the tuna industry was not large in dollar terms, it heavily influenced several congressmen. Congress thus passed legislation providing that the U.S. government, not the fishermen, had to pay the fines. Moreover, the United States was required to cut off military aid to any country that played this game and deduct the amount of the fines from U.S. economic assistance!

Ecuador picked up seventeen U.S. boats, fined them some $800,000, and then, showing astonishing chutzpah, complained that the United States had violated the OAS rule against economic coercion. It reminded me of the old joke of the boy who murdered his parents and asked for leniency because he was an orphan.

After endless hours of OAS maneuvering, a weasel-worded compromise that satisfied — more or less — both sides was reached. The two-hundred-mile territorial limit became, in the end, the norm for developing countries, while the United States went to a twelve-mile limit and later to two hundred miles for resource claims.

Occasionally in our OAS dealings, we tried appealing to common sense and self-interest, and once in a while, the pervasive anti-gringo front cracked. In December 1970 I took the ambassadors of Mexico, Argentina, and Brazil for lunch at the F Street Club, a handsome converted home at 1925 F Street in Washington. My idea was to convince the Latin "Big Three," who with ourselves were the major donors to the OAS, that we should cooperate. After an excellent meal, and a bit of wine, we talked through the afternoon about how to get more for our money from the creaky OAS bureaucracy. I felt rapport had been established, but nothing came of the effort.

Perhaps the voice most critical of U.S. policy in Latin America was Senator Fulbright's. As chair of the Foreign Relations Committee and an implacable foe of military aid, he could make any administration official writhe while testifying. In a typical incident in 1971, Deputy Assistant Secretary of State John Crimmins went to the Senate to testify for the U.S. contribution to the Inter-American Development Bank (IADB), an important dispenser of aid. No matter how gamely Crimmins, a very large and imposing man, tried to steer talk to the topic at hand, Fulbright tugged it back to military sales. He felt that Latin countries did not need arms, they needed resources for development. Crimmins retorted that if we didn't sell what the Latins felt sovereignty demanded, the French or others would. "Then let the French contribute to the IADB," Fulbright snorted. No amount of patient explanation that Latin countries felt they could judge better than we the level of arms they needed would convince the brilliant, irascible Arkansan; he knew best and that was that. And the dispute outlived Fulbright: a ban on military sales was finally lifted during the Clinton administration in 1997.

Making like Marco Polo

I WAS not exactly well traveled when I went to Washington, my excursions having been limited to Western Europe, Mexico, and Jamaica. Naturally, I was eager to extend my knowledge of the OAS area, and various trips were put on the drawing board. But before any such southerly venture could be organized, an opportunity arose that was too good to miss.

The Israelis had long been active in Latin America, in search of both markets and influence. The United Nations, under Arab pressure, was often the focus of anti-Israeli agitation, and the twenty-plus OAS countries offered potential for Israeli courting. Trips to Israel were a powerful magnet, and when I was invited to go along with a number of OAS colleagues, I quickly said yes — and so did Jessica.

We were scheduled to travel on January 17, 1969, nonstop from New York to Tel Aviv on El Al, the Israeli airline, but El Al's scheduling people are opportunists. When the chance to pick up passengers in Paris arose, we went to get them, schedule be damned.

Israelis reminded me a bit of the Americans of the frontier: no nonsense and, at a certain level, minimum subtlety. (Their diplomats, of course, could be very subtle indeed.) At one point on our flight, a passenger rose before the plane had quite gotten to the gate. The flight attendant wasted no time with the speaker system; she simply pushed him back down into his seat. My first morning in Jerusalem, I was still in bed in a darkened room, de-jet-lagging myself. Suddenly the door flew open, the lights came on, and an annoyed maid chastised me for being a slugabed.

Our tour was impressive. Visits included the Knesset, the Hadassah Hospital, and the wonderful synagogue where Marc Chagall's stained-glass windows illustrate the joys and sorrows of an ancient people. Symposia included a fascinating talk by Dr. Albert Sabin of polio vaccine fame. We saw the ineffably moving Yad Vashem, memorial to the Holocaust, and the Dead Sea Scrolls housed in their teardrop-shaped shrine.

One night several of us dined at a nightclub where part of the entertainment was a folksinger who wrote his own material. At one point, he dedicated a song to the amputee veterans of Israel's wars. The refrain went:

> You know it breaks my heart
> To see you've lost a part.
> But boy you did so well
> For your country, Is-roy-ell.

Everyone clapped, but I didn't know whether to laugh or cry.

Jessica joined me on the twenty-third for excursions, punctuated by visits with Israeli and U.S. officials, to Cana, the Dead Sea, solar power projects, and Tel Aviv. The purpose of the trip was admirably served; certainly the Cattos returned to the United States understanding and admiring the doughty little country. In spite of all odds, Israel was determined — like a modern David — to survive and to remain a lively democracy.

Other trips followed. Les Scott and I did a turn through El Salvador, Peru, and Venezuela in May, seeing OAS projects. In September we went to Brazil, Argentina, and Chile. Chile was in turmoil, and Washington was very worried that the just-elected Marxist Salvador Allende would end up another Castro. An OAS meeting was the reason for the trip, and our time was spent trying to get Americans elected to the various permanent committees.

I became tangentially involved in the Chilean political situation as well. At a social event I met a former Chilean journalist named Cristian Casanova, and in a boozy conversation we became amigos. I expressed the hope that Allende would not turn out to be too radical. The next day Casanova invited me to lunch at a grand old Santiago men's club, reminiscent of the British clubs on which it was patterned, for serious talk. He said he had called his friend Allende and told him of having met me. He asked the president-elect if he might use me to send a reassuring message to Washington, which permission Allende apparently gave. Cristian then proceeded to assure me that democracy would remain healthy; the Socialists would only tinker a bit at the edges, such as breaking up the press holdings of the powerful Edwards family and giving them to the press unions. I was not encouraged, but I dutifully reported the démarche to Washington. The administration's hostility was somehow unaffected by my friend's assurances, and icy opposition to Allende lasted until his overthrow by the Chilean army and his suicide.

In Argentina we called on U.S. ambassador John Davis Lodge, a former actor, a Republican political appointee, and brother of Henry Cabot Lodge, Nixon's 1960 running mate. A big and hospitable man, he nonetheless terrorized his employees, and I developed from him a strong sense of what an ambassador should *not* be like. Playing that most courtesy-conscious of games, tennis, he would call an opponent's shot out when it was a foot inside the line, and his bullying of his partner (the embassy science adviser) made me cringe. He had appeared in the 1930s in a movie with Shirley Temple, and he frequently showed the film, forcing his glassy-eyed embassy staff to watch him cavort in his salad days. He was wonderfully courteous to Les and me, but we were glad we didn't work for him.

In February 1971 I accompanied my leader, Ambassador John Jova, to Lima, Peru, where there was to be an OAS money-pledging session at which the extent of OAS assistance programs would be determined. Such meetings were always elaborate ritual dances. Since the United States matched with two dollars each dollar the Latin Americans put up, our interest was keen. In their turn the Latins, always short of cash, did not want to get out ahead of one another and an "after you, dear Alphonse" routine became a ritual.

Jova had a cousin in Lima, a Peruvian aristocrat who invited us to her home for a drink and then to dinner at the Tambo de Oro, a fine restaurant. I learned a bit about Peruvian social attitudes when one of the guests, chic and arch, criticized the wife of the U.S. ambassador to Peru, Toby Belcher. She asked me, "Why does Mrs. Belcher spend all that time working in Lima's slums? If she makes them too nice, more people will move in and the problem will get worse."

Life at US/OAS, as our office was designated at the Department of State, was far from all travel and glamour. The average day of dealing with OAS problems could be paralyzingly boring. In the committee meetings where much of the work took place, endless arguments over fine points of Spanish grammar and syntax were the rule. The English speakers—that is, those from the Caribbean islands and ourselves—would glance at each other and roll our eyes in frustration when these sessions bogged down; together we constituted an informal biracial linguistic alliance spurred by a desperate wish to get on with it.

Latin sensitivities, a constant worry, arose all the time. The OAS holds an annual meeting of foreign ministers called the General Assembly, and the question of how much time the U.S. secretary of state would spend with his Latin American colleagues invariably created tensions. At the

1970 assembly, Chile and Colombia did not send their foreign ministers, so sure were they that Secretary of State William Rogers would not spend any time at the meeting. Rogers fooled them; he spent two full days and charmed all concerned.

I had a constant flow of visitors from Texas to my office. Indeed, I felt that I was a sort of fourth congressman for San Antonio as people came by with requests. One concerned funding for a new federal office building in San Antonio. The city fathers thought it a sure thing until a congressman from Michigan named Gerald Ford put a hold on the money, hoping to siphon it off for his own district. I went to see a friend at the Office of Management and Budget (OMB) and learned that we were indeed in trouble and that only intervention by Senator John Tower of Texas at the highest level could save the project, which eventually went down the drain.

One day an OAS employee came by and told me that the organization was really run by a cabal of Cubans and Jews and that he couldn't get anything done. I eased him out of my office as best I could, though I gladly would have booted him in the rump.

On a typical day, I was called on by a man asking for U.S. support to create a new foundation to improve health conditions in developing countries; by a Haitian embassy acquaintance wanting a U.S. residence permit; and by a New York advertising woman wanting to work for the president. Why me? Perhaps I radiated vibes of goodwill — or of an easy mark.

George Bush sent a couple of men by to see me, Messrs. Tye and Holloway, whom I suspected Bush wanted to be rid of. Some years earlier, Tye had gone to Bolivia with an idea for commercial use of tailings, tiny pieces of tin that are normally just waste. The government, doubting that his idea was viable, gave him a concession, but sure enough, the plan worked and he soon had a small going concern. Alas, in one of the innumerable coups that marked that country's history, the victorious new government rewarded some of its supporters by giving them the company. Mr. Holloway, Tye's attorney, asked me, quite seriously, "Why don't we just change the Bolivian government?" I tried to explain that those days were over and that the U.S. mission to the OAS was not the place to seek redress in any case. They left, and I heard no more of the matter.

A pleasant aspect of life at the State Department's Latin American bureau consisted of occasional retreats, during which the country officers, area directors, our OAS mission, and others would retire for two days of meetings and brainstorming about problems in the hemisphere. Henry Kissinger once said that no one above the rank of assistant secretary had time to think, given the vast and time-consuming problems of simply running the bureaucracy. He was probably right. Unfortunately, when we lesser mortals did get together to think, we frequently got it wrong. In the fall of 1970, such a meeting took place at Airlie House, in rural northern Virginia. The principal result was a consensus that U.S. policy toward Cuba was sure to fall apart soon and that it needed reassessing. Keen young analyst that I had become, I solemnly concurred with this prediction, which twenty-three years later had yet to come true.

The Social Tightrope

SOCIAL LIFE looms large in Washington, but it is not all fun and food. It is hard work as well. Contacts are made and business gets done in the guise of a dinner party. Careers are made or ruined by a whispered exchange at a crowded reception. As a newcomer to Washington and to this intriguing, important game, I would have been dubbed terminally naive but for one thing — Jessica. Raised in a political household in both Washington and Houston, she caught on quickly. When she entertained, she did so with flair, and we soon found ourselves invited to all manner of functions.

We had a head start in another area. President Johnson's ranch was near San Antonio, where we had lived, and the press corps that covered his activities when he was at the ranch was billeted in that colorful city. Since Jessica had been asked by the president to look after the press, we became friends with many of the top reporters, among them Max Frankel of the *New York Times*, Bob Pierpoint of CBS, Richard Valeriani of NBC, and Hugh Sidey of *Time*. When we moved to Washington, they provided a warm welcome and an entrée to a vital part of the political scene. Max and Tobi Frankel had children who more or less matched ours in age, and we spent many a weekend with them. Bob Pierpoint and Pat were close as well. Bob had been a student in Sweden, spoke Swedish, and knew many Swedes. I soon developed the naive idea that he would make a good ambassador to that country, with which our relations were quite strained. My näiveté lay not in my judgment of Bob's ability but in the likelihood that the Nixon administration would appoint a journalist of independent mind to anything. Indeed, during the Watergate days, the president was asked if he was angry with Pierpoint about a story Bob had done on *CBS Evening News*. Nixon snapped illogically, "To be angry at someone, you have to first respect them."

Sightings of Nixon were rarer than seeing a prothonotary warbler, at least at my level of government. My feelings about the president were mixed. I wanted desperately to like and admire him; to be troubled by him cast doubt on our whole Washington adventure. For the most part, I approved of his actions. I noted in my daybook in November 1971 some pros and cons of the president. The pros, to me, included getting out of Vietnam with honor (I later concluded the cost was far too high); setting up the Environmental Protection Agency; proposing his imaginative Family Assistance ideas; opening China; negotiating the strategic arms limitations; and expanding the national parks. The cons included what to me seemed dreadful appointments, like Carswell to the Supreme Court, and the way he handled the shooting of the students at Kent State University. I felt strongly that a Cabinet member should have been sent to the funerals, but when I suggested that to aide Peter Flanigan, he scoffed.

Seeing the president was beyond hope, I feared, but I nonetheless dropped hints to Bush and others that we would dearly love to be invited to a state dinner at the White House. Miraculously, in October 1970 an envelope addressed in calligraphy appeared, and we, Latin Americanists, found ourselves bidden to a dinner for President Nicolae Ceausescu, the ruthless dictator of Communist Romania. It may have been "out of area," but we of course accepted, and it turned out to be a memorable evening.

A White House dinner, always exciting, presented a sore temptation to Nixon to gild the lily. As the Nixons and Ceausescus came into the East Room to greet the guests, four flamboyantly uniformed trumpeters blew a fanfare, and as the band played "Hail to the Chief," the presidents and their wives marched solemnly in. "Hail to the Chief" is quite enough to tingle the spine, and it has a certain democratic dignity, but trumpeters in Middle European costumes struck me as too much. When we were presented to the presidents, Nixon asked Jessica about her mother, with whom he had served in the Eisenhower administration. Extremely cordial, the president asked me about the OAS, proving that he had studied his guest list carefully and knew who was who.

After all the guests had been met, we filed into the state dining room, and as Mr. Lincoln looked benignly down from his portrait above the fireplace, we found our places. Nixon insisted on seating his guests banquet style, along E-shaped tables. That meant very stiff protocol, with all people of rank ghettoized, while probably more interesting guests without rank sat on the periphery. It was clumsy, and Jessica and I approved when Gerald Ford became president and switched to round tables.

During the toast after dinner, often a boring event, President Nixon referred to "the People's Republic of China." I had been woolgathering during the platitudes of the toast, but when he uttered those words, I nearly fell off my chair. Never had Richard Nixon called the PRC anything but "Red China" or "Mainland China" at best. I didn't know what it meant, but I knew something was up, and I excitedly talked to Jessica about it after dinner. Sure enough, it turned out to be part of the elaborate courting dance that the United States and China were going through, preparatory to Nixon's historic trip to China that ended decades of loathing and war. Romania, a friend of China, was playing a role as intermediary.

Ceausescu's toast, amazingly, had a flash of humor. He said, "I want to assure the people of the United States, they have nothing to fear from Romania," and then, slyly digging at the United States for its worldwide role, he added, "Next time I am in the United States I hope all Romanian troops will have returned to Romania and all U.S. troops are home in America." After dinner, soprano Anna Moffo gave a staggeringly beautiful recital, greeted the Ceausescus in Romanian, and sang a song for them in their language.

I had another glimpse of Nixon in action, as both man and politician, in May of the next year. The White House Press Corps salutes itself each year at a lighthearted white-tie banquet to which the president often comes and trades barbs with the reporters. In 1970, Max Frankel, head of the *New York Times* Washington bureau, was to be honored as the recipient of the prestigious Clapper Award. As Max strode to the podium to accept, Nixon, at the head table, turned away seemingly deliberately, snubbing Max. (The *Times* had been particularly critical of the administration.) John Connally, by contrast, got up, slapped Max on the back, and congratulated him. Nixon and the press seldom were at less than swordpoint, but Connally knew that snubbing was dumb.

Among our greatest friends, to be sure, were George and Barbara Bush. By 1969 the Bushes were veterans of the capital, George having been elected in 1966 and returned without opposition in 1968. In October they gave us a welcome party at the Alibi Club, an old, unobtrusive building on I Street, whose walls were lined with caricatures of members, while other memorabilia crowded every surface. It was the quintessential Washington insiders' party: journalists, senators, and administration officials in a relaxed atmosphere, conversation informed and off the record.

A larger party in November was also typical. Chief of Protocol Emil "Bus" Mosbacher and his wife, Pat, had a dinner at Blair House, the president's guest house across Pennsylvania Avenue from the White House. Wall-to-wall ambassadors, the gathering fairly glittered in the nineteenth-century elegance of the handsomely furnished old mansion. Jessica sat between the ambassadors from Iran and Malaysia, while I was bracketed by the latter's wife and the Uruguayan ambassador's wife. It was our first exposure to Iran's remarkable Ardisher Zahedi, later to become a friend and our host for many an evening. After dinner, a singer accompanied by a harpsichordist, both in period costume, performed eighteenth-century music into the small hours. The Bushes were there, and I was not the only one to get a bit restless; George had the fidgets and that glazed look in the eye that meant "Will this never end?"

On November 6 I dropped by George's office and learned momentous news: he had determined to run again in 1970 for the Senate. His 1964 campaign against Senator Ralph Yarborough had been hard-fought, but he was swept away in the Goldwater debacle. In 1970, with no presidential election and Yarborough looking weak, he decided to go for it again. I wasn't too sanguine about his chances; Republicans were still a rare breed in Texas, and though the liberal Yarborough was out of step with the Texas outlook on many issues, he was nonetheless a Democrat and an incumbent.

A totally unforeseen event reshuffled the political deck. A rather conservative former congressman and shrewd businessman from Houston, Lloyd Bentsen, beat Yarborough in the May 2 Democratic primary. George had handily beaten a right-wing opponent and I called with congratulations. Elated by Yarborough's defeat, he felt the little-known Bentsen would be an easier target. In contrast, Jessica was not so sure, feeling that many conservatives would be comfortable with Bentsen and dubious about having two Republican senators. Her concerns turned out to be prescient.

Jessica and I both became involved in the campaign. In September we had a party at the F Street Club in Washington, a fundraiser for George and Robert Taft Jr. running in Ohio. President Nixon was eager to help and invited a select few to the White House to underline the importance of these races. And while I traveled in Latin America, Jessica stepped in and, with some help from my father, had a very successful fundraiser in San Antonio. I had warned her not to expect much; off-year races in Texas frequently don't generate much juice. Still, she determined to raise the then very substantial goal of $10,000; she exceeded it. Money was not the only object at such functions, and Bush, as always, radiated goodwill and charm. Pic Swartz, a Democratic friend who attended, told Jessica afterward, "I just want you to know the party was terrific and George Bush is the most impressive politician I've ever met."

On November 3, election day, we were in Houston, to visit Jessica's mother (her father had died in 1964) and be with the Bushes that election night. I smelled defeat, probably less from political acuity than from the ingrained pessimism of a 1960s Texas Republican. As the evening wore on, gloom settled in. About nine o'clock the CBS crew gave the race to Bentsen, but on learning that no votes from Houston, strong Bush country, had been counted, they rescinded their prediction. Our elation was short-lived, however, and even the hoped-for big victory in his home city couldn't save him.

We were sad; the Bushes were crushed. Back in Washington, we went to a party November 7 at columnist Charles Bartlett's, a "cheer up the Bushes" effort by him and his wife, Martha. It didn't work. Even speculation that Nixon might give him a Cabinet post, such as Treasury, failed to lift George's spirits. Jessica called on Bar at home shortly thereafter, and found her even more down than George was. She said she had simply wept for forty-eight hours, and that it was like a death in the family: there is no appeal.

Buoyed by support from Bar, his friends, and his family, George's natural ebullience soon reasserted itself. I went to lunch with him on November 19 at the House of Representatives dining room, and no fewer than five waitresses stopped by our table to commiserate with him. He clearly wanted an administration job, and Nixon seemed inclined to offer one. We speculated on his future path. He ruled out NASA or the Small Business Administration; his eye was on the Cabinet, particularly Treasury.

That bubble burst on December 14. I was at my office when Jessica

called, urged me to sit down, and told me that John Connally had just
been named Secretary of the Treasury. It was, to a Texas Republican, truly
unbelievable. In 1968, in spite of having told Texas Republican chairman
Peter O'Donnell that he favored Nixon, Connally had supported Hubert
Humphrey, albeit lukewarmly, and as a conservative Democratic governor he represented everything Texas Republicans were trying to expunge.
That he be clasped to our bosom took the breath away and proved once
more than the ways of the White House were mysterious indeed. Political
gossip had it that Nixon admired Connally's strength, forcefulness, and
charm; perhaps he had in mind replacing Agnew in 1972. What did it
mean for our hero, Senator John Tower? No one outside 1600 Pennsylvania Avenue knew for sure.

In the end, George Bush landed on his feet, in spite of the apparent
setback: the president named him our ambassador to the United Nations,
with Cabinet rank.

Jessica's political intuition came to the fore. If Connally was to be
among us, we might as well make the best of it, erstwhile enemy or not,
and she began to plan a party in the Connallys' honor. A welcome by
Texas Republicans would signal to John that the past was forgotten (sort
of) and would indicate to our stunned colleagues back home that they
should toe the line.

The Connallys readily agreed; March 15 was set as the date, the F
Street Club the venue. Jessica arranged a star-studded guest list (including older brother Bill Hobby), a trio to enliven the party with music, special tablecloths, and an elegant menu.

The event proved her efforts worthwhile. The black-tie crowd was in
a festive mood, my after-dinner toast was warm in its welcome, and we
anticipated John's response with pleasure. Sure enough, the silver-tongued
and silver-headed former governor proved to be at his best. A superb
extemporaneous speaker, he talked of having known the Cattos and of
having hunted at their ranch. He praised the senior Hobbys for their government service. Then he said, "And in this generation, we have their offspring, Bill and Jessica, one so smart, one so beautiful . . ." Jessica, gorgeous and full of the spirit of the moment, broke in: "Which is which,
John?" There was a roar of laughter, including from Connally himself.

Washington social life, by nature always in flux as the government cast
came and went, had nonetheless a certain structure bestowed upon it by
a number of rather grand women, permanent fixtures who stayed on

through Republican and Democratic administrations. Most of them were shrewd, highly intelligent ladies, and they played a role by bringing together the political stars in creative combinations. The grandest of them all when we got there was Alice Roosevelt Longworth. Daughter of Theodore Roosevelt and widow of longtime House Speaker Nicholas Longworth, she was quick of wit and often funny. Though Jessica and I met her only once, we were fascinated. With remarks like "If you don't have anything nice to say, come sit next to me," she was much in demand until her death in her nineties.

One story, possibly apocryphal, about Mrs. Longworth tickled me greatly and illustrated her spirit. In 1901, when President McKinley was assassinated and her father became president, the young Alice was asked sympathetically how she felt, her interlocutor expecting her to confess shock or horror. Her reply: "Ecstatic!"

Susan Mary Alsop—both with her husband, columnist Joseph Alsop, and, after their divorce, alone—was (and is) one of the best. So was Lorraine Cooper, wife of Kentucky senator John Sherman Cooper. Mrs. Cooper took us under her wing as well. Arch and stylish, she could be terribly funny. At a December 1969 dinner party in the Coopers' Georgetown home, she told of deciding to go to see a soft-core porn film then much in vogue, *I Am Curious—Yellow?*. She invited the beautiful Evangeline Bruce, wife of the distinguished former ambassador David Bruce and a fine hostess herself, and Mrs. Longworth to join her. Mrs. Longworth volunteered to have the driver of her ancient Rolls-Royce pick up tickets in advance so they would not have to stand in line and—God forbid—be seen. What they did not count on was that the line to enter the theater exceeded that to get tickets, so the three women had to stand, very much revealed to public view, the Rolls-Royce in the background matching their slow pace toward the door.

At one Cooper party I was listening to the immaculately dressed, acerbic, and elegant Alsop hold forth to a small group that included the wife of the postmaster general, Winton "Red" Blount. The hors d'oeuvres consisted of bite-size tomatoes, and Mrs. Blount, rapt at Alsop's comments and always the lady, bit into one rather than popping it whole into her mouth. A jet of bright-red juice shot out, splattering Alsop's pristine white vest. He simply could not believe, at first, that it was an accident. The horrified perpetrator tried to clean him up, but he retired to his nearby home for a change of clothes.

Social life can be trying for the hosts. In May 1971 we were invited to a dinner by Margo and Gil Hahn, president of the D.C. City Council. Margo, a consummate party giver, a superb cook, and someone I enjoyed talking with, pulled me aside shortly after the guests arrived. She demanded breathlessly, "Do you know what I've done?" I admitted to ignorance and she confessed, "I have invited Art Buchwald and Joe Alsop to the same party!" In a brief cause célèbre of the time, Buchwald had written a play in which he made fun of an Alsop-like character. Happily for Margo, there were no punches between the two columnists, but a lively exchange took place between Henry Kissinger and Mary McGrory, an outspoken and very liberal *Washington Star* columnist. Kissinger, a frequent target of Mary's barbs, always tried to win over his critics. Arriving late with Ambassador Yitzhak Rabin from Israel (who was to be assassinated in 1995), he sat at our table for dessert and, his deep rumbling voice tuned to please, asked Mary when she was going to invite him to dinner. McGrory, whose social graces were not improved by alcohol, snapped, "When you have the last American out of Vietnam!" Henry gave up.

In January 1970 we were invited to a gala at the Shoreham Hotel, given by the fabled hostess Perle Mesta for Ethel Merman, who had played a Mesta-like character in the Broadway musical *Call Me Madam*. Mesta, who at one point was LBJ's ambassador to Luxembourg, apparently did not earn her fame as a Washington hostess for the small, candlelit kind of dinner. The Merman bash was far too crowded, with poor champagne, and in a hotel ballroom at that. Ethel did, however, sing "There's No Business Like Show Business," proving that her voice and presence still could dominate an audience.

A hostess of a different sort, fellow Texan and Lady Bird Johnson's press secretary Liz Carpenter, was very kind to us. She and her husband, Les, had dinners at which the focus was on issues. Rather than following the usual form, of polite conversation with the woman on your left followed at the "turning of the table" by more talk with the dinner partner to your right, Liz would call guests to order, throw out a topic, and expect everyone to comment. She was quick-witted. When longtime Democrat John Connally became a Republican in the midst of the Watergate scandal, Liz cracked, "It's the first time in history where a rat swam *toward* a sinking ship." At Liz's table you had fun.

Washington life benefits from the diplomatic corps. Most countries send their best here, and the result is an enriched social scene. Jessica and I learned this early. For example, our Israeli trip created a natural tie with Israeli ambassador to the United States Rabin and his smart, handsome, tennis-playing wife, Leah. A visit to this country by Israeli's top Latin expert, Netanel Lorch, gave me an excuse to have him to lunch, with John Jova, Ambassador Rabin, and Max Frankel of the *New York Times* to leaven the mix.

We gathered at the 1925 F Street Club, and Rabin, later to be elected Israel's prime minister, spun a theory about the failure of a recent American raid on a North Vietnamese prison camp. The idea had been to release prisoners. None were found and the administration, especially the Pentagon, was left with egg on its face.

Rabin demurred, "I don't know whether you Americans think the way we do, but here is the way I would have figured it out if I had been in the president's place."

In the first place, he mused, what were your problems? Your problems were two: Number one, you wanted to convince the North Vietnamese that you were capable of a very vigorous strike near their capital and you wanted to indicate to them that you still had plenty of sting left even though you were withdrawing. Number two, you wanted to indicate that you didn't like having your reconnaissance planes shot down and you really wanted to speak to your constituency in Hanoi. Well, that's fine, except that speaking strongly to your constituency in Hanoi involved speaking also to people who didn't want to see the war escalated. If you did anything very dramatic, you'd most likely get Senator Fulbright and all the people of his ilk furious and start a new great tidal wave of dissent that would hurt you in other areas. So how could you combine these problems and overcome them? The answer was try to rescue the prisoners. That had been the thing that caught the interest of the American people and what could be better than to try a rescue? Well, that was fine, except there was a problem there too, and that problem was, suppose you went in and before you could get them out, their captors murdered most of them or they were killed in the fighting; that was an ever-present danger. I knew because we had been involved in it and you had to have inside help to make sure that the people you intended to help didn't get hurt.

And, he continued, the answer to that, since you probably didn't have anybody inside the prison camp, was to hit a prison camp that was already vacant. Clearly, you got credit with the American people for trying a rescue. You scared the very daylights out of Hanoi because they were unwilling to admit that it happened and they would have gladly let it pass and never made a peep about it because it was humiliating. And finally, you completely neutralized Fulbright and people of his type. Who was to blame? Well, you blamed it on some faceless intelligence type who goofed things up, and the result was a very happy situation.

Max thought the idea preposterous, and I was inclined to agree. Yet the next day Senator Fulbright himself, quoted in the *Washington Post*, said he thought we knew the camp contained no prisoners.

Perhaps the most elegant dinner that Jessica and I attended during our OAS days took place in the New York City Fifth Avenue apartment of New York governor Nelson Rockefeller and his wife, Happy. We had gone to New York at the invitation of the Bushes and had stayed at their official UN residence, a flat in the Waldorf Towers. Although Rockefeller had been Jessica's mother's deputy at the Department of Health, Education, and Welfare in Eisenhower's administration, we did not know them well and were pleased to be invited. Jessica looked particularly lovely as we gawked at the Matisse and Léger murals, the most beautiful Picasso we had ever seen, and the fabulous view of the city and Central Park.

The guests included Nelson's brother David and his wife, Peggy, Mr. and Mrs. Russell Baker, and the Douglas Dillons (Dillon having been secretary of the Treasury in the Kennedy administration). When we met the former secretary, he looked a bit puzzled and then a light turned on. "I just today voted against you," he said to Jessica. She was totally mystified as to what he was talking about and showed it. He went on: "You were an independent candidate for AT&T's board, and it fell my lot to vote our proxies against you. If I had seen you first, I might not have!" Dillon was a director of AT&T. Eventually we found out that a strange corporate gadfly we had met in Washington had nominated Jessica for the board, without her knowledge or consent. But Dillon gained two fans that night.

Rockefeller, a superb host and a fine politician, put all his guests at ease, with gracious toasts and amusing stories. At a House hearing at which he reported on a trip to Latin America, he was lectured to by a particularly priggish congressman from New York named John Bingham. How could you, the indignant legislator asked, appear in public with the brutal dictator of Haiti, Papa Doc Duvalier? Nelson responded, "Jack, put yourself in my position. There I was, representing the president of the United States with the president of a country we have relations with, even though the relations are cool, and he says come out on the balcony and greet the crowd, and it's very hard not to go." Bingham primly asked, "Did you have to smile?" Rocky replied, "A politician with three hundred fifty thousand smiling, waving people in front of him? Who *wouldn't* smile?"

Rocky sometimes played straight man. At a party at Joan and Tom Braden's in 1971, he made a toast to Israeli ambassador Rabin. Carried away on a wave of goodwill and gemütlichkeit, he said, "The people of Israel are the most industrious, attractive, and grandest people I know of and I want to drink a toast to their health and the success of their country."

Ambassador Rabin rose to reply: "Thank you, Governor. Coming from you, the Governor of New York, it is doubly appreciated. You surely know the Jews well, since you control more of them than we do!"

Everyone roared, Rocky most of all.

D.C. *Family Life*

OUR LIVES were not all glamour and cavorting with the great. Indeed, as I go over my calendars, I am gratified to note how many things we did with the children and how many nights we spent quietly at home.

Having bitterly resisted the idea of leaving San Antonio, the children adapted surprisingly quickly to the Washington area. Heather attended the local public school in Montgomery County, John and Will went to Sidwell Friends School, and Isa enlivened the scene at Norwood School. The pleasures of a real winter entranced all of us. Our pool froze over, and someone borrowed a pair of skates from next door. No sooner was it determined that the ice would hold than Jessica was off to the store. Soon everyone had skates, and we went to the nearby C&O canal for some serious skating. A nonskater myself, I looked out at this brightly clad group and felt I had stumbled into a Pieter Brueghel painting of sixteenth-century Holland.

A hard winter yielded a gorgeous spring, and we were all awed by the color and variety of it. Spring in South Texas has its beauties and, above all, its scents, but for flamboyance, Washington can't be bested. First the forsythia in March dots the neighborhoods with vivid yellow. Azaleas in pink and red appear everywhere, and in recent years, thanks to Lady Bird Johnson, the tulips she had planted are bright enough to cause the viewer to squint. April's cherries and dogwoods hypnotize any newcomer. Five-year-old Isa, seeing bursts of blossoms fall from a cherry tree in a breeze, said, "Look, Mother, it's snowing flowers."

Our rotund and beloved mutt, Ginger, gave birth to nine—count them, nine—puppies. Our excitement gave way to a race to see who could park them with friends fastest, but two stayed with us to make up for the loss of Pancho, a giant, gentle, aged Belgian shepherd that had to be put away.

One day I pulled car pool duty and overheard seven-year-old Will and his classmate discussing strength. The friend commented on his own father's physical prowess, and I waited expectantly for Will to counter with an illustration of my own. Instead, I heard him say, "Aw, that's nothing. My grandfather is so strong he can even lift my sister." Ten-year-old Heather was not amused; I was.

One night I came home early and we decided to eat with the children for a change. Our habit had been to eat late, after feeding the young, so this represented a bit of a departure from the usual. Heather, seeing places set at the table for us, asked with disgust, "You're going to eat with us? Weird." As time passed, the "weird" became the usual as I clung to the quaint idea that family meals provide quality time together. For all the inevitable squabbles and sulks, I still think it worthwhile, though occasionally hard on the digestion.

Our house in Bethesda suffered from poor planning such that the easiest way to the backyard, pool, and neighboring homes led through our bedroom. This meant little privacy for Jessica and me, so occasionally we would sneak off to the guest room for a moment alone. On one such day, sure that we had escaped the children, we retreated, locked the door, and got ready for a bit of solitude. How futile! About five minutes after the click of the lock, a great pounding on the door began. It was John with news of an emergency: "Mom, come quick!" he demanded. "Isa's throwing perfume on the throw-up."

Jessica's main activities focused on raising the young, running the home, and promoting my career in a thousand subtle ways (her political acumen and people savvy far outstripped mine). On top of all that, she devoted time to volunteer efforts as well, such as working with Marg McNamara, wife of former secretary of defense Robert McNamara, in the literacy-promoting organization Reading Is Fundamental.

Marg, incidentally, had told us an interesting story as we hiked one day in Colorado. Recalling her husband's early days as secretary of defense, she said the conventional wisdom of how John Connally got to be secretary of the navy — that LBJ forced him on President Kennedy — was wrong. When McNamara agreed to leave Ford Motor Company, where he was CEO, and come to Washington, he told the president he wanted to choose his own team at the Defense Department. Kennedy concurred, but shortly thereafter he began to push Franklin Roosevelt Jr. for secretary of the navy. An interview with Roosevelt turned McNamara off, and he began to look elsewhere. Someone, she thought Sam Rayburn, suggested Connally, who quickly sold himself. McNamara called Kennedy in Florida to inform him. The president concurred and said there was someone else there McNamara would want to tell, handing the phone to LBJ, who learned for the first time that his longtime ally would be joining the administration.

Part 2

El Salvador

The Next Step

BY EARLY 1971 I began to lobby for a new challenge. The OAS job had been a fine introductory course to the world of government and diplomacy. My Spanish skills had been polished, I knew how the Department of State worked, and I knew the cast of characters, both political and career. Latin America continued to fascinate me, and Jessica, partly in the spirit of adventure and partly because she had come to loathe our house in Bethesda, was willing to give it a try. The children were game for a change.

I spread the word to Peter Flanigan, personnel chief at the White House, to the seventh floor at the State Department, where such decisions originated, and to George Bush. Then I sat back, did my job, and waited.

One of my duties at OAS lay in matters cultural, and occasionally that meant good duty. In May 1971 Secretary General Galo Plaza honored ninety-something cellist Pablo Casals, who was perhaps the greatest American musician at that time. First came a luncheon at the Pan American Union. Flags of member nations brightened the tropical ambience of that extraordinary place, and Casals's talk afterward, on how music could provide the path to international understanding, moved us all; his voice may have quavered, but his eyes sparkled with strength and understanding. That evening Jessica and I picked up Pamela Jova, John being out of town, and returned to the PAU for a concert with Casals conducting the National Symphony Orchestra in Schubert's Fifth Symphony. After the concert, which was vigorously led by the maestro, Galo gave Casals an award from the inter-American community. As he accepted the award, Casals spoke out clearly, saying, "It is nice to be back in Washington. You know, the first time I ever played here was for President Roosevelt . . . Theodore Roosevelt!" He enjoyed the reaction, a burst of laughter tinged with amazement.

My efforts to find a new job bore fruit, and I was asked to be the ambassador to El Salvador. Having been there, I knew that it was an interesting country, and the political situation seemed to present no danger to the family. Granting it to be small and little known, I accepted, realizing at last that ambition must be grounded in reality, and I could not reasonably expect a plum post. Besides, I would probably, at forty, be the youngest American ambassador. Diplomatic usage requires that the name of a prospective ambassador be approved by the host government. *Agrément,* as this step is called, is seldom denied, and on May 19, 1971, the Salvadoran Ministry of Foreign Relations gave me thumbs-up. We were elated.

The run-up to an ambassadorship consists of innumerable briefings, at State and other agencies with interest in the country. Since I already worked for the government, no further security clearances were needed, but the papers that must go to the White House for the president's final approval and then to the Senate for hearings and confirmation do not move speedily. The man I was to replace, William Bowdler (who in turn was being shifted to Guatemala), came by during a Washington visit, sharing with me much useful information on Salvadoran politics and society, and on the embassy and its personnel. Jessica and I went to the Foreign Buildings Office of State to see pictures of the residence, discuss furniture, paint, and other decorative matters. Leslie Scott had advised us to be tough with the FBO staff: "Tell them to be prepared to turn the house three degrees to the west and then bargain down from there." On her second visit, Jessica followed his advice, and the previously unforthcoming decorators came nicely into line.

I toured the communications center at State and admired the huge computer that sent an average of three thousand telegrams a day at twelve hundred words per minute to posts abroad. The man showing me about referred to the computer as "he" and "him," which interested me. I asked if the "H" was capitalized, but he didn't think that was funny.

Although El Salvador was safe at the time, I learned that, just in case, I would travel everywhere with a Salvadoran guard. We were briefed on "bugs" (listening devices), which can be planted in embassies and on people. The deputy chief of mission in Budapest, for example, had sent out a pair of shoes to be repaired. He later found out, thanks to alert U.S. counterintelligence, that Hungarian intelligence had planted listening devices in the heels of his shoes.

The White House was maddeningly slow in announcing the ambassadorial shift of Nathaniel Davis from Guatemala to Chile, Bowdler from Salvador to Guatemala, and me to El Salvador. I never learned why it kept being postponed, but it frustrated our whole family. I had already resigned the OAS job, and in July we simply pulled up stakes, kids, dogs, and all and went to our newly purchased vacation home in Aspen, Colorado, to await events. A State Department car took us to Dulles Airport, an event that today would be unthinkable as Congress in a righteous frenzy increasingly squeezes administration perks.

It turned out to be a fine summer: hikes in the mountains, tennis with the young, music at the incomparable Aspen Music Festival, and visits from good friends like Stevie and Lewis Tucker from San Antonio. Congress adjourned without acting on confirmation, and I finally relaxed and stopped worrying.

The great event of that summer was the president's dramatic announcement that Henry Kissinger had been to Peking and that Nixon himself would follow. I approved of the move, but John Tower and Colorado senator Peter Dominick questioned its wisdom. World public opinion, however, saw a Nixon-Kissinger coup, and time would prove the world's view correct as Kissinger brilliantly played the Communist giants off against one another. Jessica felt that Vice President Spiro Agnew, who had placed himself politically on the far right, would be hurt, and I noted in my diary, "I fervently hope so" and that it would be great if he would quit the ticket in '72 out of principle. (Since his selection in 1968, I had disliked Agnew, as, incidentally, did George Bush. Our instincts proved sound, as the vice president was forced to resign in 1973 to avoid an indictment for corruption.)

In early September I returned to Washington to resume calls on Cabinet members, receive more briefings, and await confirmation hearings. A call on Deputy Secretary of Commerce James Lynn revealed problems between the United States and El Salvador. As was the case with many countries, the United States limited the amount of textiles that could be imported from El Salvador, and the limit was fast approaching. Some charged that the country's shrimp exports to us were unclean. I sensed headaches ahead. Calls on the secretaries of the Treasury, Agriculture, and Labor, as well as the Peace Corps director and the director of the CIA, Richard Helms, revealed no great problems.

At the confirmation hearing on September 21, things went smoothly as both Texas senators, Lloyd Bentsen and John Tower, testified on my behalf, and on September 28, we (Bowdler, Davis, and I) were confirmed. Chief of Protocol Emil "Bus" Mosbacher swore me in shortly thereafter at the State Department. We had a reception afterward in the handsome eighth-floor facilities, with Jessica's mother in attendance. The formalities were over. A trip to Texas to say "adios" to the grandparents, and we were on our way.

Anatomy of an Embassy

THE FLIGHT time between Texas and El Salvador is under three hours, but the psychic leap is light-years. Terrain, people, customs—all differ extravagantly. As we six, in our great Pan Am plane (Pan Am, poor Pan Am, was the umbilical cord to Latin America; how I miss it!), swooped down toward the capital, San Salvador, I thought the mountainous land resembled nothing so much as crumpled green velvet.

The flight was broken in Guatemala City, and to my surprise and pleasure, the new ambassador to Guatemala (and my predecessor in El Salvador), Bill Bowdler and his wife, Peggy, greeted us. They stayed to visit with us during the forty-five-minute layover; their thoughtfulness became the first building block in a warm friendship that included the Bowdler children and our own.

Our ties with El Salvador are old. In November 1822, the Colossus of the North, Mexico, began to look hungrily at the newly independent (from Spain) countries of Central America. Distrustful of Mexico, a Salvadoran congress declared the province a state of the Union. Alas, the U.S. Congress declined to go along with this unique move, and El Salvador joined the United Provinces of Central America.

We arrived in San Salvador, the capital city, at about five o'clock on the rainy afternoon of October 13, 1971. Waiting to greet us was the "country team" (the heads of various components of the embassy) and their spouses, led by Deputy Chief of Mission Terry Leonhardy. A man from the foreign ministry protocol office added his welcome, and a large battery of photographers and reporters made us feel like celebrities.

A reception in the VIP lounge took a few minutes, and then we were off to our new home, through swiftly drying streets and the slanting rays of the setting tropical sun.

Located in a suburb called San Benito, the embassy residence was built in the open and inviting white stucco architecture typical of that part of the world. A soldier at the front gate gave us a smart (well, sort of) salute as the motorcade stopped and disgorged us. Waiting at the door, the house staff of eight smilingly offered "Bienvenidos"; they were soon to become fixtures in our lives, as well as friends. Bright flowers waited on every table. The children immediately raced about, picking out rooms and then comparing notes to see who had the best deal. Will and John had to bunk together, a disadvantage, but the two-level feature of their room was considered chic, so everyone was content. Heather's room had a large closet that became her hideout. There she did her homework, wrote her letters, and secretly (so she thought) smoked.

The pleasant and airy living area gave onto a large covered porch and a beautifully lighted pool, tropical trees and flowers in abundance. The pool was officially termed an "auxiliary water supply," lest Congress think that American ambassadors had too luxe a life, with swimming pools.

Shortly, the house filled up with embassy people, champagne flowed, and we began to sort out faces and names. One couple was easy: my old colleague from OAS days, Leslie Scott, his wife, Sandee, and son, Phillip, had recently been posted to El Salvador, Les being the head of the embassy's political section. After an hour or so, the guests were shoved out by the indomitable Lee Leonhardy, Terry's wife, and we just as quickly sneaked the Scotts back in to join us for supper. (Les had been much in demand as the only officer who could expatiate upon the new ambassador's crotchets, always a topic of intense interest at an embassy. A good ambassador can be career-enhancing for his staff; a bad one can make life hell.)

The first night, the two younger children had the night wanders, so sleep was in short supply. Heather, at twelve mature and confident, nonetheless suffered *tristesse*. She feared a school full of strangers and sobbed to her mother, "John has Will, Isa will have Ginger [the soon-to arrive dog], you have Dad, but I don't have *anybody*."

Next morning we were, if not rested, at least excited. Jessica began her redecorating efforts by taking down a large big-brother kind of photo of President Nixon and consigning it to the closet, where it stayed. Heather discovered and found it strange that the house had two parts: ours and the staff's (each wing had five bedrooms). I checked out the bathhouse and stumbled onto two more full bathrooms, previously unknown.

The weather was soft and beautiful, the colors of the sky vivid and the contrast with storm clouds exciting. There are two seasons in tropical Central America, wet and dry (Salvadorans call the first winter, the second summer). "Winter" begins in May and runs to late October, with frequent—and dramatic—evening storms. "Summer" has little or no rain, the land's lurid green giving way to brown; the return of May and rain is most welcome. Each morning, winter or summer, a large and colorful flight of parrots flew over our house, toward we knew not where. In the evening, like commuters, they noisily returned.

My arrival at the office on Day One was later than usual. The chancellery, as an embassy office is called, was a strikingly handsome building, vaguely Mayan in feel, done by a St. Louis architect. My desk groaned under accumulated *papelería* (paperwork), but my assistant, Edna Long, had preceded me and had things shipshape. It was my good fortune to inherit her, a career foreign service secretary, at the OAS mission, and she put up with me through all my posts until we left government in 1977.

Arrival at the chancellery had been impressive. The U.S. Marine guards were lined up in full dress uniform, and as we drove into the basement garage, they snapped to a very crisp salute. Their leader, a gunnery sergeant, led me to inspect them. Marines traditionally guard U.S. embassies abroad and the duty is much prized. Add to the usual rigors of Marine life the necessity to become a bit diplomatic, and you have a challenge, as I was to learn.

The day slipped by quickly, as I toured the building, spoke to the warm and welcoming staff, and went home for lunch. (El Salvador, like much of Latin America, closed down at midday, though the custom is fading today.) That afternoon, Ed Brown, the administrative officer, briefed me on security. To a North American (Latin Americans consider themselves Americans too and often make the distinction formal via the "North") it was a shock. Brown said that should I ever be driving myself in the countryside and hit a pedestrian, under no circumstances was I to stop. I should go quickly to the nearest police station and report the accident, but *never* should I get out of the car. Salvadorans are a violent people, he explained, and on more than one occasion, relatives of a person injured in an accident would appear and administer curbside justice to the driver—with machetes. In one memorable case, a physician who was trying to attend to a person he had injured lost his hand for his trouble; he was lucky not to have lost his life.

Most Americans haven't the faintest idea what goes on at an embassy. They know it's where you turn if you lose your passport or get arrested, but beyond that, it is a mystery. I wasn't quite that ignorant; I had by then traveled a good bit and had had dealings with a number of embassies, but I was to learn much more.

At the top of an embassy sits the ambassador, who orchestrates a variety of agencies in what he or she hopes will be a coherent whole. He is the president's personal representative to the country to which he is accredited, and within the country he has real authority over U.S government employees and great influence within the American community if there is one—and there almost always is. If he is serving in a foreign country, as opposed to being "at large," he is called "ambassador extraordinary and plenipotentiary," which might make you think he's calling himself "plenty powerful," but what it really means is that he can negotiate treaties. I looked the word up once and was delighted to learn of its derivation from the French *ambassadeur,* from the vulgar Latin *ambactiator* (a messenger), and from the Latin *ambactus,* meaning "vassal." I was Nixon's vassal.

The number two person is the deputy chief of mission (DCM), who runs the show as "chargé d'affaires" when the boss is away and acts as his executive officer. Terry Leonhardy proved a strong right hand, amusing, well connected, and wise. At his next post, in Guadalajara, Mexico, he was kidnapped by leftists and held for ransom, a frightening and difficult experience that, fortunately, he survived.

Senior officers include the heads of the political and economic sections, the consul general, and the administrative officer, all of them usually State Department officers. The commercial attaché, a Commerce Department officer, works to improve U.S. business relations, and the United States Information Agency's representative, known as the public affairs officer, or PAO, provides guidance in the areas of press and educational exchanges. Other agencies include Agriculture, Labor, the Pentagon's defense attaché, in developing countries an Agency for International Development (AID) contingent; a Peace Corps director, and often Central Intelligence Agency representation. The Federal Bureau of Investigation (FBI) is sometimes on board as legal attaché, and depending on embassy size and importance, there may be people from the Federal Aviation Administration, the Food and Drug Administration, the Customs Service, and so on. In El Salvador we were about two hundred strong, with many of those working on various AID projects.

Almost every embassy has local employees, or foreign service nationals (FSNs), as they are called. They provide the basic support service for the mission and serve as a channel of knowledge and advice about the host country. They represent the corporate memory of the operation; we come and go, but often the FSNs provide a lifetime of capable service to the U.S. government, and doing without them, as the U.S. embassy in Moscow had to do for an achingly long time, makes life extremely difficult.[1]

A post like mine, I realized, has four constituencies that clamor for time and attention: the host government and its people, the embassy itself, the American business community, and the diplomatic corps — the other ambassadors. The first three clearly rank as vital; the last just takes time. (Though if you ignored it you would soon hear complaints — ambassadors take themselves seriously.)

In a way, an embassy resembles a newspaper. A group of highly skilled and trained people endeavor to find out what's happening. They report and interpret what they learn, and they try to anticipate pitfalls. Clearly the audience for this reporting can't compare with that of a great metropolitan paper; the target is, after all, a handful of offices at State, Commerce, and other agencies. Still, the impact can be important, for the audience determines policy and allocates resources.

El Salvador Overview

EL SALVADOR, the most densely populated country in the Americas save Haiti, nestles between Honduras and Guatemala at the heart of the Central American isthmus. The people are a mixture of Mayan and Spanish.

Their history does not distinguish itself for peace and nonviolence: dictators are the rule, revolt the norm, as strong men struggle for control. In the 1960s, however, a tradition of guided democracy began to take root. Two main parties developed: the one allied with the military (the Partido de Conciliación Nacional, or PCN) always won the presidency and most legislative seats, but a second, the Christian Democrats (the PDC), controlled most mayoralties and a respectable number of assembly seats. There was hope that a genuine democracy would develop, a hope soon tested by an election.

The country's economy depended primarily on coffee, and the rich green highland terrain produced some of the world's best. Rice and cotton were important, and a good sprinkling of small manufacturing plants had begun to spring up, reflecting a native industriousness and entrepreneurial spirit. Some Salvadorans even dreamed of themselves as the Japan of Central America, a prospect made remote in my mind by the grinding poverty, poor education, and exploding population growth (3.4 percent a year). A number of wealthy families, dubbed "the Catorce" (the Fourteen) by *Time* magazine but probably numbering one hundred, operated vast *fincas,* or plantations.

U.S. development help, provided by USAID, was concentrated in education, housing, and population control. Sometimes the U.S. vision of development and the Salvadoran vision diverged. The Salvadorans asked us to provide $8 million for new rural schools. Okay, we said, but you must, of course, have running water for toilets and electricity at each. No way, the Ministry of Education replied. We're talking about *rural* schools—in most areas, running water and electricity don't exist; chemical toilets will be fine. No, USAID's people said, learning about sanitation is part of the education experience. Okay, was the riposte, but who will fix flush toilets when they break down? We can at least teach proper methods of digging privies. And so it went, a dialogue of the deaf. The Nordic approach versus the Latin. Eventually, a compromise allowed for water and lights wherever it was feasible.

Other assistance projects showed greater imagination. We helped with *vivienda minima* (minimal housing), a program in which the government organized the urban poor to build a cluster of houses that were shells, with only walls and roofs. Then each man who helped with the organized work would draw lots for a house and finish it himself, the costs being borne by subsidized loans at very low interest. In another scenario, the Peace Corps helped a group of fishermen form a highly successful cooperative that cut out the gouging wholesalers.

Land reform in a country like El Salvador had an appealing ring to it. The population being dense and the supply of land finite, politicians from center to far left often called for the breakup of the large estates and redistribution of the land to the peasants.

Landowners viewed this idea with fear and loathing but traditionally did little more than point to the undeniably high productivity of the great estates in defense of the status quo. Their argument suffered, however, from the existence of large spreads of totally unused land — property belonging to city dwellers who were uninterested in agriculture, farms made idle by the death of the owners, or whatever.

Noting this anomaly and eager to blunt reform efforts, a group of businessmen led by the always imaginative Francisco "Chico" de Sola came up with a unique idea. Contributing $1 million in capital, they began to buy idle property, subdivide it, and sell it on easy terms to peasants. The results of this program, two years old when I became aware of it, were astounding. A drive down a dusty rural road where the private reformers had operated revealed a startling difference. On one side were dozens of tidily fenced green fields, obviously highly productive. On the other side, sere grass nourished an occasional forlorn, flat-flanked cow. Deeply impressed, I tried to interest the widely read *Readers Digest* in doing an article on the Salvadoran effort but had no success.

One day I noted a telegram from USAID Washington, saying they were prepared to send us "100 gross colored condoms" for our important population control efforts. I contemplated wiring back, "Which color do you consider gross?" but doubting the sense of humor of AID bureaucrats, I resisted.

The routine at the embassy became familiar. Staff meetings of the country team took place in a frigid plastic "bubble," a room secure from eavesdroppers. (Years later, Marxist guerrillas put a rocket through it, accidentally, I feel sure; fortunately no one was hurt.)

Early on in Washington I learned that State Department prose had little relation to English as I knew it. As in all government offices, acronyms abound. I learned that "GOES" was not a verb but the Government of El Salvador. "HIM" didn't replace a noun as a pronoun, it meant "His Imperial Majesty." "GOP" was not the party that was the light of my life, it was the Government of Peru. Letters between governments kept the old, stilted styles, and correspondence between ambassadors would close with "Accept, excellency, the renewed assurances of my highest consideration." A declaration of war might have been the topic at hand, but we did it politely.

The remarkable Edna Long kept me moving through the endless diplomatic calls. Usage dictated that each of my fellow resident ambassadors (there were about twenty-five) would come by my office and call on me. I would then reciprocate, calling on them. With turnover, I was expected to call on and receive ambassadors who came to the country after I had, so it never ended.

The quality of the diplomatic corps was, well, spotty. The Italian, a very lively and bright man named Erberto Casagrandi, could have fit in anywhere in the world. Others, frequently given the job to get them out of their country and thus avoid potential political mischief, left something to be desired.

Our call on the ambassador of the Dominican Republic and his wife remains memorable. (Jessica, a saint, often went with me in order to meet ambassadorial spouses.) On arrival, we were ushered into a small living room (this was no grand embassy residence; indeed, it was quite modest). Once we had gotten past how many children we each had and how long we had served in El Salvador, the talk lagged a bit. Fortunately, there sat on a perch in the middle of the room a large and colorful parrot. I was about to comment on the bird when he preempted me, letting go with a great plop on the carpet below him.

Jessica and I assumed that a servant would soon be summoned or that our host, at least, would clean up. Not so. When the conversation slowed, all eyes — especially ours — would hypnotically turn, riveted, to the mess on the rug. No one came. We went.

The British ambassador was a career man on his last post before retirement, a bachelor, rotund, pink-cheeked, and vaguely distracted. His days — and presumably his nights — were made light by a portly Spanish woman of a certain age whom he introduced as his cousin. The matter caused a great scandal, with Mrs. Sánchez, the president's wife, refusing to receive the "cousin." In due course, the obstacle to holy matrimony, whatever it may have been, disappeared, they were wed, and the new ambassadress basked in the light of Mrs. Sánchez's approval.

Jessica also called on El Salvador's first lady, a day seared in her memory. Delia Maynes, wife of defense attaché George Maynes and a fluent Spanish speaker from El Paso, went along for moral and, if needed, linguistic support. They assumed that the visit would be merely a brief formality. It was not to be. Mrs. Sánchez surrounded herself with a large retinue, and all sat around chatting — for two hours. The conversation ranged from the inevitable "Y cuantos niños tiene?" (How many children have you?), to explicit detailing of the agonies of the colonically distressed, to kidney stones. Delia and Jessica glanced at each other from time to time, their eyes rolled upward, but they persevered.

I, of course, had called on President Fidel Sánchez to "present credentials," a hoary diplomatic tradition in which the new representative of a foreign power assures the local authority of his bona fides. The great day arrived with a roar of motorcycle escorts pulling up in our driveway at 11 A.M. Two senior embassy officers, the Salvadoran chief of protocol, and I hopped aboard my ancient black Buick and sped away, ambassadorial and U.S. flags flapping on the fenders. Stopping all traffic, we soon drew up to the presidential palace, a large, agreeable white stucco building in a downtown park. I emerged, walked to the fourth step of the entrance, and did an about-face. Troops were lined up in front, and a band played the Salvadoran national anthem, at three and a half minutes surely the world's longest. I did a sort of Episcopalian genuflection (a nod) to the Salvadoran flag, and we entered the building. The deputy minister of foreign affairs presented me to the minister, who took me in to the president.

Fidel Sánchez Hernández was a personable career military man of little over five feet, a fact that even his erect carriage could not disguise. Behind his back, he was called *tapon* (the cork, or in slang, a short, fat person). We had been told there would be no substantive talks, but the president apparently hadn't read that script, for he launched at once into the matter of how rural schools should be equipped. After fifteen minutes, the chief of protocol came in, and we understood the meeting had ended. At the entrance to the palace the band again played, this time a superbly rendered "Star-Spangled Banner." Moved, I went to greet and thank the bandleader, thus cementing U.S. relations with at least one Salvadoran. Back at the house with the protocol chief and our senior staff, much champagne flowed and many toasts to friendship and other eternal verities were offered. The afternoon was not too productive.

Highlights such as credentials presentation proved the exception; the rule was more mundane. Each of the cabinet members required a get-acquainted session, as did the various police and military organs. Trips to see provincial governors and mayors took time, and frequently a cast-iron stomach, for these rural barons liked to eat and especially to imbibe Scotch whisky, which Les Scott laughingly called the national drink.

The newspaper and TV merited special attention. All Salvadorans assured me there was no censorship, and indeed, no musty blue-pencil office existed in the Ministry of the Interior. There was no need: the three dailies knew exactly what to print and what not to, and articles that might annoy the government were rare.

The system of justice was deeply flawed as well. The courts, often manned by incompetent judges, lacked any semblance of impartiality. Police restraint did not exist, and investigative procedures were at best primitive. The embassy had on staff a fine American public safety adviser, Richard Martinez, but one man, a foreigner at that, cannot undo history. Furthermore, there were eventually successful pressures in Congress to abolish the public safety program because of fears that our people trained the locals in torture techniques. I found that idea particularly odious. Quite to the contrary, Martinez and his colleagues did much to inculcate compassionate handling of prisoners, safe crowd-control measures, and effective modern police techniques.

Within a few months, the pattern of *subdesarollo,* or underdevelopment, became clear. No matter where one starts, the facets of it are mutually reinforcing. Bad government leads to bad education, which leads to poor health practices and little family planning, which leads to too many people, which leads to a backward economy, which contributes to bad government. It is not a merry- but a sad-go-round, and dismounting can easily seem impossible. Dependence on foreign assistance just won't do it. Somehow it has to come from within, and thus far, thanks at least partly to twelve years of civil war, in El Salvador that hasn't happened.

A Day in the Life . . .

AN AMBASSADOR'S day is like a dentist's: people come to see you in unending procession. In El Salvador, they frequently came with requests for help. In July 1972, the vice president of the Social Security Institute came. His request: a helicopter, which would enable his people to deal directly with cases in the remote areas. I pointed out that these machines were expensive, hellishly difficult to fly and even more so to maintain, and that I really didn't have any in inventory, in any case. He scoffed at my objections, and in the end I inquired of the military assistance ground commander if anything could be done. Nothing could be.

More realistic but no more successful, a delegation of coffee growers dropped by to request a higher quota for Salvadoran coffee. A group of businessmen who were volunteer firemen in the suburban town of Santa Tecla came by to ask for a fire truck. They had no tax base with which to work and thought Uncle Sam might be their Santa Claus. The State Department having few to no fire engines, I wrote San Antonio mayor Jack Gatti to see about the chances of a hand-me-down from an American city. Not likely, he replied.

Requests for help occasionally were truly imaginative. For example, one day in May 1972, the following letter arrived:

Dear Mr. Ambassador:

As I was wandering around my house the other day, I noticed the statue of the late great President John F. Kennedy. It was a little dusty so I picked it up to dust it off and as I did, you can imagine my surprise when I saw a slight movement of the nose of the statue and the appearance of a smile on the mouth. I shook my head as if in a dream and said to the statue, "Kennedy, I certainly admire you and wish you were here to help me with the formation of my Baby Football Team." At that point the statue said to me, "Paniagua, I want you to go right now to the ambassador of my country because I know he will help you get the money to form your Baby Football Team." Therefore, Mr. Ambassador, I urge you to give me an appointment at your earliest convenience.

Attentively,
Amarilis Paniagua Cedillos

Uncle Sam wasn't always niggardly, and when we could do small but symbolic things, appreciation made water come to the eye. In June 1972 I went to the annual Fourth of July festival at the school in a remote, grindingly poor village called Comesaqua. The school, called Escuela Estados Unidos de América, had received AID help some years before, and each year it celebrated its tie to the great northern neighbor. A queen, a beautiful five-year-old, suffered herself to be crowned by me, and an Uncle Sam, also five, with long striped trousers, a tall blue hat, and white whiskers, came and sat at the queen's feet. Dancers performed, and speeches (one by me) extolled the United States, its philosophy, and its history. Doug Ellerby of the United States Information Service (USIS) presented the school with a loudspeaker system, books, and a model of the

Apollo rocket. A parade followed, watched by a crowd of perhaps two hundred, impressive for so small a place. Everyone cheered and waved small paper American flags as the queen and Uncle Sam circled the village square. Doug and I had serious cases of lump in the throat as we drove away down the dusty rural road.

Another touching example of the importance of the United States in even the remotest places came from a tiny village called Santa Teresa. One day I received a visit from the mayor, who said he had seen my picture in the paper doing things around the country and he and his people would like for me to come to inaugurate their new water system. Four kilometers off a highway, the town typified rural El Salvador. As usual, a square and a church dominated the center, with adobe houses of decreasing size spreading out from there. No streets were paved, and chickens scratched about in the dust. Water had to be carried, usually in pots balanced miraculously on women's heads, from a filthy river that lay a couple of hundred yards away.

The object of my visit, a freshly drilled, centrally located well, had washing and shower stations and, above all, made relatively clean water easily available. Flags and bunting welcomed the visitors. I shared honors as platform guest and speaker with an exiled ex-president of Guatemala, a dignified chap whose presence in so tiny a place mystified me. Also on the platform sat a barefoot village elder who had partaken of far too much local rum and who frequently had to be elbowed awake by a colleague. The importance of such changes in these people's lives was hard to overestimate, and the event defined for me the satisfaction of my job more than all the diplomatic dinners combined.

USIS's role went far beyond small gifts to remote schools. Perhaps the best program the embassy had was its Leader Grants (now called International Visitor Grants), in which future leaders from foreign countries are sent to the United States for a month to do what they like, all expenses paid. Although arranged by the USIA (USIA refers to the whole agency; in the specific country the operation is called USIS), the trips are made possible by an array of volunteers nationwide. A young attorney and Christian Democrat activist with anti-U.S. leanings named Fidel Chávez Mena went on a grant at Les Scott's suggestion. On his return he came by to say thank you. With stars in his eyes, he recounted the details; clearly America had a new friend. Some dozen years later, he became foreign minister and, still later, a candidate for president.

An American ambassador, especially in a small or remote post, inevitably acts a bit in loco parentis, as leader and ceremonial head of the American community. This role came as a surprise to me, since I had never thought of myself as a leader.

For many years it had been traditional for ambassadors everywhere to have a giant Fourth of July reception for the diplomatic corps, local leaders, and the American community. Over time, however, as budgets shrank and our numbers abroad grew, it became impossible to continue this celebration. Fortunately, in most countries there is an American society, and in El Salvador and many other places, that organization took up the slack by staging a picnic or a reception.

Our first year in El Salvador this event took place at a lakeside park not far from town. There must have been two hundred people, munching hot dogs, boating, drinking beer, playing softball, having relays, competing in sack races, and enjoying all the things we do. One event I had never seen was an egg toss. Two teams line up facing one another. An egg is handed from each team member in line A to his counterpart in line B. Both then take a step back and toss the egg. In short order, eggs are splattering like shells over Fort McHenry — on clothes, faces, and hair — amidst high hilarity. Jessica and I didn't make it past the third toss, but John and his friend came in runners-up, thus upholding Catto honor.

At dusk, the U.S. Marine guard in full uniform presented the colors, we sang "The Star-Spangled Banner" to recorded accompaniment, and I read the president's moving message to the American people. (Speaking in public had once left me mute with terror. Fortunately, over the years the stomach-wrenching fear abated and the latent ham in me took over.)

The business community also requested guidance. A respectable number of U.S. companies had Salvadoran operations, but there was no single voice to speak for common interests. I suggested and helped found an American Chamber of Commerce, today a useful advocate for U.S. commercial activity and the promotion of U.S. exports.

In October 1972 we were informed of a new Federal Women's Program, the purpose of which was to correct instances of career discrimination or poor working conditions. I called a meeting of senior women employees and appointed a coordinator, Mary Keany, a USIS employee who had become a good friend. Mary had a specific idea. Each weekend, on a rotating basis, someone served as duty secretary, in case of emergency need. (There was a duty officer as well.) This meant that the lucky one could not go anywhere, and with only a small pool of secretaries, each name came up frequently. Mary said, "Let's abolish it! It's never been used and it's a drag." I agreed, and weekend duty became a relic of the past.

Among the most difficult problems were those that would tax a psychiatrist, which I most certainly was not. An AID officer came by one day, ostensibly on business, but it soon became clear he wanted to talk about his troubled twenty-year-old son. Another day a Peace Corps official, looking as downcast as a *putto* from the Sistine ceiling, revealed an affair with the wife of an economic officer (I eventually had to send both couples back to the States, as they seemed unable to resolve their problems).

Occasionally zeal overcame judgment. Lieutenant Colonel Bill Willis, commander of our military group, came by one day looking very abashed. "Sir," he said, "something happened yesterday you should know about." "What was that?" I asked. "Well," he replied, "I was driving myself out to Santa Ana and just as I crested a hill, a truck coming the other way was passing a car, and he forced me off the road." "Terrible," I said. "Were you hurt?" "No, sir, but I was sure mad. I turned around and chased him." "Go on," I said. "Sir, I curbed him. I know it wasn't right, but I wanted to explain how dangerous what he did was." (Bill's Spanish would not have passed muster at the Madrid Academy, but he could be understood.) "And when I finished, well, I was really mad and so I pulled out my revolver and shot out his tires."

Visions of both of us being declared persona non grata flew through my head as I imagined what would happen when the horrified trucker reported being assaulted by a crazed gringo. I said, "That wasn't very wise, Bill, but let's see what happens." Amazingly, nothing happened. We heard from no authority, civil or military, and we could do nothing ourselves, as Bill had no idea of the trucker's identity. I speculated that the poor man decided to let it drop rather than risk another encounter with *norteamericanos*.

Violence was a way of life in El Salvador. One day, returning from a Sunday at the beach with the family, I had to swerve the car to avoid running over a seriously dead man on the highway. I later learned he had been killed by *machetazos* (machete chops) in a drunken brawl.

Domestic and Social Conventions

LIFE AT home developed a leisurely rhythm. Most days, I lunched with
Jessica, according to Salvadoran custom. This at first assaulted my Puri-
tan conscience; it seemed vaguely wrong to break the day, perhaps even
(sweet sin) to nap briefly after lunch.

Our house, open and perfumed with tropical flowers, lent itself to outdoor life. The staff, led by cook Genoveva Crespín and house man David
Arriaza, looked after us beautifully, and, not for the first time, Calvinis-
tic hard edges softened in the dulcet air.

Social life differed from that in Washington as well. Functions started
later; sitting down to eat at ten-thirty or eleven o'clock at night was not
uncommon. Guests, especially government officials, sometimes failed to
show up, an event that caused considerable consternation as table seat-
ings underwent last-minute reshuffling. El Salvador's *gratin,* the wealthy
families, usually sent their scions to Europe or the United States to be
educated, and the resultant sophistication made socializing pleasant.
Government figures, on the other hand, especially the leadership of the
so-called official party (PCN) were frequently of rural or lower-middle-
class origin, and that led to social patterns of a different nature. The men
would inevitably cluster and talk while the women would do the same.
Social mixing of the wealthy planters and businesspeople with the military and government people was rare.

Jessica, as ambassador's wife, had certain "duties" thrust upon her.
These she handled supremely well, but in her own way. Lee Leonhardy,
the DCM's wife, soon learned that telling Jessica "this is how it's done"
was counterproductive. One of the customs of embassy life was for foreign service officers' wives to call on Mrs. Ambassador, complete with
calling card. Frequently talented people, these women were even expected
to help their superiors unpack china, serve at teas, or bake cookies. Jessica put an end to all that. She received the wives in groups, dispensed with
formalities, and in an amazingly brief time, she was simply "Jessica" to
all concerned.

One day early in our tenure the doorbell rang. Jessica and I had just
returned from a tennis game and she was still in her tennis dress. Being

close by, she answered the door. Outside stood a tall, handsome, gray-haired man. He took one look at Jessica in the short dress, barefoot, and said, "Hello, young lady, is your mother here?" Irish blarney or genuine mistake, neighbor Terry O'Sullivan made a friend for life.

All the children attended the Escuela Americana, the American School, located a couple of blocks from our house. Most of the time Jessica's driver and a guard took them to school, but occasionally that duty fell to me and I would drop them off on my way to the office. Once, doing so left me very red of face.

Some weeks previous, administrative officer Ed Brown had come by my office, excited as a child with a new toy. It seems he had received a new security device for my car. It involved putting a microphone in the backseat, next to where I always sat. On the floor, near my feet, lay a hardly visible button that, when touched, turned on all the radios in the private embassy radio network. Thus, if bad guys stopped my car in a kidnap attempt, all I had to do was touch the button with my foot and call for help into the mike. The U.S. Marines at the embassy would be alerted, as would all senior officers who had radios in their homes. Rescue — or at least revenge — would be swift.

On the morning in question, John was the only one of the children that I was to ferry. For whatever reason, he had been sullen and difficult during breakfast and when the others were left behind, I lost my temper and let him have it verbally. The minute I dropped him off, of course, I was swept by guilt. Poor lad, he was only eleven. I'm supposed to be cool and reasoned and civilized, and I had been quite the opposite. "Oh, well," I thought, "I'll try to do better next time," and I put it out of my mind.

Shortly thereafter we arrived at the embassy, but the scene was unusual: As we turned in, a pair of anxious-looking Marines rushed breathlessly to the car.

"Are you all right, sir?" one asked.

"Of course, as you can clearly see," I replied.

"But you kicked the button a few minutes ago, and we were concerned," he said.

"My God," I thought, "my tantrum has been broadcast into every receiver we have." Apparently, my foot hit the "hot button" when I got into the car, and the alarm had sounded. Thenceforth, I treated the wretched device the way Dracula treated the Cross.

Dinner generally was served under a flower-covered arbor just beyond the patio, with all children present. I felt that this idyllic spot would lend itself to family harmony and, indeed, harmony generally obtained. One night, however, I felt that Jessica had been short with one of the young. When we left the table, I took her arm and guided her out of earshot in a walk around the pool, telling her rather pompously that she had been too harsh. In a flash, she pushed me, clothes and all, into the pool with a great splash. The children saw what had gone on, and they soon had their mother and each other pushed in. All anger quickly washed away in the moment of high hilarity.

Halloween, American style, had never been observed in El Salvador until the American community grew large, but it had caught on, and I decided the first year that we would do the traditional trick-or-treat routine. Security, however, made for problems, so the poor children (save for Heather, who, feeling too old for such, stayed home) found themselves bundled into my car while my driver, Mario Pérez, slowly drove us around San Benito, our neighborhood. The pickings proved slim, but good enough to satisfy the younger three, who raced from house to house in search of loot. The next year a damper was put on such activities when the Israeli embassy reportedly passed the word that Jewish children would be well advised to abstain — and not for any religious overtones that the holiday might still have. The massacre of Israeli Olympic athletes in Munich had made for nervousness among Jews, even as far away as Salvador, and it took time for it to wear off.

Like international terrorism, narcotics abuse had become a problem. El Salvador did not appear to be a major center for drug trafficking, but marijuana use, especially among the young, was common. The country team discussed the matter in detail, and I decided to call a meeting of all the children twelve and over in the U.S. embassy community.

This move did not spring from anti-marijuana zeal alone. I was fairly sure Heather had experimented with it and perhaps John as well, and I thought that mobilizing peer pressure might somehow make it less fashionable. Beyond that, El Salvador, like most Latin American countries, took a very dim view of drugs, and we at the embassy were fearful of the young being thrown in jail, diplomatic immunity notwithstanding. Indeed, the bright and attractive seventeen-year-old son of a USAID officer was caught with pot on his person and spent a night in jail. It was bad for him and bad for our country's image.

Trying to avoid future problems, I invited the twenty-five or so embassy teenagers for Cokes and a stern lecture one evening. The results were yawns among the young and embarrassment among my own children. But there were no more incidents.

Culture Shock

LATIN AMERICAN resentment in the face of American power colored all our dealings. It pervaded all sectors of society, except for the lowest stratum, where goodwill, acceptance, and fading pictures of John F. Kennedy in the humblest homes gave witness to a genuine warmth toward the United States. The Catorce in El Salvador frequently received their education among the gringos. They spoke perfect English, lived gracious lives, and took fashion cues from the north, though many had close ties with Europe as well. It was not uncommon, nonetheless, to detect a barb in conversation or an eyebrow lifted in if not scorn at least skepticism, when talk turned to American culture. The growing middle class ironically nurtured the bright and increasingly militant Marxists, who would soon unleash more than a decade of bloody war against a society they viewed as hopelessly corrupt.

The conflicts of approach revealed themselves in many areas of life. In a move to improve the quality of the Salvadoran Symphony Orchestra, its board decided to hire a young Mexican, Alejandro Kahan, as conductor. The Peace Corps at the time had a volunteer working with the orchestra, and she greeted the move with enthusiasm. Before Kahan arrived, however, a Guatemalan came to town, performed as guest conductor, and on hearing complaints about Kahan, proclaimed that the orchestra had no problems and the musicians were fine. The Peace Corps volunteer, whose knowledge of the musicians by then was quite thorough, publicly disagreed. The press picked it up, and a full-blown squabble ensued, as cultural nationalists decried Yankee interference in local matters, cultural condescension, and endangering of fine musicians' jobs. I received a letter asking that I throw the volunteer out of the country, which I declined to do. Eventually, Alejandro arrived and with talent, diplomacy, and a new program of free concerts, quieted the fracas.

A similar problem arose in the Escuela Americana, but the outcome was not so happy. An able new headmaster, Bob Hayden, had been hired by the board, but alas, his diplomatic ability did not match his pedagogy. Early on, he opined at a cocktail party that the problem with the school could be solved by firing about half the faculty. The word spread, and sixteen elementary school teachers decided to bypass the board and take their insulted dignity straight to the Ministry of the Interior and the Ministry of Labor. Of the first they demanded Hayden's expulsion from the country, and they reminded the latter that the law said no more than 10 percent of a faculty could be foreign and the ratio at Escuela Americana was closer to half. No one had been fired, nor had the board given serious thought to it, but nationalistic sensitivities had quickly been rubbed raw.

At first I tried to stay out of it, but I soon decided that would not work. I met with the board and urged them to control the complainers lest they totally lose sway. By way of sanction I said that if Hayden were thrown out, I would withdraw the $25,000 subsidy the embassy provided. The board responded positively and girded its loins for a fight. At this point, poor Bob Hayden decided that no matter who won he was damaged goods. He left, and the school relapsed into its comfortable mediocrity.

Cold War thinking being pervasive in the 1970s, I noted with some concern in November 1971 that the Siberian Ballet planned a visit to San Salvador as part of the opening of the new Teatro Presidente. The Mexican Folklórico and a Colombian ballet group were also coming. After seeing the Siberians perform beautifully, I determined to get an American artist of stature to perform and join in the celebration.

About that time I learned that Duke Ellington and his orchestra were to tour several South American countries, and I asked Doug Ellerby, the USIS public affairs officer, to see if we could get him. Though he had no such appearance budgeted, Doug said let's see if he'll come and then worry about the money. Sure enough, Ellington's schedule permitted a Central American stop, and we signed him up. I bludgeoned a reluctant USIA into providing $3,500. (The fee was $6,000 plus expenses.) The American business community underwrote any loss. We were in business.

The theater, a handsome newly completed hall not far from our house, was standing room only on concert night. USIS had promoted the concert widely and effectively. That the brochure showed a caricature of pianist Ellington blowing a horn proved no serious detriment beyond a red face or two. The concert left us all hoarse from shouting our approval, as those great musicians left no doubt that they were world-class talents.

Duke stayed with us and kindly agreed to play a bit afterward at the house for a reception. It turned into a jam session as the maestro, his son Mercer, and several of the other musicians played and partook of spirituous beverages until the small hours. As I escorted the orchestra to their bus at about two-thirty, one of the members looked up, saw the bright tropical crescent moon, and, thunderstruck, exclaimed, "My God, we're so far south, the moon is upside down!"

The next morning the group had to leave fairly early, so I got up at about seven and went to check on Duke. Hearing no sound, I opened the door and found our guest still fast asleep. Slow to awaken, he finally propped himself up, opened a rheumy eye, and said, "Ambassador, baby, you're a doll." Throughout the brief visit, Duke and Mercer — indeed, all the troupe — comported themselves like diplomats and left us feeling not only proud but also that we had been in the presence of greatness.

Cultural understanding between the United States and El Salvador did not come easily. Salvadorans feared "cultural imperialism," and indeed, our music, literature, television, styles, and movies must have seemed pervasive. And there was the plain old matter of taste.

One Sunday, Jessica, the children, and I drove the easy half hour to a club at the coast near La Libertad. We loved to go there, lie in the sun, play on the beautiful black sand, and bathe in the sometimes treacherous waters of the Pacific.

When we arrived, we could not believe our eyes. There, out in the middle of the cove, loomed a thirty-foot-high replica of a bottle of Pilsner beer, perfect in every respect. The week before, beauty; today, a beer bottle. Shock (far too mild a word) gave way to anger.

Jessica, not as constrained by diplomatic nicety as I, determined to act. The next day she sat down and wrote our friend Roberto Quiñónez Meza, president of the brewery, and in language not even vaguely diplomatic told him his ad was an abomination. The following week, we returned to the beach, and lo! the "bottle" had disappeared as mysteriously as it had arrived. In addition, a case of Pilsner appeared at our door with an amusing letter from Roberto. At least one cultural gap had been closed.

Another cultural difference surprised me. At Eastertime in 1972, Jessica and children had taken a short trip to the States. A temporary bachelor, I readily accepted when Chico and Leonora de Sola invited me to an overnight at their six-thousand-foot-high *finca* in the western part of the country. It took a drive of a couple of hours, but the goal was worth it. Often the house lay above the clouds, views were breathtaking, and the de Solas, the best of company, set a fine table. That I traveled on Good Friday had not seeped into my consciousness until, as we passed through small villages, some of the people threw rocks at my car. Alarmed, I asked Mario, my driver, "Qué pasa?" He explained that had it been twenty years earlier we would have had real trouble, not just glaring women and a rock or two. Travel on that holiest of days was regarded as very poor form, and getting past roadblocks set up by the faithful on country lanes would have made the trip impossible back then.

I found a cultural gap of a more serious nature on the university campuses. I had thought that a visit to the big University of El Salvador would be a high priority, but our security people said it would be a serious error. Total anarchy reigned at UES, for the Latin American tradition of university autonomy, born for good reasons long before, had gotten completely out of hand. I was told that the rector, a man of the far left, probably would not have received me, but even if he had been amenable to a visit, the student body would have rioted in protest. Feeling against the Vietnam problem ran even higher here than in the United States, and the students did not have any discipline, self- or otherwise. Naturally, the whole country suffered as Marxists, Castroites, Trotskyites, and other extremists constantly closed down this or that department for bizarre reasons. Eventually, the government simply closed the university for several years, at huge cost to the society. I was disappointed to have no chance to meet with the students.

A Catholic university had been founded some years before, partially as a response to anomie at UES, and it had thrived. I learned why during a visit with its rector, a Jesuit priest named Father Archiarandio.

Students from UES, sensing an opportunity to proselytize, organized a movement to fire a certain Catholic university teacher, who was unpopular and a U.S. citizen to boot. The rector refused, and a strike by the students loomed. Archiarandio, young, dynamic, and tough, told them to go right ahead and close the university down. At the end of six months, he promised, he would simply close it for good. The serious students heeded him, no strike took place, radical demands and leftist thought were defeated. When Archiarandio told of it, his eyes sparkled, and it was clear that he enjoyed the challenge. I liked him.

Protoloco

PROTOCOL IN El Salvador, like protocol everywhere, was meant to lend strength to human frailty, avoid embarrassment, and grease the machinery of government. (Irreverent Spanish speakers called it *protoloco* instead of *protocolo,* and indeed, it did sometimes seem "loco.")

In addition to the endless calls that ambassadors made on each other, the government managed, under the stern eye of the chief of protocol, to waste a good bit of our time. For example, it was the custom to have the diplomatic corps go en masse to the airport to greet high-ranking foreign dignitaries and then to repeat the performance upon their departure. I became aware of this early on, with the arrival of Spanish foreign minister López Bravo in November 1971. That good man had undertaken a lengthy trip through Latin America to cement ties of *hispanidad,* or Spanishness, the aim being to increase trade in particular and Spanish influence in general among the former colonies.

There was, incidentally, a Día de Hispanidad, to which I went. Finding myself standing next to the British minister counsellor during an interminable speech, I scribbled a note to him suggesting that we English speakers have an Englishness Day. He wrote back: "We could do it on July 4, and celebrate getting rid of each other!"

With muted enthusiasm, I joined my peers to welcome the peripatetic Spaniard. Troops in large numbers were massed at Ilopango Airport, bands played, and flags slapped the air as the guest's great plane pulled up to a red carpet and disgorged him. Speeches, inevitably lengthy, by López Bravo, the mayor of San Salvador, and the acting foreign minister ensued. (The Salvadoran foreign minister, with exquisite timing, managed to miss the occasion; he was off touring China trying to sell coffee, the sanguine thought being that if every Chinese learned to drink just one cup a day, El Salvador would be on easy street.)

The guest then went to a reception in the VIP lounge, met the diplomatic corps and other dignitaries, and sped off amid the screech of tires and the scream of sirens.

The official opening of the Teatro Presidente, a handsome new theater, presented another occasion for great ceremony. The day being a warm one, the guests, myself among them, anticipated a cool drink once they succeeded in getting through the vast crowd and into the building. Seared by thirst, I searched out a bar, strangely uncrowded, only to learn that no refreshment was to be served until the president arrived. Naturally, he did not arrive on time, so a thousand people stood as if on leash, drink and tables laden with food within easy reach, doing—nothing. I wondered if this was a subtle political ploy, for every person in the building was most sincerely happy to see the chief executive when at last he hove into view.

I enjoyed—or suffered from—the same routine. No embassy officer could (theoretically) leave a function before the ambassador did, or if the need were pressing, permission had to be asked. In reality I liked the arrangement. If a party was tedious, Jessica and I could depart, using the excuse of consideration for the other officers. And once or twice I used a trick that Queen Elizabeth was said to use. At a really good party, she would take leave formally and then come right back, informally, without inconveniencing the other guests.

Definitions of correct behavior obviously vary from country to country. For many years I had been an enthusiastic runner, and arriving in Salvador gave me no reason to change habit. Indeed, soon after I got there, I joined the fitness-conscious Marines in one of their dawn runs. If time was short, I went to the roof of the embassy building and did laps. If I had time, I liked to lope through the hilly neighborhoods, the faithful Buick and the *pistolero* (bodyguard) cruising slowly along beside me. The habit did not go unnoticed.

One evening at the Spanish embassy, one of the grandest of grandes dames pulled me aside and told me of a comment her driver had made. En route somewhere, he turned and said, "Señora, did you know the Americans have sent a crazy man here? The new ambassador runs in his underwear through the streets of San Benito with an Indian rag wrapped round his head."

One custom that I originated violated precedent and made the security people nervous. Idle on a Saturday afternoon, I noticed a tour bus parked outside, Americans straining to catch a glimpse of the embassy residence. "What the hell," I thought. "Why not invite them in for a quick look at the house?" They were ecstatic and so was their driver, his eyes shining at the thought of large tips for this coup. Cameras around every neck meant many pictures with the ambassador, and I gladly obliged those friendly Indianans.

The following week, Saturday found me busy (probably napping). At any rate, the house man knocked at my door and said, "Mr. Ambassador, there is a man at the door insisting on seeing you." I went down, and there was the same bus driver, with another load of tourists. I acquiesced but let him know in no uncertain terms that it was my choice whether to invite tourists in, not his.

Sad Day for Democracy

THOSE OF us at the embassy who followed Salvadoran politics—and who among us didn't?—felt moderately optimistic about the development of democracy. Granted, the "official" PCN had to be the favorite in the February 1972 presidential election, but still the Christian Democrats (PDC) clearly planned a lively scrap. They nominated San Salvador mayor José Napoleon Duarte, a scrappy, articulate, mildly leftist engineer, as their presidential candidate, and he clearly took his chances seriously. The PCN candidate, Arturo Armando Molina, was a former army colonel (the law required that the president be a civilian, so Molina, and Sánchez before him, had retired from active duty). Molina was rotund and pleasant but uninspiring. Both parties were well financed, and media coverage seemed fairly evenhanded. I instructed embassy officers to keep hands off, thus decreasing the chance for the loser to claim that he lost because of *norteamericano* interference. Indeed, I refused even to meet Molina at all until after the election.

On election eve, CBS correspondent Bob Pierpoint and his wife, Pat, arrived. Bob was not on assignment; they were on holiday, and we rejoiced to see them and have them as house guests. Holiday or not, Bob couldn't resist joining me for a tour of the polls the next morning. We got going about nine o'clock (it was a Sunday), and what we saw was amazing: everywhere the crowds were enormous. Embassy officers observing the process throughout the country reported similar turnout and response. It was fiesta, as hawkers sold soft drinks, chili, bread, and beans to good-natured people waiting in endless serpentine lines at every voting station. Moving about town took time, as traffic clogged all streets that were even vaguely near a polling place. Bob said, expressing a sentiment that I shared, "You know, it's really exciting to see democracy in action."

We played tennis that afternoon, and that evening, with economic section head Henry McCown and his wife, Arlene, joining us, we supped and awaited the returns on the local media.

From the beginning, the incumbent PCN ran comfortably ahead. Molina seemed to be getting about 51 percent and Duarte 39 percent, but by the time we left the table the race had narrowed, with Molina's lead cut to 46 to 39 (the balance going to minor parties). The odd thing was that there were still no returns from San Salvador, where Duarte's strength lay. About midnight, all reporting of returns stopped. We looked at each other in wonder and alarm. Anyone raised in South Texas, as Jessica and I had been, knew that to be an ominous sign. Still, I went to bed fairly sure that Molina had won.

The morning papers had nothing definitive to report; their antiquated presses had to be "put to bed" early, and I wasn't too surprised. Although Monday was a holiday (Washington's Birthday), much of the embassy staff wandered in to trade stories and try to divine what was up. Terry Leonhardy and Les Scott stopped by Election Central and learned something startling: Duarte had carried San Salvador, 126,000 to 63,000. As the day wore on, both candidates claimed victory. By late afternoon, Election Central announced final results: Molina led by 334,000 to 324,000 for Duarte; minor parties garnered 10,000 and 16,000. But the ratio in the capital had changed. Instead of a 63,000-vote margin, Duarte's lead in San Salvador had dropped to half of what Terry and Les had been told only hours before, throwing it to Molina. In the end, as no candidate had a majority, the National Assembly had to decide. Unsurprisingly, it chose Molina, who claimed the most votes.

We at the embassy were appalled, and our studied neutrality evaporated in the face of the clear rape of democracy; I felt unclean. Many of my Salvadoran friends, to be sure, were elated. With straight faces, they often called Duarte a communist, making a mockery of rational labeling; political subtlety never was a strong suit among the Catorce, who viewed anyone to their left as a tool of Moscow.

On Tuesday the city braced for massive demonstrations. There was nothing. Apathy reigned, and I noted in my diary: "They are giving up on the democratic process . . . it's a shame." Indeed, it proved far more than a shame; it proved a disaster. From that day on, many disillusioned liberals turned their backs on the democratic process or joined the hardline Marxists, and by the middle of the decade the kidnappings and murders, the death squads, and the grizzly warfare that eventually killed so many and cost so much had begun. One statistic struck me as particularly poignant: In the previous presidential election, 39 percent of the voters had turned out. This time, the turnout soared to 70 percent. Democracy, struggling to see light, was stillborn.

A couple of weeks after the election, I went to see Duarte. Though depressed, he talked freely. The thing that puzzled him was why the government would manipulate the vote when it became clear that neither man had a majority and the Assembly, being dominated by the PCN, would have elected Molina anyway. To have let that happen would at least have kept the fabric of democracy intact, avoiding the vast cynicism that swept all the opposition sectors and parties. He said there were fifty thousand people at a rally in the city square the night after the election. "I could have sent them on a rampage, but that's not my style. I didn't want to be on either end of a gun." As we left Duarte, almost as depressed as he, I said to Terry Leonhardy, "That is a good man; he may make it to the top yet." The prediction turned out to be correct. He became president in 1980.

Democracy in El Salvador suffered its coup de grâce two weeks after the presidential election, with the holding of legislative elections. The Christian Democrats were denied on a technicality the right to run candidates in their stronghold, the capital, and the PCN swept to a landslide victory. It was a sad day.

Coup d'État

AT TWO o'clock on the morning of Saturday, March 25, 1972, I awoke, startled. Jessica and the children had taken advantage of school vacation to get in a bit of skiing in Colorado, so I was alone. The cause of my waking, I soon realized, was the absence of the comforting "white noise" of the air-conditioning unit; the electricity had gone off. Although I went back to sleep quickly, at four I woke again. This time my prosaic subconscious was speaking to me: "The freezer is full of expensive beef; go call the electric company." Staggering downstairs, I found the number. No answer. The curious popping noise I heard far away didn't really register; Salvadorans were firecracker wackos and were likely to set them off at any time of the day or night. New Year's Eve sounded like D day — squared. And so to bed. This time, however, sleep would not come.

At almost six, I heard a great pounding on the front door. I found a distracted Les Scott there, saying there were reports of a coup d'état and that we'd better head for the embassy. Dressing quickly and grabbing a bit of breakfast, I hopped in Les's car and we sped through empty streets, arriving just as Jessica heard news of the revolt on her car radio in Aspen. Alarmed, she called the El Salvador desk at the State Department and learned—twenty-four hours later—that I was safe. Although the city was without power, the embassy's emergency generators kept us in touch with Washington.

Sunlight crested the rugged volcano to our east. By then the sound of firing could be heard clearly; no firecrackers ever sounded like that.

Red Gremilion, our CIA station chief, had been there since three that morning; all efforts to reach Les and me had failed. He reported low-flying aircraft buzzing close above the embassy as they hit—or tried to—the rebel-held military barracks, or *cuartel*, a few blocks away. The phones began to ring, as worried Americans called, anxious to know what was going on. USIS head Doug Ellerby reported that a Colonel Benjamin Mejía led the insurrection and two other ranking officers had joined him to form a junta. Two *cuarteles*, one near the embassy, the other near the presidential palace, were controlled by rebels who apparently consisted of one infantry and one artillery brigade. We later learned that rebels had taken over the main utility services and some radio stations. Electric power to the entire city was cut at 2:10 A.M. A unit from the first brigade had attacked the headquarters of the National Guard, an armed service independent of the army, but they met resistance and, in spite of pleas to join them, the Guard stayed stoutly loyal to Sánchez and the government.

Several of us gathered in Les Scott's office, on the east side of our building, for it looked out over the San Carlos *cuartel*. Suddenly, the roar of a World War II P-51 fighter-bomber flying low startled us, and seconds later a cloud appeared near the fort, followed by a great boom. With the next sound of aircraft, anti-aircraft fire chattered wildly. I bravely hit the deck, peeking up like Kilroy to snap photos. Clearly, the air force had not defected to the insurgents.

Sometime during the night, Colonel Mejía must have decided that he could not succeed without popular support. Just after midnight, he called defeated candidate Duarte and apparently convinced him that the rebellion was a success and was directed against the same evils of the government that Duarte opposed and against the corruption that had cost

Duarte the election. Strapping on a gun, the once peaceful engineer joined the rebels at their fort. At 12:15 P.M. he went on the radio, urged the Guard to surrender, called on the citizens to rise, and in a display of spectacular misunderstanding of matters military, urged that nails be strewn in the streets to hinder reinforcements from the provinces. These exhortations failed to rouse the public and succeeded in frightening rebel officers, who suddenly feared they would be fighting alongside "communists."

About the same time, businessman Chico de Sola came by with his son, Francisco Junior. Driving in from Guatemala, they had noted that the garrison in the eastern city of Santa Ana seemed to be returning to its post rather than proceeding toward the capital. This was later confirmed, providing further proof of the uprising's difficulties.

Shortly after noon the sound of heavy artillery, its boom felt deep within our chests, ricocheted across the city as the garrison in the other *cuartel*, El Zapote, let fly at we knew not what. Apparently they knew not what either. Their target, we later learned, was National Guard headquarters. What they hit was the National Geographic Institute, a scientific center of no military importance; three shells wreaked sad havoc on the national mapping project, housed therein and used to help in levying taxes. (Landowners probably rejoiced; paying taxes was not the national pastime.)

We learned during the morning something of the fate of the president, Fidel Sánchez. Shortly after midnight one of the plotters led troops to Sánchez's private home, demanding his surrender. He refused, and a lively firefight ensued, leaving the house pockmarked by countless bullets. After running out of ammunition, the president and his daughter and several aides surrendered and were taken, frightened and dismayed, to El Zapote, where they were unceremoniously thrown in a cell.

About eleven that morning, our defense attaché, Lieutenant Colonel George Maynes, drove himself to El Zapote to see what he could learn. Worried about Sánchez's fate, Maynes was escorted to the cell and shown that the president was indeed alive. On his way back to the embassy, Maynes was shot at but arrived unharmed. I was later sharply criticized by Deputy Assistant Secretary of State Bob Hurwich for letting Maynes go to El Zapote. He feared it would look as if we were supporting the coup. Hurwich was wrong; at no point during or after did the embassy come under attack for partisanship.

Although we did not know it, the revolt had begun to collapse by midday. During the noon break (even revolutions break at noon in El Salvador), several officers drifted away from El Zapote and never returned. The papal nuncio, as the ambassador of the Vatican is called, had negotiated the release of President Sánchez's daughter; then, widening his scope, he began to negotiate a settlement. Colonel Mejía attended this meeting, but while he was absent from El Zapote a number of officers fled. By five o'clock that afternoon, Sánchez had been released and resumed command, furious with his fellow officers and with Duarte and the PDC. Noting aerial activity and anxious to see for myself, I drove around town in the late afternoon, finally posting myself at a vantage point overlooking El Zapote (at a safe distance, to be sure). From there I saw a final attack by P-51s that damaged the old crenellated barracks and a nearby youth center. Almost simultaneously, a white flag began to flutter above the building. The fighting was over, and the rebel leaders slipped out of their strongholds and into foreign embassies, seeking asylum.

One of the oldest diplomatic usages concerns the sanctity of persons and premises; dating from the Congress of Vienna of 1815, it says a host government may not violate an embassy or search any foreigner who has diplomatic immunity. Yet so great was the anger of Fidel Sánchez that upon learning that Napoleon Duarte had taken sanctuary in a Venezuelan embassy home, he tore up the rule book.[2]

For a while, Duarte's whereabouts were a mystery. Mrs. Duarte, distraught, called me at home Saturday night, begging me to help find and save her husband. Like us all, she assumed that if he were captured, he was as good as dead. I could give her neither information nor help.

Les Scott received visitors Saturday. Two Christian Democrat leaders, Fidel Chávez Mena[3] and Abraham Rodríguez, descended on him in high dudgeon, keen to find Duarte. Their concern differed from that of Mrs. Duarte: they were ready to lynch him. By throwing in with a harebrained coup, he had not only endangered the PDC politically but had also placed the lives of colleagues like Chávez Mena and Rodríguez in danger. Duarte's electoral running mate, Guillermo Ungo, had fled to an embassy, even though he had absolutely no connection with the revolt. It seemed that Duarte had not consulted anyone about casting his lot with the coup plot. Seeing his madcap gamble crumble, he fled to the house of a Venezuelan diplomat, a first secretary, a friend, and a fellow Christian Democrat. (The Venezuelan PDC was in power at the time.) Duarte's benefactor showed goodwill but not good sense. As Napo (Duarte's nickname) got cleaned up, his host called Mrs. Duarte to assure her that all was well. It proved a grave error. The phone was tapped, and within minutes security forces arrived. (At the embassy, we always assumed that the phones were tapped, and we occasionally used that knowledge to suggest ideas to the host government that might have been difficult to suggest otherwise.)

The intruders, eight or ten men in civilian clothes, demanded access. The terrified diplomat said no way, this is a diplomatic residence.[4] "Let us in or we will machine-gun the house and then come in," was the reply. Finding that argument to be more persuasive, the Venezuelans opened the door, the men swarmed in, and poor Duarte was badly roughed up and dragged away.

When news of this outrage reached the papal nuncio, dean of the diplomatic corps, he called a meeting for four o'clock Sunday afternoon. The usually fractious and verbose ambassadors, after two hours of debate, were unanimous in their judgment: Duarte's life was in danger. The demands of mercy and the good name (such as it was) of the country mandated that he not be executed. A committee, consisting of the ambassadors from the United States, Brazil, and Italy and chaired by the nuncio, was named. Our task: call on the president and talk sense to him. Alas, the president was in no mood to be talked to at all, sense or otherwise.

He had gone on TV just after midnight, dressed in fatigues and looking wan. He condemned the disloyalty and criminality of the small groups who led the attempt and denounced Duarte for "irresponsible subversion." Claiming that one hundred had died and that two hundred had been hurt, he promised that the perpetrators would be prosecuted.

Since our request to meet Sánchez was refused, we had to settle for the acting foreign minister, Guillermo Paz Larín. We met at my house at eight o'clock Saturday evening, and at nine, escorted by police through streets made eerily menacing and empty by a curfew, we drove to the Foreign Ministry. I felt a strong sense of seriousness and purpose during the drive; a man's life might well depend on our success.

Paz Larín, a career diplomat, received us politely and assured us that the president was not known for hotheadedness or a thirst for revenge. After fifteen minutes, our point made, we left, unsure if we had accomplished anything. Paz Larín was not a Sánchez intimate, and we had no

way of knowing if he were in reality just patting us on the head and sending us on our way or if indeed he had any idea of what the president would
do. Feeling let down and apprehensive, I dropped by Les and Sandee
Scott's for a solemn supper.

The next day the country team gathered to assess events. Feeling that
my concern for Duarte might be misunderstood at the Casa Presidencial,
I called Sanchez to inquire as to his health and try to detect any hostility
toward the United States. There was none. Indeed, he knew of the inquiries that our defense attaché had made in his behalf when he was being held prisoner. He did say, however, that the "intellectual authors" of
the event would have to be punished, a comment that clearly referred to
Duarte.

Late Sunday afternoon, a rumor swept the city that twenty-five people
were to be summarily executed, Duarte among them. I doubted it and
predicted that Sánchez, no fool, would rather have Duarte gone than mar-
tyred; my bet was that he would be shipped to Venezuela. By Tuesday,
my prediction looked far too sanguine. Sánchez gave a press conference
and, asked as to Duarte's whereabouts, said he did not know where
Duarte was. I feared that meant he didn't know where the body had been
dumped, but by that evening all became clear. Duarte had been put on
an air force plane and shipped, bruised and forlorn, to Guatemala. There
he met with American ambassador Bill Bowdler, who confirmed that he
had been badly beaten. From Guatemala, he did indeed go to Venezuela,
where he lived until the early 1980s, plotting the return that would eventually make him president.[5]

Trying to understand just what had happened and what it meant for
the embassy, we concluded several things. The coup was very poorly
planned. As Les Scott put it, "It must have been hatched during happy
hour at the officers' club." The rebels' failure to secure Ilopango Airfield,
and thus neutralize the air force, was costly. Ideological content was nonexistent until Mejía talked Duarte into climbing aboard, and Duarte's
presence probably made things worse. His luster was dimmed by this es-
capade, since it made him appear to be impulsive and not a team player.
The embassy showed concern for human life, both Sánchez's and Duarte's,
and yet managed not to be blamed for interference in the country's internal affairs. I felt proud of our role and our reporting. Indeed, in his
autobiography Duarte wrote: "I am sure the United States intervened to

save me, because only U.S. pressure could have kept the military from eliminating me."[6]

A curious footnote to the affair: In writing about the coup attempt, journalists and historians got it wrong. It is common to see reports that the election was stolen from Duarte, who was then forced by the military to leave the country. That he brought it on himself by his support for a military uprising has been lost in the mists of ideology and sloppy research.

The Bill Collector

AND WHERE was the president-elect, Colonel Molina, during all the excitement? (Les Scott recalled the old doggerel "Little man so spick and span, where were *you* when it hit the fan?")

Molina in fact had had the good fortune to be invited by the Taiwanese government to visit the island nation, El Salvador being one of the few countries that still recognized Taiwan as the true government of China. He had a two-month interregnum before his inauguration, and the trip presented an excellent chance to polish his foreign policy credentials. En route, he learned of the situation, probably early Saturday morning. Naturally, he was intensely anxious to get home; trouble was, there was no quick way to accomplish his aim. Molina therefore turned—guess where?—to the American embassy.

Intrigued, I called the State Department, which consulted the Pentagon, and rather quickly we were able to get the president-elect flown by a U.S. Air Force plane to Guatemala City, where a Salvadoran plane picked him up and brought him home. The whole thing was dubbed a training mission for the pilots involved.

I was pleased. Surely I would be off to a solid start with the new administration. To cement relations, I called on Molina shortly after his return. Of medium height, dark-complexioned, and rotund, he was a serious contender for the Ten Worst-Dressed List, but he could not have been nicer during our hour-long visit. We chatted about his challenge, United States–El Salvador ties, the makeup of his administration. This was to be the high point of our relationship.

The first disappointment came when the National Security Council turned down my request for a Molina-Nixon visit before the inauguration. Unlike many of his successors, Nixon had no time for the Third World, a fact that was made quite clear to me on the phone. Still, Molina did not seem too upset.

Then came big trouble. About a month after Molina's return and inauguration (in an endless ceremony at National Stadium), I got a cable from State requesting in a rather offhand way that I collect $20,800 from the Salvadoran government to cover the cost of Molina's plane trip from Hawaii to Guatemala City.

Amazed, I called Deputy Assistant Secretary of State Bob Hurwich and asked him what in heaven's name Washington was thinking about. He could not have been less sympathetic. "Salvador is an independent country run by mature men," he snapped. "They should pay their debts." I protested that we had never been told anything, ever, about reimbursement, but my pleas fell on totally deaf ears.

To me, the move was wildly irrational. We spent millions in aid to El Salvador; we constantly requested its support in the UN and the OAS. Asking for such a sum, to the constantly strapped Salvadoran government, was huge, nothing short of political idiocy. Nonetheless, I took a deep breath and went to see President Molina.

On hearing my message, he sat passively, pensively, for what seemed forever. Finally he spoke. "I suppose I'll have to pay it myself. I had no government job at that time, having resigned from the army to run but not having been inaugurated president." Another silence. "Could I make monthly payments? I am not a wealthy man."

When I left his office, I could have walked under his door, so small did I feel. Back at the embassy, I picked up the phone, called Secretary of the Air Force Bob Seamans, and told him my story. Unfamiliar with the situation, Bob promised to call me back. His return call, several days later, was like one of those "good news, bad news" jokes. The good news was the Air Force had made an error in its calculations of some $7,000. Furthermore, by billing the State Department and getting it wholesale, the amount could be cut to $10,400. The bad news was: pay up. I conveyed the message to President Molina and in short order, the amount was paid (whether by the government or not, I never learned). But from that day on, within the Molina administration, I was known as "the bill collector."

Abroad and at Home

THE EVENTS of the election, the coup, and the relations with Molina kept adrenaline levels at the embassy high for the first quarter of 1972, but then life once again settled down to a somewhat slower pace.

We exchanged visits with the ambassador to Honduras, Hewson Ryan, and his wife, Helene. In San Salvador, the Ryans marveled at the paved streets, manicured lawns, and signs of economic activity, and in truth, though El Salvador was poor, it was better off than its neighbor. Hew told the doubtless apocryphal story of a French ambassador in Honduras who had been there too long. One day something snapped. Wild-eyed, he strode to his car and ordered his driver, "To Paris!" Without a word, the driver set out for San Salvador.

When the time came for us to return the visit, a faithful old U.S. Air Force DC-3 came to fetch us, commercial air links not having been restored after the Soccer War. I feared Jessica would not be too happy about the flight; she loathed flying. (I once asked her after a particularly stormy airline flight why she didn't have a martini to calm herself. "Oh, I wouldn't do that," she explained. "I have too many responsibilities to the other passengers. I've got to keep the plane aloft.") The Air Force, however, delivered us in good shape, and the visit turned out to be worthwhile. Jessica took a number of superb photos of Tegucigalpa, a city of dusty, unpaved streets, urchins shooting marbles, and a certain primitive charm. She later incorporated them into a Central American calendar that sold well throughout the region, with proceeds going to charity.

Hew and I called on officials. The foreign minister urged us to involve Henry Kissinger in settling the thorny Honduras–El Salvador problem: "He is the Prince of Peace," the man opined, in one of the more interesting descriptions ever given the good professor. Henry, tied up with Vietnam, let the opportunity pass.

Returning to his office, Hew—always ebullient, bright and amusing—asked if I would like to call on President Cruz. "Sure," I replied. Hew placed a call and ten minutes later we marched into Cruz's office. (An embassy official commented, "He must have finished the crossword puzzle to see you on such short notice.")

Short and seventy, Cruz was an international lawyer of judicial mien and Bugs Bunny teeth. As we entered his office, his choler was evident. Throwing a sheaf of telegrams on his desk, he invited us to read them, as they dealt with the Salvador-Honduras crisis. "How can you deal with savages such as these?" he demanded. His hang-up? He wanted a judicial settlement at the World Court (where, presumably, his talent could be brought to bear), as opposed to an agreement negotiated by fallible politicians and diplomats. He urged me to pass along his concerns to the Salvadoran government, which I later did. Oddly, Cruz's foreign minister heartily backed a negotiated peace. He realized the harm done both countries by the war and its aftermath and thought a court case would be too time-consuming.

Hew essayed to change the subject. "There are rumors of a military coup d'état in the making against you, Mr. President. Have you any comment?" The little man snapped, "That's ridiculous. If I give up what is by right Honduran I would be committing treason and should be killed. Any soldier who comes in and makes a nonjudicial settlement would have the same fate awaiting him." On hearing of the president's comment, one of Hew's political officers said, "It won't be too difficult. One morning the military just won't send the limousine to pick him up for work and that will be that." As we left, the harried foreign minister, who was waiting outside, whispered, "What kind of mood is he in today?" We could not offer him much comfort.

Jessica and I also went to Panama, to meet the officers of the United States Southern Command and see the Panama Canal. (Jessica opened a lock as easily as she would have turned on the tap.) We dropped in on Managua, where the U.S. ambassador, Turner Shelton, and I lunched with strongman Anastacio "Tacho" Somoza. Meanwhile, Jessica struggled through a luncheon given by the obsessive and difficult Mrs. Shelton in honor of Somoza's handsome wife, Hope.

To say that Shelton and Somoza had a symbiotic relationship would have been understatement: they virtually finished each other's sentences. Somoza, a West Point graduate, a fierce anti-communist, and the son of a dictator, never made a move without checking with Shelton, a career diplomat whose eyes were always shrouded by dark glasses. Washington knew it could count on Somoza, always, but we—and the Nicaraguan people—paid a price for his support, not the least part of which was the squalid communist government that was installed after his overthrow.

Over lunch, the maximum leader told us an amusing story of the recent coup attempt in El Salvador. Apparently, Salvadoran minister of defense Torres came apart when his president was captured. He called Tacho and, virtually in tears, asked, "What do I do?" Somoza snapped, "You're the minister of defense, you idiot; fight!" Torres did, of course, and the day was carried, but not without many calls to Somoza for ongoing counsel—at least, according to Somoza.

Our best trip, maybe ever, was to Guatemala, where Ambassador Bowdler and his wife, Peggy, organized an expedition to the ruins at Tikal and a float on pirogues down the Rio Dulce (Sweet River) to the Gulf town of Livingston. The six Catto and Bowdler children scurried over ancient Mayan monuments, haggled like veteran shoppers in the markets, and generally amused both themselves and their elders. Bill and Peggy, richly learned and superb company, provided Jessica and me with countless insights. Excitement came from motorcades conducted, for security reasons, at speeds up to eighty miles an hour, mostly on the wrong side of the road (Guatemalan leftists specialized in killing Western ambassadors). "Some security," I thought. "If I am to be killed, a terrorist bullet might be preferable."

We followed events back home in Texas closely, as Bill Hobby, Jessica's brother, announced that he would follow in his father's footsteps and run for lieutenant governor. His opponent, Wayne Connally, was John's brother, and we feared that the vaunted Connally political machine would prove too tough. But in the Democratic primary of 1972, Bill thrashed Wayne soundly (Jessica returned to San Antonio to campaign for him in the city's Spanish-speaking neighborhoods). Beating the obscure Republican nominee in November, Bill went on to be the best "light governor" in Texas history, serving until 1991, when he retired undefeated and highly respected by Republican and Democrat alike.

I liked being ambassador. No day passed without interesting problems or suppliant callers, and my respect for the foreign service grew as I came to know the embassy officers better. Tested by the Foreign Service Institute, my Spanish came out a "4 – 4," the stage just below native speaker, although my Salvadoran friends thought I had a rather quaint Mexican accent. A noncareer ambassador always has to prove himself to his career colleagues, and my willingness to cut through the bureaucratic undergrowth (as in calling the secretary of the U.S. Air Force direct) earned respect and acceptance. Jessica's breezy informality and low tolerance for puffery or cant helped enormously.

In 1972 Richard Nixon was reelected. I had done my bit by giving the campaign $25,000 during the spring. The connection between a political job and a donation weighed on my mind, but since I was already in office, I felt that the lack of quid pro quo was clear. I was distressed, therefore, when CBS reporter Dan Schorr, an old friend, did a story that lumped me with other donor-ambassadors in describing instances of suspicious timing and size of gifts. In any case, I was never asked to donate by any Nixon operative, much less pressured to do so.

Jessica and I returned to Washington for the election. While we had gone to one inauguration and vowed never to do it again, elections were different, especially this one, which we expected to win. Our joy, however, was soon diluted. Summoned to the State Department shortly after the returns were in, all presidential appointees, career and noncareer alike, who were in town were asked to submit their resignations. Exact wording of the letters we were to write was provided, and the senior people with whom I got this news were astonished and angry. As we sat around the large table in the deputy secretary's elegant conference room, I asked the hatchet man from personnel who broke the news if we had to sign the letters "sincerely." The laughter was gratifying. Asking for resignations did strike me as graceless and callous, characteristics I increasingly associated with Nixon's way of doing things. Fortunately, in my case the resignation letter proved to be a bomb that never went off.

My personal feelings about the administration continued to be ambiguous. I happened to be at the State Department one day at a function where Treasury secretary David M. Kennedy spoke. At one point, he astounded me and everyone else by saying, "Just because I'm in charge of the Treasury, don't expect me to say something Jewish about spending money." That seemed all too typical of the attitude at the higher levels; inevitably it is the leader who sets the tone. I feared Nixon was not setting it too well.

As the Watergate matter unfolded in 1973 and 1974, my suspicions were confirmed. I groaned at the way it was handled, and I was particularly sad to learn of Jeb Magruder's involvement. During one of my visits to Washington before the scandal broke, I had been introduced to him, and we ended up having lunch. Both being Williams College graduates as well as Nixon appointees, we had much to talk about, and I thoroughly liked him. Looking back on Watergate in my rare moments of midnight introspection, I realized how easily someone like Jeb could have been swallowed up by the Nixon zeitgeist. I had always reflexively resisted wearing in my lapel the tiny U.S. flag that became standard for the president and his employees, but I am not at all sure that calls for loyalty and team spirit would have left me unmoved had I been closer to the center of things and subject to intense peer pressure.

Marxist Terrorism

AN EVENT that had earlier disturbed the surface calm of El Salvador was the kidnapping and murder in February 1971 of Ernesto Regalado.

A young and handsome businessman, he was a member of one of the great families. His wife, Ellen, tall and strikingly beautiful, was the daughter of Terry O'Sullivan, an American, and her mother was a member of the aristocratic Catorce. The typical Salvadoran life did not interest "Neto," as he was called. He atypically recognized that the country had social problems, and he tried to make it a better place.

On the surface, he would have seemed an unlikely target for Marxist terrorism. In reality, he was a natural, reform being the enemy of revolution. Nonetheless, his car was stopped on his way to work by what looked like a road repair crew but turned out to be Marxist guerrillas. In spite of ransom paid by his wife and the families, he was murdered and his body dumped alongside an obscure road, an event that was to be repeated three years later with another prominent citizen.

Although Salvadoran society held its breath in the hope that the Regalado case was an aberration, that did not prove to be so. Acts of terrorism began to accumulate. In June 1972, we found incendiary devices at the Salvadoran-American Bi-National Center, site of our library. (Why do totalitarians operating in the name of "the people" always want to burn books?) The devices did not explode, but I worried nonetheless. The IBM building on Calle Roosevelt, a main thoroughfare, suffered damage in an explosion, perpetrators unknown. Pamphlets from the previously unknown Salvadoran Liberation Army proclaimed:

> Following is a list (small) of those who will be submitted to the popular justice. We have the courage to give the names of the persons who will no longer have peace, not only in their homes, their places of work, streets, amusements, churches, because whenever the circumstances and plans

permit, they will be arrested, and if they should make resistance, they will be put to death on the spot: Undesirable Foreigners: Amb. Catto & his Gang.

The "Gang" and I laughed at the extravagant language, and no more was heard of the "Liberation Army."

Rough stuff did not come only from the left side of the spectrum. The AFL-CIO sponsored, worldwide, the American Institute of Free Labor Development (AIFLD). Assisted by USAID funds, the operation tried to promote non-communist unions in developing countries. Often, however, Latin American businesspeople resented the idea of Yankees supporting any labor unions at all, and AIFLD was controversial. In July 1973 I got word that an AIFLD employee, a Salvadoran living in Santa Ana, had had his home ransacked; two years earlier he had been shot. An angry call to the minister of labor got me assurances that it was an "accident" and that it would not happen again. The matter became moot in mid-1973 when the government tossed AIFLD out altogether for interfering in internal matters.

Such incidents were but premonitory rumbles of the eruption that was coming, an eruption that would end the lives of several of our friends, including Molina's young foreign minister, Mauricio Borgonovo.

When President Molina appointed Mauricio, we were delighted. Educated at MIT, married to a woman who had become one of Jessica's friends, he represented everything good about the country. At our Fourth of July party in 1972, Mauricio had tapped on his glass for attention and then had said, "Here's to the United States and its 196 years of independence. I hope you have another 196, for your independence is ours." From then on, he naturally had a secure place in my esteem, and we began to talk with unusual frankness and tried to help each other when possible.

I began to call on him at the Foreign Office frequently, visits sometimes enlivened with a late-afternoon scotch. Returning from a meeting of Latin American foreign ministers with Secretary of State William Rogers, he told me frankly that Rogers left his colleagues cold. He arrived at a luncheon forty-five minutes late and left before dessert. Mauricio said, "I understand the pressures on his time. But the United States could afford to spend less on AID and pay more attention to such little things. Latins are sensitive and that kind of thing doesn't sit well."

He kept me posted privately on events such as Honduras-Salvador border negotiations, speaking very much off the record on the details of the two countries' positions, including Salvador's fears of a pre-cooked arbitration of the dispute. It was the kind of information that State liked to know, and it earned me points back home.

I reciprocated. Before an OAS foreign ministers meeting in Washington, Mauricio told me that Nicaraguan president Somoza had called President Molina to urge El Salvador to vote against readmitting Cuba to the OAS. "Did the U.S. put Somoza up to it?" he inquired. I asked why he cared and with his usual bluntness, he said, "If keeping Cuba out was a Central American initiative, we could probably favor it. But if it came from the U.S., we might not go along." (Occasional singeing of Uncle Sam's beard was often good politics in Latin America.) I made inquiries later and shared with him that Somoza was operating on his own.

Mauricio met death with credit. Some months after our assignment ended, a guerrilla group came to his house early in the morning. Fortunately, Patricia and the children were away; only Mauricio and his father were at home. A maid foolishly let the men in, and they began to search the house. Hearing the commotion, Borgonovo slipped out of an upstairs window and was poised to escape entirely when he realized his father had been taken hostage. In trade for his father's release, he gave himself up to the intruders. Ransom was demanded and negotiations ensued, but either by design or as the result of panic, Mauricio's body turned up in a remote area near the capital, encased in a plastic bag. By then, kidnapping had become routine, as ransom money fueled the spreading guerrilla war that eventually took thousands of lives.

The El Salvador Tour Winds Up

IN SPITE of being thought of by President Molina as "the bill collector," I was still the U.S. ambassador, and occasionally I could be useful. Jet planes were a good example.

Because of the war against Honduras, military sales to both countries had been cut off. The P-51s of the Salvadoran Air Force (SAF), flying death traps, badly needed replacing, and after the loyalty shown the government by the SAF during the coup, favors could be expected. The trouble was that those in the State Department charged with giving thumbs-up or thumbs-down had qualms. What, they wondered, would happen if war broke out again and newly purchased U.S. A-37s proved a pivotal factor? A career could be ruined. A degree of caution could serve to obviate that danger and keep Senator Fulbright quiet to boot.

Meanwhile, in Honduras, a similar situation obtained, but there, the Hondurans did what I had often warned the State Department that the Salvadorans would do: disgusted by U.S. pettifoggery, the Hondurans bought French planes. That they took months uncrating them, much less getting them assembled, perhaps eased Washington's concerns; in any case, after strenuous effort by the embassy, the okay for the sale to the SAF was given.

The next problem concerned what to sell. The Salvadorans wanted used trainers, but the USAF wanted to sell new planes. The reason? The more planes sold worldwide, the cheaper they became for the USAF, as large-scale production worked its magic on per-unit cost. After struggling with a USAF team, I finally won: the Salvadorans got their used planes and all were wreathed in smiles.

My embassy continued to delight me. Our employees proved bright and imaginative, and I learned that, contrary to the prejudices of many noncareer ambassadors, the career service was willing and eager to serve the administration that was in power. Nixon loathed the foreign service, viewing it as a fifth column that planned to frustrate his objectives. I decided he was mistaken, a conclusion that subsequent experience proved sound.

Friends and family brought welcome tastes of home. My parents and Jessica's mother, brother, and sister-in-law enlivened one Christmas. Stevie and Lewis Tucker came, as did our longtime secretary and dear friend Marty Hollinger and her husband, Byron. (Byron's memories of El Salvador were probably a bit sour; he got sick on arrival and stayed that way throughout the visit.)

Occasionally I wandered about the embassy to see what was going on. One day I strolled through the commissary, a convenience store that sold groceries, sundries, and other things that were hard to find in local markets. Browsing the same aisle by himself was a lad of about three or four, blond and cherubic-looking. As he passed me, I patted his head. With a howl, he cried, "Mama, a man just hit me!" I disappeared pronto.

In June 1972, one of our communications people named George

Morrow came by and asked if I would, as required by regulations, approve his application to adopt a baby. (I did not begin to know how powerful I was.) I, of course, was happy to do so, and some time thereafter, the Morrows asked permission to name the baby after me, which annoyed me not at all.

Staying active in the American community, I refereed a football game billed as a contest between "the War Corps and the Peace Corps," the former being our military personnel. (My memory is conveniently vague as to the victor.) I spent an afternoon vending drinks at an American school fundraiser. With Sam Moskowitz, the DCM who succeeded Terry Leonhardy, plus the political and economic counselors, I regularly briefed two groups of American businessmen on local events as viewed from the embassy.

Efficiency reports, wherein I reported on the job performance of senior embassy officers, took large chunks of time each year. Though they were a tool necessary to running the personnel system, over time they had become totally divorced from reality. Any honest criticism, voiced in the climate of keen competition for promotion, could ruin a career, so each person had to be portrayed as a "water walker," with complaint limited to how far above the surface.

On one occasion two U.S. Marine guards drank far too much Pilsner beer at a local nightclub and got into a nasty brawl with several Salvadorans. Local authorities were not lenient, and I found myself, in spite of tearful appeals from the young participants, obliged to send them home.

The population problem continued to haunt us. The country lacked adequate industrial growth to absorb each succeeding generation into the job market, and consequently unemployment grew inexorably. Our AID people concentrated on birth control methods common in developed countries, but the habit of large families proved hard to break. The idea that improved public health results in decreased infant mortality and increased longevity took years to sink into public consciousness. Governments always decided the deluge would come in the next administration, thus avoiding conflict with the traditional stand of the Catholic Church. Nicaragua's Somoza talked occasionally of taking vast numbers of Salvadorans as immigrants to his underpopulated nation, but lethargy, logistics, and questions of long-term loyalty aborted such dreams. Even more dramatic, a delegation of Brazilian senators came to explore moving 100,000 Salvadorans to the vast Brazilian northeast. Again, the idea fell through. Later, in the Reagan administration, the very idea of birth control assistance came under fire, and programs were curtailed, a decision that to my mind was a serious error.

In the spring of 1973 Jessica suggested it was time to head home. The Escuela Americana had not improved, and she feared the children would suffer long-term disadvantage should we stay. I agreed and began to do some gentle probing as to what job might be available back in Washington.

My first feeler went to George Bush. I had visited him in April 1973 at his new job as chairman of the Republican National Committee and found him looking wan and feeling frustrated. For instance, in spite of assurances that the increasingly serious Watergate affair would not be allowed to sink the party, a man George had hired from the Committee to Re-elect the President lied to him about Watergate involvement. Though the man confessed and resigned quickly, the incident symbolized Bush's predicament. In July, when I next saw him, he was distracted by pressure to come back and run for governor of Texas. With my usual perspicacity I predicted to Jessica that he would do so. (He did not.) Always ready to help, he inquired as to my prospects and found that the number one job at the OAS would soon come open. Another possibility was even more intriguing: chief of protocol.

Although I was aware of which fork to use and how to make polite conversation, my knowledge of the protocol job was not extensive. What I did know was that it was very high-profile and involved being at the heart of diplomatic action both as to visits by foreign heads of government and visits abroad by the U.S. president. Jessica had reservations. She feared it was perceived as nonsubstantive, often filled by social butterflies fluttering above the honey pots of Washington. Nonetheless, I was tempted.

In any case, we decided to move back, with or without a secure job. Tobi Frankel had called us one day in June to tell us that the sprawling Virginia home of Tim and Ann Hoopes was for sale. Though we did not know the house well, we had been there, and its ample size, good location in McLean, Virginia, and reasonable price convinced us to make a bid. We did so, and to our pleasure it was accepted.

The children, ever conservative, moaned a bit at the time, but descriptions of their new house and good memories of the Washington area tipped the balance and enabled them to view moving with equanimity.

Besides, two previous moves within four years had begun to make gypsies of them.

The plan was for Jessica and the young to head for Colorado during the summer, returning to the Washington area in time for school. I would join them in the fall after saying farewell in El Salvador. Friend Bernard Lifshutz from San Antonio came down to taste Salvadoran life and keep me company during my last days there. Taking leave of friends, colleagues, and the staff at the house proved painful; I got through it, though moist of eye more than once.

Looking back on the experience, what had I learned? What had two tropical years contributed to the education of Henry Catto?

First, I learned something of how to run an embassy. Through luck, good staff, and wise counsel from Les Scott and others, I realized that the foreign service and the FSNs could be counted on. I learned how helpless one could feel when faced with other people's problems and how little I knew of the human soul. On the personal side, I realized that although the Cattos had paid a price in our uprooting from home soil, grandparents, and tradition, there were dividends. For Jessica, the children, and me, solidarity and a shared experience seemed a rich reward. There were, however, moments of darkness of the soul, when other thoughts crept in. Could it be that I was rationalizing what was in essence a giant ego massage for me? At times, I was not at all sure.

Subsequent events in El Salvador left uncertainties as well. Often I was asked if the bloody civil war that began in the 1970s and took tens of thousands of lives could have been foreseen — or prevented — by wiser U.S. policy.

Were we justified in our all-out support of the Salvadoran government? Wouldn't a victorious communism have withered in El Salvador just as it has withered in Nicaragua, after the Soviet Union's demise? "Think," I am urged, "of all the lives that would have been saved."

These questions are beguiling — but not convincing. Grant the brutal behavior of the Salvadoran government and military; grant the blindness of the oligarchy; grant all the weaknesses of the society. I conclude, in spite of it all, that we were justified in our assistance. One has only to look at the spiritual and physical devastation, revealed by the Soviet Union's collapse, in Red-ruled Eastern Europe and Russia. One has only to read telegrams of postwar interviews with rebel leaders — interviews revealing breathtaking cynicism, the use of well-meaning dupes in the church, and the manipulation of a gullible American media — to realize that these guerrillas were moral lepers, not the liberators pictured by liberation theologians.

Leftist ideologues continue to this day to insist that the guerrillas were idealistic freedom fighters, but information uncovered since the signing of the Salvadoran peace accords make clear the vicious nature of the *muchachos* (boys), as they were called in the countryside.

For one thing, the leftists were responsible for virtually every kidnapping and extortion from the 1970s onward. They eventually realized, too late, that targeting socially aware businessmen like Francisco de Sola and Ernesto Regalado was an error. The urban terror unleashed against civilian leaders in the early 1980s also proved counterproductive, for the rightwing death squads were far from indiscriminate in their retaliation, wiping out dozens of guerrillas. The postwar revelations demonstrated again the bottomless gullibility of some well-intentioned people.

Part 3

Protocol

"Never, But Never, Miss the Motorcade"

THE WASHINGTON to which we returned in September 1973 looked familiar, but it had changed. The Kennedy Center had been finished and had opened, making a huge difference in the cultural life of the capital. Designed by famous architect Edward Durrell Stone, it looked like a fat lady with thin legs, but it quickly became a tourist attraction as well as a cultural center. We explored it with the children, seeing Christopher Plummer in a show of Shakespeare scenes and poetry called *Love and Master Will,* Alvin Ailey's superb dance troupe, and other theatrical events.

The political changes, though less visible, had even more impact, as the Nixon administration began to come apart at the seams. On October 10, Vice President Agnew resigned rather than face trial. I was pleased to be shed of him, having always felt that he was an embarrassment to the country and to the president. Describing the media, as Agnew had, as "nattering nabobs of negativism" (a line written by then White House speechwriter Bill Safire) struck me as dumb. Granted that the media did in large part loathe the administration, to go to war against them was quixotic, a war we could not win. Gerald Ford, Republican leader in the House, struck me favorably when Nixon chose him to succeed to the vice presidency, though the cynical proclaimed him merely to be impeachment insurance. We had met him at Senator John Sherman Cooper's once or twice, and I had liked his relaxed, pipe-smoking approach to life.

On September 22, Nixon named Henry Kissinger as secretary of state, to replace William P. Rogers. A shrewd move, it added a lively, articulate figure to a bland Cabinet and ended the bickering between the secretary and the national security adviser, since Kissinger would henceforth hold both jobs.

We had met Kissinger early on in the administration; indeed, Jessica had been his dinner partner at a party and had pronounced him fascinating, a good listener as well as talker, though she was surprised by his bitten-to-the-quick nails.

Our first exposure to him after our return came at a small dinner at Joan and Tom Braden's in October. (Nancy Maginnes, later to become Henry's wife and a good friend of Jessica's, was there as well.) Negotiations for peace in the endlessly painful Vietnam struggle were always intense, and Henry's reminiscences intrigued us all. He felt that his counterpart, Lee Duc Tho, did occasionally show signs of humanity but that Lee's fifty years as a communist fanatic allowed such signs to show only rarely. Even then, Kissinger was not sure whether he was seeing warmth or calculation. At one point during the Paris negotiations Lee said in a confidential tone, "Dr. Kissinger, I am going to speak to you frankly and honestly: you are a liar." When the city of Kwangtre fell to communist forces, Lee was very hard to deal with. Yet after the devastating Christmas bombing of Hanoi by the U.S. Air Force in 1972, he became much friendlier. "At one point," Henry laughingly recalled, "I thought he was making a pass at me, because he couldn't keep his hands off me." To Kissinger, the lesson was obvious: the tougher the Allies, the more pliable the communists.

Exposures to Henry were important to me. The *Washington Star* reported upon our return from El Salvador that I was to be named chief of protocol, a job that by then I was eager to get; Kissinger was not happy with the Office of Protocol as it then existed, and he would determine who was appointed to the post. In his dealings with China he had been struck by the Chinese way of handling foreign visitors. They divided all functions into eight-minute segments in their planning. Thus, in case of delays, one section could simply be deleted without adding additional time at the end of an event. He wanted our protocol office to be equally crisp.

Unhappily for me, filling the job proved a lengthy proposition. George Bush later told me what had happened. Henry apparently decided on me, but the acting incumbent, longtime deputy chief Marion Smoak, felt he should move into the position, and he weighed in with his senator, the powerful Strom Thurmond of South Carolina. Weeks later, the White House decided to appease both Kissinger and Thurmond: Smoak was made chief and immediately resigned, thus polishing his ego and resume. On March 30, my appointment was announced.

The intervening six months had been busy. Having no full-time employment (I did a special assignment on cultural relations with Latin America for the State Department) proved a blessing. Though tempted, I managed to resist a strong push from Texas Republicans to return to San Antonio to run for Congress—likely a good decision, since 1974 saw a Republican electoral slaughter.

Our new house, with its ample wooded grounds, provided a magic place for children. Neighbors Al and Carol Moses became our closest friends, and Al became our trusted lawyer and skilled adviser.

Another family also enriched our lives. Genoveva Crespín and David Arriaza, who had run the residence in San Salvador, came to live with us to do the same in McLean. As our children went to college, their three boys moved into the vacant rooms of our young, and this "second wave" of homework to help with and sleepy morning plaints of "Have you seen my shoes?" kept us young. Six quiet months ended abruptly. On April 2, President Georges Pompidou of France died. On April 3, I was sworn in, and that evening I was off to Paris, cushioned in the luxury of a plane that had once been *Air Force One*.

My traveling companions on this trip, the purpose of which was to prepare for President Nixon's attendance at the funeral, were people I came to know well. Brigadier General Richard Lawson, the military assistant to the president, had control of the considerable fleet of planes available to transport not only the president but also congressional and other dignitaries. William Henkel headed the White House advance office, charged with seeing that presidential travel went smoothly. The highly complicated matter of communications fell to Brigadier General Lawrence Adams. Given the president's need to react instantly and awesomely in the event of war, he had to be able to be in touch with the military at all times, whether he was in a car, on a plane, in a submarine, or on a bicycle. In all we were about forty on board, Secret Service people, press people, and technicians galore. Lawson and I, being senior in rank, got the stateroom.

Sitting in Lyndon B. Johnson's great swivel chair in the main compartment was a thrill, and I commented on it to the pilot. "It's comfortable, but it didn't quite suit Lyndon," he replied. The trouble, it seemed, was that he could not directly control the cabin heat; a call to the pilot was required. He could chat with the world, see a movie, summon a whiskey, all by pressing buttons, but there was no heat button. "Fix that," he demanded. The aircraft commander thoroughly checked it out and learned that actually to extend the control from the pilot's cabin to the president's chair would require $30,000 worth of modifications. A resourceful man, the pilot arranged an alternative at negligible cost. A button was installed within Johnson's easy reach. When he turned it higher or lower, lights came on up front. The pilot would then quickly adjust the heat up or down. The president never knew the difference and the taxpayer was spared, a win/win situation not common in Washington.

Although the chief of protocol had traditionally traveled on advance trips, my functions struck me as a bit vague. One involved providing ambassadorial rank. I called briefly on my harried French counterpart, an idea gleaned from previous talks with predecessors Mosbacher and Smoak, and assured him of our sympathy and concern. I soothed nerves at the U.S. embassy, sore beset by our demands and the unexpectedness of our invasion; that I knew our able ambassador, John Irwin, was helpful. I made small talk with foreign heads of government as they waited to call on Nixon after the ceremony. That was exciting. It was *all* exciting. To Bill Henkel, I was a nuisance. Curt and impatient, he had little time for diplomatic niceties, and I am sure he resented that I had the visibility but little responsibility. His lack of finesse gave me heartburn, and through many miles and many trips we maintained at best a wary truce.

Typical of our problems in Paris was a labor dispute. We had been booked by the embassy at the nearby Hotel Crillon. A strike hit the establishment the second day, and while some wanted to stay in spite of reduced service, Bill argued that it would be regarded as strikebreaking and the attendant publicity could be bad. I agreed with him, and we moved to a more distant hostelry.

The two working days we had before Nixon's arrival proved frantic, with calls on the French; meetings at the embassy; visits to Notre Dame, site of the service; and for me, picking up the required full-dress morning suit that was to be the uniform of the event. I did manage to get in a run through the Tuilleries Gardens, catch a late dinner with Dick Lawson at the famed Maxim's restaurant, and glimpse the first signs of spring in that ancient and achingly beautiful city.

Nixon's arrival was to have been at ten o'clock on a Friday night. The stream of planes carrying heads of state or government meant split-second timing, and to be sure that all went well, I arrived two hours early at Orly airport. With Deputy Assistant Secretary of State Welles Stabler, I watched the arrivals and noted French procedures. Though the day had been beautiful, clouds closed in around nine o'clock and at ten o'clock it poured. The rain did not deter the president. On landing, he slogged over to the waiting press and made a moving statement about the loss of Pompidou. That done, we boarded the motorcade and raced through wet and silent streets, depositing Nixon at the embassy residence. The rest of us trooped dripping back to our hotel. I had spoken not a word to the president, but I felt involved, close to the center.

Notre Dame, square and squat for all its height, had never looked more imposing or more ready to do honor to a fallen Frenchman. The British are generally thought the world's masters of ceremonial occasions (a wag once said the British are to ceremony what the Israelis are to commando raids), but on that overcast spring morning, the French were superb. My driver made the brief trip to the cathedral with ease; I had feared that the presence of dozens of the powerful would tie traffic in knots.

Dropping me off, the driver assured me he would be in the motorcade, several cars behind the president, at the end of the service. Although it was an hour beforehand, the huge church was filled. Behind the altar, hanging diagonally, was a hundred-foot-long tricolor, the French red, white, and blue flag. The U.S. delegation was allotted four seats, designated for the president, the ambassador, and Generals Haig and Scowcroft, so, dressed in gray tailcoat, striped trousers, pearl-gray tie, stickpin, and wing collar, I stood against the wall and marveled at the procession: first, the Church in all its schisms, colorful among a sea of black and gray; next, presidents, prime ministers, and royalty progressed slowly down the center aisle. Lined up in order of precedence, determined by number of years in office, they were led by the tiny but strong figure of Haile Selassie of Ethiopia, King of Kings, Lion of Judah, defier of Mussolini. Nixon, a short-termer in that league, nonetheless had a front-row seat. Princess Grace of Monaco, looking so very young, beautiful, and regal, came in on Prince Rainier's arm. Prince Philip represented the queen; not being a head of state, he did not make the "A list" and had to be content with the second row, a situation to which he was doubtless reconciled but at which he doubtless bridled. Bach filled the giant building, mass was offered, the great words, blessedly brief, were spoken, and within forty-five minutes the service was over and the orderly withdrawal began.

Since the aisle was jammed with mourners, I exited at a snail's pace. Seeing a priest who had helped me translate the order of service into English so that RN (as his staff and now I, catching on fast, referred to him) could understand what was happening, I paused to say thanks and then pushed on through the great door to the bright outside. Just in front of the church I noted Nixon's long, communications-laden Cadillac, which had been flown across the Atlantic so he would be always in touch; a security car followed, a swarm of motorcycles led the way. Then the ambassador's car, flags snapping on the fenders (I always liked that). Then — my God! There was my car, empty, slow but gaining speed as the motorcade pulled away. Adrenaline shot through me. I was a jogger, I could catch up —. No such luck. They were gone.

Alone, absurdly dressed, a total stranger, taxis out of the question, I stood and slowly assimilated the first commandment of protocol: "Never, but never, miss the motorcade."

At that moment an archangel of mercy appeared at my elbow. Trying to hide his amusement, a man of about my age said, "Problems, Mr. Ambassador? Follow me." Weak with gratitude, I loped along behind a form that turned out to be named Bill Marsh, a foreign service officer from the U.S. embassy. Speaking faultless French and displaying awesome knowledge, he escorted me down a long flight of stairs to — what else? — the Metro. Ignoring the curious stares at my formal dress, we were whisked to the subway stop near the embassy. I ambled nonchalantly into the compound, where no one was the wiser (until I confessed). As of that day, Marsh assumed a special place in my pantheon.

Nixon had originally planned a Saturday return to Washington, but clamor for "bi-lats," or face-to-face meetings with him, prevailed, and he decided to stay over until Sunday. I suffered a pang upon learning of the change. Sunday was Heather's birthday, and we were not scheduled to leave until 12:45 P.M.; I feared I would miss the events of the day altogether. Relief came as I realized that Paris was six hours ahead of Washington. I would be home in plenty of time, good news since I had bought her a sweater in Paris that I wanted to present with due ceremony.

Our suddenly relaxed time schedule meant that RN could attend a reception for the visiting delegations at the Quai d'Orsay, the French Foreign Office. It was jammed. Each top leader (Nixon, Harold Wilson of Britain, Tanaka of Japan, Podgorny of the USSR) was surrounded by courtiers, well-wishers, and favor-seekers. I hung around Nixon, just in case I could be useful, though I was not at all sure he knew who I was. One of the pilot fish nibbling at his attention turned out to be the head of the Bolivian delegation. She was not the head of government; she was not even the ambassador. She was an embassy official, and after she had introduced herself to the Leader of the Free World, I caught her attention and, showing off, spoke to her in Spanish. Quick to grasp an opportunity, upon learning who I was, she said, "Ay, Señor embajador: puede Vd. conseguirme una visa para los Estados Unidos?" ("Mr. Ambassador, can you get me a visa to the U.S.?") And I had assumed I'd left all the visa supplicants back in El Salvador! I had discovered the second commandment of protocol: "Never show off by speaking a foreign tongue."

On Sunday, after a run through the Tuilleries Gardens, I reported for duty at the embassy, welcoming Soviet president Podgorny and Japanese prime minister Tanaka for talks with RN. At midday the president took off from Orly, and fifteen minutes later our plane rose to follow. Eight hours later we were landing at Andrews Air Force Base, in good time for me to help Heather celebrate her fifteenth birthday.

Occupational Hazards

ON APRIL 9 I got my first taste of Henry Kissinger's royalist streak. He and his new bride, Nancy, returning from an Acapulco honeymoon, were to arrive at Washington's close-in National Airport at about eight-thirty that evening. Larry Eagleburger, Henry's assistant, had told me that it would be nice if the senior State Department officers came to greet the couple. I made contact accordingly, informing my colleagues of the unwelcome news. His needy ego surprised me. All these people worked long, grinding hours anyway; having to troop out to National Airport seemed useless and thoughtless. As it turned out, the plane (one of Nelson Rockefeller's) came in early, and only the Eagleburgers and Jessica and I were there. It was, however, too late to call off the operation, so we had the unhappy task of waiting around to tell the others that their trip was in vain. Henry had long since departed the airport for home.

I was to learn, to my distress, that mistakes were all too possible in my job. The president of Algeria, Houari Boumedienne, on a brief visit to the United States, was to lunch in the State Department's elegant eighth-floor rooms. Good protocol form required that the secretary be at the building entrance when a head of government arrived, to escort the guests in. The Secret Service (USSS), providing protection for visitors, always had an advance man at any given location to be visited, to coordinate movements and give exact times of arrival; they were, therefore, very important to the protocol people. Furthermore, since the secretary of state had USSS protection, communication between the guest and Henry's detail could be easy and instantaneous. On this occasion, the lead agent with the Algerians told his colleagues at State by radio, "We are now leaving." That should have been the cue for Kissinger to hop on his private elevator and be at the door in plenty of time. Unfortunately, the agent at State heard, "We are *not* leaving." So moments later, when the motorcade, sirens blaring and lights flashing, arrived from the president's guest quarters at nearby Blair House, we were aghast. There being no secretary to greet his guest, I had to do the honors. We strode into the building. The usual claque of lunchtime employees milling about the lobby applauded the visitor (they are not diplomats for nothing), and I led him to Henry's private elevator. At that moment, a USSS man poked me and said, "Here's the secretary." Henry, his face black with rage, had made it down; someone standing by a window in his office had seen the motorcade arrive, and he had rushed to the first floor. Muttering comments like "those protocol idiots," Henry and his guest whooshed up to eat an elegant lunch. Not invited, I was left to contemplate my fate over a salad in the cafeteria.

The day's troubles were not over. At three o'clock that afternoon I was to have taken the guest on a tour of Washington. As we planned the trip in advance with the Algerian ambassador, it became clear that Boumedienne wanted to go to the top of the Washington Monument. My office informed the Parks Department, and they duly closed that great obelisk to visitors at three-thirty. The problem was that Boumedienne and Kissinger did not finish their talks as scheduled; they went on until five o'clock. Learning of the delay, we had the monument reopen at about four o'clock, and when we finally took the tour our guest had to be content with a drive-by, during rush hour at that. The hundreds of tourists who could not enter the monument were doubtless furious. Fortunately, they never knew whom to blame.

When the Algerians first arrived, Jessica and I had met them at the airport. U.S. relations with their very left-wing government had not been good; their anti-American propaganda had been very critical of capitalism and "imperialism," and we had not had diplomatic relations with them since 1967. I expressed surprise, therefore, that the Algerian first lady had on a fur coat as she swept off the plane. Fur didn't strike me as very proletarian, and I asked Jessica's guess as to the coat's value. "Oh," she replied, "I'd guess she has about thirty thousand dollars on her back—and that doesn't count the designer dress."

The next day, I drove with the departing guests out to Andrews Air Force Base, a thirty-minute trip. It provided a useful chance to visit, and I asked Boumedienne if he expected a renewal of U.S.-Algerian relations. His reply surprised me. "No," he said. "I can be helpful in calming Arab-Israeli tensions, because we *don't* have relations with you. No Arab would ever call me a tool of the Americans." I made a mental note to report the conversation to the Algeria desk at State, happy in the realization that although this new job might be weighted toward ceremony, it could also have substantive input, a thought that was proved true by countless backseat conversations with world leaders.

The meeting of the OAS foreign ministers was held that year in Atlanta. For reasons that were obscure to me, Kissinger had agreed to go, so I decided to go down in advance to become familiar with the layout of the airport, to see the arrangements at the handsome new Hyatt Hotel, and to get to know the key Atlantans who would be our hosts. (One was the governor, a pleasant chap named Jimmy Carter.) When Henry arrived at the airport, a huge crowd awaited him, and to my amazement, he and Nancy were cheered like rock stars.

Doubtless pleased by his reception, Kissinger nonetheless was not too happy to be there. He considered Latin America a bit of a sideshow, having once described Chile as a "dagger pointed at the heart of Antarctica." Jessica and I, on the other hand, looked forward to the event and to the chance to see, for the last time as it turned out, our friends the Salvadoran foreign minister, Mauricio Borgonovo, and his wife, Patricia. Henry's general unhappiness showed when, after sitting through several typically florid and lengthy speeches, his turn came. Said he: "Most people think the United States is a developed country, but in one area the United States is distinctly underdeveloped compared to our Latin friends. I refer to the area of epic oratory." The laughter was restrained—except from those of us who knew how right he was.

Kissinger used humor constantly. We went to one party at Joan and Tom Braden's, a varied group that included the Rockefellers, the George Schultzes, Mrs. Alice Roosevelt Longworth (excited to be turning ninety), and the Iranian ambassador, Ardisher Zahedi. As we were all leaving,

Ardisher pulled Henry aside and said, "May I speak to you alone for a moment?" Henry replied, "Only if you lower the price of oil." Another evening, Zahedi was the host and Henry the honoree. The ambassador gave his after-dinner toast to his guest in good but heavily accented English. In his response, Kissinger said jokingly that his assistant had once thought he was listening to a code language, but it was only Zahedi speaking English.

Shortly after returning from Paris, I called on Alexander Haig, the former career Army officer whose meteoric rise culminated in four stars on his shoulders and the job of chief of staff to Nixon, replacing the fired Bob Haldeman. (He would later become President Reagan's secretary of state.) My purposes were two: to make the man's acquaintance and to get tips on the care and feeding of Richard Nixon.

Haig was appealing. He looked me straight in the eye, seemed unhurried and relaxed, and was totally accommodating. The word he used to describe the president was "shy," about the last thing I would have expected from so successful and driven a politician. Haig cautioned me never to speak to the president either before or after a speech; he made it sound as if the man put himself into a virtual trance of concentration, requiring an intense buildup and a slow cooling down after a public utterance. I commented that on the flight back from Paris I had not asked to ride on *Air Force One* with the president. "Good move," Haig said. "Had he known you were on board, he would have felt he had to come back and visit with you and he would have resented it." With members of Congress aboard, Haig went on, Nixon always felt impelled to chat with them, though such time-wasting niceties annoyed him.

Not all days involved White House meetings. I was much more likely to have mundane problems to solve. The Cypriot ambassador, Andreas Jacovides, presented me with one early on. An able man with an American wife, he liked to entertain, and he wanted a new house to do it in. Finding a handsome place just off Massachusetts Avenue, he asked and received permission from his government to buy. The $315,000 price proving more than the Cyprus government wanted to pay in one lump, the ambassador arranged for the owner to accept $100,000 down, the balance in three years at 9 percent interest. Everyone happy? No. The government of the District of Columbia threw a wrench in the machinery by saying that it wanted taxes paid (embassy property is tax-exempt) until title passed, which would not happen until the mortgage was paid.

It fell my lot to carry this unwelcome message to the ambassador, who was not at all pleased.

The chief of protocol being important on the diplomatic circuit, we were often invited out. Most embassy dinners are alike, and such functions came to be routine at best, dreadfully dull at worst. The program was standard: An 8:00 P.M. arrival, black tie for the men, long dresses for the women. Drinks and small talk followed until 8:30 or 8:45, with junior embassy officers stirring the social pot, seeing to it that no one felt left out. Meanwhile, the ambassador and his wife, invariably charming, chatted with the senior and ranking guests. Dinner, served by candlelight on handsome china in a paneled room, might be national food or standard French cuisine; superb wine, usually a white, a red, and champagne with dessert, would be carefully poured into handsome cut crystal. (A drop of wine on the immaculate tablecloth—or worse, on a guest's gown—was not tolerated.) Conversation with one's dinner partner usually began to the right for two courses; the table then "turned," and we all segued into talk with the person to our left. After dessert, the host would rise and offer a toast to the guest of honor, accompanied by a graceful, diplomatic, and, if we were lucky, short speech. Said guest would then respond in kind, and all would withdraw for coffee.

At this point in the evening, the ambassador had a choice to make. If a traditionalist, he would shoo the ladies upstairs to powder their noses while the men retired to the library for cigars, brandy, and "serious" talk. If, on the other hand, the ambassador was young and smart, he would usher us all to coffee together and cigars would remain in their humidors. Smoking was, in those days, increasingly unpopular, and women, Jessica among them, often resented being segregated.

On one occasion, the absurdity of separating the sexes became clear. We went to the Luxembourg embassy to honor fellow Texan Anne Armstrong, then counselor to the president and a key member of the administration. Our host, the ambassador, remained firmly mired in the nineteenth century, and at dinner's end he sent Anne upstairs with the other ladies while we men sulked below in a miasma of cigar smoke. Later, I asked Jessica what had gone on upstairs with the really important person at the party. Nothing, she replied. "Anne just tossed it off, amused, not offended."

Among the varied duties of the chief of protocol was one that proved to be an ongoing headache. U.S. law prohibits—wisely, I think—U.S.

officials from accepting gifts from foreign governments. Gifts of more than nominal value ($50 in my day, $250 now) must be turned in by all Executive Branch officials to the Office of Protocol, which in turn passes them to the General Services Administration. The GSA offers them to museums (a donor can suggest a suitable museum if desired) or else sells everything at auction, with proceeds going to the general fund of the government.

The problem lies with two facets of human frailty: avarice and inertia. Given a handsome silver horse or a Persian rug by a head of state, the tendency is to forget to turn it in. It is legal, furthermore, to display such items in one's office while one works for the government. Finally, there is no enforcement mechanism, save for needling reminders from the protocol office; it is the honor system all the way. Until, that is, a reporter gets a tip and begins to dig.

One morning a *Washington Post* reporter named Maxine Cheshire called me. Half-threatening, half-cajoling, she told me that former secretary of state Rogers had failed to turn in a highly valuable necklace given him by a foreign head of state. I called first his secretary and then Rogers, who was in New York recuperating from an operation. Both said the necklace was in a safe at the State Department, a claim that Cheshire denied, saying it was at Rogers's house. Though I reported their response to Maxine, she said if it was at State, Rogers must have sneaked it in in the dark of night. The necklace was finally found — at the State Department.

In an effort to minimize this kind of brouhaha, I attempted to short-circuit the process. Over the years, as ambassadors came to call to arrange state visits by their leaders, I would make it a point to say that the president and other American officials could not under any circumstances accept gifts. If your leader wants to bring a memento, I suggested, a photo of him or her would be the nicest possible item. They would nod in full accord — and when the foreign leader arrived he invariably brought gifts fit for the Magi.

Some foreigners were incredibly profligate. Marylou Sheils, a visits officer at Protocol who was to work with me in later years both in and out of government, recalls the visit of the sultan of Oman, of which she was in charge. As he was about to leave, having spread gifts around Washington like a turbanned Santa, one of his minions pressed $10,000 cash into Marylou's hand. Explaining she couldn't keep such a gift, she suggested it be given to the drivers who had chauffeured the party around town. Marylou—and the sultan—became very popular, very fast, with Marylou singing Christmas carols as she passed out the largesse.

On a visit to Saudi Arabia I was given a very valuable and handsome watch with the crest of the Saudi monarchy on the face. I turned it in but decided later that, as was permitted by the rules, I might buy it back from the GSA, at a price to be appraised independently. Going over one day to the GSA to see it, I was surprised by how long finding it took. Finally, a red-faced official came out and confessed he could not find it at all. He promised to get to the bottom of the matter quickly. A couple of days later, he came to my office with a remarkable tale. The FBI, in setting up an influence-peddling sting (later to be known as Abscam), had asked the GSA if it had any watches that the agents posing as influential Saudis might use. Mine fit the bill, and it was turned over to the FBI. The sting was a success—but the watch somehow got lost in the shuffle and was never found. Oh, well, I would not have bought it anyway—it turned out to be valued at $5,000.

In Japan, we goofed on one occasion. When President Ford went to Tokyo, we took along a series of audiotapes to give to the Japanese prime minister. They consisted of one tape on each U.S. state, and I thought they would be useful for a Japanese school. Alas, I failed to note that the tapes were made in Japan, a fact that the press took great glee in exposing.

From time to time, the bands that provided music during state visits caused red faces. During Queen Elizabeth's bicentennial visit, the first song played as after-dinner dancing began at the White House was " The Lady Is a Tramp." And at one of the first state dinners after President Johnson succeeded the assassinated President Kennedy, the guests were serenaded with "Dallas," with its rousing refrain, "Big *D,* little *a,* double *l, a, s.*" Accidents? Surely . . .

When Nixon went to Moscow to see Brezhnev, he took along a Chevrolet sedan as a gift. General Motors had kindly donated it, knowing that the Soviet general secretary was a car buff. One morning I was having breakfast in the dining room at the vast Rossiya Hotel when a Secret Service agent found me and whispered, "Mr. Antinov [a key KGB officer] wants to see you in the Kremlin right away." Gulping my coffee, I rushed across to the great, brooding palace and found Antinov. He whisked me to a quiet corner of one of the great reception rooms and said conspiratorially, "Where are keys?" "Huh?" I crisply replied. "Keys, keys to car!" he responded in heavily accented English. I finally caught on. He knew what Nixon's gift was and wanted the keys, fast; his boss wanted to try out the gift. I hurried back to the hotel, found the keys, and had them quickly delivered.

Hitting the Road with Nixon, Part 1

ON JUNE 3 I flew on a plane packed with advance people en route to Austria. Nixon, his presidency moribund though he did not yet realize it, was planning a trip to the Middle East and the Soviet Union. Foreign travel, though physically hard, often provides a president with relief from domestic troubles. The TV news is full of the pomp and ceremony of a trip, and the voter is reminded that the Leader is hard at work, protecting the Republic. Travel is, in short, a seductive ego trip. Being part of this last bright flowering of Nixon's tenure proved riveting.

The Austrian stop would serve as a night of rest for the president before he flew on to the Middle East, Brussels for a NATO summit, and finally, a second triumphal tour of the Soviet Union. In typical Nixon fashion, we of the advance party were adjured to schedule no meetings with Austrian leaders; Austrian-American relations being solid, Nixon regarded the prospect as a waste of time. I was thunderstruck. I did not see how he could visit the country, if only for a few hours, and not see its leaders. In the end, he relented, spending thirty minutes with Chancellor Kreisky at Schloss Klessheim, before leaving for Cairo. Secretary Kissinger's aide Larry Eagleburger had, incidentally, cautioned me to be sure that Henry was billeted in suitable quarters near the president's at each stop, a task I did not neglect.

Our advance party flew in to Salzburg after a stop at Lajes Air Force Base in the Azores, arriving at 10:00 P.M. Waking early the next day, I ran several miles along the Salzburger River and enjoyed the scenery of town and country. We checked out what would be the president's quarters, found them satisfactory, and took off for Cairo.

The Egyptian capital was dirty, crowded, smelly, loud, and wonderful. Met by Ambassador Herman Eilts, we sped (thanks to a police escort, without which the traffic would have permanently trapped us) toward the U.S. embassy. I asked about the huge, seemingly endless cemetery by which we passed. Eilts explained that it was called the City of the Dead and stretched for miles. Now, however, the dead had to put up with the living, for countless thousands of Palestinian refugees had settled there. Later we met with Egyptian officials, matters going smoothly until we broke the news that the American party would number some five hundred. They quite simply could not believe it, and finding space for us all presented a huge challenge for our hosts, who nonetheless rose to the occasion. (This Nixon trip proved the largest in history. Discipline had been sapped by the Watergate crisis, and with no Bob Haldeman to intervene, everyone with even a flimsy excuse clamored, most successfully, to come along. The Egyptians got even on Sadat's return visit. They came "not as single spies but in battalions," and each apparently charged three steak dinners a day to their hotel rooms—tabs picked up by Uncle Sam.)

The main issue of the advance was whether we should schedule a train trip to the coastal city of Alexandria, so redolent of ancient empires and sultry seduction, and if we went, how we would get back. (We went by train and returned by helicopter.) Fortunately, the issue that plagued us on every other stop caused no problem at all for the Egyptians. Whether Presidents Nixon and Sadat rode in Egyptian or U.S. cars and helicopters could not have concerned our hosts less. Sadat had a great sense of self and was not hung up on the kind of protocolary nit-picking that characterized lesser leaders.

After two nights in Cairo, we flew two hours to Jidda, Saudi Arabia. Flat and staggeringly hot, it rose shimmering where the desert met the sea, more of a city than I had expected. The Saudi protocol chief, an engaging young sheik called Ahmed Abdul Wahab, met us. I liked him, for he was quick and direct. (One of our party, an old Saudi hand, quipped, "He must be an Egyptian; I never met a Saudi that smart.") His first two points, however, caused us problems. The king refused to ride in any but a Saudi car, and Mrs. Nixon would not be invited to the state dinner, which was a stag affair. Furthermore, Mrs. Nixon's security detail would not be allowed into the queen's party in the first lady's honor unless the guards were female. One thing the Saudi side announced did please us, however: "There will be no movement in Jidda when the president arrives." I asked what they meant. "Just that—no one will be on the streets." This contrasted starkly with Cairo, where President Sadat had planned a large public welcome.

The palace in which we stayed was splendid. The furniture glowed in pastel pinks, greens, and blues, all of it overstuffed, with handsome oriental rugs everywhere. The air-conditioning stayed turned to just above freezing, or so it seemed. The shuttered windows did not open, giving a dark quietness to the entire building. To avoid the murderous heat, I ran early in the morning, watched by skeptical palace guards doubtless musing on the insanity of Americans.

After meetings at the embassy Friday morning, we were off to Damascus and the dilapidated Semiramis Hotel. Negotiations with the Syrians proved surprisingly easy, in spite of the permanently sour nature of our diplomatic relations. The city, on a hillside, had a minareted beauty and the *souk,* or market, tempted us with gold and handsome woven goods. The duty owed to Allah was seldom out of mind, with calls to worship broadcast over loudspeakers. Blended with the endless blare of automobile horns, din, not matters transcendent, seemed the purpose. Our business finished in twenty-four hours, we sped at 150 kilometers an hour to the airport and the plane waiting to take us to Israel.

The visit to Israel produced two problems: Teddy Kolleck's ego and Richard Nixon's hat. Kolleck, Jerusalem's longtime mayor, wanted to take the president on a tour of the city. A hugely energetic and charming man, he doubtless would have proved a superb guide. But the State Department, in the person of Chargé d'Affaires Nick Velliotes, feared Arab sensitivities over East Jerusalem, the status of which the Arabs (and ourselves) did not recognize as settled. Should Kolleck show too proprietary an attitude, mischief could result. Indeed, the Saudi embassy in Washington had been unusually blunt in warning us away from any move that could be construed as recognition of Israeli sovereignty over the once Arab-controlled half of the city. In the end, Kolleck's tour and the welcome by representatives of the Jewish, Christian, and Muslim religions were scrubbed. The Israelis were grumpy. One newspaper said, "Israel is fourth of the President's five stops. This shows us where we stand."

That Richard Nixon's hat should prove a problem resulted from his aversion to head cover. Our team had in no uncertain terms been told that the president did *not* wear headgear, not cowboy hats or yarmulkes. The sine qua non of a visit to Jerusalem, however, was paying respects to the victims of the Holocaust at the moving, beautiful Yad Vashem memorial, and that, in accord with Jewish custom, meant a covered head.

To solve the matter, our team suggested to the White House that a yarmulke was hardly a hat, and the wearing of it would be brief, etc., etc. The reaction was Vesuvian: "No hats!" After much back and forth, however, Nixon did agree to wear a homburg. The difficulty was that he had already left and one had to be found, a problem solved by an embassy officer in Vienna, who found a suitable model and had it waiting when the president arrived.

With Israel more or less nailed down, we flew to Jordan on June 9, where Ambassador Tom Pickering, an extremely able foreign service officer, greeted us. As usual, the car in which King Hussein and President Nixon would ride presented a problem. Indeed, we even got word that the Egyptians, perhaps hearing that other countries cared, had had second thoughts and wanted Nixon to use Sadat's car. In the end, reason (or our version of it) prevailed, and the American vehicle carried the leaders. The Jordanian variety of Islam being far more relaxed than that in Saudi Arabia, other matters fell easily into place, and on the tenth we flew, exhausted, to Salzburg to await RN. Only rain marred an otherwise smooth arrival.

Nixon's June 11 meeting with Austrian chancellor Bruno Kreisky demonstrated a pattern of behavior that proved typical of the president: vigorous resistance to a reasonable request, then last-minute capitulation. The Austrian visit and the matter of the hat at Yad Vashem were good examples of this strange pattern. I often wondered if he was aware of the grief his crotchets gave his advance people.

The Salzburg stop, meant for presidential rest, turned dramatic, courtesy of Henry Kissinger. Congressional Democrats, in full pursuit of Nixon, had latched on to Henry's role in telephone taps of various journalists, administration figures, and others, and the resulting leaks to the press made the secretary's job even more difficult. In Salzburg, his ire flared up, and he called a press conference at which he planned, in effect, to say, "Get off my case or I quit." While RN met with the Austrians, I had a visit with a worried Al Haig, who also feared the gamble would not work. It almost didn't. An emotional Kissinger took the podium but could not speak for a full five minutes, according to CBS's Bob Pierpoint, who was there. In the end, however, he gained control of both himself and the situation. The mandarins of the press rallied to his defense, the leaks stopped, and the spotlight shifted elsewhere. At dinner that night, Bob, Connie Chung, and NBC's Richard Valeriani agreed he had pulled off a tour de force.

Presidential travel, I had learned, was a very high-pressure operation, and not just at Kissinger's level. On our plane, the White House advance people continued to be unappealing. Status-conscious, humorless, and blunt, they were characterized by Larry Eagleburger as "thugs," and he wasn't far off the mark. They delighted in playing insider games, always using the Secret Service's code names, such as "Searchlight" (Nixon) or "Woodchopper" (Kissinger), and their sole interest lay in public relations, substance be damned. Everyone loathed Ron Ziegler, Nixon's press secretary, whose whining concern for his own status and perks was legendary. The president's military assistant, Brigadier General Richard Lawson, felt pretty much the way I did about this troupe, a flying circus without benefit of a Monty Python. Dick proved a welcome sounding board when the interests of State and the advance office clashed — for example, when Haig or Ziegler had a hotel room closer to the president's than Kissinger's was.

On Wednesday at 10:00 A.M. we were off to Cairo. Greeted by literally millions of Egyptians, Nixon's motorcade crept through the streets, the piercing, high-pitched ululations of the women and the rhythmic chants of "Nick-son, Nick-son" drowning out nagging worries of the deteriorating scene in Washington.

From the 2:45 P.M. arrival, the Nixons suffered through one ceremony after another (always with "light refreshments," as the program put it). They visited the Sadats; the Sadats called on them. The two presidents met for serious talk for two hours. Sadat gave Nixon the Collar of the Nile, an elaborate decoration; Nixon gave Sadat a nuclear power plant.

The state dinner was exotic and exhausting. At 9:20 P.M., the heads of state greeted four hundred guests at a palace reception. (I went through the line just to get one more exposure to my new boss; I still wasn't sure he had placed me.) At ten o'clock the dinner began. Literally hundreds of waiters, turbanned and in elaborately scrolled red jackets, marched in, each carrying dishes held high. Oriental rugs covered the sandy and beautifully lighted garden. Speeches and toasts (offered with sparking Catawba juice; Muslims theoretically don't drink). The inevitable price that the guests pay for having been fed began after eleven o'clock. At eleven-thirty the two national anthems were played, and we adjourned to the opposite end of the garden for coffee. At midnight, the entertainment began, and the poor Nixons, comatose with fatigue, had to try to look entranced as dozens of comely lasses wiggled their way through elaborate and endless dances, showing preternatural control of their stomach muscles. A jazz band then played a salute to Duke Ellington, and finally, at two, we dragged ourselves glassy-eyed off to bed.

The next day we departed by train for Alexandria, a trip of three and a half hours. Every inch of the way, wall-to-wall cheering, sign-waving people greeted the train, as Nixon and Sadat waved till they wilted. The signs read, NIXON, MAN OF PEACE, and NIXON, WE TRUST YOU. It was a triumph of organization, and Walter Cronkite, Helen Thomas, John Chancellor, and other press barons who accompanied us could not help being impressed.

In "Alex," as we had all begun to call it, we stayed at the Ras el Tin Palace, perched on the shore of the Mediterranean's blue, blue water. Another summit meeting between the two leaders preceded the return dinner, with the Americans entertaining the Egyptians. The press and TV covered every appropriate event, the U.S. Air Force Strolling Strings provided music, and with only sixty-nine guests, this event was far less elaborate and ended far earlier than the other one.

Two protocolary boo-boos enlivened the evening: During the receiving line I presented Mrs. Fahmy, wife of the Egyptian foreign minister, to Nixon. Alas, she turned out not to be Mrs. Fahmy. At dinner we managed to slight U.S. ambassador Herman Eilts in the seating order, an oversight that he brought volubly to my attention the next day. To the vast gratification of the American guests, wine was served—Dom Perignon champagne, no less. Four naval vessels, their silhouettes outlined in lights, provided a glamorous backdrop out in the bay; we needed every conversation topic we could find, for as is often the case, language problems made for tough sledding. Sadat, on the other hand, spoke powerfully in excellent English of the strong new ties his country and ours were forming. At evening's end (around midnight) General Lawson, a beautiful White House calligrapher, and I liberated some sparkling wine and watched the sparkling sea.

Breakfast the next day was made sprightly by Henry Kissinger, his ebullience likely the result of the successful Sadat-Nixon talks and his own role in detaching Egypt from its former dependence on the Soviet Union. He came into the dining room laden with a number of packages. I offered to help him, but recalling rules of turning foreign gifts over to the chief of protocol, he growled in mock alarm, "Get away from me, Catto; I bought all these items with my own money." During breakfast he reminisced about Nixon's famous and fatuous comment on seeing the Great Wall during the visit to China: "That *is* a great wall." "I wonder," mused the secretary, "if he'll say 'That *is* a pyramid' when he sees the Pyramids."

Our return to Cairo was somewhat less glamorous than the trip up. The Nixons, Kissinger, and the ambassador flew down on a U.S. Army chopper, in great comfort, to view the Pyramids. Lesser mortals like me were assigned to an Egyptian Army bird with no doors, and I viewed the prospect with the same degree of enthusiasm as I would view being night manager at a convenience store. Safely there, however, we were treated to a superb show of Egyptian horsemanship and visits to those ancient tombs, the Pyramids.

Our greeting on arrival in Jidda turned out livelier than we had anticipated. Having been told by Saudi security that there "would be no movement," we found instead considerable crowds. Clearly, the Saudi government reacted to Nixon's tumultuous reception in Egypt and decided that hospitality demanded similar outbursts in Jidda. Large numbers therefore appeared, but the sense of genuine enthusiasm was not there.

Nixon had been met by the king at the airport, where a royal pavilion had been built. There, coffee was served; then the president was driven in his host's car (we lost that one) to the Royal Guest Palace, where coffee was again served. The coffee ceremony, incidentally, is not stand up and chitchat. The principals sit in the center, while the official parties flank their leaders, sitting in descending protocol order.

Following a welcome siesta, we assembled for the stag state dinner. (Mrs. Nixon had been shuffled off to a separate party given by the queen.) All the Saudis were handsomely turned out in traditional robes and kaffiyehs, the headdress of diagonally folded square cloth held in place by an *agal,* or band. The distinctive smell of Arrid deodorant suffused the crowded room. There being, of course, no cocktail hour, we quickly sat at long banquet tables, while at the raised royal table the king was flanked by the president and Kissinger. This seating arrangement made conversation difficult. The king, naturally, spent his time talking to Nixon. Kissinger, bored, fidgeted, yawned, picked his teeth, and looked generally miserable.

I sat next to the minister of agriculture, who spoke English and translated for the three princes seated across from me. It was hard work for us all, from Nixon on down, and I suspect the same was true for our hosts. After dinner and the inevitable speeches, we mercifully were able to leave, and so to bed.

The next day, Saturday, the principals had a two-hour meeting, farewell ceremonies took place at the airport, and we were off to Syria.

Hitting the Road with Nixon, Part 2

FLYING FROM one Middle Eastern country to another offers no spectacular views; all one sees is desert. Unless, that is, one happens to go near or over Israel. It is green, an astonishing sight in the sea of dun dunes. Indeed, it was the only sight between Jidda and Damascus, a flight of more than two hours.

If the flight was uneventful, so too was the visit. President Hafez el-Assad and his retinue turned out to be courteous in their welcome. As had become the norm, we drove through huge crowds of cheering Syrians, the two presidents leading the parade in an open car. (Here again, we lost the Battle of the Vehicles.) Courtesy in diplomacy might not seem curious, but U.S.-Syrian relations had been long since broken as a result of U.S. support for Israel, and we were represented in Damascus not by an embassy and an ambassador but by an "interests section." The social events I found quite enjoyable, since I was seated next to Syrians who spoke English. The speeches were not unduly long, and toasting was not a Syrian custom; the folkloric dancers were better than Cairo's. I might mention that throughout the trip, whenever Nixon spoke at such an event, he did so without notes, brilliantly; I was proud of him.

During the head-to-head meetings of Assad and Nixon, I roamed the *souk,* or market, and teamed with NBC reporter John Chancellor to see the beautiful Ommiad Mosque, a giant structure that contained within its elaborately tiled walls what used to be a Christian church.

My impression of Syria as we left for Israel was that while one must always recall it as a ruthlessly authoritarian government, the people were warm and had the sophistication of a civilization of great antiquity.

Our arrival in Tel Aviv proved to be an episode of déjà vu: as President and Mrs. Nixon came down the ramp from the plane, herald trumpets blared their welcome, just as at the White House. Two liberal democracies playing royalist games; it did not seem quite, well, kosher.

The state dinner, held at the handsome Knesset (parliament) in Jerusalem, made us feel as if we were in an oasis, not only in the genuine warmth of the Israeli welcome but also because wine flowed with biblical abundance. A glass of the grape makes potentially stiff diplomatic events vastly easier for all concerned. Nixon, in a moving talk, urged Israel to take a chance for peace. The atmosphere was warm and, as they say in Yiddish, *heimisch*.[1]

Release from Muslim temperance took its toll; a heavy head early Monday morning caused me to do laps in the hotel pool, followed by a brisk walk through the Old City of Jerusalem, so full of rich and exotic sights and sounds and smells. The president, meanwhile, toured the Holocaust memorial, Yad Vashem, wearing the troublesome, much discussed, and never-to-be-seen-again homburg.

After the usual summit meeting, our vast entourage flew the thirty minutes to Amman in Jordan. Twenty-one guns boomed their welcome, but monarchy or not, there were no herald trumpets. King Hussein and his queen, Alia (who was later to perish in a plane crash), welcomed the Nixons. Troops were inspected, speeches made—the normal routine.

The state dinner that evening, a black-tie event, took place in Basmad Palace. The Jordanians, from the hosts on down, were strikingly handsome people, men and women alike. The U-shaped table was set with china and silver, all bearing the royal crest, perfectly matched, though the salt and pepper shakers, oddly, could have come from Woolworth's. An orchestra, hidden behind closed doors to avoid competing with the conversation, played Cole Porter and Broadway tunes.

Recovered from the previous evening's excess, I had a nightcap with CBS's John Shahan and NBC's Peter Jennings at the comfortable bar of the Continental Hotel. (Jordan's version of Islam is more relaxed on the issue of alcoholic beverages.) Shahan told of an event in 1970, just before King Hussein ran the Palestine Liberation Organization out of Jordan. Sitting one evening in this same hotel, he saw a helicopter hover briefly over the swimming pool. No one thought much about it; the only chopper in the country at the time was the king's and he frequently used it. Later, however, Shahan learned that it was piloted not by Hussein but by two audacious Israelis dropping by to ogle the scenery around the pool.

Jordan was Nixon's last stop, and he returned to Washington for a week before setting out for the USSR. Our mission, however, continued to Brussels for a day and then off to Moscow on June 20 (our eighteenth day of advance work).

I was excited. Moscow—the very name was redolent of history, mystery, and a touch of the dangerous. The Soviet chief of protocol, an engaging career diplomat (or was he KGB, the secret police? one never knew for sure) met us. We sped at fifty miles per hour down the middle lane of boulevards so wide as to make Pennsylvania Avenue seem an alley. Common folk drove to the left or right, but bureaucrats used the middle lane, reserved for the sleek black Zils or Chaikas of the elite.

Our goal, the three-thousand-room Rossiya Hotel, turned out to be a bit primitive by Western standards. On arrival, I received my book of instructions, the rules of the house. It read:

1. The payment for the hotel is made according to the price list. There is a unique checking hour at the hotel 12 o'clock.

2. If you keep money or jewelry in your room it is your own responsibility and not of the hotel.

3. At the request of the guest and with the administration's approval visitors can stay in the guest's room from 9 A.M. until 11 P.M.

4. When leaving the room the guest must not leave taps open, close the windows, put out the light, the radio and the TV set and give the key to the floor keeper.

5. The guest must keep everything in order. He will have to repay the damage if anything is broken or damaged.

6. The coupons for the hotel should be delivered to the reception desk.

7. You are not permitted to have some strangers in the room while you are absent. Be careful with the fire. Don't have big luggage in your room.

The hotel's bathrooms were little better than privies. First of all, there was no escape trap for noxious odors. There were no shower curtains, assuring that one sprayed water like kids in a water fight (the showers were the gooseneck type). The basin had no stopper, but that really didn't matter. The drain was so clogged that the water rose to the rim and took five minutes to empty.

All meals, some of them very good, were paid for by the Soviets. The refrigerator in the room was stocked with sodas; concerts and the circus were on the house. Water in public places, however, cost three kopeks, but there was only one glass, for use by all.

The "floor keeper" referred to was invariably wide as a barge, shabby, and gruff. No amount of jollying could evoke even a slight smile. Her job was to keep track of the guests, doubtless for the KGB's benefit, and she took it seriously.

On my first arrival in Moscow, I was greeted at the airport by a Soviet Foreign Office man named Viktor Lessiovski. Short, round, and rumpled, he spoke excellent English and had a wry way about him. I bumped into him frequently and found him good company. At one point he gave me a set of Russian textbooks, since I had expressed an interest in the language. He carped about his career and generally seemed normal, agreeable, and interesting.

On returning to Washington, I stumbled upon a book called *Who's Who in the KGB* by an American Sovietologist. Flipping through the pages, I could scarcely believe my eyes: there was a biography of my friend Viktor—a full KGB colonel!

Our negotiations with the Soviets hit bumpy air almost at once. This was not a surprise. Two years before, on Nixon's first Soviet visit, every proposal put forward by the Americans was greeted by the phrase "No problem; impossible." This time they were not quite so difficult, but they were genuinely horrified by the gargantuan U.S. traveling party of more than five hundred people. Second, their plan was for Nixon and Brezhnev to fly to the Black Sea to relax. We agreed, until we discovered that the Soviet leader's *dacha,* or country house, was at Yalta. We flashed alarm signals to Washington, which quickly replied, "Richard Nixon does not go to Yalta," a name synonymous with Franklin Roosevelt's appeasement of the Soviets after World War II. We explained our position. Our hosts said they understood but that a huge effort at sprucing up the entire city had already been made; they vigorously denied any attempt at embarrassing Nixon with old ghosts. The stalemate finally ended thus: we agreed to go, but no public announcement of a trip to Yalta would be made. Technically, the *dacha* was in the Yalta suburb of Orienda, and so it was announced. The briefing books referred only to a trip to "the Black Sea," not mentioning any city at all. Needless to say, the press was not fooled.

On Saturday our advance party flew to the Black Sea on a Soviet Ilushin 62 executive aircraft. As ranking American, I was paired in an elegant stateroom with the Soviet deputy protocol chief, an unprepossessing man of middle years named Chernikhov. My host's English was imperfect, my Russian nonexistent. A further factor impeding conversation lay in the fact that the left lens of his glasses was shattered, making eye contact iffy, his left eye being totally invisible.

As we cruised along at thirty thousand feet, the Soviet suggested a vodka toast to the summit's success. As it was eight o'clock in the morning, I agreed reluctantly. Still, conversation did get easier after the toast.

I commented on the two red phones on the table between us. One had a hammer and sickle on the receiver, the other the Stars and Stripes. The Russian said, "Pick up one, get Kremlin. Pick up other, White House answers. Try." I did. The White House operator asked whom I wished to speak to. I said, "Call Mrs. Catto."

A very sleepy-sounding Jessica answered. I had forgotten that the time difference meant it was the middle of the night in Washington. Jessica was not amused.

I essayed a new approach with my Soviet colleague.

"The young interpreter you have assigned us, Mr. Feakov, is superb. His English is faultless."

My host giggled and poured more vodka.

"Name not Feakov," he said.

An awful thought crossed my mind: he must be KGB, traveling under an assumed name.

"No," the Russian explained, "name Fukov. But he cannot bear to say it in front of Americans."

Arrival at the Black Sea led to a drive through freshly painted, spic-and-span Orienda, visits to the *dacha* and the Brezhnevs' yacht, and a swim in the icy sea, a welcome and usefully sobering experience. Next day we returned to Moscow via Minsk, Chernikhov and I by then awash in boozy camaraderie. Indeed, as we parted he gave me a box of chocolates.

Our stop in Minsk, capital of the Belorussian Soviet Republic, was brief but memorable. There we visited a memorial to a village called Khatyn, whose 149 residents were marched into a barn by the Germans in 1943. The barn was then set afire; only one person survived. Dozens of such villages were wiped out during the war, when one of every four Belorussians died by fighting or murder.

The memorial centered on a giant statue of a man holding his dead son. A marble peak-roof slab commemorated the barn, and a belled tower marked where each chimney had been; every thirty seconds, the bells quietly tolled. Three corners of a flowered plaza were marked by three birch trees, while the fourth was a perpetual flame; the trees stood for the population's survivors, the flame for the one quarter who died. It rivaled Jerusalem's Yad Vashem in impact, and in a country known for the ugly gigantism of its public sculpture, it was a rare example of understatement and taste.

On June 24, our beleaguered band returned to Brussels to await the president, who arrived on schedule, was feted at a luncheon by the king of the Belgians, and attended a NATO meeting. At the luncheon, RN sat to the king's right, the German chancellor to the king's left. On noting this, British ambassador Muirhead dryly remarked, "I suppose they are now seating nations by gross national product rather than seniority." Ah, protocol.

After the reception by U.S. NATO ambassador Don Rumsfeld, I sneaked off for dinner with CBS's Bob Pierpoint, the *Guardian*'s Hella Pick, and columnist Joe Kraft. The press, always good company, frequently figured that I would be good for a story, but for the most part, I learned more than they did.

Our 3:00 P.M. arrival next day in Moscow surprised us. The Big Four of the Soviet lineup were on hand to greet the president: General Secretary Brezhnev, President Podgorny, Prime Minister Kosygin, and Foreign Minister Gromyko. Two years before, none of them had been at the airport; clearly, a major thaw in relations had taken place. The honor guard of Soviet troops passing in review were quite the best-drilled soldiers I had ever seen. Fortunately, Nixon was not required to do any wreath-laying. Frequently, ceremonial events required a salute with a sword as flowers were laid on a memorial, but Nixon's manual dexterity left something to be desired. To avoid accidental beheading of bystanders with the ceremonial sword, Major Jack Brennan, Nixon's Marine aide, would present the sword to the president. Nixon would lay hands on it, and Brennan would turn smartly with the sword and give the salute; the Occupational Safety and Health Administration would have approved.

We rode into town in a motorcade of some 150 gleaming black limos, each with an oriental rug on the floor of the back compartment. The opening event of the visit was a huge dinner in the Kremlin, in a hall whose roof was supported by a giant central pillar from which sprang four great vaulted arches. Extraordinary gold paintings of Adam and Eve, the Last Supper, and Jesus' baptism graced the room, which was finished in 1491, a rich if ironic tribute to Christianity in an officially atheist state. The guest list was flexible, and in effect, the Soviets graciously said, "Y'all come." As a result, we were able to invite stenos, security people, and baggage handlers, a rare treat on such trips.

Toasts with icy vodka took place before dinner, rather than after, as in our country. Whether this was for reasons of press deadlines or to ensure a sober toaster I did not find out. The menu was formidable. We started with fresh caviar, followed by fish puff pies; jellied besta (another fish); venison with pickles and a salad; a delicious cold vegetable soup called *okroshka,* followed by white baked salmon; then a filet of hazel grouse stuffed with mushrooms; and finally, strawberry ice cream, fruit, and coffee. The above was washed down with mediocre red and white wines and very good champagne. A final cognac assured the unwary of total collapse the next day. My dinner partners were Jacob Malik, the Soviet UN delegate and frequent sparring partner of our George Bush, and Georgi Arbatov, head of the USA-Canada Institute. I noted with a twinge of regret that the protocol chief and his assistants were seated far "below the salt," that is, at the foot of the table.

The following day, feeling a bit mushy, I slept in, my job done. I was not to accompany RN to the meetings or to the Black Sea, so tourism beckoned. An art lover, I went first to the Tretiakov Gallery, which was awash with people; I had never seen so many human beings slogging dully by so much dull art. The Pushkin was a different story. There, the *Mona Lisa* was on display, on loan from the Louvre. Dismayed by the length of the entry queue, I was wondering what to do when a pretty pink-cheeked girl pushed her way up to me and said in good English (having seen my car), "Are you an important foreigner?" Nothing loath, I admitted to foreignness and lied about my importance. She said, "Wait here." A moment later she returned and, pulling me by the hand, guided me past the entire line and waltzed me into the museum. "How on earth did you do that?" I asked. "It was simple. I pointed out you and your car, and told the guard he must let us in at once; that way we *both* got in quickly!" Mission accomplished, she went merrily on her way, returning, I presumed, to the poor husband she had left waiting in the line.

That afternoon I got word I was to sit in the plush and comfortable presidential box at the Bolshoi Theatre, where a special program had been laid on for the visitors. Totally unexpected, it was that much more of a rare treat: only the Nixons, the Soviet Big Four, the Soviet culture minister, Henry Kissinger, American ambassador Walter Stoessel and his effervescent wife, Mary Ann, and I were so honored.[2]

The minute the honored guests arrived, the program began. The first half, ballet selections by world-famous Soviet artists, was followed by operatic arias and dazzling folk dances by performers in vivid costumes from the various republics. At intermission, we were treated to a fast but elegant dinner. The climax of the event came with a huge chorus, singing—I am not making this up—"Way Down Upon the Swanee River" in English. I thought at first it might be a put-down of American racial difficulties, but I decided, perhaps naively, that it was not.

Returning to the hotel, I found the London *Times*'s U.S. correspondent, Henry Brandon, wanting to talk, a hot rumor having come his way. Was I, he wanted to know, about to be appointed U.S. ambassador to Britain? I was amazed, having heard no such thing, a fact I quickly shared with Brandon. Later, I found out where the rumor had originated. Knowing that I would dearly love such an appointment, Jessica had planted the item at strategic points back in Washington, where it quickly found its way to the reporter's ear. Jessica's ploy didn't work out, of course, and I was not named, but it showed how adept she was at playing the game.

The Nixons and their hosts fled south the next day and my tourism continued, with a visit to the famed, crowded, colorful Moscow Circus and a tour of the Kremlin's public areas.

Sunday night I went alone to the Tschaikovsky Competitions, where young pianists from over the world vied for a prize sure to jump-start their careers. Though it began forty minutes late, I enjoyed it. The audience, clearly knowledgeable about music, would collectively gasp with horror at any small error by a nervous contestant, errors I had not even noticed. At intermission, I decided to buy an ice cream cone, on sale in the cavernous lobby. There was—typical in the USSR—an endless line, but feeling hot and cramped, I decided to tough it out. Some forty minutes later, as the warning buzzers squawked, I finally got to the head of the line and learned why it had taken so long. The babushka who was serving, her sweating head swathed in a babushka, was putting each laden cone on a scale. If it weighed a bit much, she would slice off a chunk and try again. Finally satisfied, she would hand it gruffly to the tantalized and famished customer. How, I wondered, could a society capable of sending people into space put up with such an infuriating, inefficient distribution system?

A United States Information Service officer, David Nalle, introduced me to an extraordinary woman named Nina Stevens. A Russian, she was the wife of the longtime *U.S. News and World Report* Moscow correspondent, and she dabbled in art. Indeed, the Stevenses lived in a private house (a rarity in Moscow) that groaned with art, both old and contemporary. Astonishingly, the items that graced the walls were for sale, and I bought three naïf paintings by a man who signed himself Arkharov. By day Arkharov (not his real name) was a loyal member of the Union of Soviet Artists, or some such proletarian organization. By day he painted tractors and heroes of Soviet labor. But by night his talented brushes created wonderful worlds of onion-domed churches, religious symbolism, blue skies, and crowds of happy people. Underground art flourished in Moscow.

Again under the tutelage of the Nalles, I visited the flat of a Greek-born Canadian citizen named George Kostakis. That remarkable man had presciently begun to collect early twentieth-century Russian art during the many years when such work was proscribed by the communist authorities, who considered it degenerate. The result was a collection of astounding variety and beauty, worth millions of dollars, stored on every inch of wall space and under every bed of a high-rise Moscow apartment. Kostakis was happy to show it off, both for the pleasure it gave him and for the insurance it provided against confiscation by the ignorant hooligans of the Ministry of Art. With well-known foreigners such as Senator Ted Kennedy visiting, the owner felt he was safe from the art police.

A farewell reception in the huge St. George's Hall of the Kremlin closed the visit. With tables and glasses overflowing, our Soviet hosts bade us farewell, while an orchestra in the balcony played "Old Folks at Home" and "Old Black Joe" in bizarre counterpoint to the event below.

From the Kremlin, another lengthy motorcade sped to Vnukuvo II Airport. Once again, the top Soviets were there, anthems were smartly played, splendid troops passed in review, Richard Nixon boarded the *Spirit of '76,* and we were away, feeling a bit breathless and wondering what, if anything, it all meant.

The Fall of a President

OUR 11 P.M. arrival in Washington (delayed by a forty-five-minute phone conversation by Julie Nixon Eisenhower, who had joined us in Maine when we stopped to refuel and who flew to Washington not with her parents but with us) was joyous. Jessica, who met us, said I was so bleary-eyed as I alit from thirty-three days of grueling travel that I introduced myself to her and mumbled, "I am so pleased to be in your country." A late but equally joyous welcome from the children at home was like Christmas in July, for I had collected many goodies for them, as expiation for having been away for so long.

For Richard Nixon, return meant the eye of the Watergate storm and resignation thirty-six days later. For me, return meant most-welcome normality: ping-pong with the children (Will beat me the first time), dinners with friends, movies, and the slower life of summer.

At the office, the deputy chief of protocol, Ambassador Stuart Rockwell, and I battled with Pan American over luggage inspection. Diplomats from abroad do not expect to have their bags searched, but terrorism had made such a procedure standard and feathers were often ruffled. These were the days before X-ray machines did the job quietly, and when the sister of the Shah of Iran and the first lady of Liberia, traveling incognito, had their luggage brazenly opened for all to see, there was hell to pay. Stuart and I urged Pan Am to be aware of itinerant VIPs and to stroke them a bit.

One day I stopped by the White House and told Greg Lebedev of the personnel office that I could be persuaded to fill the vacant ambassadorship to the United Kingdom. That evening, Jessica and I dined at the Sri Lanka embassy, where the ambassador was astonished to learn that my grandfather had been born in his country. A fellow guest was Senator Vance Hartke, who spent dinner loudly and unpleasantly denouncing Undersecretary of State Joe Sisco, seated across the table. It was the kind of scene that embarrassed all within hearing. (Hartke had distinguished himself a year before by refusing to have his luggage searched at the Albuquerque airport, loudly proclaiming that he was a United States senator. The airline officials said he could be searched or walk; he chose the frisking.)

Looking back, these days seem idyllic when no account is given of the tumult at the White House and in Congress. With my usual genius for prognostication, I stoutly denied, even as August neared, that Nixon could be forced out. (I will admit, however, that when Vice President Ford came to the State Department for breakfast one morning, I took pains to be helpful.) Jessica was more perceptive. Indeed, as early as June she had bet me a hundred dollars that Richard Nixon would be out of office by year's end. (I paid up on August 9, the day after Nixon left.) On

July 29, George Bush came by for dinner. As chairman of the Republican National Committee, he was despondent about the political scene and glum at the mess Nixon had gotten himself and the country into. He discussed resigning, an idea that jolted me. If loyalist George was that disturbed, the situation clearly was worse than I, absorbed in my daily routine, had realized.

An incident at a diplomatic dinner on August 7 illustrated the depth of some people's feelings. The Jordanian prime minister was on an official visit to Washington, and a dinner and theater evening was arranged at the Kennedy Center. Among the guests were the State Department's Jordan desk officer and his wife. I had thought her a bit odd when I met her. Very informally dressed in slacks and a blouse, she asked for a doggie bag at the dinner's end, a move perhaps appropriate at a family restaurant but not at a dinner for a visiting official. Then, when the inevitable after-dinner toast was offered, the young woman sat during the toast "To the President." It was a painful moment, and it cost her and her husband an invitation to the White House when President Ford subsequently entertained King Hussein. Theoretically, since wives of State Department officers are not government employees, their behavior is not taken into account as their husband's performance is being judged, but there are limits. (Spouses are never mentioned in officers' efficiency reports, but the word gets around.)

On August 5, Jessica and I attended a fiery and delicious dinner at the Chinese embassy. It was an electric evening. Kay Graham, whose *Washington Post* had done so much to bring Nixon to his low state, was there as well, and we all sensed the end was near. On the eighth, my stubborn disbelief was shattered as the president announced his intention to resign.

Thursday and Friday, August 8 and 9, were a blur of constant movement, as our office shuffled ambassadors in and out of the Oval Office for farewell calls. Friday morning, at 9:30 A.M., the president said good-bye to a large crowd of administration officials gathered in the East Room. Amid muffled snuffles and wet eyes, he managed to be as confounding in humiliation as in victory. With the first lady at his side, his voice a mixture of pathos and defiance, he recounted how difficult the recent days had been. He said he could not have survived without the love of a wonderful woman. I expected him to turn and embrace his wife, Pat, and when he said, "my mother," I almost keeled over. Mrs. Nixon had been a tower of quiet and uncomplaining strength, but given the chance to acknowledge her he did not, remaining graceless to the end.

The first family then left, the crowd surging behind; tearfully they embraced the Fords and climbed aboard the helicopter that took them to Andrews Air Force Base. There, the *Spirit of '76* waited to take this star-crossed man back to California.[3] With a final clumsy wave, he was gone.

I never again witnessed a moment so riveting. Richard Nixon had been on the national scene for a quarter of a century, hated intensely by legions of Americans but admired by others, who watched his tragedy play out in mute puzzlement.

Even today, ask an American—or even more so, a foreigner—who lived through those days, what Nixon did to deserve his fate, and chances are you will receive a blank stare; many people just don't quite recall anything heinous enough to warrant the outcome, though reading the long-secret tapes may make it clearer.

Jessica felt his flaw lay in being so full of hate and anger, defying his enemies in a way that precluded admissions of error. I felt that style played a role. While his language could soar, he often sounded like Uriah Heep, whining in 1952 that he would *not* return the puppy a man in Texas had sent his girls or feeling that the press would not have Nixon to kick around anymore when he lost the California gubernatorial race in 1962. And I never heard anyone accuse him of having a sense of humor, that great leavener. In a funny way, those who hated him may have created him. For all his tragic faults, he had one powerful virtue: self-discipline. A supremely shy man, he nonetheless forced himself throughout a lifetime to mix and mingle with total strangers as he clawed his way to the top. How he must have hated it; getting there was *not* half the fun.

Later on Friday, August 9, 1974, Gerald R. Ford was sworn in as the thirty-eighth president, and the nation heaved a great sigh of relief, his inaugural address having struck just the right note of healing. Jessica and I witnessed the moment in the packed White House. Looking back, she taps Ford as her favorite among the many presidents we have known. She felt he kept his sense of balance and destiny better than the others. The transfer of so much power so easily struck me as amazing at the time—and still does. It leaves one with a deep pride in this country's institutions—and in its people.

Back to Business as Usual

ASTONISHINGLY, MY life as chief of protocol settled quickly down to normal. I went to Andrews Air Force Base to welcome Egyptian foreign minister Fahmy on Sunday. Alas, the visitor came in a bit early. Kissinger, concerned by the state of Israeli-Egyptian negotiations, decided to come to Andrews as well, but—typically—he arrived late. The result was a Kissinger tantrum: strictly normal.

The new president decided to address a joint session of Congress on Monday night, and of course, the diplomatic corps was invited. The House chamber is always crowded when Senate and House are packed in together during a joint session; add 150 diplomats and chaos becomes likely. My team had enough chairs to seat all of our ambassadorial charges, but by the time they arrived and were ushered in, a fair number of the chairs had been expropriated by hands unknown—likely members of Congress. In any case, several of the diplomats, among them the French chargé d'affaires, had to stand through the event, Knowing the French, I sought him out afterward to apologize. It was a waste of time, for his indignation was white-hot; had Americans exploded a small nuclear device in downtown Paris, he would not have been in greater distress. The more earnest my regrets, the greater his fury. I finally decided he was a hopeless ass and went about my business.

Tuesday, August 13, all political appointees sent Ford a resignation letter, as was customary. To ease the potential pain, he invited us all to the White House that afternoon for a "photo op," thus providing that element essential for every politico, a framed picture with the new boss.

After much thought, the president finally tapped Governor Nelson Rockefeller of New York to be vice president. Jessica and I thought him a good choice. Though we would have preferred George Bush, Nelson was well versed in government, widely experienced, and a canny politician. One day he came by State for lunch with Henry Kissinger and the Russian ambassador, Anatoly Dobrynin. Since Henry was late, we chatted, and Dobrynin told a story on himself and the fabled Rockefeller family, long the bête noire of the communists.

It seems that the Russian had been in Arkansas, where Nelson's brother Winthrop was running for governor. On being introduced to the Soviet visitor, the candidate promptly pinned a "Rockefeller" button on the Russian's lapel. The two had a good laugh, and then each went on his way.

Returning to Washington, Dobrynin quickly packed and flew off to Moscow. The following day, he walked into a politburo meeting. His colleagues, being Russians and therefore fascinated with lapel buttons, all crowded around to examine this strange button in the foreign lettering. Dobrynin, having totally forgotten he was wearing it from the previous day, said, "This was a very dangerous error I made; you all will think I have defected to the West!"

Russians did not always have a sense of humor. In mid-September, Gromyko made a quick visit to Washington. Kissinger always met his Russian colleague at the airport, and Gromyko reciprocated. It was a small diplomatic courtesy that symbolized the importance each granted the other. This time, however, Kissinger had a long-standing date to escort the prickly Indian ambassador personally to see the president. Henry, of course, had a tantrum and demanded that somehow we solve the conflicting demands on his time. We tried to arrange for the Soviet plane to land at nearby National Airport, as opposed to distant Andrews Air Force Base, but the plane was too large. I called the Russian embassy and spoke to the chargé d'affaires, explaining our problem. He was cold and grumpy. "Gromyko always cancels everything to meet Henry," he whined, and no amount of selling could change his mind. In the end, Kissinger chose his new boss over his old adversary, and Bob Ingersoll, the deputy secretary, met the Russians. No war ensued.

The next day I took Gromyko and Dobrynin to the White House for a meeting with Ford. The president was a bit late, so we waited in the Cabinet Room and the president's irrepressible photographer, David Hume Kennerly, snapped a number of photos. Quickly developing them, he gave me a particularly good shot of me and the Soviets. I asked the two to autograph it, but to my surprise, they refused. Instead, they passed it to an aide who sent it to me a few days later, framed. Instead of signing the picture, each suspicious Russian had signed a piece of paper, and each signature was mounted just below the picture. What devious trick they thought could come from signing the photo itself I never found out.

As the days went by, I learned even more lessons about the job. The first was that while much of it was pomp, ceremony, fuss and feathers, its symbolism could be important. One Saturday morning, the Argentine foreign minister had an early appointment with the president. Although we had been out late the evening before at a charity ball, I dragged myself up and went to the White House myself, rather than asking the deputy chief of protocol, Ambassador Stuart Rockwell, to cover for me. I later learned that the Argentine, like all Latin Americans, would have taken it amiss had the deputy been there to receive him; he would have felt a subtle message was being sent.

My second lesson was that plans change and one had better be ready for the unexpected. That same day, in the afternoon, Prime Minister Tanaka of Japan came to call on President Ford. Their meeting was scheduled for an hour and a half, and rather than waste time doing a crossword puzzle while I waited, I decided to get in my daily three-mile run. Returning to State, I suited up and went out, but as I loped along, a still, small voice began to whisper, "What will you do if they should by any chance finish early?" Heeding it, I turned around after a mile and came back. Dressing in a leisurely way, I returned to the White House and saw to my horror that the motorcade was just pulling out of the drive. I pulled my car in as the last vehicle, and away we went to the heliport. Trying to look collected, I climbed on board for the ten-minute flight to Andrews, said *sayonara* to the Japanese guest, and saw him off to Tokyo with a great sigh of relief. The relationship with our most important trading partner would not have suffered; indeed, the prime minister probably would not have noticed. But *someone* would have, and some meaning — other than pure carelessness — might have been attributed to the incident.

In late September, I experienced my first full-blown state visit, a long-planned call by Italian president Leone and his staggeringly beautiful wife, Vittoria.

There is something wonderful about the Italians. Somehow they have more charm, more worldliness, and more beautiful women than any nationality I know. Sure, their government may be a mess and their streets may be dirty and they drive like maniacs, but I like them, and the prospect of having them descend on us was inviting.

The Italian ambassador at the time was a very senior career man named Egidio Ortona. A fine diplomat, he was blessed as well by talent (he played the piano at a professional level and gave recitals after his own lively dinner parties). His wife, Giulia, was perhaps the handsomest woman in the world, looking like one of those exquisite Renaissance portraits that hang in the Pitti, with snow-white hair and perfect skin, the kind of looks that demand a velvet backdrop.

As was our custom, we had suggested to the Italians that the visiting party land in Williamsburg, Virginia. That old restored town is charming and provides the guest a chance to rest and recover from jet lag before the rigors of the visit really begin. I had wheedled a jet from my friend General Lawson, the president's military assistant, and we asked the Ortonas to fly down with us. Alas, the pilot landed at the wrong airport, an ordeal for Mrs. Ortona, who loathed flying, perhaps even more than Jessica does. Mercifully, we finally made it.

The visitors got the Williamsburg Treatment. They were shown the restored old colonial town in a carriage, were serenaded by musicians in colonial costume, and were formally welcomed at the beautiful Governor's Mansion, after which they retreated to their suite to recover from the trip. We joined them for supper and went early to bed.

As was typical for a state visit, the official welcome was to be at the White House, so the next morning we went by helicopter from the golf course at the Williamsburg Inn for the one-hour flight to the Ellipse, the circular park across the street from the mansion. Limousines whisked us up the long drive to where the Fords waited. Bands played, soldiers marched, the presidents reviewed the troops, speeches were made, and the principals retired to the Oval Office to conduct their business while the rest of us took coffee in the Blue Room.

A lunch was to be given in the Leones' honor by the Kissingers at the handsome old building of the Organization of American States on Seventeenth Street, and it provided by accident a lovely example of the idiocy that protocol can sometime achieve.

The chief of protocol of the OAS was a man I had known from my days with the U.S. delegation, a man named Manuel Ramírez, a Peruvian. I had asked him if Henry could use the OAS building, since State's entertainment rooms were being redone. He graciously acceded. The day of the luncheon, I went into Manuel's office to borrow the phone, and to my surprise, he seemed very cold and distant. Not beating around the bush, I asked him what his problem was. Ice dripping from every word, he said, "Why didn't you invite the secretary general [Galo Plaza] of the OAS to the luncheon? You really should have." He was right, but, as I explained, I simply hadn't thought of it. It was not a Latin American function, and the idea had not crossed my mind. He would not be put off in spite of my apologies. I finally tired of his outburst and asked him why in the world he hadn't just called me to suggest the idea; I would have been glad to do it. At that point, he bowled me over by sniffing indignantly, "Of course, Galo is abroad, and he won't know about it."

The visit, which proved to be a typical one, continued with a state dinner, black tie at the White House. Just before eight o'clock, Jessica and I went to Blair House to collect the Leones and escort them to the party. Arriving at the north portico, we were met by the Fords and taken up to the family quarters for a glass of champagne.

I came to believe this was a particularly nice way to entertain. There were never more than a handful of people in the Yellow Oval Room, an exceptionally handsome room lined with fine nineteenth-century American paintings. The guests consisted of the two families, the foreign ministers and their wives, the Italian ambassador, the chiefs of protocol, and perhaps one or two others. It gave the guests a glimpse of where the president really lived and started the evening with warm informality.

At eight-thirty, a military aide appeared and escorted all save the two principals and their wives down to join the other guests, eight o'clock arrivals by then enjoying drinks in the spacious East Room. Social aides began to move people into the receiving line, ranking guests at the front. At eight-thirty-five, the strains of the ever-stirring "Hail to the Chief" were heard, and the Fords and the Leones were announced and marched four abreast into the room to receive the guests.

My role was to stand by President Ford and introduce each guest to him. How did I know who they were? I didn't, but a strategically placed military aide would ask the guest's name and whisper it to me, and I would then boldly say, "Mr. President, may I present Mr. So-and-So."

This rigmarole was inherently clumsy, for often the aide mangled the name, or the person being introduced turned out to be the president's nephew. At the dinner for President Sadat some months later, I thought the aide said, "General Gazala," and I so introduced the man to Ford. Later, thinking the man somehow looked familiar, I asked Jessica who he might be. She said, "Dummy, that's Omar Sharif, the actor." No wonder he looked familiar.

Introductions made, the Fords escorted their guests into the State

Dining Room, beautifully laid out and beflowered. The tables were a Ford change, and a very good one. Nixon's E-shaped tables made conversation stiff and difficult, but round ones invited generalized talk—as opposed to speaking only to the person to right or left. Nixon's herald trumpets blaring as the principals entered had also been abandoned, another move away from pretentious show toward republican simplicity.

Typically, there would be tables of eight or ten, the number depending on how many guests there were. (The maximum the room will hold is 120.) Generally there were four courses—appetizer, entrée, salad, and dessert—and three wines, usually domestic. I never had a bad meal at the White House, or even a bad dish, for that matter. The American people can be proud of the way we entertain; it is elegant but never extravagant.

As dessert was served, the Air Force's Strolling Strings provided a musical interlude. The guests then moved into the other rooms for coffee and then back to the East Room for a concert. That evening, it was the New England Ragtime Ensemble from the New England Conservatory in Boston, playing mostly Scott Joplin music. Afterward there was dancing, something the Fords liked to do and did well. (Often they stayed late to dance, which the Nixons had seldom done.)

At about eleven o'clock, Jessica and I sought out the Leones and upon learning they were ready to go, escorted them after warm good-byes back to Blair House. From there our superb driver, Robert Hill, took us home, tired but elated by our first state dinner in the new job.

The next day was again typical. I called for Leone fairly early and took him to Georgetown University, where he received an honorary degree. Our motorcade, leaving jammed traffic and annoyed commuters in its wake (the Secret Service protection detail, of course, stopped all traffic to allow easy and safe access), we then went to Arlington Cemetery for a wreath-laying ceremony at the Tomb of the Unknown Soldier. There we were met by a black two-star general who, to Leone's delight, greeted the president in excellent Italian. I thought to myself, "Only in America"; it was a wonderful moment.

Next we sped to a prayer service at Holy Rosary Church, where many Americans of Italian descent had gathered. The service concluded with the singing of "God Bless America," another nice touch by the trip's planners.

Then, with a tip of the hat to the separation of powers, we drove to the Capitol for meetings with congressional leaders, presentation of all congressmen of Italian descent, and a luncheon by the Senate Foreign Relations Committee. All the lawmakers I met assumed that with a name like Catto, I was a *paisan;* I did not disabuse them. (Indeed, for years I was on the mailing list of the Sons of Italy.)

The visitor's afternoon was devoted to meetings with American Cabinet members, and that evening we suffered through a giant reception at the Italian embassy for the diplomatic corps.

After a brief farewell ceremony, at which Kissinger bade our guests Godspeed and bands played the national anthems, we flew by helicopter to Andrews Air Force Base and then by Air Force Convair to New York.

Again, the pace was hectic. Greeted by former ambassador Angier Biddle Duke, then New York's protocol chief, we drove directly to the Union Club, where the Morgan Guaranty Bank had most of the city's business barons for lunch. There followed a speech to the United Nations General Assembly and a dinner by Secretary General Kurt Waldheim, to which I was mercifully not invited. Instead, I went to dinner with old friends Lois and Tom Evans, a welcome change of pace.

Saturday, after an early run in Central Park, I escorted the Leones on a Staten Island ferry tour of lower Manhattan, with a good look at the Statue of Liberty. Lunch was with Mayor Abraham Beame at Gracie Mansion, his official residence, followed by a motor trip to the Rockefellers' estate, Pocantico Hills in Tarrytown. Nelson and David Rockefeller closeted themselves with Leone, and I and the other straphangers ogled the art and the beauty of four thousand acres of autumnal New York. I had driven up with the U.S. ambassador to Italy, John Volpe, a Massachusetts politician of Italian parentage and numbing verbosity, whom I nonetheless enjoyed. That evening the Sons of Italy gave a huge reception; I accompanied Leone and, assured he was in good hands, melted into the evening for Mexican food with two of my Protocol colleagues, Marylou Sheils and Bill Codus. The following day the official party slowly got itself together and drove to JFK airport for farewells and the return to *bella Italia.* The weary protocol group engaged in a tradition: as the guest's plane[3] lifted off, we lifted a glass of whatever was available in a "wheels up" toast. The ironist could interpret this as he pleased: "Godspeed" or "Thank God, you're gone." We never told — but we knew. In the Leones' case it was the former.

A Refreshing Change in Command

FORD CHANGED things. Not overarching policies but little things. For example, when a new ambassador arrives in Washington (or any national capital), he "presents his credentials" to the head of state, the president. In so doing, he officially begins his mission. In Nixon's time, this was usually considered a nuisance: While herald trumpets announced the arrival of the ambassador's limousine, the actual presentation amounted to nothing. The ambassador entered, flashbulbs popped, and he was out of there. No conversation, *nada*.

Ford did it differently. Trumpets were forgotten, but the ambassadors were asked to sit down in the Oval Office to chat with the president, albeit in most cases briefly, before the guest departed. The ambassadors were happy, for with the resulting pictures to each nation's press, a telegram might begin: "As I said today to President Ford . . ." Sure, it took a bit of time, but I think it was worth it, a grace note all too rare in frenetic Washington.

In a similar vein, in October Ford gave a ball for the entire ambassadorial corps, white tie and tails (or traditional national dress), with decorations, the kind of thing ambassadors really get a hoot out of doing. Due at nine o'clock in the evening, they began arriving at the White House shortly after eight. They were ushered up to the East Room, where the deputy chief of protocol, Ambassador Stuart Rockwell, and I greeted them and saw to it that they were given a glass of champagne. And they were splendid! Medals in republican America are not a big deal, but almost everywhere else they are treasured and displayed. Some of the ambassadors, such as dean of the diplomatic corps Guillermo Sevilla Sacasa of Nicaragua, clanked like tanks as they walked, so laden were they with stars, crosses, sashes, and the other paraphernalia of diplomatic honor. Getting all those peacocks in line in order of precedence (those who have served the longest come first, the recent arrivals last) required patience, but eventually we succeeded.

The president came in at nine o'clock, daughter Susan on his arm (Mrs. Ford was ill), and after his words of welcome, I proceeded to present all 130-odd to him. While I knew many of them, having assiduously called on them, the majority were strangers, and doing a queue that long was hot and tiring. Afterward, there was dancing. We danced and so did the president. The music was good and Jessica and I were—literally—the last to leave.

Another innovation of Ford's White House concerned gifts to foreign leaders. Not long after I began the job, the terminally tenacious Maxine Cheshire of the *Post* called and told me she had proof that the Nixons had stolen an emerald worth $300,000, a gift of the Shah of Iran. The Office of Protocol was the record keeper on gifts for all branches of government save the White House; gifts to the president were recorded separately, and apparently the record keeping was not good. Criticism of this sloppiness caused the White House to turn over its records to Protocol, where they were carefully checked. No alarming abuse was found. (The Nixons had not kept the emerald.)

On the other hand, carelessness had been rampant. One record, for example, mentioned an ornate clock given to the president's secretary, Rosemary Woods, by the Iranian ambassador. I called Rosemary to ask. She said no, it was a gift to the Nixons, but it didn't count under the gift rules. "Why?" I queried. "Because," she explained, "it was not from the head of state." I told her that *any* gift from a foreigner was covered; she was, she said, unaware of that. Indeed, the records showed no evidence of any of the president's entourage ever having turned in any gifts, though they were doubtless the recipients of many.

Aware of this brouhaha, Ford decided that not only would we discourage gifts from visiting delegations but also the U.S. government would not pay for any gift. If protocol demanded a return gift for a visiting leader, Catto would have to find a donor. The result was that I spent countless hours as Scrounger General, asking U.S. companies and individuals to come through for the good old USA. The living former ambassadors to Paris gave money to buy a bust of Lafayette for French president Giscard d'Estaing. Washington sculptor (and my good friend) John Safer donated one of his handsome works for Ford to give the king of Spain. (He liked it; I subsequently saw it at the royal palace outside Madrid.)[4] Kodak gave an elaborate camera set for Egyptian president Anwar Sadat. It was not a satisfactory system, but it kept Ford far from problems that plagued the Nixons.

In October I learned of a pleasant perk of my office and was quick to take advantage of it. There is a presidential box at the Kennedy Center, and inasmuch as the president seldom uses it, senior government people are free to do so for official entertainment. When the American Ballet Theatre was in town, I asked the British, Mexican, Portuguese, and Sri Lankan ambassadors to be our guests for a performance. The Mexican had children of John's and Isa's ages, so for good measure we invited the young as well. A foyer outside the box enabled us to serve champagne and sandwiches at intermission, privately and quite elegantly.

Press interest in the doings of the chief of protocol continued. Barbara Walters interviewed Jessica and me for a show she was doing on the diplomatic corps, and CBS's *60 Minutes* followed me on my rounds for two weeks for a segment to be broadcast the following year. It was to be called "The Other Henry," the real Henry, of course, being Kissinger. My trial by fire, Morley Safer presiding, turned out to be good-humored and lighthearted. For example, the crew had filmed me at the Vietnamese national day reception. There I ran into the new Chinese ambassador and pinned one of President Ford's "Whip Inflation Now" buttons on him, to the amusement of all except, probably, the poor ambassador himself.

The next major foreign policy event in Ford's young presidency was a trip to Japan, Korea, and the Soviet Union. As I had during the previous summer, I led the advance party, and found, to my delight, that the atmosphere was now entirely different. Ford's people had none of the turf-conscious angst of Nixon's and working with them was fun.

The trip took us to Tokyo and Kyoto, where I was exposed to the pickiness of the Imperial Palace protocol people, whom I found humorless, parochial, and dull. Protocol at the foreign office was an entirely different cup of tea, the people relaxed and easy to work with.

Our schedule offered ample time for substance but with fun on the side. In the latter category fell a visit to the Shogun's Palace, site of the famed "nightingale floors," whose squeak guaranteed that no malefactor could sneak up on a sleeping shogun with ill intent. A traditional geisha party was planned, and a visit to the serenity of the Golden Pavilion, a Buddhist shrine.

In Korea we found a warm welcome and an introduction to *kimchi*, the garlic-laden traditional dish that caused us to wilt roses at thirty paces. There also I ran into Don Gregg, the CIA's man in Seoul[5] and an acquaintance from my Williams College days. We inadvertently gave the Koreans a hard time by not being able to say exactly when the president would arrive or leave. That arose from tardiness on the part of the Soviets, with whom Ford was to meet in Vladivostok after he left Korea. Our hosts, though frustrated, nonetheless made our job easy. We came, furthermore, to understand some of the Koreans' resentment of the Japanese, who had turned their country into a colony for decades. For example, the Koreans were so anxious to throw off Japanese ways that upon liberation in 1945, they almost overnight began to drive on the right, the Japanese having forced left-hand motoring on them. Chaos and carnage resulted, but national pride was served.

Our last stop, the icy and heretofore closed-to-foreigners Vladivostok, turned out to be a bit of a reunion, since the Soviets were people we had worked with the previous summer. Remoteness and Soviet sensitivities made that stop strictly business. Our hosts were proud to point out, however, that the spa where we were to be housed boasted a warm indoor pool for the athletic president's exercise.

The presidential trip itself took place six days after the advance party's return to Washington, into which time we shoehorned a visit by Austria's chancellor, Bruno Kreisky.

A flap arose over what kind of collar and tie the Americans would wear with their morning suits for the call on the emperor of Japan. We came with wing collars, but it turned out that the Japanese would wear pointed collars with ties, not the ascots we had. Some rat leaked this crisis to the press, and great fun was made by the American reporters, especially the loathsome Maxine Cheshire, about how ridiculous we would look, out of uniform, as it were. Furthermore, the president's pants were adjudged by reporters to be too short, for which I was blamed. The joke made the rounds that the president's tailor must have played football at Michigan State without his helmet on.

As previously mentioned, the president's gift for the emperor turned out to have been made in Japan (the set of audiotapes, one on each state of the Union). Again, the press made a great to-do and Kissinger rumbled to me at one point, "Well, Catto, it could have been worse—the tapes might have been made in Taiwan." The woes of protocol are many.

In spite of such tempests, the visit was a great success. Dinner at the Imperial Palace, the spare and serene architecture of which I found deeply appealing, went off without problems. And the geisha party at the Tsuruya Restaurant in Osaka was a treat. Seated shoeless on the floor, each member of the American party had a beautifully costumed hostess, her face painted the traditional stark white, to serve him and to try to get through impenetrable language barriers to amuse us. A traditional dance with samisen accompaniment did just that. Then, after a superb ten-course meal and a good bit of sake, the potent Japanese rice wine, the ladies played a game with us in which a pipe cleaner was passed from person to person using only lips, noses, and chins, no hands allowed. Most of us, Ford, Chief of Staff Don Rumsfeld, Press Secretary Ron Nesson, Ambassador James Hodgson, and I managed reasonably well, but Henry Kissinger had problems. As we left, he growled at me, "Catto, there better not be any photos of this!" There were, but none found its way to the press.

One sight surprised me. At our hotel in Kyoto, the old imperial capital, there was a staff dining room. I went in for a bit of lunch on our last day, and there sat Gerald Ford, eating a burger along with everyone else. Did this sort of "fraternizing" demean him? Richard Nixon would probably have said yes; remoteness to him was a key element of leadership, and he would not have been caught dead eating and visiting the baggage handlers and secretaries. My guess is that Ford's approach was better. It certainly endeared him to me, and I was not alone.

The president's welcome in Seoul amazed us, especially the Secret Service security men. The broad boulevard linking the airport to the downtown seethed with people; literally millions lined the twelve-mile route. Pushing throngs broke police lines, and our pace slowed to a creep. My car, about ten behind the president's, was surrounded, and I opened the window to shake hands with the flag-waving and clearly ecstatic crowd. It reminded me of Nixon's welcome in Cairo, but the Seoul greeting seemed not to be organized and orchestrated but spontaneous. (I suspect my naïveté is showing here.) As we finally reached town center, confetti slithered down from tall buildings and balloons appeared everywhere.

After laying a wreath on the grave of the late Mrs. Park, recently assassinated in a failed attempt to kill the president, the presidential party visited a U.S. military installation. From there Ford went to call on President Park at the Blue House, his official residence.

I rejoined the party for a giant reception at which poor Ford had to shake seven hundred hands and then attend a state dinner. The contrast with Japan was vivid: We sat at banquet tables and used knives and forks. Military bands played U.S. show tunes and waltzes, which was good, given the difficulty of conversation. One of my dinner partners was a Buddhist monk, the other a Presbyterian minister. The latter spoke

English, a rare treat, since few of the Koreans spoke our tongue and none of us save embassy people spoke theirs. Entertainment included Korean dancers and a chorus of children, who charmed us by singing in English the Michigan fight song, the anthem of Ford's alma mater.

The following day Ford and key aides left for Siberia, and I flew home, fourteen hours on a C-141, a military transport plane packed with people and equipment.

"Super K" in Action

BACK AT the office, I tried an idea to help U.S.–Latin American relations. I suggested to the assistant secretary for Latin America that he and I give a luncheon for several key ambassadors at the State Department. We cleared the date on Kissinger's calendar, for the idea was to have him drop by unannounced for coffee with the sure-to-be-delighted envoys, who could cable home what they said to the Great Man (*Newsweek* magazine had run a cover of Henry dubbing him "Super K," and he was riding high). Alas, and not surprisingly, Henry got stuck testifying on Capitol Hill and didn't make it. The guests, I am happy to say, remained ignorant, but it disappointed me.

German chancellor Helmut Schmidt came to town in December, engaging all who met him. The interesting thing, however, was not his coming but who the Fords invited to the White House dinner. Among the guests were Kay Graham and Ben Bradlee, publisher and editor of the *Washington Post*. During the Johnson and Nixon years, neither had been a guest at the mansion; both were cordially loathed by the residents. With Ford, things were different. The *Post*, Democratic in outlook, had said scathing things about Ford on countless occasions, particularly when he pardoned Nixon. The president, however, knew the game and played it well, as inviting the *Post* people showed. Washington noticed and nodded in approval.

Kissinger gave a dinner at State for the Trilateral Commission, an international think tank of North Americans, Europeans, and Japanese, all prominent and distinguished people. After dinner he spoke briefly and then answered questions. A windy Englishman rose, with a question that took him eight minutes to ask (I timed him). As he at last sat, Governor

Jimmy Carter of Georgia popped up and said, "Mr. Secretary, those of us in back could not hear; could you repeat the question?" The audience was amused, and Henry was up to the occasion. With a twinkle, he said, "There goes my opportunity to give an obscure answer." He then proceeded to distill the lengthy question into a statement of about thirty seconds, leaving out nothing of importance, and his answer was equally brilliant. At moments like those, I forgot his childish tantrums and felt proud to work for such an extraordinary man.

Entertainment of another sort came from Italian ambassador Egidio Ortona. Knowing how much work had gone into President Leone's visit, he gave a luncheon at his handsome Sixteenth Street residence for the Office of Protocol. Secretaries, drivers, baggage handlers, officers — all came and all had a ball. Marylou Sheils, the one who had done most of the work, was given a pair of Gucci shoes, which she sadly turned in. Ortona showed himself not only a first-rate "pro" but also a first-rate human being.

Christmas slowed official life. We celebrated Hanukkah with Al and Carol Moses, our neighbors. My parents (and my aunt Liz Pritchett) came to town to visit, and we had an early Christmas with them. Then we six were off to Aspen for a white Christmas and lots of skiing. Isa, 9, and I began a tradition by sneaking off for a pancake breakfast, just the two of us. It was a good holiday, but for me Christmas is always somehow tinged with sadness, in spite of the joyous event it represents.

The first visitor of the New Year, Sultan Qabus of Oman, arrived on January 9 for a visit memorable mostly for an event incidental to his ride into town from Andrews Air Force Base. Arriving there to meet him, I was pulled aside by the head of the Secret Service protection detail. In tones furtive, he told me not to be alarmed if we took a different route driving into town. "A bank is about to be robbed," he explained, "and we don't want to drive past it during the robbery." That seemed reasonable enough, but I inquired how in the world he knew in advance. "Oh," he deadpanned, "the police tipped us off. They will be lying in wait when the robbers come." We switched routes, and the serenity of His Highness was not disturbed. I was disappointed: it might have been exciting. The tip, incidentally, proved correct, and the robbers were caught as planned.

The flow of visits included Israeli foreign minister Ygal Alon, for whom Henry Kissinger had a luncheon. I was seated next to Israeli ambassador Simcha Dinitz, who told a story on Henry. As was frequently the case, Henry was mad at the Israelis in general and at Dinitz in particular, and he said, "Dinitz, if you don't behave yourself, I'm going to serve you pork chops for lunch and then leak it to the Israeli press. It will ruin your career." The ambassador gave as good as he got: "Henry, I could stand having that leaked to the Israeli press, but you couldn't stand your father knowing *you* ate pork chops!" (Kissinger's father was an Observant Jew.)

In January I also began to take French lessons at the Foreign Service Institute. French, though no longer the language of diplomacy that it once was, is nonetheless extremely useful; for about half the countries in Africa, it is the lingua franca. Ability to speak French, Spanish, and English enables one to communicate in more than eighty of the world's countries.

British prime minister Harold Wilson came to see Ford, giving me a chance for good chats with that thoroughly charming man. He had committed to memory reams of light verse, one piece of which stuck in my mind:

> You cannot hope to bribe or twist,
> Thank God, the British journalist.
> But seeing what unbribed he'll do,
> There isn't any reason to.

Wilson liked Ford. He told me, "He fits one like an old shoe, though it may not be dignified to say it." I passed that along to Ford, doing my bit for British-American relations.

George Bush came for consultations at State from his post as U.S. representative in Beijing, but he came down with dysentery and had to be admitted to Georgetown Hospital. Barbara had remained in China, and he wanted company, so I went by for an hour and heard what it was like to live in that remote, closed, sometimes hostile society. He and Bar enjoyed it; they rode bikes frequently and found the Chinese polite if not forthcoming. They were, however, isolated. Two Chinese seemed to be assigned to play tennis with him, and when the Bushes went to restaurants, they (and indeed all foreigners) were seated apart, where they could not contaminate the locals.

A dinner at Vice President Rockefeller's turned out to be fun. Besides two Rockefeller staffers, the guests included only the Kissingers, Tom and Joan Braden, and us, and Henry was on a storytelling roll. He recalled meeting with Saudi's King Faisal and how His Majesty began an anti-Zionist tirade. First, the king said, the Zionists took over Palestine, then Russia, and they were well on toward capturing the United States. Naturally, Kissinger became very uncomfortable. During a pause in the king's rantings, Henry pointed to a picture on the wall and asked, by way of changing the subject, what it was. "I couldn't have asked a more inappropriate question," Henry chuckled. "First, because most religious Muslims don't allow any pictures at all and second, because it was a picture of the Holy Arabian Desert. I might as well have asked a Catholic if a picture of the Virgin Mary was his mother-in-law."

He told how the Saudi foreign minister, whose English was faultless, suddenly turned personally quite cool and began using an interpreter in dealing with Henry. Kissinger was puzzled: "You speak English better than I do and with less accent. After all these years of using English, why this change? What is wrong?" Finally, the Saudi diplomat confessed. His rival, the Saudi oil minister Sheik Yamani, had been invited to dinner at the home of American secretary of the Treasury Bill Simon, but he, the foreign minister, had never been to Kissinger's home; this apparently made Yamani "one up." Kissinger quickly arranged a party at home for his colleague's next trip, but alas, the man carelessly died before coming back to Washington. To Kissinger, this incident illustrated the disruptive power of human emotions in foreign affairs.

As our dinner drew to a close, Henry ruminated on the psychic state of America, lamenting that we were sick in spirit and unable to deal with other nations. With no little prescience, he said he would not be surprised to see a strong right-winger elected by 1980. He did not view the prospect with pleasure, but given the way Congress was tying the hands of the executive and generally making a mess of things, he felt it inevitable.

Finally, he told wryly of *New York Times* columnist Anthony Lewis, a frequent and strident critic of Kissinger. "One day he calls me in print a fascist pig; the next he calls me on the phone and asks me to get one of his Russian Jewish relatives out of the Soviet Union." But what really riled him was another *Times* columnist, Bill Safire, who accused Kissinger of conspiring with the Soviet ambassador to derail the presidential campaign of vigorously pro-Israel senator Henry Jackson. To be accused of political footsie with a foreigner over American politics made Henry livid.

A visit by Pakistani prime minister Zulfikar Ali Bhutto proved instructive. A polished and bright man, he and his wife left all who met them impressed, as did their ambassador, Yaqub Khan and his wife, Tuba. Charm, however, did not carry the day for the Pakistanis. Their main objective was to get the United States to lift its arms embargo. Since rival India was perfectly free to buy arms from the Soviets, it struck the Pakistanis as unfair that they could not buy from us. The administration agreed, but congressional doves did not, thus the embargo. India being always a self-righteous and vocal critic of America, this galled me; India was in those days to hypocrisy what Rome was to the Church: the home office.

In 1975 the Freedom of Information Act (FOIA) became law. The idea struck me as good; there is a tendency in government to overclassify documents. For example, when in El Salvador I noticed that our CIA station routinely classified newspaper articles that they wanted me to see. That seemed bizarre, and I asked the station chief why he would classify something read by millions. He explained that the classification arose not from the information contained in the article but from the fact that the CIA was interested in it.

On the other hand, with the FOIA, a Soviet journalist could theoretically come to State and demand the declassification and release of documents. The government would have to prove that to release them would harm the national interest. That was not hard in many cases, but the end result increased the flow of information to the public. Furthermore, there was less tendency to slap a classification of "Secret" on a document that was of little importance. On the whole, it has, I think, proved to be a good law, but at the time the very mention of it caused us bureaucrats to hold up a cross to ward it off. One result was undeniable: the law created an explosion of employees whose job it was to implement it.

Lessons in Hardball Diplomacy

IN MID-MARCH of 1975 Iranian ambassador Ardisher Zahedi wanted to discuss the Shah's forthcoming visit, set for May. We had been to many of Ardisher's lavish parties, where champagne and caviar were scarfed down like hot dogs and soda pop at a baseball game. We considered him a friend, and I anticipated no problems with the proposed trip. I was surprised, therefore, when over lunch at the Hay Adams Hotel, he started us off by saying, in effect, "Here's how it's going to be." I had no problems until he said, "We will have a dinner at the embassy on the second evening, and the president will come."

At that point, I demurred. "President Ford has a firm policy of not attending dinners given by visiting heads of state; he won't be able to be there. Vice President Rockefeller will represent him." Ardisher lifted a heavy black eyebrow and said, "Well, we might as well leave, because there will be no state visit by the Shah," and he pushed back his chair as if to go.

"Whoa," I said, beating an inglorious retreat. "Let me talk to Brent Scowcroft at the White House and explain your position." At that, we finished our coffee and talked of other things.

When he departed, I bolted across Lafayette Square to the White House and told Brent what had happened. He was annoyed; the demands on the president's time are huge and one more party was not what he needed. Furthermore, it would set a precedent: if we did it for Iran, it would be hard to resist doing it for other countries. (Like a wolf in the wilds, precedent constantly stalks diplomacy.)

In the end, as I knew they would, Scowcroft and Kissinger caved in and the president agreed to attend. Our fallback policy became, in effect, if the country is big enough or rich enough, the president will attend. Otherwise, forget it. Life's not fair.

A contrast to developing-but-rich Iran came the following month in a visit from developing-but-poor Zambia. Its president, Kenneth Kaunda, the deeply religious son of a Presbyterian missionary, became the first African head of state to visit President Ford.

I welcomed the official party at Andrews and got them settled at Blair House. Kaunda, 50, struck me as an open, pleasant, friendly man. He and his wife, who always wore traditional Zambian dress, both spoke excellent English. Rumor had it that he was a bit emotional, though he clearly had dedicated his life to eliminating racial injustice in southern Africa.

The visit began well. The first event, a luncheon at State given by Secretary Kissinger, went smoothly. At three o'clock, I took Kaunda to the White House for his private visit with the president, and afterward I asked how it had gone. His response was contagiously positive, and I felt keenly his honesty and integrity.

While Henry entertained Kaunda, Nancy honored the Zambian first lady with a luncheon in a different State Dining Room, with Jessica among the guests. All went well until the wine, a Johannesburger Riesling from California, was poured. One of the guests noticed that the label mentioned Johannesburg, the largest city of South Africa's hated racist regime. Indignant, the guest of honor asked the meaning of being served a South African wine, calming down only after being shown that in spite of its name, the wine was American.

Back at Blair House, the Zambian foreign minister pulled me aside in conspiratorial fashion and shared an interesting piece of information. The Kaundas, he said, had recently been to the Soviet Union, and while there, they had sung for General Secretary Brezhnev. They would, if we liked, be prepared to do the same for the Fords. All they would need would be to borrow a guitar.

In ready agreement, I hurried back over to the White House to ask social secretary Nancy Ruwe what she thought. Nancy on board, I returned to Blair and sought out Kaunda. "President Ford has heard you are a fine guitarist," I said. "Would you perchance be willing to sing after the White House dinner tonight?" Wreathed in smiles, he acceded.

As usual, we escorted the guests across Pennsylvania Avenue, where they were warmly greeted by the Fords. The receiving line went smoothly, dinner was excellent, and when it came time for after-dinner toasts, Ford outdid himself in the warmth of his welcome. Then came Kaunda's turn to respond.

I settled back with a bit of champagne, comfortably awaiting a gracious response from our visitor. Was I surprised! My mild-mannered new friend arose and made not a toast but a speech. For twenty minutes — a long twenty minutes — he excoriated the United States and everything American. "The U.S. has no African policy," he announced. He blasted the new assistant secretary of state for African affairs, Nat Davis, comparing him most unfavorably to a Democratic predecessor, Mennen "Soapy" Williams. (Davis, a career officer, had been ambassador in Chile and had become a target of shrill African leftists when first nominated; attacking Chile and its military government was much in vogue in those days.)

As Kaunda's vitriol increased, the Americans' resentment matched it; the ice in the air was palpable. One of my dinner partners, the wife of Hollywood mogul and Democratic activist Lew Wasserman, turned and expressed her disbelief. The diamond-draped woman to my other side whispered, "I wish I had something to place in a certain position in that man's body." Nancy Kissinger turned to her dinner partner, the Zambian foreign minister, and demanded, "Who wrote that speech?" He replied proudly, "Oh, I wrote most of it." Nancy turned her back and spoke to him no more.

The press, meanwhile, was having a field day. Traditionally invited to cover the toasts at dinner, reporters, their mouths agape, scribbled frantically and TV cameras whirred. Ford, meanwhile, kept his calm demeanor, face a mask, pipe billowing smoke.

After Kaunda had finished his speech and nodded jovially to what most would have considered scant applause, I found Kissinger. "Do you want to go to the Zambian reception as planned tomorrow night?" I asked. "I don't know," he responded. "This sort of thing is simply not acceptable."

We then left the dining room and went to the East Room, where a young husband and wife piano team gave a fine recital. When their performance was over, Ford stood up and said, "I hear our guest of honor is quite an artist, quite a musician. I wonder if he would be good enough to play for us now on the banjo."

With a whoop, Mrs. Ford ran over to him and said, "Guitar, not banjo!" The president corrected himself, and as he came down off the stage, I heard him say, sotto voce with a grin, "Guess I really screwed that one up!"

President and Mrs. Kaunda then mounted the stage and to my surprise, asked the entire official Zambian party to join them—thirty or so in all. Assembled, the group proceeded to sing an African folk song of haunting beauty; they could have sung professionally. After that, all left the stage save the two Kaundas, who sang a duet, again very well.

The following day, a Sunday, I picked Kaunda up to take him to Arlington to lay the traditional wreath at the Tomb of the Unknown Soldier. Afterward he asked if we could go by President Kennedy's grave, which we did. He walked by himself up to the eternal flame that marks Kennedy's resting place. To my total surprise, he began softly to sing, and I quickly recognized "Rock of Ages." As if on cue, the Zambian party joined in, in their own tongue. Was I moved? Absolutely.

In the car alone with President Kaunda for perhaps a half hour, I asked about the events of the previous evening. He was serene, not the least repentant. I asked who his audience was. "The American people," he replied. "President Ford and Secretary Kissinger are very much on the same wavelength about racial injustice in southern Africa, but this is a democracy and you have to reach the Congress and the people before you can have an impact." Clearly, he had understood completely how the press works. A press conference would not have earned a line in the American press; a public tirade would — and did — get headlines. He guessed, correctly, that President Ford could stand the embarrassment and discomfort, and so he made his move. It was a masterstroke; I never saw the like of it in all the visits to come.

I also asked Kaunda about his visit to the Soviet Union. The memories rankled. First he was put off, then told that Brezhnev would not have time to see him; he would have to make do with Podgorny and Kosygin, lesser figures in the trio then in charge. "I won't come," he replied. In the end, he did go and, world-class player of political poker that he was, he saw Brezhnev.

With some bitterness he recounted riding in a car with the two lesser leaders. They condescendingly asked if he really believed in God, reflecting official, and probably their own personal, atheism. Kaunda, exposed to the prejudices toward Africans that have long marred Russian society, was not amused.

I later wrote a memo of our talks for the secretary of state, and in the end he decided to attend the Zambian reception that night. It turned out, however, to be a hot and crowded madhouse and, not given to suffering gladly, he left after about fifteen minutes. I escaped with him, eager to get home. But I never forgot Kenneth Kaunda.

Two Weeks, One King,
Four Prime Ministers,
and a Shah

THE FOLLOWING two weeks took a prize for being hectic. Starting with King Hussein of Jordan, we had prime ministers from Cyprus, Britain, New Zealand, Australia, Singapore, and, climactically, the Shah of Iran.

The Shah's visit was strenuous: two white-tie dinners, a ride on an

AWACS radar plane, a trip to Pocantico, the Rockefeller estate, caviar and champagne in quantities not good for girth or sobriety. Jessica and I concluded at the end: loved her, not so sure about him. He was far too, well, regal for our republican tastes. One small incident summed it all up for us. As they left, we were presented with a handsome photo of the two of them, he in uniform, she in a beautiful gown, posed at the bottom of a flight of steps. As I looked carefully, I noticed an amusing detail: the tall empress was standing on the ground floor, while His Majesty stood on the first step, thus making him seem the taller. Her gown disguised, but could not hide, this small vanity.

Three days later, British diplomat Edward Glover came by to begin planning for the visit of Her Majesty, Queen Elizabeth II. Given that the visit was scheduled for July 1976 and this was May 1975, I thought we had ample lead time, to put it mildly.

Life in Protocol never lacked unexpected challenges and crises. Jessica and I went to the Kennedy Center to see *Spartacus,* a ballet by the Russian Bolshoi Company. I noticed extremist Jewish Defense League (JDL) pickets outside, protesting Soviet treatment of Jews, but thought little about it. As was customary, the Russian orchestra played "The Star-Spangled Banner," which was greeted with polite applause. Then, as they were about to play the Soviet anthem, several JDL members jumped to their feet and began to toot foghorns, causing a great cacophony but not stopping the unflappable musicians. At the end of the piece, the audience stood, with rousing applause; no matter how little we liked Soviet communism, we liked rudeness even less. I doubt, however, that the young JDLers got the picture.

A different case involved the government's ever-zealous narcotics hunters. The president of Lebanon came into New York for a visit to the UN. Our office, having no branch there, was not on hand to meet him, and the narcs, for reasons best known to themselves, decided to check the visitors' luggage for illicit drugs, a grotesque violation of diplomatic immunity and a seriously dumb move. Alas, the Lebanese caught them at it and a dreadful row ensued. There was nonetheless a happy ending: we created an assistant chief of protocol post in New York, making such flubs less likely in the future.

Under the rubric of "Henry Will Be Henry," a phone call rolled me out of bed early one Saturday morning, the week following the New York flap. My grumpy "Hello" was trumped by an even grumpier Larry Eagleburger, Kissinger's right-hand man, growling, "Where were you last night?" "At home," I replied. "Why weren't you at Andrews at twelve o'clock? The secretary came home from a trip."

I couldn't believe it. "First of all, I didn't know it. Second, why on earth would he want me there?" I protested, thinking the secretary might have mellowed.

"Believe me, he does. He wants you and me and Ingersoll [the deputy secretary] on tap *whenever* he returns from abroad," Larry explained. It was an old story, and I consoled myself with the unsatisfactory explanation that the ways of genius were not for the likes of me to question.

Visits slowed somewhat during the summer and we had time for the family. Visits did not, however, stop. They run together in the mind, with only shards of memory remaining.

President Walter Scheel of Germany came. We took him to Chicago and watched the remarkable Mayor Richard Daley entertain in royal style. The mayor's social skills were limited; indeed, the well-briefed German knew more about Chicago history, architecture, and art than our host did. But Daley's entertainment budget was apparently unlimited, and he put on a wonderful show, with musicians in colonial costume, a parade, and an elegant lunch.

In July, I took my last presidential trip, this time to Finland for the Helsinki Conference, which proved so productive for the cause of the West in the subsequent years of the Cold War. Dick Cheney had replaced Don Rumsfeld as chief of staff and had set about seriously to reduce the size of the traveling parties. I protested vigorously being cut out of trips. Although I knew too many people traveled, I nonetheless suspected there was an element of Kissinger-tweaking involved. That I had always looked diligently after his interests had not gone unnoticed by the White House staff. Henry's paranoia may have been well founded. On the other hand, maybe it was contagious and I had caught it. Either way, I traveled abroad no more.

My last trip proved a good one. The thirty-five nations whose leaders met in Helsinki produced, as I mentioned, a historical agreement, the founding of the Conference on Security and Cooperation in Europe (CSCE). In it, the Soviets agreed for the first time to comply with certain norms of human rights. The right wing in the United States howled that the agreement was a sellout, which was nonsense, for the Helsinki agreement proved a splendid club with which to whack the Soviets when they violated human rights.

Being there was exciting. At the plenary meetings, it was fun to watch the leaders of so many nations — indeed, to meet many of them. Brezhnev, combing his eyebrows during idle moments, looked ill and spoke haltingly. Ford, by contrast, spoke brilliantly, the best I had ever heard him, and received twice the applause of the Soviet. He was given to wandering the halls of the Finlandia Conference Center in a typical fashion, greeting and chatting.

A Kissinger aide, Helmut (Hal) Sonnenfeldt, provided a bit of excitement. On the last day, he and Kissinger had a breakfast meeting with Ford. Afterward, the president and the secretary went to their cars for the drive to Finlandia Hall. Hal, too, had a car and driver, but he was not part of the official motorcade. So as not to lose time, he told his driver just to get in the motorcade, up close to the president's car.

It was not a good move. Finnish security and the U.S. Secret Service stopped the motorcade, swarmed around poor Hal and demanded to know what he was doing. Terrified, he explained who he was. The burly, hard-eyed guards were not impressed. Apparently, we had told the Finns our motorcade would always have ten cars. Suddenly, here was an eleventh, and that would not do. "Do it again," they explained, "and we will shoot you dead." The embarrassed Sonnenfeldt didn't have to be told twice.

Sometimes You Win One . . .

THE GREAT event of the fall, toward which we had all been working for a year, was the visit of the emperor of Japan. Never had I encountered people so meticulous. Every step of every event had to be planned, rehearsed, talked out until not a nit was left to pick. The ghost of Pearl Harbor and World War II stalked us all. We even got into matters such as the trajectory of his plane as it left Honolulu (he was to visit Hawaii), so there would be no chance of flying over Pearl on departure. At one point, I noted a military band playing Stephen Foster songs at the Lincoln Memorial. I asked visit coordinator Roger Wallace if the band had picked the songs to be played. "Oh, no," he replied. "The songs were a matter of intense negotiations with the Japanese advance party."

For my own part, I bought a biography of the emperor and read it, rapt, looking toward what I thought might be the most interesting encounter of my life. There turned out to be a good bit of evidence that Hirohito, one of the demons of my childhood days during the war, had in reality tried to head it off, and he undoubtedly contributed to bringing it to an end. A faction of fanatics wanted to bleed America white for the glory of the emperor, atom bomb or no, by fighting to the last man. The emperor, however, had a better idea, and the surrender at Tokyo Bay was the result.

During one of the planning sessions I confessed innocently to a State Department Japanologist that I was storing up questions to ask our visitor about his past actions, an idea quickly squelched by the expert. The Japanese, he explained, were extremely sensitive, not only about the mythical "persona" of their emperor but also about nosy foreigners probing him for dubious reasons. I abandoned any idea of serious historical talk.

Nonetheless, I was prepared, carefully reviewing U.S. history and facts such as the height of the Washington Monument so as to be able to answer any questions he might have. I learned, however, that conversational silence gave the Japanese no problems. A hiatus of talk that would leave an American in a nervous twit would disturb a Japanese not at all.

A welcome relief from preparations for the imperial visit came in the form of a trip to Washington by a representative of the other great monarchy, as Margaret Thatcher, newly elected head of the Conservative Party, popped in to make the rounds. Given Henry's habitual tardiness, I got to spend a good bit of time with her, including questioning her about the emperor, who had visited Britain not long before. Katharine Graham, publisher of the *Washington Post,* gave a dinner for her at which she and Henry got off in a corner for a very lengthy chat. Oblivious to all save the riveting Briton, Kissinger did not notice the hour getting later and later. He being the senior guest at the party, people nervously wondered when he would leave and thus permit lesser lights to depart as well. Finally, puckish Ed Levi, the attorney general, broke in on the tête-à-tête and asked, "Mr. Secretary, may I have your permission to withdraw?" Kissinger came back quickly, as always: "Well, I guess it's all right, as long as you recognize the principle!" giving all within earshot a great laugh.

The bright and charming president of Colombia, Alfonso Lopes Michelson, came as well, and I had a good chance to practice Spanish, though his English was excellent. One remark that he made stuck in my mind: "The last time I was here, an American had just walked on the moon. But impressive as that achievement was, it did not impress me as much as the achievement you made nearly two hundred years ago when you wrote your Constitution. The former came out of science and was perhaps inevitable given the knowledge man now has. But the achievement of writing the document came from a different kind of genius and was not inevitable at all." He noticed that Jessica was carrying a book of Mexican poetry in Spanish, and they had a great time reading the originals and the translations. Moments like those made the job worthwhile.

The plane that brought the Japanese emperor and empress touched down near Williamsburg, Virginia, at 10:40 A.M. on October 30, 1975. I had arrived earlier, my ever-patient driver, Robert Hill, getting up before dawn to deliver me on time. Jessica flew down later.

Our oft-rehearsed plan had me climbing the stairs to the plane alone, immediately after the door opened. There I was to be met by a Royal Household protocol officer, and, when His Majesty was ready, I was to be ushered into his presence. The prime rule to remember, I kept repeating to myself was, "Don't be a chatty Texan; the emperor speaks first; then and only then do you welcome him."

I loped up the stairs and was greeted as per plan. After a brief wait, the great moment arrived.

As I entered his cabin, the emperor arose. Although a short and rather frail man (he was seventy-four at the time), he nonetheless managed in getting up to whack his head very sharply on the overhead storage bin. Abruptly, he sat down again. The startled staff quickly moved to help him, and I, protocol forgotten, asked, "Are you all right, sir?" Oh, well, so much for plans. He then greeted me, and I gave my oft-rehearsed brief words of welcome.

Getting him down the stairs proved a challenge. Not steady on his feet, he tottered down one step at a time. I decided to precede him close enough to cushion any fall, but far enough ahead to stay out of the pictures, for cameras clicked like summer locusts. The empress, as was customary, followed.

Waiting below were Japanese ambassador Yasukawa and various dignitaries, including a senator, the governor of Virginia, and local representatives. The quality of the welcoming party put to rest one worry: that Americans remembering Pearl Harbor as adjured to do would resent this former enemy coming to our shores; it did not happen.

Serenaded by a piper band in colonial costume, Their Majesties boarded their car and were taken swiftly to their quarters to rest. Jessica and I took a leaf from the Royal Notebook and had dinner sent to our house. Assistant Chief of Protocol Bill Codus and trip coordinator Roger Wallace came by for a drink. Someone made me laugh with a comment: "The emperor must be a Democrat." "Why?" I asked. "He wears double-knit suits."

The next day Jessica was presented to the visitors, having not met them the previous day; they and we explored the colonial legislature, then Jessica took the lovely and gentle empress on a brief shopping tour.

Everywhere we went, hoards of press followed close behind, some 450 from Japan alone. The trip was very important to the Japanese government, for it was seen as the final stamp of approval on Japan as a reliable partner and friend. Not surprisingly, the Japanese were holding their breath to a certain extent, but they had nothing to worry about.

In the afternoon, Their Majesties took a stroll through the immaculate gardens of colonial Williamsburg, feeding the ducks and the fish and stopping to admire Bill Codus and me pretending we knew how to bowl on the green. Though our guests retired again, we joined Mary and Carl Hummelsine (the president of Williamsburg) for an early, excellent dinner.

I noted an example of the downright weirdness of imperial protocol. The first night, the emperor and empress went to their second-floor suite via the stairs. Given their age, it seemed that an elevator would have been more fitting, so I inquired of our people if there was one. Indeed, there was, but it would hold only four people. The official party could never have chosen among the hangers-on (the grand steward, the grand chamberlain, the grand master, etc.) who would accompany the couple, and thus the compromise: they walked up the stairs.

The following day we flew in the royal plane to Washington, Their Majesties not being given to helicopter flights. The arrival, White House tour, and state dinner, starring pianist Van Cliburn, all went smoothly. Increasingly, we were charmed by our guests. Jessica, in a display of republican lèse-majesté, told me the emperor was the cutest thing she ever saw and that she wanted to pick him up and pat him; I felt the same way about Her Majesty, a very talented artist whose shy smile won everyone she met.

A visit to Arlington Cemetery and the Tomb of the Unknown Soldier led off the following day. There were many stairs to navigate, and I decided to ignore the injunction that they were not to be touched, offering the empress an arm, which she readily took.

Jessica and I hosted the visitors at lunch on the Potomac on the presidential yacht *Sequoia*. A press boat followed, and a police helicopter kept benign watch above. A Secret Service man explained the tight security: "This is a good day not to own a blue Camaro," he said. Apparently, there had been a report that the Japanese Red Army (a particularly virulent terrorist group) had infiltrated the United States and were going to attack the visitors. "We're stopping every blue Camaro in the U.S.," the agent said.

The luncheon itself turned out to be less stiff than we had feared. The Royal Household Protocol Office had tried to convince us that there should be no interpreters; they simply do not like for Their Majesties to have to talk. I drew the line at that and won. Helped by U.S. ambassador to Japan Jim Hodgson and his wife, we talked to the empress about her art and her grandchildren (she had trouble recalling how many there were). Jessica and the emperor, a world-recognized marine biologist, discussed history and the environment. After a wreath-laying ceremony at George Washington's home, Mount Vernon, we drove back to Washington, and Their Majesties took advantage of the thirty-minute ride to nap.

That evening the guests gave a return banquet in honor of the Fords at the Smithsonian Institution, fittingly in the wonderfully medieval vaulted "castle" that is the Smithsonian's headquarters. The Japanese had brought their own silver, china, and even cigarettes, all encrested with the royal seal, a chrysanthemum. The event went well; indeed, the emperor in his toast apologized—sort of—for World War II. "Gemütlich" may not have been the word to describe the atmosphere—but what white-tie dinner could qualify? Still, it was warm. The Speaker of the House, Carl Albert, got very much into the spirit of it all, taking on perhaps more sake than was wise. At the end of the party he was reluctant to leave, though I tried to encourage him toward the door. Instead, he wove his jovial way to the kitchen, where he addressed the chef's staff with a hearty "Viva la huelga" ("Long live the strike"), the motto of the grape pickers' union. It added a certain cross-cultured charm to the evening. Fortunately, no press were there to observe.

The Stately Procession, the tour of America that ought to put me in the Guinness Book of Records as the only *gaijin* (foreigner) to spend thirteen days with the emperor of Japan, began the next day with a flight to the Woods Hole Marine Laboratory in Massachusetts. There, the emperor peered into microscopes, enchanted, as American biologists showed him examples of their work. It was the only time I saw him really relaxed and involved, and we virtually had to drag him away for the flight to New York.

Everywhere, there were crowds gathered to see him go by, all friendly, many waving Japanese flags. The motorcade stopped at a park in the city, where a multicultural group of children serenaded the visitors with a wonderful rendition of "Consider yourself at home, consider yourself one of the family" from the musical *Oliver!*

Visits to the two Rockefeller homes [6] preceded, believe it or not, a football game, the Jets versus the Patriots. Why we dreamed this up I don't know. The Japanese play baseball, not football. Besides, rough types go to football, and they might boo our gentle guest, and that would be bad.

Nonetheless, football it was, and poor Ambassador Yasukawa took a cram course in it so he could explain everything to His Majesty, which he animatedly did. The emperor got polite applause on arrival. Then the crowd returned to the matter at hand and after watching this strenuous spectacle for about forty minutes, the ambassador abandoned his instruction and we left. I was glad we didn't cancel the event, as fear of adverse reaction nearly caused us to do; chaotic or not, I think the emperor enjoyed it.

Monday was given to the UN, the Botanical Gardens in the Bronx, and a luncheon, memorable mostly for undrinkable wine, at Mayor Abraham Beame's official residence, Gracie Mansion.

Tuesday we provoked a lovely tiff in Chicago. Mayor Daley and Governor Walker, both Democrats, got into a near shoving match at the foot of the aircraft steps. Normally, a governor outranks a mayor and would be first in the greeting line, but this was Chicago and the two officials did not constitute a mutual admiration society. The mayor won and was the first to welcome Their Majesties. Furthermore, he got to ride into town in their car.

Therein arose another problem we had to wrestle with: where in the limousine to seat him. The Japanese would not hear of Daley sitting between the royal couple, and certainly neither of them would sit in the middle. In the end, the mayor was consigned to the limousine's cramped jump seat.

Daley outdid himself at the luncheon in honor of the visitors. There was a parade in front of the hotel with mounted, uniformed men; a somewhat reedy band in wigs and Continental uniforms played Handel's "Water Music" as the emperor and the mayor entered the giant, packed banquet room; and the Chicago Symphony played a brief concert at meal's end. During the meal I noted that conversation between host and guest was marked by, well, a lot of chewing.

After lunch we drove to a 2,200-acre farm belonging to a family named Balz, so the visitors could see the wonders of American farming. The emperor was photographed holding piglets, rabbits, and other benign creatures, and we then moved into the Balzes' parlor for a chat and more pictures. This domestic scene was interrupted by the grandmother of the thirty-five-year-old younger Balz; she was horrified that he was chatting with the emperor of Japan, wearing a baseball cap. Young Balz couldn't have cared less, and I thought the scene wonderfully American, straight out of a Norman Rockwell painting.

The flight to Los Angeles took us over the Grand Canyon, which the emperor viewed with great interest. What he and the empress really wanted to see, however, was Disneyland, so it was arranged. As the visitors, surrounded by a large crowd, approached the entrance, Mickey Mouse came out to greet them. To the evident amusement of the royals, Mickey danced and capered about in charming fashion. Indeed, no one was more charmed by his performance than Mickey himself; though the script had him appear and then leave, he kept it up to a point where our progress was a bit impeded.

At that point, I was walking slowly along next to one of the numerous Secret Service men. Tiring of Mickey's antics, the agent bent over and barked into the mouse's large ear, "Fuck off, mouse." Mickey obliged, at warp speed.

California is home to countless Japanese and Japanese Americans, so we built in visits for them with the emperor and empress. I found the ritualistic nature of these events amazing. The first took place at the Beverly Wilshire Hotel, where we stayed. A crowd of several hundred was packed three or four deep around the periphery of a large meeting room. Two chairs, at the far end of the room, awaited the royal couple. After they were seated, a welcome was read, followed by the emperor's reply. The couple then circuited the room, bowing every few steps; with no handshaking allowed, it was almost eerily reserved.

I asked Ambassador Takeshi Yasukawa about His Majesty's eyesight.

"We don't know, really," he replied. "He wears the same glasses for reading and distant vision and says he sees fine."

At several stops during the visit, there were pickets complaining of Japanese whaling practices. I doubted the emperor noticed, but in a conversation with the grand steward, a member of the royal household, I learned that the emperor received about thirty letters a month from Americans complaining about whaling. The Japanese thought it astonishing that so many ordinary Americans cared.

San Francisco provided an example of how plans can go awry. Everywhere, greeting committees had been warned not to touch the royals, but Mayor Alioto's wife, Angelina, overcome by the feeling of the moment, gave the empress a big hug at the foot of the plane steps. All the Japanese, horrified, did what we irreverently referred to as a "double gum suck," the sharp intake of air that was a characteristic Japanese reaction to the unexpected. We had briefed the royal party that Japanese citizens would bow while Japanese Americans would, in receiving lines, thrust out a hand, so the visitors would know which was which. Hugs, we hadn't counted on.

My hope for meaningful conversation with the emperor took on life during a motorcade in California. I had grown used to long stretches of silence, so when the interpreter tapped me on the back and said, "His Majesty wishes to tell you something," my heart leapt. Eagerly, I turned (I was riding on the jump seat of the limo) to see what he might say. A rattle of Japanese sprang forth as I nodded my head in anticipation. The interpreter said, "His Majesty wishes you to know eggs in United States are better than eggs in Japan." My riposte, the only thing I could think of to say, was "Ah, so?"[7] So much for a meaningful relationship.

During motorcades through San Francisco's streets, I watched reactions of the thick crowds, mostly Japanese. Many, especially older people, stood with their backs to the street, reflecting the old idea that the emperor is divine and one should not look directly at him.

Our last stop, Hawaii, went smoothly. Mayor Frank Fasi of Honolulu decided that rather than ask only the rich and famous to his reception, he would ask the general populace, by lot. The Secret Service, as was customary, did brief background checks on all the lucky invitees and of the 1,100 names checked, 960 had had some sort of problem with the police. Other than that little difficulty, all went well: huge crowds, leis, Hawaiian music, the warmest possible welcome.

For the last two days, the plan called for rest, and we flew to the island of Hawaii to the beautiful and tasteful Mauna Kea Hotel. The emperor and empress had no appearances scheduled, so our group played tennis, swam, drank exotic beverages, and recovered. The Japanese learned that October 12 was our trip coordinator Roger Wallace's birthday and had a cake baked in celebration. On the final day, I was summoned to the presence of our visitors, and given warm thanks and a beautiful silver vase (that I sadly relinquished upon my return).

The departure of their plane to the west, steering carefully clear of Pearl Harbor, was a wistful moment. These gentle people had lived such stormy lives and had done so many things they doubtless did not want to do. I did not envy them.

A footnote: Shortly after our return, Henry Kissinger pulled me aside and said, "The Japanese are out of their cotton-picking minds over the success of the trip." Peculiar phraseology, perhaps, but gratifying nevertheless.

. . . And Sometimes You Lose One

IF THE Japanese visit ran like a Swiss watch, the visit of Egyptian president Anwar Sadat ran like a snorting, backfiring jalopy. Kissinger felt the visit vital to his efforts for peace in the Middle East and was anxious that it go smoothly. Alas, he failed to take into account the Egyptian character.

For openers, Sadat arrived at Williamsburg an hour late, leaving Henry in a snit. Naturally, Protocol felt the lash. Tired on arrival, Sadat canceled the planned dinner and went to bed. Egyptian foreign minister Ismail Fahmy cordially loathed Egyptian ambassador to the United States Ashraf Ghorbal, and we tried to keep them apart insofar as it was possible. We were told that Mrs. Sadat and Mrs. Fahmy must not ride together. (They did; we often had no sensible choice.)

Then there was the Great Get Even. The Egyptians remembered with crystal clarity what we had cost them on Nixon's 1974 visit, and they put their ample imagination toward outdoing us. They frequently ordered three entrées each from room service in their hotels, to sample a range of American cuisine—and there were 170 of them. We marshaled eight U.S. aircraft to move our guests: a presidential plane and a backup, a baggage plane, a Convair for the advance team, an Egyptian plane for hangers-on, and three helicopters. President Sadat, incidentally, brought his own chef, who prepared all the boss's meals, including the one at the White House.

The visitors annoyed one of our team, luggage master James Payne, by filling out baggage tags in Arabic and then complaining about tardy delivery. Poor Mr. Payne, pained, told me, "Mr. Ambassador, I don't read Arabic!"

The manifests for plane flights became a source of contention; the Egyptians were never satisfied with who was on what plane. The Sadat children (six of them, counting spouses) canceled events at a moment's notice, causing problems of transport, logistics, and security.

Recalling the vast crowds that greeted Nixon, I hoped to have on-lookers for Sadat. At the time, however, he was not well known, and I ended up having to bus Washington schoolchildren into the White House to assure a minimally enthusiastic welcome. It worked.

The administration took a long view on costs. The president's briefing book for the visit urged him to try to mute Egyptian hostility toward the Soviets, Egypt's onetime ally. The purpose: keep the Russians a bit interested, lest we end up picking up the bill for all development assistance to the shaky Egyptian economy.

Sadat spoke to the National Press Club and in his answers to questions inadvertently revealed the challenge that Kissinger faced. In describing the supposed Zionist attitude toward Arabs, he recounted how in 1948 he had tried to buy a radio in Cairo from a Jewish merchant. Citing Sadat's record of fighting for the Palestinians, the merchant refused to sell it. I told my neighbor Al Moses, later to become president of the American Jewish Committee, the story. Al let out a great guffaw. "What nonsense!" he said. "Can you imagine a Jewish merchant refusing to sell something?"

The state dinner provided no surprises, and afterward, Pearl Bailey sang in her inimitable style. With her deep, rich voice and quick ad-libs, I felt sure she would be a hit with the guests. Kissinger, however, was horrified when he heard who was to entertain: "She'll make a stage prop out of him," he moaned.

To make matters worse, the Egyptians told us they feared that if Sadat were to be seen dancing, the Egyptian people would consider the trip frivolous; fundamentalist Muslims, no friends of Sadat (whom they later assassinated), would have a field day. Knowing all this, we sent word to Pearl to treat Sadat with deference.

The show was good. Pearl, mercilessly teasing Kissinger, could not have been funnier or better. But she did run on a bit long. I leaned over to Henry and whispered, "You should make her an ambassador." He growled, "I'd do anything to get her off the stage so I could go home."

Done at last, she swooped up President Ford and twirled him around the stage, to his delight. (He was a good dancer.)

I held my breath. In vain. Forgetting her briefing, she pulled Sadat out of his seat and waltzed him vigorously about. The Egyptian party was scandalized, as was American ambassador Herman Eilts. An Egyptian public relations adviser demanded that any pictures of the event be destroyed, clearly an impossibility.

Shortly afterward, in a state of shock, I escorted the guests home to Blair House. I apologized to President Sadat. He could not have been less concerned. "The problem," he said, "is that I don't know how to dance. If I had, I surely would have!"

Gremlins continued to plague the visit. The Egyptians gave a return banquet honoring the Fords at Anderson House, an elegant former residence on Massachusetts Avenue. The Muslim hosts served sparkling Catawba juice, which may have been just as well. In his after-dinner toast, President Ford rose, made a rather rambling speech, and then said, "I ask you to join me in a toast to the president of Israel." He quickly corrected himself but not before a vast "oooh" went through the room. Afterward, no one spoke a word about it. It reminded me of the parrot at the Dominican ambassador's house back in El Salvador: it was there, but no one wanted to — or could — clean it up.

Pro-Sadat demonstrators — mostly American Black Muslims — lined many of the routes we traveled, chanting, "Long live Sadat." A check by the Secret Service revealed that most of them had criminal records; I never learned who organized them.

In New York City, where the Economic Club of New York hosted a dinner speech for the Sadats, once again the jinx struck. First, while we had explained to the club that the Sadats, for domestic political reasons, were not bringing tuxedos to the United States, the ancient crank in charge huffed, "We've always worn black tie; we will continue to wear black tie." Then at the event, Undersecretary of State Joe Sisco let me know that he was not pleased with me. Though he was placed at the three-tier head table, his seat was at the bottom level. "Henry," he said, "you know I don't care about protocol, but . . ." a statement that should rank with "The check is in the mail" and "I'm from the government, here to help you" among life's great lies. I assured the irate diplomat that it was not my office but the club that had prepared the seating arrangements. He was neither convinced nor mollified.

The next glitch came when Mayor Beame, doing his bit for peace in the Middle East, canceled a planned call on Sadat. Governor Carey did the same, then rescheduled, then courageously said he would call if there were no photographers. That insult was more than the Egyptians were prepared to take, and there was no meeting. I was annoyed at this shamelessly political behavior, a pandering to Jewish voters, who were, I suspected, as embarrassed by their officials as we were. In a welcome gesture, Senator Charles Percy of Illinois went out of his way, accompanying us to Chicago and showing that not all U.S. politicians were ill-mannered.

Our next stop, Houston, saw the bizarre events continue. In setting up the dinner in Sadat's honor, our office had asked Texas governor Dolph Briscoe to be the ranking guest. At the last minute he canceled, and I turned quickly to my brother-in-law, Bill Hobby, Texas' lieutenant governor. To my relief and pleasure, Bill accepted.

The dinner organizers in Houston had, unbeknownst to me, asked former governor John Connally to be master of ceremonies. That disturbed me; Connally had not been supportive of Ford. I called Chief of Staff Don Rumsfeld to check the idea out. Rummy okayed it, but as a balance to Connally and as a courtesy to Sadat, Vice President Rockefeller decided he should join the Houston leg of the trip.

At the reception before the dinner, I spotted Connally and went over to say hello. He almost literally exploded: "Catto, you are a disgrace to the State of Texas and your home city. The way the head table is seated is inexcusable. The people who have done the most for Sadat's visit are seated far, far away from him." He ranted on in blind, uncontrolled fury until I finally walked away.

Jessica and I concluded later that the problem lay in Connally's not being seated next to Sadat; Hobby and Rockefeller correctly had that honor. John was seated down the table, for as a former official, he had less rank. What really galled him, we speculated, was that Bill Hobby had beaten John's brother, Wayne, in the race for lieutenant governor three years earlier. Whatever it was, his outburst was unpleasant and made me wonder about his stability.

About halfway through one of the speeches, a female voice close to the head table began to scream, "No, no!" I spotted her as her husband tried to shove a napkin in her mouth to shut her up. She switched to "Please, please!"

At that point, the speaker of the moment said, "There seems to be something wrong with that lady down there." By then, the Secret Service had leapt into the fray, but a moment too late. She had retreated under the table and was shouting, "There's nothing wrong with me!" She was finally led from the room, and we later learned that she had medical problems and perhaps had imbibed a touch too much of the fruit of the vine.

The next day the Hugh Marshalls had an indoor rodeo at their ranch near Houston, an event that the Sadats loved (he was a great fan of western movies). From Houston we flew to Jacksonville, Florida, where Minerva and Raymond Mason turned their great house over to the visitors and, indeed, persuaded several nearby neighbors to house the senior members of the traveling party. (Jessica and I shared a house with the totally charming Egyptian ambassador, Ashraf Ghorbal, and his wife, Ahmal, and the able U.S. ambassador and Mrs. Herman Eilts.)

Governor Ruben Askew had agreed to have a dinner in the Sadats' honor, his only requirement being that it not be at a club that excludes Jews. That proved a problem, but we overcame it, sort of. We found a club that had no exclusionary language in its charter but "just happened" not to have any Jewish members. There being no alternative, we took it.

The visit was relaxed, so much so that the Egyptians decided to stay over another day. (I will spare the details of the problems caused by that decision.) President Ford and Secretary Kissinger came down for further meetings, and the Masons took us all on a yacht cruise. Ford announced a number of Cabinet changes during this time, and while intending to nominate as secretary of commerce the man of all seasons Elliot Richardson, then ambassador to Great Britain, he said, "my good friend Elliot Roosevelt." The regnant gremlin had struck again.

While the renewed summit reconvened, Jessica and I played hosts to Mrs. Sadat and her children at Disney World, flying to Orlando in a military aircraft. There, a bus took us to the theme park for a delightful day of sights, rides, and shopping.

Late in the afternoon, tired but happy, we all piled back onto the bus to return to the naval air station for the return flight. About ten minutes from the base, the lead Secret Service agent pulled me aside. "I hope you won't be alarmed," he said, "but a threat has been phoned to the control tower at the base, saying the plane would blow up if we tried to take off."

I passed this happy news to the always serene Mrs. Sadat, and she agreed that caution was called for. We drove around aimlessly while base security summoned the sheriff's office to bring their bomb-sniffer dog. After assiduous sniffing, the dog reported all clear. (I hoped his detecting ability was better than his house training: he left a puddle in the aisle of the plane.)

Just as we were about to drive to the plane, Jessica, always logical, said to the agent, "How do we know the bus doesn't have a bomb on it? It was parked in an insecure place at Disney World."

"Good thinking," said the agent, and we all got out while the bus, every package, and the ladies' purses were searched.

Just as we reboarded, another call came in. This time the man said, "The tower and the plane will both be bombed if you take off." Clearly, it was a hoax and we took off about two hours behind schedule. Later, a third call came in. "I won't tell you who I am, but I'm in room 303 of the mental hospital."

Sure enough, a patient had learned of our arrival from TV and, having access to a phone, decided to have some fun. We all laughed at the absurdity of it, but it was nervous laughter. As Sadat's assassination in 1981 proved, that man of peace had no shortage of real enemies.

Our return to Washington at midweek featured Sadat speaking to a joint session of Congress. To my relief, he refrained from gratuitous remarks about Zionism and delivered an altogether excellent and well-received address.[8]

A final Ford-Sadat meeting had been scheduled for the late afternoon of November 5, and it provided an example of Henry Kissinger's never-far-from-the-surface insecurity. As Henry and Egyptian foreign minister Fahmy parted after a congressional luncheon honoring Sadat, Henry said airily, "See you at four-thirty," the hour of the presidents' meeting. Fahmy said, "I'm not scheduled to be at that meeting." Henry was thunderstruck: could it be that Ford would meet without him? He had just been relieved of his job as national security adviser, leaving him as "only" the secretary of state; to be excluded from a meeting would be too much. He showed up at the appointed hour and went into the Oval Office with Sadat (Fahmy was not there). But sure enough, a few minutes later he emerged; Ford did indeed want to deal with Sadat alone, a sign of his increasing self-confidence in the job.

That evening the Sadats left for Cairo, with Kissinger and me bidding them farewell at Andrews. I never saw him again. As they flew off into the night, Kissinger made all the effort, angst, and sweat worth it: "You've done a marvelous job," he told me. "All the arrangements were perfect."

Equal Time for Israel

THERE WERE no more visits for the balance of the year, and our office subsided into routine. This meant much more quality time with the family, and I managed also to address some personnel problems. One that galled me particularly was that Marylou Sheils and Roger Wallace, both excellent visits officers, did not receive equal pay. Although I argued with the paymasters until blue in the face, I could not get her the special promotion that would have resulted in parity. In the end, she had to resign from her job-secure civil service position and be renamed in a political slot. A year later, when Ford lost, she found herself among the jobless.

Knowing the "supporting cast" at State, the people who really made things run behind the scenes, proved useful and sometimes amusing.

One of these people was the cook at the secretary's dining room on the eighth floor, a black man with a nice sense of humor. He told me that on a recent night, he had gotten word that the Kissingers and Henry's two children might have dinner at the department, *en famille,* and that he should have steaks for four. For some reason, the children's arrival was delayed, so he was told to prepare only two steaks. Still later, he was told to cook three.

When at last the secretary and Nancy arrived, they had no guest, just the two of them. Still, having been told to prepare three steaks, the chef put three on the table. "I didn't know what was going on," my friend grumbled, "so after a while I looked in there. There was no third guest. They had put the extra steak on the floor for that damn dog, Tyler. While they ate theirs, he ate his!" Tyler, much loved by both Nancy and Henry, enjoyed a high standard of living.

The daily tasks of the office always interested me. On any given day, any number of unanticipated situations would arise that had to be resolved. An employee of the Ecuadorian delegation came by to beg me not to send him out of the country and ruin his career. His problem? His wife so loved the good things of America that she helped herself to them, neglecting the detail of paying for them. The Swedish and Danish kings planned to make private visits to the United States, but I couldn't get the White House to decide whether or not the president would receive them, causing great anxiety for the ambassadors involved. (In the end, they were, of course, entertained—royally.) The Israeli ambassador came by to stress the importance of treating the Israeli prime minister, Yitzhak Rabin, with as much pomp as we had treated Sadat. And so it went.

Jessica had lunch one day with Happy Rockefeller, wife of the vice president. We had always liked her contagious enthusiasm, and on this day she told Jessica an amusing story. She and Nelson Junior, 11, had been given a private tour of the White House. A guide (mischievously, I suspect) asked Nelson if he would like to live there. "No," he said impishly, "It doesn't have a golf course." Not long thereafter Jessica lunched at the White House with Nelson Senior, who had been her mother's deputy in the Eisenhower administration. He told her that he believed the Chinese had given money to Richard Nixon, an idea so preposterous that I wondered if he were headed around the bend.

This phrase came to mind again when the newly named American ambassador to Luxembourg came to see me. A longtime Republican activist from the Midwest, she burbled charmingly as we were seated, "Don't you just love the Luxembourgers? They all have such ample foreheads over the new brain." A phrenologist, no less! We could carpetbomb the capital of that ancient and distinguished grand duchy and not do serious harm to U.S.-Luxembourg relations, so I guessed they would survive this latest envoy.

Press sniping was fairly continuous. *Washington Post* reporter Maxine Cheshire picked up a tip from the House Intelligence Committee that led her to conclude that Henry Kissinger was stealing from the government. (She had no sense of proportion; maybe that's what makes a good reporter.) It seems that a Kurdish nationalist leader named Barzani had come to the United States under the auspices of the CIA to plead the case for Kurdish independence before President Ford. He brought a three-foot-by-five-foot rug for Henry Kissinger, but the CIA asked that it not be registered with Protocol since that would give away the fact of his presence. The rug ended up on Kissinger's office floor, but his office told Maxine it was never in his "personal possession." She thought that was a lie, a scandal; I thought it a tempest in a teapot. Poor Henry, often totally unaware of his physical surroundings, had not a clue that the rug was there.

For years the diplomatic "dean" or senior ambassador had been Guillermo Sevilla Sacasa of Nicaragua. Short, round, and voluble, he was the brother-in-law of the dictator, Anastacio Somoza. We had frequent contact, and while recognizing his limitations, I had a soft spot for him. One day he called me on the phone and in his heavily accented English said, "Henry, people are parking illegally in front of my house. I want you to put up a third No Parking sign. If you don't, I will go out there and take an ice pick and stab their tires!" He got his extra sign; punching out all those tires would have been far too strenuous for Guillermo.

The Rabin visit turned out to be the equal of the Sadat visit in pomp but not in mischance. There were, however, amusing sidelights.

ITEM: Mayor Rizzo of Philadelphia, riding in from the airport with the prime minister, peppered his conversation half a dozen times with the phrase "Holy Moses!"—not the suavest thing to say to a Jewish leader.

ITEM: The White House dining room tried valiantly but unsuccessfully to present a kosher meal. It was not suitable for the Orthodox because the kitchen was not kosher; those who cared ate fruit.

ITEM: Jessica, Vivien Dinitz (wife of the Israeli ambassador to the United States), Barbara Bush, and Leah Rabin played tennis one afternoon. Riding in the car the next day with Leah, I was surprised when she thanked me effusively for the tennis racket. Seeing my puzzlement, she explained: she had not brought a racket, so Jessica gave her mine—for keeps.

ITEM: Rabin got the name of "Stone Face." He was the only politician I ever met who could be greeted by wildly cheering crowds without smiling or waving.

ITEM: Illinois politics cropped up again. An assistant to Governor Dan Walker called me before the trip to demand that I arrange for Mrs. Walker to be at the head table for Mayor Daley's luncheon. I declined involvement in that tempest but asked who would be first to greet Rabin on arrival in Chicago at the foot of the plane's steps. His reply:

"Walker, even if we have to use force." I thought, "I'd hate to bet on it," and sure enough, Daley headed the reception line.

ITEM: In conversation about autistic children, the wife of a Supreme Court justice said, to my horror, to Mrs. Rabin, "Oh, you are interested in the autistic? People of your race are so intelligent I didn't think you had autistic children."

ITEM: Rabin told us of substantial numbers of North Koreans, Vietnamese, and Cubans in Syria, there to help in case of another Syria-Israel war. That the most squalid dictatorships of the world were joined in opposition to the pluckiest democracy in the world left me angry if unsurprised.

Preparing for the Next Challenge

IN MIDWINTER of 1976 I began to cast about for a new job. Jessica felt that chiefs of protocol were regarded by those serious about foreign affairs as two pounds lighter than a straw hat. I agreed that that perception existed among those who didn't know the job's opportunities, but it had given us a profile high enough to justify hopes for something better.

Elliot Richardson's nomination as secretary of commerce having opened up the job, I followed up on the groundwork laid by Jessica and made a run at being named ambassador to Great Britain. In all likelihood, it was a naive thing to do; presidents do not name ambassadors as the result of lobbying. Nonetheless, I let my wishes be known to senators, White House staffers, State Department bureaucrats, George Bush, and anyone else I could think of. I even called on Bob Strauss, then chairman of the Democratic National Committee. The ebullient Strauss, a friend and fellow Texan, said, "Catto, if you get named, the Democratic National Committee will pass a resolution praising the appointment!"

I talked to Anne Armstrong, then a White House counselor, who was enthusiastic and supportive. In the end, of course, Ford named her to the job, which she handled beautifully.

So the door to London had been closed. The UN job in New York, soon to be vacated by Daniel Patrick Moynihan, seemed equally out of reach. But one bright day Brent Scowcroft, the national security adviser who had become a friend, called with encouraging news. Two jobs were to become vacant, ambassador to Bogotá and to Geneva, where the UN had its far-flung European headquarters. Jessica agreed with my inclination: we had served in Latin America; why not try Europe? The job was a serious one, and my newly acquired French would come in handy. So informed, Brent put things in motion.

Hurdles, however, remained, since 1976 was the American Bicentennial Year and a vast national celebration awaited July 4. Countries important to our history — Spain, France, and above all, Britain — planned state visits. Jordanians, Danes, Swedes, and Sierra Leonese were coming as well. That meant endless work for Protocol and for me before we could get away.

Each visit by a foreign head of state or government spawned a frenzy of activity at the State Department. One of the results of this bureaucratic whirlwind was the president's briefing book, a detailed look at every issue that could conceivably come up. By its nature, the book had no continuity; it was written by perhaps a dozen different agencies or departments, and the idea of editing it did not exist. The result, as I learned from reading these tomes, was a product that assumed by implication that the president was a moron. For example, the book prepared for the French visit touched on French-Chinese relations; the author, with a ready grasp of the obvious, informed the president: "A political dispute and leadership struggle of a fundamental order is occurring in China." Wow, I bet he didn't know that. The editor in me, never far beneath the surface (in spite of the evidence of this book) yearned in vain to cut it down and pull it together.

The French, in the person of tall, handsome Valery Giscard d'Estaing and his striking wife, Ann-Aymone, flew into Andrews on May 17 at 9:55 A.M. on a sleek Concorde. Jessica and I left plenty of time for the trip to the base. We did not, however, count on a massive traffic jam caused by crowds coming to greet him. (No, we didn't organize it; it was spontaneous. A show of love for *la France*? No, keen interest in viewing the supersonic, seldom-seen Concorde.)

The visit went well, at least with respect to the principals; both were attractive, and Giscard took a shine to Jessica. The two dinners, the one at the White House and the French party at the embassy, both white-tie events, vied for elegant evening of the year. The French won, hands down.

The French embassy residence, on Kalorama Road in Washington, couldn't handle the two hundred guests, so a huge tent appeared miraculously in the garden. The solid-looking walls were of a subtle red cloth adorned with Gobelin tapestries. A bewigged twenty-five-piece orchestra played eighteenth-century music during a superb meal graced by the best wine I had ever tasted. The evening brightened visibly, furthermore, with the news of President Ford's thumping win over Ronald Reagan in the Michigan primary.

The preceding doesn't mean the White House dinner had flopped; it hadn't. To be sure, jazz great Earl Hines played too long and Henry Kissinger startled the nodding guests when his chair broke with a loud crack as he tilted it back during the concert. No, it's just that the French have such élan, a sense of style that is hard to rival.

They can, however, be difficult. One of the stops on this exhausting five-day trip was New Orleans. French ambassador Jacques Kosciusko-Morizet, unhappy with his place seating at a dinner, threw a fit, his wife raging at me as well. They even began moving place cards without informing the host, the mayor. When I offered to swap places, his fury abated. The next day, Mrs. Kosciusko tried to have Jessica ride the cramped jump seat in their limo. "There is room for only two," she whined. "Move over, Yanie," Jessica snapped, annoyed. Yanie moved.

Word got out that we were not amused, and the following day, the ambassador pulled me aside. "I understand," he said, "that Jessica was a little, er, nervous last night. I hope you will tell her I love her." "Tell her yourself, Jacques," I responded. There comes a time when diplomatic nicety is best served by taking no guff.

The visit, rife with historical overtones, included stops at Yorktown to celebrate the Franco-American victory over the British, at Philadelphia's Independence Hall, at Mount Vernon for the arresting sound and light show of the history of that great home. In Louisiana, Giscard praised the preservation of French culture and courted the state's French speakers (though their French left something to be desired). Near Houston, Mac and Eleanor McCollum entertained at their ranch and Giscard gave them a Charolais bull. There I ran into vivacious Nellie Connally, John's wife. Remembering his behavior during the Sadat visit, she said, to my delight, "Oh, Henry, I'm so glad to see you. Now that old nozzlenose isn't here, we'll have some fun."

When they left on May 22 I was sad. The French can be ornery, no doubt about it. Yet a touch of history and the company of people like the Giscards make any effort worthwhile.

Between France and Spain, President Stevens of Sierra Leone popped in for an informal visit. I took him to see Ford and, as was customary, I chatted with him in the Cabinet Room. An agreeable man, he talked easily and I enjoyed him. Alas, the clock moved steadily along until half an hour had passed. I inquired and learned that Secretary Kissinger was late, making *two* presidents wait upon his perpetual tardiness. There had been rumors that Henry was slipping, that Ford, increasingly secure in his foreign policy role, no longer felt the eager dependence of his early tenure. Vice President Rockefeller, long a Kissinger ally, heard these stories and when Henry returned in late May from a European trip, went to Andrews to welcome him home — and to boost his ever-fragile ego and his standing with the press.

Spanish Successes
and Bicentennial Bloopers

ON MAY 22, King Juan Carlos and Queen Sophia came to help celebrate Spain's important role in American history. The four of us rode into town from Andrews together, and we saw at once that they were different. Young and not in the least puffed up, they chatted freely and clearly looked forward to the visit.

The next day the king addressed a joint session of Congress, and as we rode over to the Capitol, I offered him a bit of advice. Recalling Giscard's rather stiff response to the warm applause his appearance evoked, I suggested the king might want to smile, wave a bit, react to a typical American welcome. He was nervous and readily accepted my suggestion, with gratifying results. Afterward, when we returned to Blair House, the queen (who had returned before us) rushed up, threw her arms around him, kissed and congratulated him. Wreathed in smiles and relief that he had done well, the young monarch, grinning, said to me, "Looks like she's going to rape me here and now!"

Later, at a lunch given by the Senate Foreign Relations Committee, Senator Jacob Javits of New York said with self-satisfaction to the king, "I've never been to Spain because I despised Franco." (I'll bet he had an I BRAKE FOR SMALL ANIMALS bumper sticker on his car.) I asked the queen afterward how she felt about that. Clearly annoyed, she snapped, "How can he make judgments if he closes his mind and refuses to go? It accomplishes nothing and blinds him to reality." I agreed.

The state dinner, made memorable mostly by the presence among the guests of my excited and beautiful mother, took place Wednesday night. Noting a monogram "JCB" (Juan Carlos de Bourbon) on the king's shirt, I asked Her Majesty a bit about their families, both of which have been major players for so long in European history. (She is the sister of the deposed king of Greece.) She talked freely. "Oh, we're all interconnected, you know; we're just like rabbits." She said that Queen Elizabeth and Prince Philip were very nice, the queen being quite formal. At that point, Juan Carlos broke in: "Philip's just like us; you'll like him." The next day in New York, Sophia went to Bloomingdale's for some serious shopping. When she returned, it was clear that she had had a grand time. "Did you have any money?" her husband asked. "No," she laughed. "I just went through saying, 'I want this and that,' assuming someone would take care of it." Someone did.

A visit to the packed Spanish Cultural Center in New York was worse than a Japanese train at rush hour. I asked Her Majesty how she stood it. She brushed it off: "It's the kind of thing we have to do all the time," adding that their jobs resembled those of American politicians. I thought, yes, but a politician's job someday ends, while theirs goes on until they die.

In New York we went to Fort Green Park in Brooklyn to visit a monument to Spaniards killed in the American Revolution. There were, to my surprise, protesters. Pithy but dated signs said things like JOBS YES, FASCISTS NO.

Chanting leftists marred the ceremony of wreath-laying, hymns, and brief speeches. A rock landed near the queen; an egg hit a policeman. As we drove away, the demonstrators surged up to the car in which the king and I rode, their faces contorted by hate, mouthing insults.

At that moment, the king, with a wonderful look of mischief on his face, made a gesture known worldwide. We laughed and sped on our way. He told me how a tomato once hit him during a public appearance. He nonchalantly reached down, plucked a piece of it from his trouser and popped it in his mouth, remarking, "Not bad. Perhaps a bit ripe." His nonplussed hecklers left him alone thereafter.

On another public occasion, before he was king, he happened to see an egg flying his way. Young and athletic, he took a quick step back. The egg sailed by and whacked a Franco cabinet minister with full force. Juan Carlos thought it funny; the minister did not.

That evening we saw this handsome, merry young couple off for home. Often the Protocol gang felt nothing but glee to speed a parting guest. Juan Carlos and Sophia were, indeed, different. They won the affection of everyone they met by being natural, relaxed, and funny. Through the years we have seen them twice more, once in Aspen skiing and once in Spain, but not long enough to detect whether they have changed, whether time has eroded the joy of life that made them so appealing.

Before I could turn my full attention to the upcoming visit of Queen Elizabeth and Prince Philip, General Scowcroft asked me to go to Puerto Rico to greet the heads of the major industrialized nations, who were arriving there for their annual meeting, at which President Ford was to be host. Only an overnight trip, nonetheless two memorable events occurred. As I boarded French president Giscard's plane to welcome him back to the United States, he put on a long face and said plaintively, "Where is Jessica?"

Meanwhile, the governor of Puerto Rico was almost getting his head blown off by the Secret Service. Giscard having arrived on a Concorde, there were again thousands of sightseers at the airport to catch a view of that uniquely beautiful machine. The result was a horrible traffic jam that made Governor Hernández Colón late to greet the just-arriving President Ford. Desperate, the governor told his driver and escort vehicle to enter the airport via a back route. There they found that the ever-vigilant Secret Service had locked a usually open gate. "Knock it down with the car," he ordered. That failing, the governor and his guests scaled the fence and ran panting across the tarmac, only to be intercepted by agents who doubtless thought him a crazed terrorist. Fortunately, he did succeed in convincing the interceptors that he was the governor, in spite of being disheveled, sweaty, and breathless, and he greeted the debarking president as if nothing had happened.

His wife, arriving separately, was not so lucky. Though she did not have the proper pass, she was insistent that she should be allowed in. When the agents demurred, her Latin temper flared, and she scratched an agent, who then forcibly detained her and apparently roughed her up. I later tried with but modest success to heal her psychic wounds; she was seriously mad.[9]

Back in Washington, several challenges loomed before we could head to Europe. First was my Senate confirmation, and as time permitted, I went to numerous briefings on what the U.S. mission in Geneva did. The most interesting briefing was given by the treasurer (later president) of the AFL-CIO, Lane Kirkland. He was vitally concerned with the Geneva post and who held it, for the Geneva-based International Labor Organization (ILO) was currently suffering from a spasm of Arab-inspired anti-Israeli activity. (During my tenure, the United States withdrew from the ILO.) Lane and his wife, Irina, later became close friends with whom we enjoyed many evenings of spirited poker and lively conversation. In the end, with labor's support, I was easily confirmed on June 22. Indeed, Senator John Sparkman cautioned Shirley Temple, my successor as chief of protocol, who was also being heard by the Senate committee, that she had big shoes to fill.

The second hill to climb, the Great July Fourth Bicentennial Tall Ship Sail-By, proved a disaster, showing once again that for a protocol officer to commit suicide is almost a redundancy.

There being considerable interest among the diplomatic corps, my office, in cooperation with the U.S. Navy, decided to invite all the ambassadors and their families to fly to New York for the event. I knew logistics would be a problem, and I called Secretary of the Navy William Middendorf to ask for help in getting the diplomats out to the carrier USS *Forrestal*, from which the president, the vice president, and other dignitaries would be watching the tall ships. The conversation with Middendorf was, well, elliptical.

CATTO: Bill, the New York police say traffic in the city will be horrible. Could you provide helicopter service from La Guardia airport to the carrier?

MIDDENDORF: Oh, no, we couldn't do that. We have no assets there; the Brooklyn Navy Yard is closed.

CATTO: But moving them by bus and then a ferry to the *Forrestal* will be slow and difficult.

MIDDENDORF: To move so many ambassadors would be an operation as big as the evacuation of Saigon. You know, we lost some choppers evacuating Saigon.

CATTO (with visions of diplomats dangling from the struts): Oh, er, uh . . .

MIDDENDORF: Landing a chopper on a carrier at sea is very difficult.

CATTO: Bill, the carrier will be at anchor in New York harbor!

MIDDENDORF: You wouldn't want to lose thirty or thirty-five ambassadors, would you? It would cost us both our jobs.

With the Pentagon unbending, we proceeded with Plan B: planes to New York, then buses and a ferry. I sent the invitation to the diplomats, warning them that it might be rigorous.

Nothing loath, 175 accepted. We chartered two planes (at the expense of our "guests"), and at seven o'clock in the morning on the great day, away we went, Deputy Protocol Chief Stuart Rockwell and several of our officers shepherding one, I with daughter, Heather, and the balance of our staff looking after the other. At first all went well. We landed on time, piled the diplomats onto buses, and with police escort sirens a-wailing, sped to the dock. The ferry, already groaning with other invitees, was there, and after an hour's wait (which I spent playing gin rummy on a stairstep with Washington friend Joan Tobin), we chugged off in high spirits at nine-thirty.

The ferry was big, with a capacity of 2,400 people, but next to the *Forrestal* it looked like a rowboat. I leapt off first and went to check seating. The Navy had promised us front row bleachers, but as the great wave of humanity slowly debarked, confusion reigned. Clearly, the Navy had invited more than could be handled comfortably and the gaily bedecked visitors wandered like cattle at a roundup, looking for seats. The German and Dutch ambassadors suffered a serious case of the huffs, but finally all things fell into order—more or less. The president arrived. So did the vice president, Secretary Kissinger, Princess Grace and Prince Rainier, and a pair of Norwegian royals—all, incidentally, in helicopters. President Ford came by and greeted the diplomats, and all feathers were again smooth. The show began.

Dozens of sailing ships from across the world proudly passed, flags snapping, crews saluting, bands playing. A less-than-gourmet lunch of dry fried chicken, beans, potato salad, and ice cream sticks kept hunger at bay. Good humor clearly prevailed on a day with heaven-sent weather. Then it came time to go.

The special ship that the Navy had promised for debarking my charges duly awaited us. The trouble was that no one had told the non-diplomats that this was a reserved vessel, and everyone swarmed aboard. Only about half of our guests made it, among them, fortunately, Ambassador Rockwell. I, meanwhile, waited with the sweaty 1,700 souls who slowly crept onto the ferry. Loading for the trip out had been a few at a time and was painless. Loading for the return made Dunkirk seem like a holiday outing; it took two hours and twenty minutes. The wives of the Kuwaiti and Swedish ambassadors became ill.

Across the river, poor Stuart and his charges, having made the crossing fairly quickly, chafed impatiently. Finally, the British ambassador led a minor revolt, and the lucky few were taken by the police escort back to one of the two waiting planes. They, presumably, made it home for dinner.

My grumpy group also finally made it to America's shining shores; Ellis Island in 1900 would have been better — and better organized. They were not happy campers. And it got worse. On arrival at Washington's National Airport, we found that the crowds coming downtown to see the annual Fourth of July fireworks display had turned the George Washington Parkway into the George Washington Parking Lot. Bidding my guests an apologetic farewell, Heather and I climbed into my car at 8:10 P.M. The twenty-minute trip home took an hour and a half. It had been a long day, and I hoped it did not portend trouble for our last and most challenging visitor: Queen Elizabeth II.

Hail, Britannia

THE VISIT of Queen Elizabeth had taken thousands of hours of planning over a period of almost a year; our British cousins are sticklers for detail and skilled at protocol. Clearly, they have over centuries of practice learned the truth of the old Chinese proverb "Embarrassment leads to anger," and a bit of forethought can eliminate most embarrassment between heads of state.

Her Majesty and His Royal Highness Prince Philip, the Duke of Edinburgh ("HM" and "HRH" to our crew), were due to disembark the royal yacht *Britannia* at 10:35 A.M. on July 6 at Penn's Landing, Philadelphia. At 10:30 A.M. Jessica and I were to go aboard to welcome the visitors.

To be safe, we came up the night before and were treated to an elegant small dinner by the British consul general, Denis Richards, and his wife. There we met the former American ambassador to the United Kingdom, publisher and art collector Walter Annenberg, and his wife, Lee. Walter had been ridiculed mercilessly early in his tour in Britain, but by the time of his departure he had won the British over in great style. He had also rehabilitated (what he had called "elements of refurbishment" in his first visit with the queen) the official American residence in London, Winfield House, with generosity and taste that would benefit Jessica and me nearly twenty years later. At the dinner I sat next to Lee, a conversationalist of epic proportions who herself became chief of protocol in the first Reagan administration.[10]

The next morning I rose early and ran four miles through downtown Philadelphia, burning off any excess energy and angst I may have felt. At 10:00 A.M. on the dot, the great ship glided into the dock. Governor Milton Shapp and Mayor Frank Rizzo were there in good time to welcome the visitors. (Although they were both Democrats, I learned they did not speak to one another.) Jessica and I mounted the gangplank at the appointed moment. A band had appeared on deck, and flags were unfurled; we were excited and more than a little nervous. Taken directly to the queen's salon, we were presented to the principals, who put us at once at ease. We also were pleased to greet fellow Texans Anne Armstrong, U.S. ambassador to Britain, and her husband, Tobin. I left at once to be ready to present the governor and the mayor. Somehow the cover had not been put on the ridged gangplank, and it was hard to walk down it; the *Washington Post* reporter on the scene wrote later than I was walking so carefully I might have been coming down Mount Everest. At 10:30 on the nose, to a stirring musical fanfare, down marched this indomitable little woman and her consort. National anthems followed introductions, and we boarded the motorcade to proceed to the first event.

As in all such visits, activities become a tumble in the mind. The memory that stands out is that we were an on-time operation.

10:45   Depart Penn's Landing
10:55   Arrive City Hall (Queen presented with Andrew Wyeth lithographs)
11:15   Depart
11:20   Arrive Liberty Bell Pavilion
11:30   Depart
11:35   Visit observation deck, Penn Mutual Building

12:00   Depart
12:05   Arrive *Britannia*
12:45   Luncheon on board *Britannia*
 2:50   Depart
 3:00   Queen presents the Bicentennial Bell, Independence National Park
 3:15   Visit Independence Hall
 4:05   Depart
 4:10   Arrive *Britannia*
 4:30   Tea for U.S. governors aboard *Britannia*
 5:30   Presentation of gifts aboard *Britannia*
 6:00   Prince Philip gives reception honoring Royal Society of Arts
 8:15   Depart
 8:30   Black tie banquet by Mayor, Museum of Art
11:00   (with luck) Collapse into bed

As the day sped by, I wondered what Her Majesty thought as she visited scenes of American triumph and British defeat. Pickets noisily greeted her at the 3:00 P.M. Bicentennial Bell presentation. It seemed there was no mention of God in the bell's inscription, which read, "Let Freedom Ring." This offended one Rev. Carl McIntyre and his retinue, and they carried signs proclaiming TAKE BACK THE BELL. They had, furthermore, organized a letter-writing campaign to protest, and there being more than one hundred letters, the queen was informed. Some of her advisers feared they had indeed made a faux pas, but I reassured them to the contrary. If Her Majesty fretted, it didn't show. In her remarks at the presentation she said her forebears had learned a lesson at Philadelphia: "You can't keep a people subject against their will." I thought her most effective.

During the day, I got a chance to observe her closely. Shorter than I would have guessed (perhaps five-two), she was at fifty much younger-looking and prettier than in her pictures, with perfect skin. She, and thus all women around her, wore hats and gloves at all daytime functions. At one point, I took the younger children down to Blair House to meet the queen, who had on a light-blue kidney-shaped hat. Afterward, thirteen-year-old Will mischievously asked if she had been ill. "Why?" I responded. "Well, she had an ice bag on her head and I thought maybe she had a headache."

The advance party had told us that in crowds, as she "went walkabout" (greeted the public), she always carried flowers so as to avoid the often painful experience of overvigorous handshakes. Her blue eyes could radiate ice when she was annoyed, but her smile would light up the dark side of the moon.

I liked her. One never forgot who she was; neither did she. Yet at times she was delightfully human, such as one day when I was riding with her in the back of her limo after a lengthy event and noticed she had unobtrusively slipped off her shoes. I asked her how she managed such apparently animated conversations with people of startlingly different backgrounds. (I had Mayor Rizzo in mind.) "It's easy," she replied. "Just ask a few questions and they will take it from there."

Prince Philip, although popular with the vast crowds that turned out to greet the couple, struck me as remote and at times difficult. At breakfast after their first night at Blair House, he greeted me with: "I say, Catto, do you employ professional door slammers here?" Billeted on the second floor above the front door, he had been bothered by the comings and goings of the security people. We quickly had felt nailed on the doorjamb in hopes of dulling the sound, while warning the Secret Service to tread lightly.

Prince Phillip's lot was not an easy one. Addressed as "Your Royal Highness," in public appearances he always walks two or three paces behind his wife, hands clasped behind his back. When they went walkabout, he charmed all he met. Tall, handsome, and athletic, he paused with what appeared to be real interest in chatting with people.

Wednesday morning a British Royal Flight plane took the traveling party from Philadelphia to Andrews Air Force Base, where we boarded limos for the half hour trip to the White House and the first meeting with the Fords. I rode with the queen and Prince Philip and had my first chance to talk privately with them. They had recently been to Japan, and they laughed as I recounted my difficulties in communicating with the emperor.

The arrival ceremonies went well. The weather had cleared, the crowds were huge, and the Fords, never losing their common touch, charmed their guests. After lunch with the president and first lady, Her Majesty laid a wreath at Arlington Cemetery and visited the Lincoln Memorial, where, again, huge crowds greeted her and British folk dancers charmed her.

The White House state dinner that evening broke records. For months both the White House social office and my office had been driven loco by often not-too-subtle requests to be invited to the party of the year; people can think up amazing reasons to wheedle an invitation ("My company did $100 million worth of business in the U.K. last year . . .") and by the time the list closed, 200 dinner guests—instead of the usual 120—had made the cut. The dining room was too small, so a white tent had been erected over the rose garden and huge baskets of flowers and ferns hung everywhere. The wine and dinner could not have been better, nor the toasts more gracious and sincere. British-born Bob Hope provided the after-dinner entertainment and as he sang his theme song, "Thanks for the Memories," even such a practiced pro as he showed a bit of nerves: the sheet music he held quivered like an autumn aspen tree. The Armstrongs and Jessica and I initiated the ensuing dancing, inspiring the president to ask Her Majesty to dance, followed by His Royal Highness and Mrs. Ford. I tried to get up the nerve to cut in on Ford—but failed. For the Cattos, it was a magic moment. A bit before one o'clock, we escorted the guests across Pennsylvania Avenue to Blair House. I wanted to go back and dance some more; the Fords were still going strong. Fortunately, Jessica's better judgment prevailed and we went home.

Thursday, trouble. Angier Biddle Duke, a predecessor as chief of protocol and then chief for New York City, called with the news that Governor Carey of New York had decided not to greet the queen on arrival in his state. Angie gave no explanation, but I needed none: Carey's Irish ancestry and New York's huge Irish vote had given him pause. New York and Boston had long been hotbeds of Irish Republican Army supporters; what better way to make cheap points with these terrorists and their American sympathizers than to snub the queen of the Sassenachs. (We were to be greeted in Boston by pickets whose placards read, IRA THE ONLY WAY and BRITAIN OUT OF IRELAND.)

I informed the British of this unwelcome news just before the queen, officially the head of the Anglican Church, went to the National Cathedral to lay a memorial stone. The magnificent service, marked by the queen's own trumpeters and generally marvelous music capped by the "Battle Hymn of the Republic," was marred by Carey's decision. But all was not lost. At a congressional luncheon following the service, British ambassador Peter Ramsbottom managed to whisper in Vice President Rockefeller's ear what his fellow New Yorker had done. Nelson, livid, called Carey. "Hugh," he boomed, "I hear you are not planning to greet the queen. That will not do." Carey stammered, "I thought I probably wouldn't be able to make it . . ." Retorted Rocky: "I don't want any excuses. Be there." And he hung up. And there Carey was. In New York, even Democrats like Carey listened when a Rockefeller spoke, especially one who happened to be vice president.

That evening the queen gave a return dinner honoring the Fords at the elegant British embassy on Massachusetts Avenue, all of the men again in white tie and the women decked out in their finest. The queen was particularly beautiful in ice blue with the ribbon of one of her countless decorations across the front of her gown.

The next day we flew to New Jersey, boarded *Britannia,* and sailed across New York Harbor to lower Manhattan. There the reluctant Governor Carey and Mayor Abraham Beame and their wives welcomed the visitors, who were escorted to City Hall for a ceremony followed by a giant (1,800 people) luncheon at the Waldorf Ballroom, hosted by the Anglo-American Pilgrims Society and the English Speaking Union. Afterward, in Harlem, the queen visited General Washington's headquarters at the Jumel Mansion, and thousands of black Americans turned out in a welcome quite as enthusiastic as that given her in lower Manhattan.

Next stop, the queen turned tourist and hit Bloomingdale's, her first visit to an American department store. There she met fashion royalty Calvin Klein, Ralph Lauren, Donna Karan, and Louis Del Ilio. British products got a boost from the chairman of Wedgwood and the president of Aquascutum.

That evening the royal couple gave a small dinner on *Britannia.* For Jessica and me it was the first real visit aboard, and we were amazed. Very big and beautifully appointed, it was a floating palace, replete with the royal silver and china. The walls were hung with paintings and naval memorabilia, such as the buttons from Lord Nelson's tunic. The tables at which we ate were polished (by hand, of course) to such a high sheen I had to touch them to see if they were glass-covered.

Christened in 1953, the vessel carried a crew of 230 plus 20 officers and had sailed more than a million miles. The wear and tear of so much use plus the annual cost of almost $19 million dictated she be decommissioned in 1997, with a replacement in doubt. But *Britannia* was far more than a royal toy: while the queen wowed Washington, the ship wooed American businessmen by hosting a series of floating seminars on the opportunities of doing business with the British. Commercial? Maybe. But effective.

The Woody Creek Summit, August 1, 1990. President Bush and Prime
Minister Thatcher are Jessica's and my guests at our Colorado ranch on the
day the Gulf War breaks out. Left to right: Me, Charles Powell, Ambassador
Robin Renwick, General Brent Scowcroft, President Bush, and
Mrs. Thatcher. White House photo.

*Fortunately, the
Secret Service
didn't react.
February 1969.*

*First communion:
Nixon campaigns
for himself and for
the fledgling
Republican
legislative ticket
in the fall of 1960.*
Fred Winchell photo.

Ike comes to San Antonio to campaign for me and John Goode (center) in a 1961 special election. John ran for Congress, I for the state legislature. Ike or no, it was no go.
Elicson photo,
San Antonio.

No, it's not heartburn: it's the national anthem after presenting credentials to El Salvador's president, Fidel Sánchez Hernández (not shown).
October 1971.
U.S. Embassy photo.

Maestro Pablo Casals tells me and Organization of American States secretary general Galo Plaza what it was like to give a concert in the Roosevelt administration—the Theodore Roosevelt administration. 1971. State Department photo.

Nordic carols during a tropical Christmas. El Salvador. 1972. Left to right: Heather, Will, Jessica, me, Isa, and John. USIS photo.

Left to right: Unidentified orchestra member, Mercer Ellington, me, and jazz royalty Duke Ellington. El Salvador. 1972. U.S. Embassy photo.

In the protocol job, we dined out—a lot.
Today, we carry out!
Photo from *The Saturday Evening Post*, October 1975.

At home with cat Barnaby in McLean, Virginia. Probably 1975. Photographer unknown.

Left to right: Mrs. Ford, Mrs. Rockefeller, Jessica, and Mrs. Kissinger before a state dinner. We gathered for relaxed moments such as this in the family quarters. Date uncertain. White House photo.

Sharing a laugh in the White House Cabinet Room with (from front left) Egyptian ambassador Ashraf Ghorbal, General Brent Scowcroft, and Secretary of State Henry Kissinger. 1975.
White House photo by Ricardo Thomas.

Going into the White House East Room, just before the state dinner for the Shah and Empress of Iran. May 1975.
Women's Wear Daily photo.

Queen Elizabeth II arrives to help us celebrate our national bicentennial. The Royal Yacht Britannia *is in the background. July 1976.* White House photo.

The Duke of Edinburgh and Mrs. Rockefeller. July 1976. White House photo.

*Trying unsuccessfully to get up the nerve to cut in on the president, I dance
with Jessica after the state dinner. July 1976.* White House photo.

*Arrggh: Jessica (foreground right) does her bit for international amity at a
State Department luncheon for the wife of a visiting leader. April 1974.*
Department of State photo by Walter Booze.

With Jessica, Isa, John, and Will after being sworn in as U.S. ambassador to the European Office of the United Nations. July 1976. Department of State photo by Walter Booze.

Communication with the Fourth Estate: I brief the Pentagon press on Lebanon. July 1982. Pentagon photo.

I am sworn in as assistant secretary of defense by General Counsel William Howard Taft IV. Jessica, Isa, and Will are witnesses. May 1981. Pentagon photo.

At the White House with President Reagan. January 1982. White House photo.

Aboard the aircraft carrier Constellation *with Secretary Weinberger (third from left) and naval officers.*

I give a western party for leaders of the Trade Unions Congress.
Photo by Graham Wood.

*Greeting General Colin Powell at my Pentagon retirement ceremony.
September 15, 1983.* Pentagon photo.

*Meeting with future president of Poland Lech Walesa (left).
October 1987.* Bernard Lifshutz photo.

*The president comes to London and the delegation meets before calling on
Prime Minister Thatcher. June 1989.* White House photo.

*Embassies are for entertaining, among other things: I chat with authors Inga
Morath and Arthur Miller at a reception. 1992.* U.S. Embassy photo.

The man who came to dinner returns. Left to right: unidentified Secret Service man, President Bush, Jessica, me, Governor John Sununu, and General Brent Scowcroft. July 1990.

Former President and Mrs. Jimmy Carter come to London. 1992.

Photo by Barry Swaebe.

As director of the U.S. Information Agency, I call on
Japanese prime minister Kaifu. September 1991.
Office of the Prime Minister photo.

A message for the Cuban people: I broadcast in Spanish to
Cuba on the Voice of America. 1992. USIA photo.

The evening ended at about eleven o'clock and the traveling party of Assistant Chief of Protocol Bill and Rosemarie Codus and Jessica and I returned to our own hardly less regal digs. Malcolm Forbes, publisher of *Forbes* magazine, had made his yacht *Highlander* available to us for the overnight trip by sea to New Haven, Connecticut. Malcolm, surely the most genial and adventurous man I ever met, loved travel and did it by yacht, plane, balloon, and motorcycle, and where he went, he went first class. *Highlander* may not have been as big as *Britannia,* but, as they say in the South, we were in high cotton.

As the two yachts sailed out of the harbor, our group assembled at the stern. We admired the beauty of the great British ship, moon limpid above and Manhattan fading in the background. Out onto *Britannia*'s rear deck came our royal guests. We toasted them with champagne, waves, and our ship's horn. *Britannia* and the Windsors responded in kind. It was a beautiful moment. As we crawled happily into our bunks, Jessica said, "I'm not going to let you go to sleep until you get me a boat like this." Fortunately, she relented.

We docked on Saturday at New Haven, briefly greeting Governor Ella Grasso, and then streaked for the airport and a flight to Charlottesville, Virginia, there to be greeted by Governor Mills Godwin. The purpose of this southward retreat was to present a "devisal" to the University of Virginia (a devisal is a grant of something, but I can't recall what HM devised). Also they toured the university and Thomas Jefferson's other great memorial, his home at Monticello. Returning to Providence, where *Britannia* had steamed, Prince Philip essayed a comment I found germane. As we chatted about Jefferson and his genius, the frequently taciturn man said, "You know, we really miss a bet. What we ought to be talking about in this bicentennial is the success of the free-enterprise system, not silly British-American platitudes about walking into the future together. We ought to tell the world this system works better than any other." Recalling the Niagara of platitudes emitted during the trip, I uttered a silent amen.

Landing in Rhode Island, we had a drive through rural areas en route to rejoining *Britannia* in Providence. Even in the countryside, people gathered in groups to watch the motorcade speed past and to wave welcome. One group had a sign that to me summed up the spirit of America's reaction to Britain's queen. It read simply, WELCOME QUEEN, THE JONESES. I hoped she saw it.

That evening, the queen and Prince Philip entertained the Fords, Rockefellers, Kissingers, Armstrongs, Richard Cheneys, Claiborne Pell, General Scowcroft, the Coduses, the Cattos, and the British traveling party on *Britannia*. Jessica and I had a special treat: we spent the night on board, in a three-room suite whose beds had linen sheets. We slept in regal comfort as the great ship made smoothly toward Boston. The next morning Jessica took her breakfast in bed while I joined the men in the dining room for a hearty English breakfast and sleepy, desultory conversation.

Arriving at Boston Harbor, we were greeted by hundreds of small vessels, which provided escort. The great old ironside warship *Constitution* sailed out and offered a twenty-one-gun salute. As in Philadelphia, as we anchored the flags snapped into place, the band played, and once again, we felt the thrill of pomp and ceremony. Governor Michael Dukakis and his wife, Kitty, waited to greet us, as did Boston mayor Kevin White, a classmate of mine at Williams College, and his wife.

As the queen stepped onto the gangplank, gremlins struck. Something about the texture of the gangplank, its angle, and Her Majesty's shoes combined to provide no traction at all. As a result, she literally slid down the entire way, keeping her balance like an Olympic skier and grinning bemusedly all the while. *That,* I thought, was sangfroid.

The Bostonians turned out in huge numbers (the police estimated 600,000) to see the queen, her route lined by men dressed in British and American colonial uniforms. At Old North Church the minister gave a fire-and-brimstone sermon, attacking Boston's political leadership. The day was hot, the un-airconditioned church was hot, and I expect the hottest of all was Kevin White, for he seemed the target of the holy ire. His lunch at City Hall was marred by Governor Dukakis's failure to show up, and the empty chair next to the queen was glaringly obvious. Quick-thinking Secretary of Commerce Elliot Richardson slipped into the seat when it became obvious that the governor wasn't coming. A slow learner, I finally got the picture: big-city Democratic mayors don't get along with their Democratic governors, as we saw in Chicago, Philadelphia, and now Boston.

After lunch, the scheduled brief parade had been under way for fifty-five minutes before Mayor White summoned a policeman and attempted to rescue the melting queen by saying, "Tell them not to delay anymore, I don't care what you have to do." A few minutes later, Bill Codus trumped the mayor by going down and simply ending the event, to the relief of all concerned.

From that point the visit wound down quickly. We toured the USS *Constitution* and returned to *Britannia* for a final reception. Notables such as Joan Kennedy, Senator Edward Brooke, the mayor, and the governor joined the crowd. At seven-thirty this last event was due to end, and the British used a neat trick to end it gracefully. Her Majesty's Marching Band, in white uniforms and pith helmets, "beat the retreat" on the dock, playing wonderfully well all manner of marches and ending with "The Star-Spangled Banner" (dominated by soprano Leontyne Price's voice, starting softly, then building to full power) and "God Save the Queen." Naturally, the guests crowded the rails to see this precision performance. When they turned back for their next drink, the bars had firmly closed. The guests themselves soon departed. I went aboard *Highlander* to watch *Britannia* leave. As she slid out of the dock, the band played "Auld Lang Syne" and the queen and Prince Philip stood alone on the stern. Horns tooted, and the fleet of small vessels re-formed to provide escort once again. Among our group, there were many moist eyes, mine included.

Part 4

The United Nations and the Pentagon

A Post in Geneva

ON JULY 13, without fanfare, I was sworn in as ambassador to the European Office of the United Nations in my office by Stuart Rockwell, and on July 15 we were off to Europe.

At a dinner party a few weeks previous, the multi-talented Pakistani ambassador, Yaqub Khan, had said in what I thought was a weak moment that he and his wife, Tuba, would see us off. To my total surprise, he meant it, and as we waited to board our plane at Dulles Airport, in came the two of them to give us a warm farewell.

Rather than going at once to Geneva, we had planned a tour by boat of Greek historical sites. The six Cattos were joined by Bill and Diana Hobby and daughter Kate; Susan Mary Alsop and friend Stephen Graubard; Ed and Janet Harte, son Chris, and Chris's friend Abigail Havens; and our neighbor and chum of all our young, Karen Oxaal. We sailed from port to port on a ninety-foot, eleven-knot, ten-stateroom, top-heavy yacht called the *Arvi*. The captain, a good environmentalist, began storing our empty wine bottles in a lifeboat rather than throwing them overboard, and twelve days later, the lifeboat was full. John Catto devoured the *Iliad* and the *Odyssey;* we studied, toured ancient sites, hiked, swam, water-skied, and generally had the time of our lives.

On August 2, after farewells to our companions, we climbed aboard Swissair to be wafted from Athens to Geneva. There waited top officers of the U.S. mission to the European Office of the United Nations and our beloved Edna Long, my secretary in San Salvador and in Protocol, who had, with more loyalty than judgment, followed us to Geneva.

Our new home sat on four wooded acres with a view of Lake Geneva. Built in the eighteenth century, it for years had been leased by the Pierre Micheli family to the U.S. government as the residence for the U.S. ambassadors. The Michelis lived in a commodious gatehouse, and their sheep, rabbits, and dogs lent a rural feel to the property. Pierre, a retired Swiss diplomat, his wife, Marie Rose, and her ninety-year-old mother, Elvira de Maceda (soon known as "Granny" to all the Cattos), became dear and lasting friends. Indeed, son John lived with them for a year while working for a Swiss bank after he graduated from Colorado College.

New York City is the seat of the United Nations, its Security Council and General Assembly, and it is there that the light of publicity shines. Geneva, nonetheless, houses a large number of specialized agencies, such as the International Labor Organization (ILO); World International Property Organization (WIPO); the High Commission for Refugees; the International Telegraphic Union; the World Meteorological Organization; the UN Commission on Trade and Development, and so on. The resulting vast bureaucracy is housed in the old League of Nations. Given the scope and variety of operations, the UN ambassador can focus as he pleases, backed up by the mission staffers who cover each activity. Furthermore, Geneva is frequently host for international meetings, and there is a constant flow of VIPs from all over the world. During our first few days we met and entertained Senator Abe Ribicoff, Undersecretary of Housing John Rhinelander, Congressman John Brademus, Flora Lewis of the *New York Times,* and dozens of others from the States. We also met numerous permanent Geneva residents, a glittering group from many countries — even some Swiss!

A mission such as Geneva resembles an embassy, but there are differences. For one, credentials are presented not to a head of state but to a secretary general of the UN. The ambassador follows the activities of a multinational body rather than a sovereign government, and the American business community does not look to the mission for support as it would to an embassy. The main "constituencies" are the mission itself (we had ninety Americans plus forty Swiss and assorted other nationalities), the UN, and the diplomatic corps. The "Geneva Group" of the Western nations, plus Japan and often Israel, worked together to try to bring economy and order to the often fractious and difficult Third World nations that clamored for assistance yet resented interference. Of course, the rivalries of the Cold War seldom strayed far from our minds.

In October, Mao Tse-Tung, legendary but brutal leader of the Chinese Communist revolution, died, and I went to sign the customary condolence book at the Chinese mission. The ambassador escorted me to a room banked with thousands of flowers and giant photos of Mao. As I sat to sign, a hidden photographer popped out and snapped a photo, startling the daylights out of me. I never knew if it served to record my presence for the benefit of the Foreign Office in Beijing or if the intelligence people wanted a photo for their files. Probably both.

As in El Salvador, the ambassadors spent a good bit of time calling on one another, exchanging gossip and, occasionally, forming alliances. Harry Jay, the Canadian ambassador, and Reinaldo Petrignani, the Italian, became friends with whom one could play tennis or speculate on such arcane subjects as why the North Koreans canceled their National Day party on short notice. (Was dictator Kim-il-Sung sick? Was a counterrevolution brewing?)

In getting acquainted at the mission, a high priority, I took a leaf from Deputy Secretary of State Robert Ingersoll's book. On arriving at his new job, he had every assistant secretary and department head to lunch, just the two of them. I did the same with my diverse and many-talented group, and it helped me learn the ropes and judge the people. And vice versa.

We suffered a blow in September with the death by heart attack of Ed Barbier, the CIA's head man in Geneva. Ed and his wife, Marietta, had quickly become good friends and hiking companions, and we were stunned both professionally and personally by his loss. A great trumpeter, he was given a jazz send-off at his funeral in the beautiful Episcopal church by the group with which he played.

At an early staff meeting, I tackled an unspoken problem. President Ford trailed Jimmy Carter in the polls, and there existed a high probability I would be gone within six months. I told the staff that I was aware of this but that I intended to work as if I would be there for years.

I picked up rumors that the Americans working at the UN felt neglected by the mission, so I hatched an idea. I asked USIS man Dan Hafrey if he could get tapes of the Ford-Carter debates expressed over to us immediately. He could, so I invited the mission folk and the UN employees to have beer and watch the debates the night after they happened. The event proved successful but boded ill: far too many cheered when Carter scored a point. When Ford insisted that the Poles weren't under Soviet domination, I groaned silently and mentally started packing. Our only hope lay in our new friend Senator Ribicoff; we hoped he might convince the Carter administration to keep us until school let out in the spring.

The Catto young, meanwhile, had gotten settled nicely in school. John went to a shabbily genteel British boarding school called Aiglon, where he reveled in climbing, swimming, and skiing. He reported that one of the masters had scoffed at his after-hours reading, in this case a biography of Texas' Sam Houston called *The Raven*. I was not too happy with that, and I thought prohibiting blue jeans and sneakers a bit silly, but all in all, we were satisfied.

Heather postponed going to Williams College for a year in order to take advantage of a year at Franklin College in Lugano. A small American-run school in the Italian part of Switzerland, it gave her her first taste of life away from parents and she loved it. The two youngest stayed with us and went to the International School in Geneva.

Social life kept us busy. Bankers Edgar de Picciotto, Denis Severis, and Elie Zilkha and their wives became good and lasting friends. Geneva had more than its share of the "beautiful people," and watching them at play was fun. The scion of the great Rothschild family, Edmond, turned fifty and gave a lavish party at his château outside Geneva. I had never seen so many expensively gowned and heavily bejeweled women. A guest from Paris explained why so many French came all the way to Geneva: "If we do this kind of thing and dress up like this in Paris, the society photographers would take pictures that would cause the tax people to become suspicious, so when we really want to live it up, we come to Switzerland because here nobody resents this kind of lavish display."

The family of the Aga Khan also cut a broad swath in Geneva. Sadrudin Aga Khan, his uncle, did first-rate work as high commissioner for refugees. A good friend of George and Barbara Bush, he welcomed us warmly. The Aga Khan's younger brother, Amyn, managed the family business and proved to be razor-sharp and excellent company.

We became peripherally involved in the Rhodesian peace talks. State Department official Frank Wisner had come to Geneva to observe talks among the British, the white Rhodesians, and the liberation movement. He had a quiet meeting, to which I was not invited, at our house with Joshua Nkomo, one of the key African leaders. I later mentioned this to one of my friends, *Newsweek* correspondent Arnaud de Borchgrave. Arnaud scoffed and said Nkomo was a very high liver, for all his socialist rhetoric. He lived in a mansion that he owned but claimed was rented, and he drove a Mercedes. Arnaud said he couldn't report such things because *Newsweek* wouldn't print bad things about African nationalists. A State Department official I chatted with claimed Nkomo was a corrupt man of little talent, but he could not report that to the department; it would be leaked to the Congressional Black Caucus and might endanger his career. I had run into self-censorship in the Salvadoran press several years before, but learning that it existed in the U.S. government and press was discouraging.

November 2 — election day — came at last, and we joined a throng at a hotel to watch the returns. But being six hours ahead of the East Coast, there was little to learn, so we gave up and went home. I woke at 5:00 A.M., listened to the returns on Voice of America for a while, and slipped into a great blue funk. When I told Jessica, she said, "I guess we just grew up." It would indeed mean major readjustments. We decided nonetheless to enjoy our remaining time to the fullest.

Later that week, my receptionist, Brenda Januzzi, burst into my office and said, "There's a guy on the phone who says he's the king of Spain!" It might, of course, have been a nut, but Jessica and our Texas friends Stevie and Lewis Tucker had not long before spent a few days in Madrid, and Jessica had dropped Juan Carlos and Sophia a note, to say hello and reiterate what a hit they had been in the United States. I picked up the receiver and sure enough, there was HM, full of life and good cheer but annoyed that Jessica had not told them in advance of her visit. We had a good ten-minute talk. He had placed the call himself, and Brenda walked on air at having talked to the king.

Later, at a staff meeting, I learned of a Russian agent actively trying — though unsuccessfully — to recruit American students as Soviet moles. He approached the Panamanian ambassador as well, again unsuccessfully. Not too smooth, but proof of my theory that Geneva was the home office of espionage.

After the Christmas holidays, I learned more details when the Panamanian ambassador asked to come by and see me. For weeks, he had been urged to defect by the Soviet KGB, and since he did not trust anyone in his mission and was anxious to talk about it, he turned to me.

It all began at a reception at the Chinese mission, where he had met a Romanian official, who invited him to lunch. They went and my new friend enjoyed it. They lunched several more times, and eventually the purpose of these lavish meals became clear. One day the Panamanian diplomat, drowsily enjoying himself in a public sauna, looked up to see the naked truth: the Romanian had plopped down next to him, more importunate than ever. Having tired of the courtship, the Panamanian sent him packing and felt relieved that it was over.

Shortly thereafter, the pursuit began again, this time with the Russians. They wanted to know about the Panama Canal, about the negotiations for a new canal treaty. The Panamanian explained that he knew nothing about such things. Greatly agitated, he told me communists had infiltrated the Panamanian government. I assured him I would report all this, which I did. I never heard from him again.

I soon learned a lesson in bureaucracy. The U.S. government had long planned to build a new building to house our mission. Plans proceeded apace, and though I knew I would never serve there, I supported the idea, our current quarters being inconvenient, inefficient, and run-down.

Poring over the plans, I learned to my amazement that the offices of the disarmament negotiator and the trade representative hadn't been included in the building.

"How much do we pay for these offices?" I asked. After a bit of research, they came up with the rent paid annually: $550,000. I asked if we couldn't add a couple of floors to the plan we had; at more than a half million a year, it couldn't take long to pay for it. The architect said it could be done, but the State Department guy with us balked.

"For goodness' sake," he said, "don't stir that up. All it will do is cause delay, and we have the money for this thing. I grant it doesn't make sense, but we would have to have new congressional hearings and it would just take too long. We can add it later."

"No," I retorted. "I'm going to stir it up." When they left my office, I wrote to both the State Department and the head of the Office of Management and Budget. Actually, our bureaucrat friend was doubtless right. Rents and capital expenditures didn't come out of the same governmental pocket and were not controlled by the same congressional committees.

This bizarre matter illustrated two things that I had learned. First, no administration can hope to remake the government; Congress's creaky system of perks and jurisdiction makes it impossible (and the proliferation of subcommittees since those days makes it even worse today). Second, our system of having noncareer people in ambassadorial posts is not without its strengths. A career ambassador might well have simply shrugged and gone with the flow. As a noncareer person, I could afford to tilt at windmills and — occasionally — knock one over.

In mid-December, Nancy Kissinger called saying she was in Europe and wondered if she could come visit. We were delighted; Nancy and Jessica had become good friends, and I liked her as well. Having high-ranking houseguests was not, however, easy. Security men preceded her, turning the house upside down to install a complete communications system. Sixteen security guards bobbed in her wake. I had no doubt that Henry had threats made against him, but I strongly suspected that his concern, rather than any concrete danger, dictated the protection Nancy got.

Nonetheless, it was fun. We took her to lunch at the beautiful fifty-room house of our friend Pierre Sciclounoff, an attorney, and had a small dinner for her that evening. After the guests left, she and Jessica talked until the wee hours, how late I knew not, for I gave up and went to bed at two o'clock.

My parents having come for a good visit in October, we decided on a Swiss Christmas. Sandra de Borchgrave, Arnaud's wife, helped us rent a flat in Gstaad, a ski resort one hundred miles from Geneva. In spite of our years of going to Aspen, I had never learned to ski, and though a bit long in the tooth to learn now, I determined to get started. And ski we did, lots of it, helped by a fine Swiss instructor named Emanuel Welten.[1]

It turned out to be a good family vacation and glamorous to boot; We went to Elizabeth Taylor's flat for a cocktail party and met luminaries of filmdom, such as Audrey Hepburn, David Niven, and James Mason. Edna and Brenda came for Christmas Day, the children found many chums from school, and even though Jessica broke a rib in a fall, it slowed neither her nor us down. We met and thoroughly enjoyed economist and liberal guru John Kenneth Galbraith and his family. Clearly, he was liberal-minded; associating with a Republican proved it.

New Year's night we went to a black-tie dinner thrown by the Saudi ambassador to the United States, Ali Alireza, and his wife, Hugette. Heather, having a few days previously given their daughter a skiing lesson, was also invited. The ambassador held forth all evening to Jessica on the evils of presidential adviser Zbigniew Brzezinski. Never had we seen as many high people in low-cut dresses, with more diamonds than a South African mine. Heather was awed. So were we.

Returning to the mission, the reality of a desk groaning with accumulated mail was eased by a box from James Catto & Co., Scotch Whiskey Blenders and Exporters. An enclosed note read: "Dear Mr. Catto: I heard you speak on the BBC "Today" programme last week and enjoyed your quip about Henry Kissinger and offering to carry his parcels. Since our excellent Scotch whiskey bears your famous name, we thought it might be appropriate to send you a little Christmas cheer with our best wishes. Sincerely, J. R. Wray, Managing Director." Two weeks previously, BBC radio had done a farewell profile of Henry, and as one of the interviewees, I had recounted the tale of the secretary and his purchases in Egypt. My dad had always served Catto's at home, and receiving some of that velvety beverage brightened the day. Never underestimate the power of the media.

In January I headed the American delegation to the Conference on Territorial Asylum, whose aim was to draw up an agreement on when a signatory should grant asylum to refugees. As always, the delegates broke into caucuses, Western (including Australia, Japan, and Israel), Communist, Latin American, Asian, and African. The West had a candidate, an Austrian, to head the key committee, and as is the custom in multilateral diplomacy, we made gentlemen's agreements with the Asians and Africans to support our guy, and we in turn would support their man for the presidency of the convention. We did not expect or foresee the political skills of the Latin Americans. Invoking Third World solidarity, they lured away many Asians and Africans, and before it ended, their Brazilian had swamped our Austrian, 46 – 36. From this humiliation I learned two things: First, the idea of "gentlemen" in the late twentieth century was a quaint anachronism. Second, if you wanted votes you had to ask for them. We sat in our comfortable caucus room dealing with supposed power brokers. The Latins stalked the corridors and politicked, working on each delegate. It was brilliantly effective. Besides, the Brazilian was a pretty able person.

Inevitably, inauguration day arrived and James Earl Carter became what the Secret Service calls POTUS (President of the United States). Heather called to commiserate about my impending fate, which cheered me greatly. I had asked Democrats Bob Strauss, Lloyd Bentsen, and Abe Ribicoff to investigate the odds of our staying in Geneva through the school year. All of them agreed on the diagnosis: the chances were slim to none. Secretary of State Cyrus Vance had made an early European tour and had cut Republican ambassador Anne Armstrong out of his meeting in London, a gratuitous insult. Hearing about it, Ambassador Ken Rush in Paris left town to avoid a similar slight. Fortunately, Vance did not come to Geneva. Another dolorous signal came with the wholesale firing of the three ambassadors to the UN in New York and the assistant secretary of state for international organizations. One Republican holdover in New

York got a phone call and heard the following: "Say, I'm the guy that's going to take your job. When can I come by and learn what the job is all about?" Not too smooth, for the incumbent had heard nothing from State.

Democrats began to appear in Geneva. I thought it must have been like the first Germans to arrive in Paris in 1940 after France surrendered. They were suspicious and so, certainly, were we. Some of that first wave, however, charmed us, in particular Allard Lowenstein, a former member of Congress and leader in the 1968 "Dump LBJ" movement, who was sent over as head of the U.S. delegation to a human rights meeting. He was so contagiously jovial and so bright that we made friends and invited him to dinner. Both of us liked him and were deeply saddened when he was murdered by an insane man some months later.

For all his charm, Al made waves. Angered by a move to condemn Israel in one of the meetings, he came up with the idea of condemning the USSR for a recent arrest of a human rights protester. When State heard about it, he was icily informed that delegates to international meetings, even former members of Congress, did not declare unilateral verbal war without telling Washington.

An even more controversial arrival was the Reverend Brady Tyson, special assistant to the new UN ambassador, Andrew Young. Young himself had caused ulcers in Washington by publicly announcing that the Cuban mercenaries recently arrived in Angola were a force for stability. Tyson, at the Geneva meeting, met with and drafted rights resolutions with Brazilian terrorists. I was incredulous; Democrats really *were* different.

Congressman Ed Derwinski came to town and we had a dinner for him. Of Polish ancestry and able to speak Polish, he told of being head of a U.S. delegation to a meeting in Warsaw. He had been invited to a dinner at the U.S. embassy and decided to walk to get there. Seeing a bar, he went in, told the bartender who he was and that the drinks were on him. He stayed and visited for a few minutes and went on, pleased with his person-to-person diplomacy. Spotting another bar, he repeated the scenario. He arrived at the ambassador's dinner as dessert was being served, and then learned to his chagrin that he had been the guest of honor. We were relieved on hearing the story that he didn't speak French; he might never have gotten to our house.

Sometime in February we had made the difficult decision to return to

Washington. Clearly, the Carter administration had zero sympathy for the educational problems of Republican schoolchildren. John had returned to St. Albans School as a boarder, and Will had been readmitted as well. Isa would go to the Potomac School, and Heather would stay at Franklin, then enter Williams College as a freshman in September.

Our last days in Geneva involved a number of farewell parties and a good bit of skiing with Janet and Bill Walker, the U.S. deputy trade representative. We left on March 15. I was sorry to have it end. French lessons had made me, if not fluent, at least fair in that rich language. I liked the ancient city, so redolent of history. And the job's great variety made it a challenge.

Return to the Private Sector

MORE THAN once we had wondered about being in Washington but out of power. Would anyone remember our name? And, of course, what we would do loomed large. I had told several Swiss and British friends that I planned to open a consulting office, and as time went by, those contacts proved fruitful. Edgar de Picciotto's Swiss bank retained me as its Washington representative, as did the British conglomerate Hanson Industries and media mogul Rupert Murdoch. A string of such clients was less a tribute to me than a recognition that Washington, the political capital of America, had become in no small measure as important as New York, the country's financial heart. Having representation there was comforting to Swiss, Briton, and Australian alike, and having an ample income was assuredly comforting to me. Furthermore, I found a number of ad hoc clients. Marylou Sheils joined me as president of our small firm, and I felt quite content.

And Washington did, after all, quickly prove that underneath its cynical veneer lay many kind people and good friends. Susan Mary Alsop, the Rowland Evanses, the Lane Kirklands, the David Brinkleys, and many more welcomed us back, as did friends in the diplomatic corps, such as Sweden's able ambassador, Willie Wachtmeister, and his wife, Ulla, a superb painter; the Yaqub Khans of Pakistan; Iran's Ardisher Zahedi; and countless others.

So I was back to routine domestic life. Dog Ginger had nine pups.

Genoveva and David once again made the house hum, and it was then that two sons, German and Jorge, arrived from El Salvador, adding spice to our lives, as did the birth of a third, Juan Carlos.

I saw much more of the young. John and I drove through the East and West looking at colleges, and in September I drove Heather in a car groaning with her worldly goods to Williamstown to continue her college experience. Shortly thereafter she wrote us triumphantly: "Good news. I have only two AM classes, and they are both lectures and are in dark rooms!"

I stayed active in public policy. President Carter and my old friend Ambassador Sol Linowitz negotiated the highly controversial Panama Canal Treaty. While many Republicans, including Ronald Reagan, loathed it, I joined a group led by Democratic panjandrum Averell Harriman in urging its passage. While I was ambassador in El Salvador, Jessica and I had toured the canal by helicopter, and I had become convinced that without a treaty of devolution of the canal to Panama, we would find ourselves having to defend it against guerrilla attacks. A small group of men with rifles could terrorize ships inching slowly through the locks and then fade into the jungle. Failure to grant sovereignty would, I felt, leave us with a running sore and cause serious damage to our relations with the rest of Latin America.

Getting to know the Harrimans, both of them, was interesting. Averell, son of railroad magnate Edward Harriman, was tall, handsome, and lean like his father, but without the latter's large beaver mustache. Born in 1891, he lived a full life. President Franklin Roosevelt brought him to government during World War II as expediter of the provisions of the Lend-Lease Act to our allies. For three crucial years he served as ambassador to the Soviet Union, and later to Great Britain. President Kennedy appointed him assistant secretary of state for far eastern affairs, and President Johnson named him U.S. representative to the Paris Peace Talks to end the Vietnam War. As governor of New York and thus a national political power, he ran for the Democratic presidential nomination, with singular lack of success. Pamela Harriman, once Winston Churchill's daughter-in-law and later President Clinton's ambassador to France, was lively, lovely, and easy to talk to. Averell by then was crusty, deaf, and rude to his wife, but nonetheless a presence in the meetings that took place in their handsome Georgetown house.

In October 1977 I went to Europe, primarily to join Lloyds of London as a "name" or underwriter of that great insurance organization. I thought it made sense; insurance was my family's business, so I knew a good bit about it. Traditionally it had made good money for the names, though lurking in the deep background was the caveat that each name pledged his entire worth if need be to cover claims. As it turned out, Lloyds fell on troubled times and in 1985 I resigned, though ten years later I was still not entirely free of what they call "long tail run-off" claims.

From London I flew to Geneva to call on my client, banker Edgar de Picciotto, and to see our many other friends. The real excitement of the trip, however, lay in getting there, which proved to be more than half the fun. A Briton by the name of Freddie Laker had started what he called a Skytrain, a jumbo jet totally without amenities that flew New York to London in seven hours for about $150.

The antithesis of Laker was British Airways' supersonic Concorde that made the London–New York trip in three hours and forty-five minutes but cost more than ten times the fare for Laker's lumberer. I decided to fly Laker over and treat myself to Concorde on the return, averaging out at about what a normal airline would cost.

As I thought about it, a flaky idea struck. "Why not," I asked myself, "write an article about the two extremes of air travel and peddle it to enough papers to pay for the whole trip?" To my delight, it worked. How many who couldn't otherwise afford Concorde followed my lead I don't know. All I know is I had fun — especially coming home.

The year 1978, a quiet starter, didn't stay that way for long. In April, Henry Kissinger asked Jessica to read and help edit the manuscript of the first volume of his memoirs, a task she took to readily. I found his prose heavy and Germanic, and I thought Jessica's suggestions invariably good ones. The finished product, on which a number of people worked, was thoroughly readable, and his later works are first-rate.

I went to Cuba in May with a group organized by former Peace Corps director Joseph Blatchford. The ostensible purpose of the trip, promoting trade, disguised another motive: curiosity. Travel to the communist island ran contrary to U.S. policy, but for a brief time, Carter's administration opened a bit of a window and groups like ours went.

I had expected the group to be Marxist-leaning leftists, and indeed, some fit that description. Nonetheless, Tories too wanted to see our Red neighbor, and we had editors from *Readers Digest* and *Human Events* with us. What made the trip for me was a most agreeable academic named Roger Fontaine, a fellow Spanish speaker and runner.

Roger and I ran every day along the famed Malecón, the broad avenue bounding the harbor. Invariably, bands of tatterdemalions of eight or ten years, frequently barefoot, tagged along.

"*Hola, señor,*" one would say. "What are you running from?"

"Nothing, lad," we would answer. "We just like exercise."

"What will you give us? How about your shoes?" one asked one day.

"No way, *hijo mío,*" I replied. "They are the only ones I have."

Eventually, they would tire and break away, but people in Havana found a pair of scantily clad middle-aged men running through their city fascinating. Friendly, if bewildered, many would greet us and on several occasions we were saluted by "*Hola, tovarish!*" as the Cubans assumed that only a Russian, of which there were many in Cuba, would be so dumb as to run in the midday sun.

The city through which we trotted was depressing, as was the whole country. Fidel Castro might brag of his health and educational systems, but the economy was clearly a shambles. Through the streets rolled a fleet of 1950s American cars, a veritable museum of out-of-date vehicles held together with gum and baling wire. The buildings flaked paint like dandruff. Above all, it was boring. No vendors crowded the streets, no shops invited travelers or locals, neon lights meant dull revolutionary slogans. Frequently, a furtive and frightened person, assuming that we were neither Cuban nor Russian, would pull us aside and, telling a sad story about the need to buy a gift for a father or a lover, would beg us to go to the hard-currency store maintained solely for foreigners and buy what was needed. We resisted, fearing a setup by the highly effective DGI, the Cuban secret police, but my guess was they were real people, sick of being unable to purchase anything beyond revolutionary posters.

We met with officials, bankers, bureaucrats, and trading company types, all of whom wanted us to urge Carter to end the boycott. Rumors of a meeting with Castro himself proved wrong, though our guides tantalized us with the possibility until the last minute.

In early June, my parents, my aunt Liz Pritchett, and Jessica's mother converged on Washington to see John graduate. At 2:30 A.M. on the morning of the graduation I fumbled to silence the insistent phone, to learn that John, on his way home from a graduation party, had been in an accident and was at Fairfax County Hospital. They wouldn't tell us his condition.

We learned it was bad when we arrived. Hit head-on while driving my small Honda, he had multiple injuries: a broken leg, ribs, and skull; a damaged eye and general trauma. The car was a total loss, and had he not been wearing a seat belt, he would likely have been killed. As it was, he had to have surgery on an eye and his leg, could eat no solids for six weeks, and spent two months in a body cast. I went to search the crumpled remains of my car in hopes of finding salvageable teeth but had no luck. The young man who hit him was uninjured, uninsured, unsober, and unrepentant. Will accepted John's diploma later that day, and his many close and supportive friends and his siblings helped him through a long, uncomfortable, and boring — but full — recovery.

Investments in Politics and Publishing

IN 1978 George Bush took the first step on the road that would lead to the White House. In August, Jessica and I had a fundraising dinner at our house in McLean, Virginia, the first of many Bush functions across the country. I kept a fairly constant flow of ideas going to George and Jim Baker, his campaign manager. One concern was that there were more volunteers than there were jobs for them to do, at least in the Washington area. When offers of help went unheeded, lips got trembly.

Jim had asked me to run George's effort in the Puerto Rico primary. Though not a state, Puerto Rico had politics of a vigor that made the jousts on the mainland seem like croquet. Those people really cared about politics. To draw attention to the island's concerns, a decision was made to upstage all the states by having the very first political event of the 1980 election year, even before the Iowa caucuses, held in Puerto Rico. In January 1979, I flew to San Juan, met Republican leaders, including former governor Luis Ferré, and spoke at a rally of volcanic intensity.

On my return to Washington, I looked up an attorney named Luis Ginot, who practiced in both Washington and San Juan and who wanted to help George. He proved to be invaluable and became a good friend as well. Indeed, thanks to the efforts of Luis and of the Bushes' Spanish-speaking son Jeb, we won the primary, and in so doing jolted the stateside politicians who had deprecated George's candidacy.

With Heather and John in college, demands on Jessica's time abated and she began to think about a career. I heard that a local magazine of journalistic criticism, the *Washington Journalism Review* (*WJR*), might be for sale. Lacking capital, owner Roger Kranz had struggled to keep it going but had reached the end of his tether. He and I met for lunch and based on what I reported, Jessica decided it could be interesting. I bought it and she became publisher. Katherine Winton Evans, wife of columnist Rowland Evans, came aboard as editor, teaming with art director David Kidd. The three of them put together a staff that turned the struggling magazine into a respected national voice on matters journalistic, and Jessica ceased being "wife of" for good. We gave *WJR* to the school of journalism at the University of Maryland in 1985, but for more than six years it was a source of great pride, proving Jessica to be a first-class publisher.

With the prime interest rate hitting 21 percent in 1980, inflation rampant, and all America shamed by the disastrous failure of the attempt to rescue American hostages in Iran, Republicans felt hopeful. Ronald Reagan loomed large as the clear favorite for the nomination, but George Bush continued to run strongly and remained a viable candidate until May, when Reagan became unstoppable and George withdrew, the last Reagan rival to do so. We were sorry; in addition to working on the Puerto Rico primary, I had been a speaker for Bush, had raised money, and generally did what I could without going full-time. Our disappointment at his loss, however, was considerably assuaged when Reagan tapped George to be vice president.

In February, Susan Mary Alsop had a dinner party at her Georgetown home for Prince and Princess Michael of Kent, he being the queen's cousin and they being very active members of the royal family. Asked to come early, we did, and Susan Mary had everything organized as if it were the D day invasion. I was to start off the cocktail hour by sitting next to Princess Michael. After ten minutes, I was to move on, my place would be taken by someone else, and so it would go until dinner, with the royal guests never left untended.

At the appointed hour sharp, the guests arrived. He was tall, beautifully tailored, and pleasant; she was blond and gorgeous. I looked forward to my assignment.

We settled in the drawing room, and recalling the advice of her in-law the queen on keeping conversation going, I asked a question my most debonair way. "How was the trip?" I assayed. "Fine," she responded. "Do you know Washington well?" "Reasonably," she said. "Have you known our hostess well?" I offered, getting antsy. "Not too," came back.

By then, I was invoking the queen in my mind, desperately. Had I forgotten a key element of the game? Did I have halitosis?

I recalled that she liked art, and I inquired as to her interests. Just for a second, a spark seemed to have been struck. Eagerly, I followed up: "Do you collect?" "No," she sniffed, "we inherit." Defeated, I withdrew from the field.

In March I got a call from Viktor Lessiovski, my friend from Moscow who had recently become an assistant secretary general of the UN in New York. He and his wife were coming to Washington and wanted to visit. Although I knew that Viktor was KGB, I invited them to our McLean house for lunch. He was lively and I might just learn something from him.

On the appointed day, they arrived in a rental car. Mrs. Lessiovski struck me as rather unprepossessing, toting a large purse and sporting heavily hennaed hair. The four of us settled on the screen porch. With no warning, the bag opened and out popped a rheumy-eyed toy poodle, who proceeded to sit sulking in mama's lap for the rest of the visit. "We always travel with her," Mrs. Lessiovski explained dulcetly. Viktor looked vaguely embarrassed.

Conversation flowed easily. We caught each other up on our comings and goings, did a survey of the world's hot spots, and discussed the future of Soviet-American relations. At one point Viktor said he'd like to see my art, so I took him on a tour.

I showed him the three primitive oil paintings I had bought in 1975 in Moscow, thinking to pay a compliment to the quality of Soviet art. Viktor, however, looked sour, and it suddenly occurred to me that he was KGB and doubtless disapproved of underground, unauthorized art. "God," I thought, "I hope he doesn't send word to the KGB that the artist was subverting the system." I took comfort in the knowledge that the name signed in the corner was a pseudonym, but my conscience nonetheless bothered me. I never learned if "A. Arkhov" suffered from my indiscretion.

Over coffee, Viktor let his hair down. He told us he had been offered an embassy in an African country but had turned it down because the Mrs. didn't want to live there. He groused that he had not been asked to join the prestigious USA-Canada Institute, a Moscow think tank, because he didn't have a Ph.D. "I know more about America than any of those clowns," he huffed, "but they don't want me just because of a scrap of paper."

I found his comments fascinating. They said to me that Soviets have family and career problems even as we in the West do. I repeated this story later to my staunch anti-communist friend, journalist Arnaud de

Borchgrave. "What a dupe you are," Arnaud scoffed. "Communist apparatchiks go where they are told." Dupe or not, I continued to believe that no matter how dehumanizing the Soviet system was, it nonetheless couldn't stamp out human nature entirely.

The year went by swiftly, as they increasingly and annoyingly tend to do. Heather and I went to Tanzania with my old friend Bernard Lifshutz and hiked up Mount Kilimanjaro. I wrote articles from time to time for such varied publications as the *New York Times, Newsweek,* and *National Review.* And I tended my consulting clients with some success. To my great sorrow, my mother died in August, the result of complications from a fall and a broken hip. Dad, unprepared for life without her, followed her on Christmas Eve of 1981.

When November 4 rolled around at last and the Reagan-Bush ticket swept to landslide victory, Jessica and I were elated. Having voted, as always, in San Antonio, we flew over to Houston to join the Bushes in their celebration, an event made even sweeter by having the Republicans capture the Senate for the first time since Eisenhower's first term, in 1952. Jessica and I both had doubts about Reagan, but his choice of Bush as running mate and his performance in the campaign put them to rest, at least for me. His early moves as president-elect were surefooted and professional, especially naming Jim Baker chief of staff. The Reagans also showed great savvy by having a party for the Washington establishment well before the inauguration, to rave reviews in the local press.

New Administration, New Job

HAVING BEEN at Nixon's inauguration festivities, we knew better than to do that routine again. So on January 20 I went to a birthday party for Jocelyn Straus, a longtime friend and Republican activist from San Antonio, and afterward went home and to bed by ten. Jessica didn't even leave the house.

This lack of interest did not mean I was unaffected by the return of the True Faith to the White House. Four years spent as a consultant had their joys, but I was ready to get back in the government swing, and my eye was set on ambassador to the United Nations in New York. I let George know, but it quickly became clear that Bush planned a very low profile in the new administration, and until he and Reagan had established a firm relationship, he would be reluctant to push his friends for jobs.

In November, George and Madeleine Will had a dinner honoring the Reagans. George, a syndicated columnist and our close friend, knew I had hopes of serving the new administration; he also knew that I did not know the president-elect. To remedy this, he not only invited us to the dinner, he also told me he was going to seat me next to Nancy.

This was good news indeed, and I thought out in advance conversational gambits that might interest her. Meanwhile, during the cocktail hour, I listened to Reagan tell stories and charm all concerned.

Dinner served, I turned my full attention to impressing Nancy. I might as well have tried to melt an iceberg with a cigarette lighter; to say she was hard to talk to would be a grotesque understatement. I had thought Britain's Princess Michael was a conversational challenge, but she was a piece of cake by comparison. Later, we read with amusement of a conversation reported by Mrs. Reagan's biographer, Kitty Kelly. Apparently, one of the doyennes of Georgetown was telling the by-then first lady whom she might want to get to know and mentioned us among others. "The Cattos?" she sniffed. "Who needs them?"

As it turned out, the Pentagon did. Early in January, Bill Walker, a friend from Geneva days, called. He had been talking to Deputy Defense Secretary Frank Carlucci and learned that Frank and his boss, Caspar Weinberger, were looking for an assistant secretary for public affairs. Bill suggested me. While ignorant on defense matters, Bill explained, Catto knew all the media heavies in town, thanks in no small way to *WJR*. Frank agreed to talk to "Cap," as Weinberger was called, and an appointment with me was set for January 22, two days after the inauguration.

The three of us met in Weinberger's gigantic office for about ten minutes. I made no bones of my ignorance, but then neither Weinberger nor Carlucci had Pentagon experience, so I hoped they would assume me capable of learning. A few days later I got the word: I was to be assistant secretary and Pentagon spokesman. I told my consulting business associate Marylou Sheils that we would be closing down and that I hoped she would accompany me to the Pentagon. She agreed, and we were off on a new adventure.[2]

Secretary Weinberger was impatient to get me going, and I began to function well before the Senate confirmed me. Indeed, in early April of 1981 I accompanied the secretary to London, Bonn, and Rome. Danger lay in such an action. If the Senate got word that I took confirmation for granted, it could have become sticky. It did not. The only bow I made to propriety lay in not briefing the press, which suited me fine; I had little enthusiasm for entering the bear pit. On May 2, the Senate okayed me as assistant secretary of defense for public affairs.

The job I assumed was broad in its scope. For the benefit of our military personnel, we operated the biggest media conglomerate in the world. Armed Forces Radio and TV consisted of 34 television stations, 95 radio stations, and 260 cable outlets. We published a daily newspaper, *Stars and Stripes,* a tabloid magazine, and a "thought" magazine. We had a full-time satellite.

PA, as it was known, handled the freedom-of-information requests that poured into the Pentagon. Our community relations directorate saw to it that the military were good citizens of the hundreds of communities where the armed forces operated throughout the country. We reviewed all speeches given by the military to check them for policy and security considerations. We operated a full-time journalism school, graduating some two thousand persons a year. We decided whether or not the Pentagon would cooperate with Hollywood when it planned a film on the military; if a script seemed balanced and positive, we cooperated, but if it was anti-military, we sent the Hollywooders packing. Finally, PA responded to the needs of journalists from throughout the world, by briefings, interviews, visits to military installations and ships at sea (carriers were particularly popular).

Although I managed to put off my first press briefing, thanks to travel and getting confirmed, inevitably the day arrived. Hard-eyed professionals, the Pentagon reporters knew much about defense and nothing about the quality of mercy. The prospect of facing them was daunting.

I was, to be sure, prepared. Before each briefing, I met with six or eight of the PA staff for what we called a "murder board." In it, for as long as it took, they threw questions and I rehearsed answers. Topics of the day were for the most part predictable. The previous evening's TV news and the headlines from the day's *New York Times, Washington Post,* and *Wall Street Journal* set the agenda. We always read Jack Anderson's column carefully, for he often turned up matters that could prove troublesome. Curiously, I almost never got a question based on an Anderson column. He did not attend the briefings and his colleagues of the Fourth Estate never read his work, so I was spared.

The staff were good at guessing questions but from time to time we would be totally blindsided. For example, a reporter named Lester

Kinsolving constantly came at me from outer space. An Episcopal priest turned gadfly journalist, he hit me early on with the following:

LESTER: The Secretary of the Interior [James Watt] told the *Los Angeles Times* last week that President Reagan was his "soulmate" and that the Administration is engaged in a crusade which has both theological as well as military connotations and my question is, since the Secretary of the Interior has also testified to Congress that "I do not know how many future generations we can count on before the Lord returns," could you tell us if the Secretary of Defense agrees or disagrees with the Secretary of the Interior's apocalyptic view?

HENRY: Unfortunately, I guess you weren't here the day before yesterday when I compared our batting average on being able to anticipate questions with the average of the hapless Chicago Cubs. Here again, I have to confess that this was not one we anticipated.

LESTER: Henry—I'd be most interested in Cap Weinberger's view on whether the Lord is coming.

HENRY: As a Christian, I'm sure he agrees.

LESTER: He's an Episcopalian.

HENRY: You make a distinction between Christian and Episcopalian?

LESTER: No, I was just thinning it out.

The tussle with Les that got the biggest guffaw went as follows:

LESTER: If you were Secretary of Defense, Henry, and the State Department suggested that you allow armed P.L.O. people to come aboard the ships over which you had supervision, you'd resign rather than allow that, wouldn't you, Henry? (laughter)

HENRY: Lester, I'm reminded of another Henry, in this case Henry II, who at a point of exasperation with Thomas à Becket said, "Who will free me of this turbulent priest?"

LESTER: He was murdered in the north transept and Henry went and scourged himself every year for the rest of his life—remember that.

HENRY: By George, it might be worth it, Lester, I don't know. (laughter)

When Israel pre-emptively destroyed an Iraqi nuclear reactor in 1981, much debate ensued on whether their strike was defensive or offensive. The following exchange took place:

LESTER: On the way in I saw a very impressive photograph, I mean a portrait, of General Pershing, who I recall just prior to World War I took a small American army across the border into Mexico pursuing a terrorist. Does the Department of Defense feel that was a legitimate self-defense?

HENRY (to an aide): Remind me to take that picture down, will you?

Kinsolving occasionally pointed out that the king had no clothes. There was a sex scandal of some sort at the Naval Academy and Lester asked what else one could expect when 4,200 healthy young males lived in the same barracks as 277 healthy young women. Actually, Lester was useful to me. Put in a box on some difficult topic, I could always deflect the fire by calling on him, sure in the knowledge that he would radically change the subject. For this and other sins, the regulars loathed Lester; though he frustrated me, I liked him.

A Pentagon briefer found himself totally at the mercy of the senior reporter, who by tradition closed the session when there were no more questions. In my time, this puppeteer was longtime Associated Press correspondent Fred Hoffman, a man vastly knowledgeable about defense matters. As the questioning wound down (after running hot and heavy for anywhere from thirty minutes to an hour), I would begin to cross my fingers and look imploringly at Fred to say the traditional "Thank you," thus ending the session. Sometimes, if he were annoyed with me, he would sit silent, knowing I was anxious but helpless. Of course, the time of silence seemed endless and when Fred would finally relent, I would silently thank God and get out of there.

In my first briefing, I annoyed the whole group. Traditionally, the briefer would be asked how many Soviet and how many American ships were in the Mediterranean, that number being seen as an index of the state of tension between the two. Weinberger, learning of this tradition, instructed me not to tell the American number. To me that seemed foolish and quirky. Soviet intelligence likely knew how many vessels we had, and giving the exact number could do no harm. When I so informed the press, they were incredulous and seriously disturbed, seeing the new rule as an indication that the new administration planned to clam up with the media.

I took a good bit of grief on the opening day, and in every subsequent briefing, the question was asked. After a time, I got a reprieve and was allowed to give an approximate number, "about thirty" or whatever. By the end of my tenure, we had relaxed entirely and were once again giving the precise number.

One amusing sidelight of the ship matter showed that the members of the press were not all heartless. Asked the usual question about ship numbers, I was searching absentmindedly through my notes for the answer. Finding it, I said, "Let's see, there are thirty-seven Soviet shits in the Mediterranean." The room exploded with laughter and I turned suitably red, but the gaff didn't see print.

A more serious kind of embarrassment could arise when the press played their favorite game of hunting for differences among White House, State, and Pentagon. Shortly after President Sadat of Egypt died in a hail of assassins' bullets, a reporter asked about a U.S. military exercise in the Eastern Mediterranean. Had it been planned, he asked, as a response to possible unrest in the wake of Sadat's death? Knowing it had been planned for some time, I said no. The reporter leapt on me gleefully. "You are aware," he sneered, "that you are apparently contradicting what the Secretary of State said . . . you are creating an opposite impression and that is what you intend to do."

I, of course, had no idea what Secretary Haig had said; no one could keep up with the comments of all officials all the time. It did, however, provide a reporter with a splendid chance to play "Gotcha!"

The three press offices did try to coordinate via a daily conference call (incidentally, on an unclassified open phone line, available to Soviet penetration) to decide who would handle what among the foreseeable questions. We met at the White House every Thursday as well, looking to upcoming events with an eye to spinning them to our advantage. Still, lacking total prescience, we inevitably fell into traps such as I described.

A situation of a different kind arose when the *Washington Post*'s George Wilson came into my office one day, looking very serious indeed.

Without a word he handed me a letter. On Pentagon stationery and signed "Caspar," it dripped with anti-Semitism and dealt with selling AWACS radar planes to Saudi Arabia, a move vehemently opposed by Israel.

"This is serious," George said. "What do you have to say about it?"

I read the letter again and said, "George, it's a forgery." I explained. In the first place, Cap *never* signed himself "Caspar." It was "Caspar W. Weinberger" in formal situations or "Cap" to people he knew. Second, in the third paragraph lurked something everyone knew Cap loathed: a split infinitive. Weinberger, a stickler for correct grammar, would not have made such an error. George acknowledged it immediately, and though he wanted me to take him to see Cap (which I did), he had no further doubts.

All Over the Map with Cap

WEINBERGER'S ITCHY FOOT suited me very well indeed. I always accompanied him when he traveled, and we went often and in style. He usually used LBJ's old *Air Force One,* a well-appointed if elderly Boeing 707 with a cabin for Cap and his wife, Jane, and bunks for me and Cap's military assistant, a very bright Air Force two-star general named Carl Smith.

The trips could be lively. On an Asian swing we went to Korea and visited the demilitarized zone. The reporters accompanying us were eager to get as close as possible to the line, and in preparation the Army briefed us extensively.

One point made in the briefing was that we should not exchange *any* recognition, signal, wink, grimace, or even a smile and a nod with North Korean guards whose eye we might catch. Such acknowledgments of common humanity infuriated the tetchy and paranoid communists, and they tended to bring even the smallest thing up at the regular meeting of the UN–North Korean commission that supervised the shaky peace.

I reinforced these warnings to my reporter charges and took them off to bleachers where we could scan the communist post at leisure through field glasses, even as they did the same to us.

All of us silently scoped the scene, thinking how thin the line between war and peace. Suddenly, I heard a snicker from the group behind me. Whipping around, I couldn't believe what I saw. There was George Lewis, veteran NBC-TV reporter, holding up a hand-lettered sign. It read, FUCK YOU, COMMIE BASTARDS. Half horrified and half convulsed with laughter, I got him to take it down. We were probably too far away for it to be seen, and they probably couldn't read English anyway.

An autumn NATO-related trip to France, Sweden, Scotland, and England was in the offing, and I suggested to Weinberger that if Jane Weinberger was going, perhaps inviting Jessica and Marty Smith, Carl Smith's wife, would be in order. His noncommittal response wiped the idea from my mind, but two days before departure he invited them, to my delight and to Jessica's as well.

Every stop proved educational, for I learned much about NATO and its problems, but it was also fun; we even had haggis, the traditional Scottish entrail dish that requires a healthy splash of Scotch whisky to down. For me, the education lay in learning a bit about the power of anger as a tool of intimidation.

There having been dozens of press availabilities during our stops, Weinberger and I decided to inform the traveling press that we would have no briefings returning from London to Washington. This "putting the lid on" meant the press could relax, knowing we would have nothing to say.

Alas, not everyone got the word. The *Washington Post*'s George Wilson had been off on some jaunt of his own and was not aware that there would be no briefing. Learning the situation as he boarded the plane, he became surly; he needed to file something. His fury and the clout of his paper eventually won the day, and I convinced Cap at least to make a statement on our arrival at Andrews Air Force Base, thus saving George's bacon.

There were always reporters wanting to accompany Cap; the networks, the national dailies, the wire services, and the weekly magazines, such as *Time* and *Newsweek,* went along every time. Invariably, their reporters were bright and attractive, and I made friends with many of them after hours, no matter how vigorous the sparring during briefings.

One event early in my tenure troubled me. Cap sent for me and told me he wanted me to hire his Harvard classmate Ben Welles, a former *New York Times* reporter, as my deputy. My fear was that, given Cap and Ben's long relationship, I would be cut out of the action. I need not have worried. Ben, whom I had known slightly, became a close friend and confidant, never trying to bypass me by trading on his friendship with our boss, whom we dubbed "DOTFW" (Defender of the Free World).

Two career military people impressed me and helped make life easier: Colonel (later Brigadier General) Colin Powell and Lieutenant Colonel Mike Burch, Frank Carlucci's military assistant and my own, respectively. Mike, who succeeded me as assistant secretary, was a genius at foreseeing problems and offering solutions. Colin was the kind of man who made things (like paper and the decision-making process) move. Though he had a sense of humor, he inspired a bit of the awe I recall feeling in the presence of my headmaster at military school. The French would have called him an *homme serieux;* Jessica said, "He's at ease with himself."

Indeed, one of the great revelations of my tour at the Pentagon came from realizing that the services had countless men and women of extraordinary ability. At State, there had been a condescending attitude toward the military, considered clods compared to the elite of the foreign service. Wars, the cliché went, were planned by geniuses and carried out by morons. I came to realize it just wasn't so—good news for America.

The task the new administration faced would have daunted the weak-spirited, but Weinberger, fully backed by the president, would never be accused of that. As we saw it, the aftermath of Watergate followed by the Carter administration had left the United States weaker than it should have been vis-à-vis the Soviet Union. We needed to turn that equation around, increase spending well beyond Carter's levels, improve pay for the troops, modernize aging equipment, and push development of new weapons. The aim was twofold: to make us so strong that our adversaries would hesitate to be overtly hostile and at the same time to use our economic might to spend the Soviets into bankruptcy. It worked.

Certain decisions on strategic policy at last made, President Reagan called a press conference in the East Room of the White House to announce them. Cap went and I tagged along for the ride.

Reagan seemed to be at sea. He took two or three questions but muffed them badly. I writhed in embarrassed empathy. The president, over his head when queried about details, finally turned to Weinberger, to the relief of all.

Cap took the questions, answering not only with accuracy but also with remarkably sharp humor. Watching the faces of the reporters as they reacted to his tour de force was interesting. Many laughed along with everyone else. Some, however, remained stonily serious, whether from a determination for their faces to reflect the seriousness of the topic or from an atrophied funny bone, I couldn't tell. I developed a theory: anyone who could hear what we heard and not crack a smile could not conceivably be a balanced person and provide a balanced picture of events.

By the end of 1981 we had a clear plan of how to proceed from the public affairs standpoint. Our goal was to convince the Congress and the people that the threat was real and that we needed to respond. We looked at a map of the country and at a list of forthcoming events, such as holidays, dedications, congressional hearings, meetings. We then plotted trips, especially by Weinberger and Carlucci but also by other senior officials, to cover every geographic region. In the past we had been reactive: A request would come in for the secretary to speak; our office would approve it if it looked good and send it along to Weinberger. If he approved, speechwriter Seth Cropsey (and his successor, Kathy Troia) would prepare a talk. We wanted this to change, with us setting the agenda, picking the topics, and determining the dates.

In addition, we inaugurated a series of "LBH dinners" ("LBH" standing for "long ball hitters"). At these events, leaders in business, labor, the church, publishing, education, and the nonprofit world came to hear a brief, tightly written slide presentation on the Soviet threat, after which we served dinner and opened the questioning. Articulate and humorous, Cap invariably made a hit, and while we didn't convince all our guests, many went away with a far better understanding of what we faced.

We began a program of having Cap write articles for major newspapers on topics of importance. I personally undertook to write replies to ill-informed editorials. It is amazing how editorial writers are ready to hold forth on topics about which they know almost nothing; maybe it's because they don't have to sign their names. In any case, I kept a steady flow of indignant responses to ill-considered pieces. Doing so let off steam and (I hoped) brought enlightenment to the benighted. In October 1984, for instance, *New York Times* columnist Tom Wicker suggested to my great annoyance that the shooting down of Korean Air Lines Flight 007 might have been provoked by the United States. I was long out of office, but I refuted his statements in a column published in the *Washington Post;* old habits die hard.

Weinberger began a series of private briefings for the "regulars," Pentagon reporters who had covered defense issues for the major media. This move angered the specialty press and small papers, but we aimed for numbers, not justice.

We published an annual book called *Soviet Military Power.* With first-rate illustrations, it documented the breadth of the new Soviet systems with renderings of their equipment based on captured examples (mostly by the Israelis) and on secret sources (mostly pictures taken by spies or sympathizers behind the Iron Curtain).

I wooed the press at "vespers," late-afternoon sessions in my office, where we served wine and cheese to the Pentagon reporters and often had a "mystery guest," a Pentagon official to whom they could talk in a relaxed environment.

The most imaginative idea in our campaign turned out to be highly controversial. I reasoned as follows: We knew from classified sources what the Soviets were doing, but the press had to accept our word on faith, an article always in short supply between press and government, especially post-Watergate. Why not give the reporters, good Americans all, a *classified* briefing? That way, they would know what we knew, at first hand. We had a respected Soviet expert named John Hughes who could do the briefing; surely everyone would benefit.

I broached the idea to Cap and the military. The former proved intrigued; the latter went ballistic. "Classified material to reporters?" they sputtered. "Preposterous." Our people explained patiently that reporters were not the moral equivalent of the KGB. They wanted stories that would help their viewers, listeners, and readers understand the huge and costly military buildup that Reagan proposed.

After serious thought, Weinberger came down on my side and we began to set it up. The brass, however, were harder to convince. They put conditions on the proposal, insisting that all participants would have to sign a statement saying they would keep what they learned on deep background and would report to the Defense Department anyone from the outside who made inquiries about where the information came from.

Ben Welles and I went along with these caveats. We should have known better. The great day finally arrived and all were assembled to look and learn from the lecture, slide show, and questions that were to ensue. As the ground rules were read, they was a good bit of mumbling. Richard Gross of UPI got up and after an impassioned speech, stalked out. Richard Halloran of the *New York Times* refused to attend, stating that he and his paper could have no part of an activity they participated in but could not report on. (Given the number of unsourced quotes appearing daily in the *Times* and in every paper, this struck me as passing strange.)

In the end, the wording of our rules was modified and the briefing took place. Those who did stay benefited and privately said so. But the great pompous *Times* blasted us in an editorial, the pith of which was "What is the Pentagon trying to hide?," a theme picked up by the *Washington Post,* the *Philadelphia Inquirer,* and several uninvited papers. Bud Mc-Farlane of the National Security Council sent a memo to President Reagan asserting that we had done it over NSC's objection, though if they objected, I never knew it. No good deed goes unpunished, the saying goes. Chagrined, I came to believe it.

Early in my tenure I learned a lesson about bureaucracy. PA had an office in New York City. On one of our trips to the metropolis, I visited it and got a thorough briefing on its vital nature. Skeptical, I asked around a bit and concluded that it mostly served to provide support, logistics, transport, and theater tickets for high-ranking officers visiting "the Apple." On my return, I recommended to the secretary that it be closed.

The services—Army, Navy, Air Force, and Marines—were united in few things, but in the reduction of perks, they were as one. They opposed the idea with such vigor (the leases had too long to run, and so on) that the closure never took place. For all I know, that office may still exist today, if perhaps in lesser quarters.

Channels of Communication

MY RELATIONS with Weinberger on a personal level became warm as time passed. He was a thoroughgoing gentleman, patient, humorous, and bright. His idea of my job and my own, however, differed. I felt that a press spokesman should be kept plugged in to everything, using guidance and his own knowledge to determine what questions to answer and how to answer them. Cap felt that if I didn't know, I couldn't make mistakes. A crisis with Libya came up early in our tenure, and I was roused from bed by the operations center to come at once to a conference on how to handle it. I beat the secretary to the meeting, but when he arrived and saw me there, he asked an aide why I was present. He was told my predecessors had always been included in such meetings.

As our public affairs plan took hold and he made more and more speaking trips around the country, I came to criticize his greatest fault: he talked too long. Armed with excellent speeches crafted by first-class writers, he would read along nicely until something would trigger a random thought and off he would go, extemporizing and eating up time. I constantly warned him from the audience by hand signals that he was running over the ideal of twenty minutes, which I felt was the maximum a listener's rear end could take. It was useless; we dubbed him a "textual deviate." As we left a speaking engagement he would frequently ask, dreading the answer, "How long did I go?" "Thirty-three minutes, boss," I would reply, and he would promise faithfully to do better next time.

At our LBH dinners his responses to guests' questions rattled on interminably, limiting the time for widespread questioning from a variety of those present. Indeed, one guest said in a thank-you note that he had enjoyed the evening but felt frustrated that his question never got asked; the secretary's answers to one or two other queries were too long. I duly reported this to Cap, to no avail. I wondered if it was an intentional tactic but concluded it was not.

Leaks at the Pentagon gave us constant indigestion. Perversely, many in the military ranks assumed that leaks came from PA. Some did—Ben occasionally let the old *New York Times* tie loosen his tongue—but the overwhelming majority came from individuals with personal or ideological axes to grind. If a policy seemed misguided to some mole buried deep in the bureaus, he felt empowered and justified by righteousness to tip a reporter friend, often causing a public outcry that could delay or derail decisions. In my briefings, I publicly decried the practice, to the annoyance of the reporter-beneficiaries of it. They felt—with some justification—that if it weren't for leaks, the public would never learn anything. In the end, I held to my belief: leakers don't know, can't know, the big picture, and they frequently do serious harm, being necessarily parochial. In retrospect, I have come to believe the services were too secretive, too often.

One case illustrated the problem. On ABC's *Evening News* one night, Pentagon reporter John McWethy reported that the United States had sent AWACS radar planes to Sudan, which was at the time involved in a war scare with fractious, leftist Libya. We had not wanted this move revealed, Libya's Colonel Khadaffi being unpredictable and dangerous.

The brass launched a full-scale investigation in a determined effort to find and punish the leaker. The internal intelligence people called on me first. For an hour I answered questions of every sort, patiently and truthfully. It was easy; I hadn't known of the deployment in the first place. From there, the inquisition spread throughout the Pentagon (which I used to call in speeches "The World's Largest Five-Sided Sieve"). It lasted for months.

In the end, the truth came out. An alert person in Oklahoma City noticed one day that the giant AWACS planes he had been used to seeing parked at Tinker Air Force Base as he drove to work were no longer there. He passed the information along to a friend who worked at the local

ABC-TV affiliate, who in turn passed it to ABC's John McWethy. An intelligent man and an enterprising reporter, McWethy began to dig and in due course learned what had happened. No leak; just good reporting.

I called McWethy while writing this passage, to check my recollection. He told me I had it right but there was more to the story than I knew.

When the AWACS flew to Cairo, two of them had to land at Cairo International because of crowding at the more remote — and secretive — Cairo West airfield. Soviet agents could clearly see the giant aircraft, so the mission was blown from the standpoint of security.

Another tip alerted McWethy to a repositioning of the U.S. Mediterranean fleet, caused by a massing of Libyan troops and aircraft in southwestern Libya near the Sudanese border. Had Colonel Khadaffi invaded, we were ready to respond; the AWACS were in support of American forces, not Egyptian.

Armed with this knowledge and pretending to know even more than he did, McWethy went to see Undersecretary of Defense for Policy Fred Iklé, saying, "Here's what I have, where am I in error?" Iklé turned pale and told the NSC.

At the White House, National Security Adviser William Clark called Roone Arledge of ABC News, urging the network to sit on the story for forty-eight hours, lest U.S. information sources within Libya be imperiled. Unknown to Arledge and Clark, McWethy had already sat on the story for twenty-four hours, something he did not like to do.

To complicate matters, President Reagan had scheduled a press conference for that evening, and he denied any repositioning of U.S. forces in the Mediterranean. Afterward, Larry Speakes, Reagan's spokesman, had to put out the word that the president was in error; we had indeed moved our forces.

McWethy sensed a split, though he could not prove it. He felt that Clark and the NSC wanted Khadaffi to invade Sudan, so the United States could smartly slap him down with naval air power. Weinberger and Iklé, on the other hand, did not favor such a course (Weinberger was always chary about committing U.S. forces). Said McWethy: "I think there was a power play within the administration about what we wanted to achieve."

The above story doesn't prove that leakers don't exist; they do, in legions. One Monday morning I attended the weekly meeting of the Armed Forces Policy Council, at which a contentious issue came up. By the time I got back to my office after the meeting (a seven-minute walk in that giant building), AP's Fred Hoffman was waiting. His query? It concerned a matter discussed at the just concluded meeting, clearly a leak. Nonetheless, inquisitive reporters with good sources can piece together stories without benefit of leaks.

Fear of the press sometimes led to foolish ideas. In February of 1982 Weinberger was due to travel to the Middle East, his itinerary including a politically sensitive stop in Saudi Arabia, to which the administration wanted to sell AWACS radar spotter planes. Someone—I never learned who—had suggested to the secretary that we not take the usual press contingent along, and he was considering the idea.

I hit the ceiling. In a memo, I pointed out the disadvantages:

• He had always taken the press; to change that policy would unleash a howl of protest and a wave of suspicion.

• The media were rich enough and tenacious enough to go on their own, either by jointly chartering a plane, by using local "stringers" (independent on-the-scene reporters), or by sending their regulars commercially.

• Our reporters knew the score and were far more reliable than local reporters, whose stories would dominate the news in the absence of Pentagon pros.

• Press on board with us could be guided, given backgrounders en route, and generally helped in ways beneficial to all concerned.

In the end, Cap came down for taking the reporters. I was pleased; later, I was to be sorry.

We left February 4, flew to Upper Heyford in Britain for two nights, and then pressed on to Riyadh. Our Saudi hosts, far more fearful of the press than even the Pentagon brass were, segregated the reporters, took them on meaningless tours to keep them at arm's length, and generally made their lives miserable. Naturally, I took the flak, which was bitter and heavy. At one point, Dick Halloran of the *New York Times* stalked up to me and announced, "Henry, if things don't get better, if we don't get briefed on what's happening, I'm going with what I'm hearing." His threat was angry but empty. I tried my best to provide usable tidbits, but hard news proved hard to come by and the mood aboard our plane remained sour.

The Media and the Pentagon

CRISIS MODE was routine at the Pentagon; something was *always* happening, much of it of the "you've got to be kidding" variety. A joke going around in those days: You know it's going to be a bad day when you go out in the morning to pick up the paper and there's a *60 Minutes* truck parked in front of your house.

For my office, the joke imitated life. In early 1983 I had a visitor, a senior producer for *60 Minutes* named Scheffler. He came to complain that we refused to give his program on-camera interviews with Pentagon officials. I assured him that no orchestrated campaign existed but that his program suffered from a genuinely spontaneous backlash at the grassroots level. Key officers and civilians throughout the building had come to a common conclusion: *60 Minutes* had an anti-military bias that had been shown time and time again. Why, the military wondered, should we put our necks on the line when it was certain our heads would be severed? The more sophisticated went further. Give us sixty seconds of *unedited* time on camera and we will appear; otherwise, no dice. The producers indignantly refused such offers, claiming their editorial prerogatives would be at risk.

I tried to end the standoff by offering to act as an intermediary. Let me know whom you want, I told Scheffler, and I'll see if I can talk that person into it. He never called. What he did instead was write to David Gergen, assistant to the president for communications. Claiming that *60 Minutes* was President Reagan's favorite TV show, the program asked Gergen to lean on me; he refused.

A case in point concerned an anti-tank missile called Maverick. When the program asked our cooperation with a segment on this new weapon, a feisty colonel in my office, Robert O'Brien, had some fun.

Apparently the producer led off his meeting with the colonel by making a snide comment about the problem-plagued missile, tipping O'Brien as to the story's thrust.

"Sure, we'll cooperate," chirped Bob, whose mind worked at computer speed. "Here's what we'll do. We'll give you an M-1 tank. You will put Mike Wallace and Morley Safer in it and they will then hide on any testing ground they choose. We will then send in a plane armed with one Maverick missile. If it misses, your point will have been made, graphically. If it hits, think of the picture, the dust, the opportunity for 'voice-over.' Think of the ratings! It'll be a smash."

The stunned producer, momentarily silent, ended the conversation with a snarl and stalked away.

Incidentally, the Pentagon never refused contributions to the program; we always replied to queries, but in writing, not on camera.

The matter became public when the *Wall Street Journal* published a piece on the controversy. I received letters from all over the country, urging us to stick to our guns.

60 Minutes wasn't our only bête noire. One day a producer for Bill Moyers's CBS-TV program, Leslie Cockburn, called and explained she wanted to do an hour on what it's like to be secretary of defense, a sort of "twenty-four hours in the life of Cap Weinberger."

I knew Moyers from the early days when he worked as press secretary for LBJ, and I felt the program sounded attractive. Many people thought of the Pentagon as the home office of war and destruction and its leader as a bloodthirsty madman. I knew better. A chance to help dispel the negative appealed to me, and so I recommended to Cap that he accept.

He did. Shortly thereafter, crews began to follow him to meetings, social events, on journeys, wherever he went. They were agreeable, and we accommodated them.

Some months later the show aired. It was so bad that I apologized to Cap and wrote an indignant letter to Moyers and another to CBS president Tom Wyman. Instead of "a day in the life" format, they had turned it, typically of TV, into a confrontation. Unbeknownst to us, every question that had been put to Weinberger in interviews was given to a young woman called Dina Rasor, who I felt was militantly anti-military. The format thus turned into a debate, with all the advantage to our adversary. It struck me as a breach of faith; Weinberger (not knowing that he was debating) made his points but never had the last word.

Moyers and Wyman responded, denying any wrongdoing or misdirection. The former said in his reply, "When we began we did not have a point of view." He ended his letter, however, revealingly: "I will make you this promise: You help reporters for a change get at all evidence you people are sitting on about cost overruns, fraud, waste, pork barrels, inept testing, inadequate weapons, cronyism, etc., and I cheerfully will sit in the pew of your church every Sunday to Judgment Day allowing you to preach to me on the virtues of candor." Tough line, amusing polemics, but no point of view . . . ?

Briefings and Leaks

FIREWORKS CAME from all directions. A group of Catholic clergymen got word that the Navy planned to name a new nuclear submarine the *Corpus Christi*. The idea of calling an engine of death "Body of Christ" chilled them and they complained bitterly. The Navy, of course, intended only to honor the Texas city, but the men of the cloth could see it as nothing short of blasphemy. We compromised by changing the name to *City of Corpus Christi*.

Cap's daily 8:30 A.M. staff meetings, at which this kind of thing often came up, were set pieces, each senior person always sitting in the same place; a newcomer unlucky enough to trespass soon learned the error of his ways. I sat on the couch at Cap's right hand. At first I thought it symbolic: I was always the first person to report, after the secretary; I must be a big deal. Oh, well, you can't get it right every time.

Invariably I tried to see Cap alone either before or after the meeting. My briefings and their credibility depended on the perception that I truly did speak for the secretary. That was a difficult enough challenge as it was; without these fleeting meetings, even with Weinberger's mind distracted as it always was, my job would have been impossible.

Amusing things happened, which I often shared during the meetings. At one point, the CIA and the Defense Intelligence Agency (DIA) held an open briefing on the alarming buildup of Soviet arms in Nicaragua. CNN taped it. Sometime thereafter, a PA person called CNN and asked for a copy of the briefing. "Sorry," he was told, "we have only two copies. One is checked out to the Soviets, the other to the Nicaraguans."

Rank had its privileges. I accompanied Cap on a visit to an aircraft carrier. We watched from the bridge as one of our battleships loosed salvos the size of Volkswagens at targets miles away; the power of the blast singed my eyebrows. I was invited to spend a night on a submarine, an invitation that my tendency toward claustrophobia caused me politely to decline. And I flew in an F-16 fighter-bomber. I warned the young pilot that if he turned too fast, accelerated too rapidly, or otherwise caused me to throw up by pulling nine Gs, it would not be a career-enhancing move. He didn't and I didn't.

Leaks being an ongoing problem, there arose a clamor for a simple solution. One that appealed to Weinberger was a vast increase in the use of polygraphs, or lie detectors. I opposed the idea; the press would inevitably be up in arms when they learned of it and the assistant secretary for health affairs, Dr. John Beary, weighed in that he felt the tests to be unreliable. Beary told Cap that machines cannot detect lies, they can detect only stress. Aldrich Ames, a longtime CIA employee who years later sold information to the Soviets, was asked by the *New York Times* how he managed to fool so many lie detector tests. His reply: "Well, they don't work."

My own objections sprang not from scientific evidence like Beary's but from a sense of how we would look; as I put it to Weinberger, giving lie detector tests to our people in uniform and our civil servants would have about it a whiff of the jackboot. Cap did not change his mind, but the wholesale use that I had feared didn't happen, at least not on my watch.

Another ongoing controversy concerned the secretary's relations with his colleagues at State. With first Alexander Haig and later George Schultz, rumors of bad blood persisted. When reporters asked about the rumors, I invariably pooh-poohed the idea, but all was not easy camaraderie.

For example, fairly early in the first Reagan administration, the Weinbergers had a cocktail party honoring their son, Cap Junior, and his wife, newly arrived in Washington. I was bidden to attend, as were Ed Meese, Bill Clark, Jim Baker, and Al Haig, among others. Though I hadn't seen Al since the Ford days, I liked him and, on seeing him, greeted him enthusiastically.

His response was viperous. "Do you know how much trouble your boss caused me today? His comment on *Good Morning America* created such havoc I had to spend five hours undoing it." He ranted on, looking mad enough to bite the head off a chicken, sweating, eyes shining, out of control. What set Haig off was that Weinberger had said that Israeli prime minister Menachem Begin's course could "not be described as moderate."

I should not have been surprised. A month earlier Cap had told me my briefing on the Israeli attack on the Iraqi reactor had caused Haig "to walk all over the ceiling" because I "gave away Israeli secrets and upset a delicate balance." Cap added, "Soon he'll be going to China and things should calm down."

The Haig-Weinberger rivalry could not be put to bed, no matter how hard we tried. One evening I was talking to Rowland Evans, a widely syndicated columnist and a good friend. I mentioned Haig's irascibility. He laughed and recounted an experience he had had. When Rowly asked Haig to comment on rumors of troubles with Weinberger, the secretary of state snapped, "If you believe that, you're sucking on the White House sewer pipe."

In January 1983 I told Weinberger that I planned to resign before long. Jessica's mother, who had run the family communications company, was taking a smaller role now, and the Catto side of H & C Communications needed tending. Jessica's hands were full with running *Washington Journalism Review*, so that left me. Cap resisted the idea, apparently sincerely, and told me not to be in any hurry. As it turned out, I didn't hurry—my last day was September 19.

In fact, while the company did beckon, I was increasingly frustrated with Cap's approach to public affairs. He and his substantive people seldom told me anything voluntarily; I had to ask, presuming, of course, that I was lucky enough to get an inkling of what was going on, and often, asking proved to be in vain. Examples abound.

One Saturday I got a call at home from Dick Halloran of the *New York Times*. He asked if I were aware that David Gergen, a White House communications adviser, was about to hold a briefing on a major change in the administration's arms budget.

Fresh off the tennis court, I was astonished and annoyed. I called Cap and sure enough, Halloran's information proved correct. My bitter complaint about what this kind of event did to my credibility brought no satisfactory response at the time. That evening, however, Cap called me and sympathized, thus ending my black mood and my flirtation with immediate resignation. He did not, however, mend his ways.

As a former ambassador to El Salvador, I naturally had a great interest in that country and its struggles against Marxist-Leninist guerrillas. Wanting to know whether the Nicaraguans had provided most of the arms for the rebels, I one day asked Undersecretary Fred Iklé, in all seriousness, where the truth lay. Iklé countered, "What do *you* think?"—totally unforthcoming, as usual. (Ben Welles once quipped, "Machiavelli would have slept badly if Iklé had been around in the sixteenth century.")

One night at midnight I was wrenched from sleep by an insistently jangling phone. It was AP's Fred Hoffman, who requested confirmation that LTV executive Paul Thayer was soon to be announced as the new deputy secretary of defense, replacing the retiring Frank Carlucci. I had to confess I had no idea; Cap had not told me.

The arrival of Thayer caused waves. For one thing, Cap had not chosen him; he was forced on us by the White House. For another, Thayer was woefully ignorant about government. A strong-minded, take-charge person, he moved into office with an "I'll clean this place up in a hurry" attitude. The predictable result was chaos.

Cap and Frank had had a very long and close partnership. The arrival of a stranger as the Pentagon's number two made the secretary uncomfortable. For me, it was a disaster. The first thing he did was to suggest that my office be supplemented by an advertising agency. When I tried to see him to brief him on our problems and activities, he canceled appointments on short notice four times, thus sending a message, intentional or not. At one staff meeting where he was presiding, he snapped at me, "You have your orders."

Early on, he had his former LTV office invite four reporters to dinner. He wanted to get to know them, but, as one of the invitees later told me, he asked pointed questions about me and the public affairs operation. To me, he was a pain in the posterior who had little interest in press relations and whose continuing use of his former private-sector connections was dangerous.

When the Marines went to Lebanon there were reports that Israelis and Americans had had unpleasant encounters, even pointing loaded guns at one another. During a briefing, Fred Hoffman quizzed me on the topic. Bobbing, weaving, and sweating, I tried to answer with but one objective in mind: to keep it from being obvious that I did not know. I later asked Military Assistant Pete Carmack what had really happened. "Why do you need to know?" he snapped. "So I'll be as well informed as the *Baltimore Sun*," I responded.

When Britain and Argentina went to war over the Falkland Islands, I said in an early briefing that the United States would not take sides, that we would play it "straight down the middle." (Secretary Haig at the time was desperately and unsuccessfully trying to mediate between the two.) I turned out to be wrong—totally. Weinberger, his famous Anglophilia coming to the fore, was seeing to it that the British had every kind of help we could offer.

Weinberger sometimes spoke without reflection. During the 1982

Solidarity labor union crisis in Poland, he called Polish president Wojciech Jaruzelski a "Russian general in a Polish uniform." State Department spokesman Alan Romberg gave me a stern lecture on the matter during one of our regular Thursday afternoon meetings at the White House, explaining that the Pole was a fervent patriot, suspicious of Russian intentions. He felt that Cap had harmed American efforts to keep Solidarity alive. I felt that had Cap used me more widely, such problems could have been minimized.

Ben Welles asked Cap what was going on in Honduras. It later turned out that the small nation was being converted into a sanctuary and staging area for the Nicaraguan anti-communist guerrillas, the Contras. Cap refused to give Ben so much as a hint of the truth.

Often Cap would take a phone call from a favorite reporter, unbeknownst to me. On several occasions the reporter later referred to his conversation while talking to me. To have to admit I didn't know the conversation had taken place was embarrassing.

Still, it was hard to get mad at him. One day he became very annoyed with me — over what, I don't recall. Before the end of the day, however, a note of apology arrived, ending "My job description doesn't include being grumpy."

In the Carter administration, Defense Secretary Harold Brown and his spokesman, Tom Ross, had had a fine relationship. I had talked to Tom about it before taking the job and I knew it was possible. Personally, I did have a good rapport with Cap. I admired his mind, his decency, his humor.[3] The job, furthermore, had proved to be great training. It taught me to think before I spoke (at least most of the time), and it proved that if you want to win, you *never* get mad. Still, the cost-benefit equation had shifted; there were never any victories, and it was time to move on. I knew this without doubt one night when I dreamed I was helping Cap put on his cuff links.

The above incidents reflect a sad but very real deterioration in the relations between government and press. Shortly after I left the Pentagon, the rescue of American students on the chaotic, anarchic Caribbean island of Grenada took place. The media, uninvited, were incensed. What was a perfectly reasonable move by the administration to protect the one thousand Americans on the island got pilloried, as all the suspicions of the excluded reporters (who were not brought ashore until the second day) ran rampant.

Later, reading Weinberger's memoir of his Pentagon days, I learned that the commanding officer of the task force, Vice Admiral Joseph Metcalf, had pleaded urgently that no reporters be allowed. As Cap explained Metcalf's view, "The need for secrecy was urgent . . ."

I couldn't help remembering what had happened when we invaded Europe on D day in 1944. There, the stakes were infinitely higher, yet the press went, General Eisenhower clearly comfortable that they would respect the need for absolute secrecy. Recently I read the *New York Times* edition of D day, 1944. It made constant references to "our" troops. I found it hard to imagine the *Times* of today using a similar possessive pronoun. Today's reporters and publishers observe loyalty to a different entity, the concepts of press freedom and the First Amendment. I think I understand why, but I know we have lost something valuable in the change. Where lies the blame? I think it lies on neither press nor government totally, but on the real and tragic decline of trust and civility that infects our society.

There is no better place to observe democracy in action in contemporary America than at the juncture of press and government. Both have incalculable influence on the lives of us all. There is assuredly no better place to see these forces in action than the hot seat of a major department press secretary. Lest I seem a biased witness, given my history of government service, I can cite *Washington Journalism Review* and H & C Communications as the balancing private-sector experience.

The two great antagonists have one major failing in common, the Infallibility Syndrome. The White House in particular is loath to admit error, even when it is undeniable. So is the press. In the Moyers story on Weinberger cited earlier, CBS wrapped itself tightly in a cloak of indignant denial that it might conceivably have misled us. Coming from a company (CBS) that pioneered the "ambush" or surprise interview, that seemed a bit of a stretch.

Over the years I wrote dozens of letters to newspapers complaining about editorials that clearly had sprung from an inadequate information base. I had developed a theory that the first report of *any* breaking story would always prove incorrect, a theory that I have yet to see disproved. Yet too many editorialists fail to remember that the heat of the outrage one feels about a governmental action is directly proportional to one's ignorance of all the facts.

Roone Arledge of ABC News once pinpointed this media weakness:

"An opinion has grown among the public that we have gotten too arrogant. I find myself sometimes agreeing. There is a small but highly visible section of the press that says, 'Screw you—I don't have to answer to anyone. If you don't like it, that's too bad. I'll make the decisions and that's that.'" Reporters at times forget they are there to report, not to act as avenging angels of a mistreated public or as first-round prosecutors. Confrontation is their mother's milk, and if there isn't any, some are not above stirring it up. And when a reporter intoned the phrase "the public's right to know," I often suspected what he meant was "my right to beat my competitor to the story and thus keep my well-paying job."[4]

The government, particularly a segment of it as large and complex as the Pentagon, suffers from hubris as well. Given the nature of mankind, when $300 billion is being spent, not all of it will be well spent; backdoor deals will be made, and carelessness with money that is not one's own becomes inevitable. Government officials tend to forget this. The press needs to ferret out waste and fraud and help hold them to a minimum, but they need to explain thoroughly how matters sometimes evolve.

For example, what looks like waste or inefficiency may be politics and human nature. Suppose the Army asks Congress to approve a new tank in 1980. Perhaps it will be in production by 1990 and can enjoy ten years of service before it is obsolete in 2000. But when 2000 rolls around, Congress is in no mood to approve a follow-up model, so the old tank must continue to serve.

Like all things, tanks wear out. The Army originally ordered tank widgets enough to last until 2000, but by 2005 the widget supply is exhausted; more must be ordered. By then, however, the factory that manufactured them is no longer geared to make more, certainly not for the same price. So a widget that originally cost $10 now costs $200. Learning this, the press erupts. Complicating factors are forgotten or ignored.

The military services do not seem by nature to be articulate, and their innate press relations sense is stunted. (I once said on TV that the Joint Chiefs of Staff had the PR sense of Attila the Hun; that was, to be sure, after I had left the Pentagon.) Acronyms proliferate like mice, making conversations with service people difficult for the novice. And their prose tends to consist solely of euphemism. For example, I once saw a press release about a missile test failure that read, "The missile was raised and it fell and made contact with the ground." Oi.

So it went at the Pentagon. I was far from perfect at the job, and I was often ground between the insatiable curiosity of the reporter and the Berlin Wall of military secrecy. But ABC's John McWethy made it all seem worthwhile when he wrote me on my departure:

> On this your last day in office at the Pentagon I feel it my obligation to provide you with a critique on your nearly three years of public service at this job. Henry, as a friend and admirer, I feel it is only fair to be bluntly honest with you about your weaknesses which I see as being just two. One, you are at times so goddam nice and so gracious under fire that I wanted you just once to jump off the platform in the briefing room and take a swing at one of us . . . or at the very least to make some off-color remark about someone's heritage or mother. You are amazing. Grace under fire is a rare quality. You are blessed. Second, and I hope you don't take this too personally, you need some serious work on your [tennis] backhand . . . Seriously, I've enjoyed working with you in often difficult times. You have always played fairly and honestly with me and more should not be asked of an ASD [assistant secretary of defense] in public affairs. Good luck.

To me, McWethy had taken one small step toward the restoration of civility and trust between government and the Fourth Estate.

My departure from the Pentagon went according to form. Cap made pleasant remarks and presented me with a medal. I made pleasant remarks, refreshments were served, and it was over. In a way, I felt my Pentagon years made up for the fact that I had not been able to serve in the military, an organization for which I came to have great respect. And for all his keeping me in the dark and his tendency to snap judgment, Caspar Weinberger was a dedicated patriot, a tireless worker, and a thoroughly decent man.

Civilian Ventures and Explorations

RETURN TO civilian life provided many benefits. First, having a superb assistant named Christina Sagris kept me organized and on time. Second, setting my own schedule allowed opportunities for more family time. Finally, I enjoyed the television business enormously. With the purchase of Cowles Communications, our small group of TV stations became a rather large group, eventually including Houston, Daytona-Orlando, Nashville, San Antonio, Des Moines, and Tucson, with affiliates of each network. As vice chairman, I became active in industry organizations and traveled frequently to our stations, getting to know the business, the first-rate people who worked for us, and the interesting communities in which we operated.

Politics remained an interest as well. We often saw the Bushes, Bakers, and other movers. Jessica's central role in media matters via *WJR* kept us current on that important component of Washington life, and her appointment as trustee of Washington College on the Eastern Shore of Maryland opened doors to academe.

The Reagan-Bush victory in 1984 was a relief. A well-placed Democratic friend, Sarah Weddington of Texas, told us that Jesse Jackson's price for enthusiastic support of Democratic candidate Walter Mondale was to be a veto over ambassadorial appointees to Third World countries, a prospect I viewed about as enthusiastically as I would an invitation to dine with Jeffrey Dahmer.

The military in El Salvador suffered, deservedly, from bad press in the United States. Given my history as an ambassador to El Salvador and spokesman for our own military, someone in the State Department got the bright idea that I should go to that revolt-torn country and try to nudge them toward more civilized behavior and the better press that might flow from it. I went, meeting with the major players, visiting combat areas in the eastern part of the country by helicopter, and trying to explain the military's role in a democracy. They received me politely, listened attentively, and changed nothing at all.

To hone my writing and speaking skills, I began to write a regular column on whatever caught my fancy for the *San Antonio Light* and became an occasional contributor to National Public Radio's *All Things Considered,* the most interesting program on American radio. I felt that *All Things Considered* tended to present far more opinion from the left, and I tried to right the balance, as it were. It wasn't easy; the program seemed to me to harbor a suspicion of Reagan administration veterans, but I broadcast pieces dealing with a fair number of issues and enjoyed doing it.

In the spring of 1986, I took son Will on a two-week trip to South America. Starting with Argentina, we interviewed media people, including a totally charming publisher named Federico Massot, who invited us to a fine weekend of steaks and wine on his *estancia,* or ranch, near Bahia Blanca. The trip carried on a tradition I had started in 1980 (with Heather, when we climbed Mount Kilimanjaro) of taking one of the offspring on a trip alone, without siblings.

Invited by ambassador to Paraguay Clyde Taylor and his wife, Ginnie, to stay at the embassy, we had a first-class time, even though President Alfredo Stroessner would not see us. We took side trips through the countryside, enjoyed the flower-laden trees, and became admirers of the lively Paraguayan music.

One evening, the Taylors had a dinner for us. I spent a good bit of time with a cabinet minister, a charming man of great cultivation. Talking over the evening with Clyde after the guests had departed, I mentioned my new friend. "Ah, yes," said the young ambassador, "he's the one who invented Stroessner's policy of teaching political enemies how to skydive—without parachutes."

Chile proved the most exciting stop. I had written the United States Information Service chief a letter saying I would like to see the dictator, President Gustavo Pinochet. The bait I used was to say that Pinochet had gotten very poor press in the United States. I represented a magazine of press criticism, and I proposed to give the general a chance to comment on the fairness of the U.S. media.

On arrival we called on the president's press secretary. While he received us warmly, he was very vague about an appointment, but on the morning of March 5 (which, incidentally, was Will's twenty-second birthday), the public affairs officer at the embassy called to tell us the president would receive us at eleven-thirty. Will was excited; he couldn't have had a better birthday present.

We arrived at the Moneda Palace, the official residence of Chilean presidents, in good time, and a soldier of grim face and shiny boots escorted us to a large waiting room that overlooked a central plaza. Although filled with huge arrangements of fresh cut flowers, the room was dark and somber, hung with large paintings on themes of Chilean history. We checked out everything there was to see, awaiting with nervous interest the interview.

In due course, a military aide appeared, and we shortly found ourselves in Pinochet's office.

My first impressions as we (Will and I, the general, and his press aide) settled down was that this man had the sense of humor of a guillotine.

Dressed in a formal, stiff uniform of red and white, he offered minimal small talk.

My questions—naturally, it seemed to me—had to do with his image in the world press. His answers, increasingly curt, were short of revealing. Puzzled, I plowed on, but after twelve minutes, the general rose, snapped, "This is turning into an interview," and out we went. I had thought all along it was an interview; how he came to believe otherwise remains a mystery.

The summer of 1988 was to prove important in our lives. For one thing, George Bush was nominated for president. While he had the nomination sewed up by March 8, getting there had been difficult. I had visited him in his White House vice presidential office, offering to become active in the campaign in any way he might wish. I was disappointed at the vagueness of his reaction but remembered that in a national presidential campaign, there are often far more volunteers than can successfully be used. I settled for helping to raise money and giving the limit I legally could, which amounted to $10,000. Furthermore, I wrote pro-Bush op-ed pieces for the *Washington Post* when I had an angle I thought unusual enough to merit publication.

That otherwise pleasant summer was marred when a small cloud on the horizon became a storm. I had joined friend Bernard Lifshutz in investing in a real estate project in New York City. Various problems caused it to begin to unravel, and in the end it cost more than I could afford to lose. To make matters worse, the Texas real estate market simultaneously collapsed. I had foolishly failed to keep Jessica fully current on the problems; a shrewd businesswoman, she might have foreseen trouble better than I did. The only redeeming feature of that error was that she was not a signatory to any of the notes, so her separate property was not at risk. After many agonizing months, I emerged financially and spiritually damaged but, thanks to astute advice from friend and attorney Al Moses, still afloat. The lessons learned were two: don't get into businesses about which you know little, and pay attention to your own hunches, since expert opinion often isn't.

The young, meanwhile, were on their own and doing well. Heather had married Williams classmate Martin Kohout in 1985 and settled in Washington, where she was teaching at American University and raising offspring Lizzie and Tito (a third, Thea, came along in 1992). John, in San Diego, worked as a TV photojournalist. Will became engaged to and in October married an enchanting girl, Kristina Kent of New York, whom he met at Georgetown University, and Isa, having graduated from Williams, was off to London to study the practical side of fine arts at a school owned by the great auction house Christie's. Jessica, increasingly interested in environmental problems and the search for sensible solutions to them, was elected to the board of the Environmental Defense Fund, and in marked divergence from previous practice, I bobbed along behind her as "spouse of" at meetings.

My interest in the press and its role in society had triggered an idea in the summer of 1988. Op-ed page columnists in the newspapers often hold forth with far more conviction than seemed reasonable to me. What would be the result, I mused, of rereading, say, ten years of a given columnist's work and comparing his ex cathedra pronouncements with how things really turned out? If I had the patience to do it, and undertook to do several, I might have the makings of a useful (and publishable) book.

The problem involved whom to look at and how many to do. Enlisting the aid of a colleague at *Washington Journalism Review,* Shelby Sadler, I settled on Anthony Lewis of the *New York Times.* To me, his work was drearily predictable. Lewis personified the liberal outlook of that noble institution, an outlook whose sameness made the editorial and op-ed pages woefully inferior to the generally excellent quality of the news pages.

Shelby, the world's best researcher, dug up and organized ten years' worth of Lewis's columns, and I diligently plowed through them, a long and difficult task. Like drinking too much, it proved a sin that carried its own punishment. Reading through much of the summer of '88, I began to write in the fall, finishing the article late in the year. Bill Buckley at *National Review* agreed to publish it, and it appeared in January 1989.

My elation at successful completion of the job was tempered by a minor problem: while my thesis that Lewis had changed little and learned less about the world seemed accurate, I found upon interviewing the subject a thoroughly nice person. His knowledge of the law, its structures, strengths, and weaknesses, was deep, and even today, when I note a Lewis column on that subject, I read it.

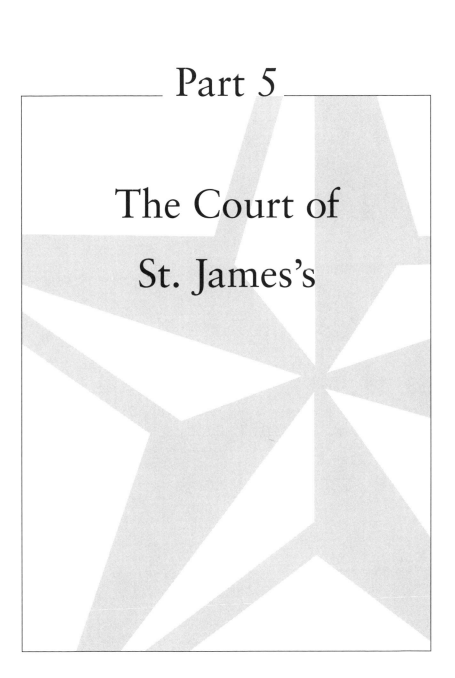

Part 5

The Court of
St. James's

Tapped for a Coveted Post

THE BOOK project, as it turned out, came to an abrupt halt on December 11. George and Barbara Bush had invited us to a Christmas brunch at the vice president's house, located on the sprawling, wooded Massachusetts Avenue grounds of the Naval Observatory. A group of Air Force musicians sang Christmas songs, and the Christmas spirit of the Bush friends and family clearly was buoyed by George's smashing victory in the presidential election of the previous month.

At one point I noticed the president-elect and Jessica engaged in serious conversation. Curious, I joined them. George didn't make me wait: "How would you like to go to London?" he asked.

I was stunned. Although my efforts in the campaign had been modest, I thought it likely I would be asked to help in some way or another. I had thought the United States Information Agency would be an interesting challenge, and *New York Times* columnist Bill Safire had even speculated on that job as a useful match. But the London embassy, a very tasty plum indeed, had not entered my mind.

Still, it had a very strong appeal. First of all, I knew the country. Grandfather Catto's being a Scot had deeply affected me, especially given the wartime British-American partnership in desperate times. We had family there. I spoke the language fluently (or thought I did). All in all, it seemed a great compliment and an exciting challenge.

I knew, nonetheless, that there would be a problem, so I asked George to let me sleep on it, to which he readily agreed.

The thing that worried me was Jessica, and as we drove home, we discussed it. She had very much found her niche in Colorado, designing and building environmentally sound houses. With four houses under construction and a family business in flux, the timing to pull up stakes and go abroad for a third time could not have been more awkward for her. Realizing this as we talked, I finally said I would turn it down. But when she, characteristically, said, "No, you must do it," I quickly acquiesced. Always expert at rationalization, I reasoned that the challenges and excitement of London would eventually win her, but I turned out to be wrong. In the end, no matter the charm of that ancient land, the pull of the American West and the demands of business held sway, and we were both to spend much time alone.

The Bush team used the transition days productively. By January 6, my impending nomination was announced. I spent the day before phoning family and friends, letting them know what lay ahead and finding no shortage of volunteers to come and visit. I went early on to the State Department to meet those concerned with United States–United Kingdom relations, and found in United Kingdom desk officer Howard Perlow an expert who quickly became a friend and ally.[1] He swiftly set about arranging the seemingly endless calls on people within the U.S. government who needed to have the ear of the ambassador or who wanted to influence him.

Having a friend become president presented protocolary problems. Calling him "George" in public sounded presumptuous, so I was careful to use "Mr. President." In private or family situations, I lapsed into the informal. George's inauguration, on January 20, 1989, was an occasion of deep satisfaction. Not only was he an old friend but he had many qualities that I thought ideal in a president. He handled the press easily and articulately. His strength had to me never been in doubt, and the campaign claptrap branding him a "wimp" made me laugh (when I wasn't fuming). The inaugural address struck the right tone. We had, I thought, just who was needed at 1600 Pennsylvania Avenue. Other than the inauguration itself, we again skipped most events.

An early chore involved picking London's new deputy chief of mission. I had gotten to know the incumbent, Raymond Seitz, by telephone, finding his advice uniformly sensible and his personality appealing. He knew, however, that he was likely to be replaced, so he discouraged me from trying to get him an extension. (As it turned out, he proved correct: he was named assistant secretary of state for European and Canadian affairs.) I interviewed six or seven candidates and finally settled on Ronald Woods, then the deputy chief of mission in Brussels.

Charles and Carol Price, the incumbents in the London embassy, came by to visit and provided much useful information on the house and the staff. A five-year veteran at the job, Charlie was big, hearty, and appealing; I knew that replacing him would not be easy.

Another early task was to persuade Marylou Sheils to come with us. She readily accepted and proved to be a first-rate staff chief, quickly learning everything there was to know and meeting everyone worth knowing. I hated to leave our longtime assistant, Tina Sagris, behind, but on that score Jessica pointed out that we could not operate without her minding the home front.

An ominous cloud turned up in an unlikely place: the State Department's medical offices.

Each officer headed overseas gets an exam to determine if he is fit for service in what are often posts with few medical amenities. London certainly was not one of those, but the exam was mandatory.

The result unsettled me. It showed an elevated white cell count, typical of leukemia. After arriving at post, I had the count checked regularly, watching it grow steadily. The embassy doctor diagnosed CLL, chronic lymphocytic leukemia, a diagnosis confirmed at Houston's MD Anderson Cancer Center on my return in March 1991. Then, miraculously, the white cell count began to diminish and I remained medicine-free until 1997.

Charlie Price had told us there was no library at Winfield House, the ambassador's Regent's Park residence, nor were there many paintings. I solved one of these problems by asking daughter Isa to set about asking the loan of American paintings from Texas museums. This she did enthusiastically and with great success. The solution to the library problem proved not so simple. I asked a number of friends and book dealers for help in donating the core of a permanent library, but I struck out completely. It proved good training, however, for budgetary stringencies frequently transform the ambassador into a mendicant, as will be seen.

In late March I joined a dozen other appointees and went to ambassador's school at the Foreign Service Institute. Unhappy, I grumbled to Jessica that it was a waste of a week; I'd been an ambassador. I couldn't have been more mistaken.

First of all, the lectures on press relations, ethics, management, and so on were amusing and informative. At midweek, our class of a dozen or so would-be ambassadors was to fly to the Federal Law Enforcement Training Center (FLETC) in North Carolina.

Laughing and relaxed, we were strapping ourselves in when suddenly a group of armed men, loud, burly, and demanding, forced their way on board.

"Hands on your heads," the leader screamed in a heavy accent. "Do not look up at us." Sneaking a peak, I decided to play along. While I felt 98 percent sure that this was a charade, I could nonetheless see how a gaggle of ambassadors-to-be might tempt a terrorist.

One of our number gave the leader a bit of lip, and I thought the thug was going to strike him. Instead, he raised the decibels and lowered the gun. After fifteen minutes, it was over and we were introduced to our "captors," who talked to us about how to react if we should really be kidnapped. They were, of course, government employees, but they should have gotten an Oscar.

The southward flight passed quickly, and a bus met us for the trip to the hotel for cocktails and dinner. Seated in the front of the bus, I noticed a well-dressed woman standing ahead at roadside by a late-model car, frantically waving for us to stop. We did, and the driver opened the door to see what she wanted.

"I've broken down," she said, almost sobbing. "I'm headed for the hotel a few miles ahead. Would you mind taking my bag while I try to get help to fix the car?"

The driver readily agreed, but the future ambassador to New Zealand, Della Newman, seated in the back, was wiser. "No!" she shouted. "It might be a bomb." The rest of us, all male, sheepishly agreed, having totally failed to see this as part of our initiation.

Our day at FLETC included training in evasive driving, firing weapons, and watching car bombs detonated, all graphic reminders of the perils of diplomacy in the Age of Terrorism.

Taking courses was good; talking to people who know the trade was even better. One foreign service officer, asked who was the best ambassador he had ever served with, replied with no hesitation, "Charles Whitehouse" (who had been U.S. ambassador to Laos and Thailand). I asked why. The answer: "Because he listens. He's not always on broadcast. He can breathe through his nose."

Lunch with Tom Pickering, whose many ambassadorial posts include El Salvador, Jordan, and Russia — among others — yielded imaginative ideas: be sure to invite new arrivals at the post to your residence; have a party every year for local employees; do a "captain's inspection" of your embassy — that is, start at the top of the building and visit every office;

ask each officer whom it would help him to know, and then arrange it; have a staff meeting to which spouses are invited; and be sure that congressional mail is answered promptly.

Ray Seitz suggested such books as *The Anatomy of Britain* and *Alliance Politics,* which proved highly useful.

Calls on most of the Cabinet and other agency heads completed, my Senate hearing was set for April 12. As an old hand, I had no problems. Senator Joseph Biden of Delaware urged me to go to Northern Ireland to see the situation there firsthand. "Don't just take the word of the British," he cautioned. I agreed (and Belfast was indeed the destination of my first in-country visit). The Senate voted unanimous confirmation on April 14, and on April 22 we were off on the great new adventure, with Al and Carol Moses taking us to the airport.

<hr />

Settling In

THE EARLY days in Britain were a whirl of activities, meeting friendly new faces, and learning not to get lost in the great mansion in which we were to live. Ray Seitz and a small embassy group were at Heathrow Airport to welcome us in spite of the 6:00 A.M. arrival. I wore for the first and only time in Britain my Stetson hat, guessing (correctly) that it would guarantee pictures in the papers. The American ambassador is automatically visible; there were countless articles in the papers before we arrived, and the curiosity level about a new ambassador is high. Eccentricities like a Western hat would pique British interest even more, and my goal was to become known as quickly as possible.

Day One proved fairly typical of what lay in store. I spoke to the foregathered embassy employees at 9:00 A.M., briefed Senators John Danforth and John Chafee at 10:00, briefed a House of Representatives delegation at noon, and popped into the embassy cafeteria for lunch at 1:00. The employees were pleased to see me there and amazed as well. It was rare for an ambassador to eat there, but I did — often. At 4:00, the father of a victim of the downed Pan Am Flight 103, blown out of the sky over Scotland by a terrorist bomb, came by, and at 5:00, Prime Minister Thatcher received me at 10 Downing Street, the prime minister's official residence.

I was pleased to be asked to call on her so soon. George, unbeknownst to me, had called her shortly after I accepted the job, urging her to grant *agrément,* the formal acceptance of a proposed ambassador, quickly; it was typical of his thoughtfulness. (The prime minister gently reminded him that it was the queen, not the prime minister, who attended to these protocolary niceties.) Her invitation to me clearly signaled that she knew I was a Bush friend. She greeted me in the reception room, very warmly; pictures were taken and she led me to her cozy private sitting room. She talked animatedly of her recent visit with Soviet president Mikhail Gorbachev, of South Africa's wrenching problems, and of the agony of Ireland. Fortunately, I didn't have any serious points to make; getting a word in proved difficult. Charles Powell, her senior adviser, sat in with us. I found him quietly prepossessing, and in time he and his effervescent wife, Carla, became valued friends to Jessica and me. That night we three (Isa had come over with Jessica on an earlier flight) had a quiet dinner in the candlelit family dining room.

Calls on British officials took much of my time in the early days. Neil Kinnock and Gerald Kaufman, the top two leaders of the Labour Party opposition, were early victims of my social blitzkrieg. Kinnock, a red-headed Welshman, told amusing stories and was almost as voluble as the prime minister. Occasionally, he let his rhetorical metaphors run away from him. When Mrs. Thatcher fired her longtime and faithful foreign minister, Geoffrey Howe, Howe fired back at her in a feisty speech in the House of Commons. Neil remarked, "Mrs. Thatcher has been bitten by the man she treated as doormat, and she deserves it." I liked him, but felt he was a bit uncomfortable with me. Though he never became prime minister, he moved his party sharply to the right, shed much of its outdated socialist baggage, and laid the groundwork for a Labour victory, though it was not to be he who engineered it.

My predecessor, Charles Price, had waged virtually open warfare with the Labour Party, but I felt that an American ambassador should keep all doors open; in a democracy, no government is forever. The *Times* ran a series on the American embassy's change of heart, speculating that we were preparing for Thatcher's defeat, and a Tory member of Parliament took me to task at a public gathering, but I felt I was correct. Occasionally I got interesting insights: Kinnock at lunch in November 1989 offered to bet me one hundred pounds that Mrs. Thatcher would not be prime minister on June 1, 1990. Unfortunately, I didn't take the bet, for she was.

Politicians were not my sole targets. The civil servants in Britain play a key role, frequently using their profound knowledge of how government works to guide the politicians, their theoretical bosses, to suit themselves. It was my experience that the British TV satire *Yes, Minister,* showing how ministers could be manipulated by high-ranking civil servants, had it about right. These "mandarins," as they were called, were often very bright and able, as I learned upon calling on the permanent undersecretary of the foreign office, Sir Patrick Wright.

I had met and instantly liked Wright in Washington, and he told me a story about his title. It seems a Japanese dignitary, whose command of English left something to be desired, translated Wright's title of permanent undersecretary as "immortal junior typist."

Other leaders I saw included Norman Willis, head of the Trade Unions Congress, and the three main religious leaders, the Archbishop of Canterbury, the Catholic archbishop, and the chief rabbi.

Winfield House ran smoothly. The staff consisted of the butler, Graham Hartley—the "CEO," if you will. Under his tutelage were a housekeeper, three maids (all Filipinos), three cooks, three footmen, and a gardener. It sounded extravagant to me, but I soon learned better. As Jessica quickly noted, "This isn't a house; it's a small four-star hotel." They worked hard and they worked well. Every need of every guest, every detail of every party, was foreseen and attended to, and, miraculously, *everyone* was nice. Surely it rivaled the White House itself. Jessica and I had, for the first time in our lives, separate bathrooms—a genuine luxury—enough closet space and dressing area, and a family room in which to unwind. Two suites, the Adams Suite (the Presidential Suite) and the Winfield Suite, provided elegant quarters for whomever might come. Two other handsome bedrooms completed the second floor, while the third floor consisted of offices and one large, rather informal suite, perfect for Heather, Martin, and family. In addition, most of the staff lived in the main house; Graham, the gardener, and driver John Bryant had housing on the grounds.

Graham had an eye for saving money. The California Winegrowers Association was keen to increase exports to Britain and had frequent tastings to promote its products. In the past the group had also donated wine to the residence, knowing that Winfield House would provide a superb showcase for these excellent wines. Graham suggested that I call David Berckley, the association's head, and see if he would oblige the new ambassador. After checking with his board, he agreed, and they shipped us some one hundred cases of the Golden State's best, making Winfield House a candidate for having the best cellar in London.

The Winfield House grounds, about twelve acres, were the largest in London save for Buckingham Palace; I was even able to put in a golf hole. The jewel of it all was a formal rose garden that perfumed the entire area in summer. A large greenhouse helped us keep fresh cut flowers in profusion throughout the house.

The furnishings came largely from the generosity of former ambassador and Mrs. Walter Annenberg, and many pieces were of museum quality. Several clocks required winding periodically, a job performed by a small and elderly man, a horologist named George Pewsey, who came by every week. He had clients all over London, a unique profession, and Dickensian charm.

One of the clocks had no glass face and I asked why. Pewsey explained that that one, given by Ambassador and Mrs. David Bruce, had no glass because in 1792 Prime Minister William Pitt put a five shilling tax on clocks with glass faces. A clever Swiss clockmaker named Justin Vulliamy promptly began making glassless models. Tax avoidance hath a hoary history.

Scotland Yard, like the U.S. Secret Service, liked code names, as we soon discovered. I was Silver Bullet (I liked that); Jessica was White Rose; and Isa, who stayed most often with us, was Yellow Rose. The house was Campground and the office, Bonanza. All the monikers were quite suitable for Texans.

Early on, I had admired the fifty-five portraits of previous ministers and ambassadors to the Court of St. James's. They hung in the great hall at the Chancery building on Grosvenor Square, and they were an imposing lot. For one thing, they traced the history of American portraiture, the older paintings given to blacks and whites, the subjects stiffly seated and of serious mien, while the more recent of my predecessors looked relaxed, perhaps taking themselves just a bit less seriously.

They included five presidents: John Adams, James Monroe, John Quincy Adams, Martin Van Buren, and James Buchanan. Robert Lincoln and Charles Francis Adams were sons of presidents. Giants of business, government, and the academy such as Andrew Mellon, Walter Hines Page, W. Averell Harriman, John Hay Whitney, Walter Annenberg, David Bruce, and Elliot Richardson, carried the burden. Joseph P. Kennedy, who didn't really like the British, had the job in the crucial years of 1938 to 1940. Anne Armstrong, a fellow Texan, was the first woman in the office. In the early days, the American representatives carried the title of minister, but in 1893, titular inflation struck and we became ambassadors. To date there have been twenty-nine of each.

Ray Seitz warned me shortly after I arrived to start looking for a portrait artist; I agreed, reasoning that I'd never look any younger. I had heard that an Israeli of Russian descent named Israel Zohar had been retained to paint Princess Diana. I called his agent, we met and haggled over what I would pay. After a false start or two, Zohar produced a satisfactory likeness that now peers down quizzically from an embassy wall. Not everyone liked it, but I did.

My official car, an armor-plated Opel, was due to be replaced by a Cadillac. Administrative counselor John Condayan bubbled with enthusiasm at the prospect. Having an identifiably American car would be appropriate, he felt, and we awaited the new machine impatiently. Months went by and it did not appear. The problem was that Cadillac didn't make right-hand-drive cars (thus dealing itself effectively out of the British, Japanese, Indian, and other markets). Instead, the steering wheel, transmission, and other components were being shifted on a standard left-hand-drive car, and apparently it wasn't easy.

Finally the great day came. I went down to the embassy garage to see the armored wonder and take a spin around the block.

Disaster. For security reasons, the windows could not be opened. Legroom was nonexistent. And every time we went over a bump, the oil pan or some such entrail came clattering off. With a greater understanding of the problems of the American auto industry, I quietly resumed using the old Opel, Charlie Price's car. The genius who had dreamed up the idea of a Cadillac had cost the taxpayers a bundle via an expensive and impractical conversion. We used the Caddy to transport members of Congress; I'm sure they liked it.

My third day I awoke very early and decided to take my daily run. Strapping on a backpack of fresh clothes, I loped off just before dawn to the embassy building in Grosvenor Square, taking care to look right before crossing streets, lest I be flattened by cars driving on the left. The embassy door, not surprisingly, was locked, and as I looked around distractedly, wondering what to do, a deep voice behind me inquired sternly, "May I help you, sir?"

Startled, I couldn't see where this Oz-like voice came from. Finally, I noticed a speaker box and said, "I'm the new ambassador. Could I come in?" The unseen young Marine guard inside looked at the sweaty, scantily clad man outside skeptically, but after due consultation, he popped the lock and in I came. The story somehow found its way into the papers, to the further amusement of the British.

This outing proved to be my last solo run. My predecessor had had Scotland Yard Special Branch protection. The British Home Office, in charge of such matters and noticing the high cost of protecting ambassadors, had informed the embassy that with the arrival of a new man, the protection would cease. The embassy security office protested. Terrorist threats were very real, and our people took pains to relate how hard it would be to understand if an unprotected American ambassador were kidnapped and held for ransom. The British reluctantly acceded, and two superb officers, Bob Gilby and Rick Persich, were assigned to accompany me wherever I went outside embassy grounds. Not enthusiastic runners, they conned their superior into buying them a rickety bike to use when their daft protectee went running. Educated and amusing people, Bob, Rick, and driver John Bryant became good friends of mine.

Indeed, all the Winfield House staff became valued colleagues, guided by the sure hand of butler Graham Hartley. The kitchen, overseen by a German named Hans Kremer, turned out four-star meals. Their culinary horizons broadened when Rosemary Kowalski, a talented and successful cateress from San Antonio, came over at her own expense as our houseguest and added Mexican food to Hans's repertoire.

Winfield House had not only a fine staff but also an intriguing history. Originally the twelve-acre property had been part of an ambitious development by famed nineteenth-century architect John Nash. In 1936 the existing house had burned, and the property was purchased by American heiress Barbara Hutton, then married to Count Haugwitz-Reventlow. (She later married actor Cary Grant.) The Georgian house she built was called Winfield after Hutton's grandfather, Frank Winfield Woolworth, founder of the store chain.

In 1939, with war looming and her marriage on the rocks, Hutton moved back to America. The Royal Air Force took the property, boarded up the house, and tethered barrage balloons in the gardens during the London blitz. In 1944, a flying "buzz bomb" hit nearby, slightly damaging the building; later, it became a U.S. Air Force officers club.

After the war, Hutton returned and decided to give the property to the U.S. government as a residence for the American ambassador. Reconstruction proved slow, and the first ambassador to live there, Winthrop Aldrich, did not move in until January 18, 1955.

At an early country team meeting, I asked each member to outline the main problems of his or her agency or department. For my part, I urged that we pay close attention to biographical reporting, an activity often given disappointing attention at embassies and by the CIA. I suggested being alert to who was in town; knowing of the presence of business, church, union, or other Americans could be helpful to our mission in countless ways. A review by the State Department's inspector general lay just ahead, and I cautioned senior officers to know their junior officers, to be alert to the need for minority representation, and to be sensitive to gender concerns. Recalling Tom Pickering's advice, I did "management by walking."

We instituted a quarterly briefing on matters British for the high-powered and numerous members of the American business community living in London. My first performance being somewhat short of brilliant, I thereafter thought out carefully in advance what I wanted to say. Relations with business were of vital interest to an administration that realized that the British were by far the largest foreign investors in America (easily outstripping the Japanese), while we held the number one position among foreign investors in the United Kingdom.

The main issues between the two countries? The thorniest was Hong Kong. Thousands of Vietnamese "boat people" had fled to that tight little island colony, and British detention facilities groaned under their numbers. The British wanted to start sending them back, forcibly if necessary. I brought the matter up with the president personally, at Camp David. His reaction was rigorous; he was not about to be party to shipping refugees back to a squalid communist dictatorship. Given that we turned back Cubans and Haitians, this struck the British as, at best, two-faced. I had learned the strength of their convictions early, in a call on prickly foreign office officials. While I could see their point and sympathize with their predicament in defying their closest ally, I staunchly maintained that the cases differed. However, when the British did indeed repatriate a number of Vietnamese in spite of U.S. objections, I shed no tears; I felt the president could have shown more sympathy to a truly nasty dilemma that could have led to riots and bloodshed. A trip to Washington for consultations at the State Department made me aware that many colleagues shared my view. Clearly, the president was driving our policy.

Other issues included Northern Ireland, where we had issued travel warnings to American tourists about the sectarian violence there, much to the distress of British officials. True to my promise to Senator Biden, I made my first trip a visit to the troubled province.

Presentation of Credentials

THE OFFICIAL start of an ambassador's tour comes when he presents his credentials to the head of the state to which he is accredited. In Britain, of course, that meant Her Majesty, Queen Elizabeth II, and to say that the whole business is highly protocolary doesn't nearly cover it.

It all began shortly after my arrival, with a call on Sir John Richards, marshal of the diplomatic corps. A tall, distinguished-looking retired general, he went over in detail everything that we would do. I learned that I would not go it alone; the top nine officers of the embassy would accompany me and be presented by me to the queen. Furthermore, we would all be dressed in white tie and tails, the official civilian uniform of the court.

The great debate that followed my sharing this information with my colleagues centered on whether we would look sillier with top hats or without. Some voices held strongly that Americans, a breezy, informal lot, would do better without. In the end, I decided—hats it was. An embassy is no democracy.

The next question was who would pay the $100 or so to rent the swallowtail suits. I felt the State Department should; it was, after all, an official function. We wired Washington and were turned down flat. "Charge it off on your income tax," they generously suggested.

My own case was not so simple. I had been warned by Charlie Price that I would need both tails and a morning suit. I dropped by Anderson and Shepherd, Bond Street tailors I had used from time to time, and learned to my horror that each suit would cost about a thousand pounds. Yankee thrift (present even in Southerners like me) quickly dispatched pride and style, and I bought them at Moss Brothers off the rack for three hundred pounds apiece, bad enough but bearable. (Naturally, this story was leaked to the press and, again, reported with glee.)

The great day arrived—May 17, clear and warm. Weather mattered. We were to be called for in carriages, and having the tops back made it all much nicer.

Nervous as debutantes, our hearty band gathered well before the appointed hour, admiring one another extravagantly. The staff turned out in large numbers to check us out and, I felt sure, to snicker a bit. A considerable crowd waited outside as Sir John led me to the first of four carriages. We clambered aboard, and off we clopped.

The trip between Grosvenor Square and Buckingham Palace[2] took little more than ten minutes, as the carriage drivers managed somehow to avoid snarling London traffic. A hopeless ham, I waved to all we encountered, suspecting that they thought us escapees from an asylum. As we arrived, the great gates of Buckingham swung open, and we dismounted.

Climbing the seemingly endless red-carpeted steps inside left some of us breathless, and on arrival at the appointed place, I was cut from the herd and guided to one corner of the huge waiting room. My colleagues, rent from my side, were led across the room, scarcely within shouting distance.

Sir Patrick Wright, permanent undersecretary of the foreign and commonwealth office, again ran through what would happen. He and I would stand in front of two ten-foot-high polished doors. As they opened, we would nod our heads, take one step forward, and nod again. We would then march in, left foot first, to where the queen waited. He would present me and depart. After I handed her my credentials and the notification of my predecessor's departure, we would chat. My officers would then one at a time repeat the procedure, and I would present them.

Thanks to a bit of history, the whole drill carried the awareness that something could go wrong. One of my predecessors, Walter Annenberg, had the misfortune to have his presentation ceremony filmed by BBC Television. (Normally, no cameras are allowed.) When the queen asked how he was settling in, he nervously replied that all was well except that the "residence was undergoing elements of refurbishment," a phrase that struck the British public when they saw it as hilariously stuffy, and poor Walter took a merciless ribbing of the sort that only the British press can administer.

At 11:00 on the dot, a bell rang, and as if by magic the doors to the reception room slid open. (I saw no one there to open them.) Inside, about twenty yards away, stood the queen. By grace, I managed to get through the nods and the endless march up to where Her Majesty waited, and from there it was easy.

The queen is surely the world's best conversationalist; she could write a manual on how to put people at ease. We chatted about her visit to the United States thirteen years before, and she made me feel as if she of course remembered me. Still, I felt a barrier, perhaps the fact that we remained standing, perhaps something in those ice-blue eyes. As in our first meeting in 1976, she never forgot who she was and neither did I. After ten minutes of such talk, she, through some alchemy undetectable by lesser mortals, let it be known it was time to get on with it, and the rest of our crew came in.

I managed not to bobble any names or titles as each person shook her hand and she asked what each did. When the CIA station chief, Bert Dunn, came in, I described him as "political coordinator." One does not identify Central Intelligence Agency officers abroad; even though the British and Americans had shared virtually all intelligence with one another for decades, I felt constrained. "And what do you coordinate?" she asked. The tall, straight, and impish Dunn replied without missing a beat: "Why, anything the ambassador wants me to coordinate!"

The last one presented, I said good-bye, turned my back, and strode to the door, turned again for a final brisk head nod, and we were done. Remounting our carriages, which had fortunately not turned pumpkin on us, we returned to Grosvenor Square and the embassy, where virtually the whole staff waited.

There, tradition called for me to give champagne to each of the carriage drivers and lumps of sugar to each of the horses. I managed the first with better grace than the second; Texan or not, I've never been relaxed around horses, and I had visions of my thumb disappearing with the sugar. Afterward, all of us retired to my office for a champagne party in honor of the various British who had helped bring off the event.

One morning in late April, Ray Seitz had come into my office with the news that former president and Mrs. Reagan were planning a trip to London, where he was to speak at the Guildhall. Their staff man had dropped an unsubtle hint that they would like to stay at Winfield House.

At home that evening, I broke this news to Jessica, who reminded me that we would have Heather, Martin, and their children with us and that the Reagans might be more comfortable in a quieter, less spirited atmosphere. She called Bar Bush for guidance, and Bar led us to believe no offense would be taken. Fortunately, Malcolm Forbes put his beautiful London home at the Reagans' disposal, thus solving the problem.

Reagan featured in another early event. One day as I drove through London I noticed a large billboard with a picture of the former president on it. An ad for a computer, it read, *ANYBODY* CAN LEARN TO USE A KONICA. Sorely annoyed by an insult to a great American, I called the head of the local Konica operation and complained. The billboard quickly disappeared.

Dinner at Buckingham Palace — and Murder

AN EVENING at Buckingham Palace doesn't happen often, even for ambassadors, so we readily accepted the invitation to attend a dinner for President Babangida of Nigeria.

White tie with decorations meant a struggle getting dressed but no problem of getting decked out, since American civilians in government service don't wear decorations. Jessica wore a yellow silk Arnold Scassi gown and looked very much as if she belonged in a palace.

Our car purred through the gates at 8:00 P.M. on the dot, preceded, as it happened, by a sleek Jaguar bearing the prime minister and Mr. Thatcher. We alit simultaneously and I introduced Jessica, since she had not met the Thatchers.

Up the red-carpeted stairs we went, to a large room where drinks were being served to a considerable crowd, including the Archbishop of Canterbury. After about fifteen minutes of chitchat, two tall doors (all the doors in the palace are tall, or so it seemed) opened, we lined up in no particular order, and the receiving line began. In it waited the queen and Prince Philip, the guest of honor and his lady, and to my delight, the "Queen Mum," Queen Elizabeth's mother, a totally engaging person of eighty-nine.

From the line, ushers guided us into the great dining hall, the ceiling of which must have been fifty feet high. The table, E-shaped, groaned with silver, china, and crystal enough to accommodate five wines. A red-coated Royal Marine Band played show tunes in the balcony as the 150 or so guests found their places.

Conversation for me proved pleasant and easy, my dinner partners being a contractor's wife, Lady Chetwood, and the wife of the head of Scotland Yard, Lady Imbert. Jessica sat at another leg of the E between a retired journalist and the Uni of Iffi, hereditary chief of a Nigerian district, a voluble man in a tailored pink dress with a small pink hat on his head. Jessica thought his dress much handsomer than her own.

After a multicourse dinner washed down by the endless flow of wine, a toastmaster enjoined us to "Pray silence" and the queen offered her guest a toast. He responded with blessed brevity. At that point, in came twelve Scottish pipers, bagpipes awheeze, tall fur hats atop their heads. They marched around the tables playing their mournful tunes, and the head table rose and left.

Bidding good-bye to my dinner partners, I went to find Jessica, who introduced me to her companions, both of whom she had enjoyed. The Uni, aglow, asked me if I had ever been to his country. When I replied in the negative, he said, "Oh, we must get you to come for a week. Perhaps two weeks." And he toddled off.

At that point, social aides with the skill of border collies herding sheep moved us into another large room, where waited members of the royal family, including Princess Anne, Prince Charles and Princess Diana, Prince Philip, the bubbly "Fergy," the Duke and Duchess of Kent, and Mrs. Angus Ogilvy. Key guests were smoothly maneuvered to one after another of the family, allowed to chat for a few moments, and then moved along to another. The queen and President Babangida, meanwhile, had retired to a smaller, adjoining room, and the politically important guests, not including the Cattos, were ushered in for more leisurely visits.

About 12:30 I found Sir John Richards and asked if we might withdraw even though the queen remained. In American protocol one does not leave before the ranking guest, and though we were tired, we didn't want to blow it so early in our tenure. Sir John assured us that departure would be entirely correct, so we managed to be abed by 1:00 A.M.

Calls on British officials continued to take up much of my time, as my foreign service officer Special Assistant Marie ("Masha") Yovanovich held me to a busy schedule. An early one was on Sir Geoffrey Howe, the secretary of state for foreign affairs. Rotund, wry, and intensely likable, he nonetheless could be starkly frank. At one point I had to tell him on short notice that the president planned to announce a revival of President Eisenhower's "open skies" idea, which would allow NATO and Warsaw Pact planes to overfly one another's territory under certain circumstances. Geoffrey minced no words telling me he thought that we should have proposed the idea to NATO first, rather than just doing it. I called Brent Scowcroft at the National Security Council to suggest such a change, but Brent said the speech, by then set in concrete, could not be amended.

Geoffrey told me a bit about a recent visit with Soviet president Gorbachev. He summed up the Russian's message to his Cuban client, Fidel Castro: "We're still with you, lads, but don't count on us," a doubtless discouraging message for Fidel, but one that proved fair warning.

I took Michael Heseltine, the British secretary of transportation, to lunch at Le Gavroche. Tall, handsome, vain, and ambitious, he waited in the parliamentary wings for Mrs. Thatcher to stumble. He made no effort to hide his disgust with American treatment of our British ally. A devout believer in the Anglo-American "special relationship," I asked what he thought of its current state. Heseltine snapped, "It doesn't exist. You proved that in the Reagan administration when you did not tell us in advance of the decision to invade Grenada." George Bush was sensitive to the value of a close United States–United Kingdom tie, but the imbalance in power inevitably created strains; Heseltine had a point.

Speaker of the House Bernard Weatherill was wonderfully amusing during my call. He reminisced on his days as Chief Whip: "If my boys didn't stay in line and vote with the government, I'd just threaten them with being put on a delegation to Nigeria!" And in a variation on Lord Acton's famous dictum, he said, "All power is wonderful. Absolute power is absolutely wonderful!"

John Major, then treasury secretary and later chancellor and prime minister, struck me very favorably. Relaxed and informal, he fell quickly to use of given names, a very un-British trait but one most appealing to Americans.

Bert Dunn had me to lunch with British intelligence chief Sir Percy Craddock, a tall, spindly, languid man given to wrapping his legs one around the other like the snakes on a caduceus. A Chinese specialist, he was good company and a good man to have on our side. We discussed the recent expulsion of fourteen Soviet embassy personnel, a much-criticized action by Her Majesty's government during a time of détente and a move quickly reciprocated by the Soviets. "We had to do it," Sir Percy said. "They were just too blatant [in their espionage activity]."

Another visit with Bert was fascinating as well. A ranking KGB officer named Oleg Gordievsky had recently defected to the British, and U.S. intelligence, as was customary, was invited to debrief him. When Bert suggested we go see him I quickly accepted.

Gordievsky told us that the food shortage in Russia was bad, the worst since 1973. He felt that a lessening of discipline was in part responsible. This opinion was reinforced some time later when Soviet ambassador to Britain Zamyatin urged in a letter to the *Times* that the British public donate food.

I asked the Russian what we in the West could do to help. Train managers, he replied, and help educate high-level people in the hundred-some ministries of the government.

Didn't Leninism and economic liberalism collide? I wondered. He didn't think so, citing the Finns and Swedes. I asked about President Nixon's idea that periods of détente were invariably times of greatest Soviet espionage activity; he quickly confirmed what Nixon had said. As tensions relaxed, KGB people became warm and cuddly, Cold War ideology was forgotten, and the first thing you know, Westerners passed along valuable information.

I told Gordievsky of a lunch I had had with Ambassador Zamyatin, and I wondered what percentage of the embassy personnel were KGB officers. He replied that at the typical embassy, 50 percent were foreign service types, but that 30 percent were likely to be KGB and 20 percent GRU (the Soviet military intelligence operation). There were, he added, tremendous financial incentives for Soviet officers to recruit Western officials.

Having run into a number of Soviet journalists over the years, I asked what percentage of them were likely to have been intelligence operatives; perhaps 10 percent, he speculated.

Western good manners gave the Soviets an advantage, because since the Revolution, Russians had not been trained to be polite. They brayed the party line, and when a Westerner would courteously grant one point or another, the Russian would think the brilliance of his arguments had carried the day; politeness was viewed as weakness.

I constantly learned lessons about the British press. One day a London *Times* reporter interviewed me. I liked him and as I walked him to the elevator, I told him my gaffe at Defense when my tongue slipped and I said there were seventeen Soviet "shits" sailing the Mediterranean. Clearly, I meant not to be quoted, and I felt safe since he had put away his tape recorder. Forget it: the story appeared next day.

Security at the embassy always carried a high priority, and lapses by Marines at the U.S. embassy in Moscow made our eager young men doubly alert in London. Sometimes they were too alert. One evening the political minister-counselor, Kim Pendleton, came storming into my office, ready to murder the next Marine he saw. It seemed that several of his political officers were, as usual, working late. A Marine guard let one of the charwomen in to the political section to clean up, and while she was there, the guard sneaked into the safe and removed classified papers. He then charged Kim with a security violation for not having been alert to the presence of someone without clearance. To Kim, it looked like game-playing, a "sting" that accomplished nothing. Knowing that such violations can hurt an officer's career, I asked the administrative officer to strike the violation, which he did.

Security questions of a deadly nature struck us in late May. One of our senior consular officers, Marie Burke, failed to report to work one day. Two of her colleagues went to the ground floor apartment where she lived alone and found her stabbed to death in bed in a pool of blood. Her purse and credit cards had disappeared and there were no fingerprints. Scotland Yard, assisted by our security office, investigated intensively for months. The case became the largest murder investigation in the history of the Metropolitan Police, with more than 700 people involved, and 250 fingerprinted. Nothing definitive turned up and no arrests were made. Having known and liked Marie, I was deeply saddened; I was also worried about the effect of the murder on morale. Could it have been a disgruntled visa applicant? Or a drug smuggler? The police sent officers to Jamaica to check the drug angle, without luck. The case remains open today.

Jessica and I managed to escape these concerns by visits to the countryside on weekends. On one occasion we visited a stately home, called Stoner, that welcomes guests (the paying kind, to be sure). As we wandered through the beautiful old place, inhabited by the same family for eight hundred years, she called my attention to several portraits of people variously named Hoby or Hobbie, and we speculated on whether they might have been her ancestors. Some of her forebears had been run out of the country for horse theft, she explained, but others were quite respectable.

A Presidential Visit

WORD CAME in May that the president and Bar would soon pay a visit to Britain, sparking frenzied preparations. A presidential visit is not taken lightly by the White House advance office or by the embassy concerned; advance people, logistics experts, communicators, and press office personnel swarmed like energetic ants. Our final planning meeting before arrival crammed the room with more than a hundred people.

To see the great blue-and-white plane with "United States of America" emblazoned on its side was always an exciting moment, and never more so than when, with President and Mrs. Bush aboard, it landed at a military airport near London. Prime Minister and Mr. Thatcher were both on hand to greet the Bushes on their first visit to Britain in his presidency. After national anthems were played, we boarded helicopters for the quick trip to Winfield House. Although the presidential craft left first, the chopper carrying Jessica and me passed the VIPs and landed first, enabling us to greet the visitors and the Thatchers when they, in turn, touched down. Our cow sculpture, whom we dubbed Udder Pendragon, grazed placidly nearby, much to the amusement of all.[3] The prime minister came in for a quick moment, and Heather and family got to greet all the visitors. After she left, we enjoyed dinner served in the small dining room, and the Bushes, tired after a week of travel, turned in early, a move that I always applaud.

Early on June 1, George was up and ready for a press interview with Don Oberdorfer of the *Washington Post*. I sat in on it and enjoyed how smoothly and knowledgeably he answered questions. It always amazed me that critics accused him of being tongue-tied; he was in my experience always highly articulate.

After the interview, a reporter asked National Security Council head Brent Scowcroft, "General, are you getting any sleep?" Brent, always quick-witted, replied, "As long as there are meetings, I get plenty of sleep." Then, looking at the tape recorder in the reporter's hand, he had second thoughts and mumbled, "I hope that thing is off."

At 10:00 we drove to 10 Downing Street for a summit meeting. The two leaders and their key aides, General Scowcroft and Charles Powell, retired to the prime minister's small sitting room while the rest of us, including Jim Baker and his British counterpart, attended a larger meeting in the Cabinet Room. I was disappointed, having hoped to be the note-taker sitting in with the principals. One always wants to be "in," participating where the action is.

A couple of weeks before, I had gotten a call from Larry Eagleburger, deputy secretary of state, a former protégé of Henry Kissinger, the world's most secretive man.[4] Larry had been a good friend since my Protocol days, and I was glad to hear from him. I did not, however, like what he said.

"Bob Gates [deputy CIA director] and I are arriving tomorrow at two o'clock in the morning. Please bed us down. Later, we'll see Thatcher. Just Bob and I."

I relayed this news to DCM Ray Seitz, who was bothered by Larry's message. If a new ambassador were cut out of a meeting between the prime minister and second-level American officials, it would send a very negative message to the prime minister about the ambassador's standing with the president.

I sweated and stewed. Larry had been brought up at Kissinger's knee, and this was pure Kissinger theatrics. "To hell with it," I thought. "I'll call George."

I did, briefly explaining what was happening. George soothed me at once: "Don't worry. You'll go to the meeting." Perhaps he recalled being blindsided by Kissinger when George was the U.S. representative in Beijing in the early 1970s and Kissinger kept him largely in the dark during highly secret negotiations with the Chinese.

The meeting with Mrs. T had a revealing side. As we settled into the comfortable chairs in the prime minister's study, she said, smiling, "Now, Larry, tell me what this is all about," with which she launched into a forty-five-minute monologue. I doubt Larry said much more than two sentences.

The queen and Prince Philip had a luncheon for the Bushes at Buckingham Palace and Bar narrowly escaped committing a faux pas. She had originally planned to wear a short-sleeved dress to the luncheon, but cool weather changed her mind. We later learned that one *does not* wear short sleeves at Buckingham Palace.

Having Mrs. Thatcher as my luncheon partner gave me a good chance to talk seriously with her, and I welcomed it. Indeed, there was no other visit with her save a serious one. She liked issues and talking about them, and she did not have a bubbly sense of humor. We spent most of our time talking about what a world without a communist enemy would be like. I told her that Daniel Ortega, the Nicaraguan communist leader, now called himself a Scandinavian-style socialist. She snorted and, showing extraordinary knowledge of world events, mentioned that that was strange, given that Lenin's picture graces Nicaraguan stamps.

Meanwhile, Jessica enjoyed being placed between Prince Philip and Denis Thatcher. The prince had long been involved with the World Wildlife Fund, and that gave him and Jessica the common bond of interest in environmental matters. At one point, while discussing animals, His Royal Highness complained, rather grumpily she thought, that in the animal kingdom it is the females that select the breeding stock. They also compared notes on Nigeria's Uni of Iffi, Jessica's dinner partner at Buckingham Palace, with the prince explaining the Uni's importance on the Nigerian scene.

From the palace we returned to the embassy, where the president and Secretary of State Jim Baker addressed the gathered employees. George spoke well and movingly, mentioning, as I had suggested, the murder of Marie Burke. Evangelist Billy Graham dropped by just before the meeting, and George introduced him to the crowd.

Jessica and I rode with the president and the first lady in their limo back to Winfield House. On the way, George played a game: As we drove past pedestrians, he would wave, trying to guess in advance which ones would wave back and which would simply stare, mute and uncomprehending. He would say, "I'll get the one on the corner in the white dress," and most often he guessed right, eliciting a wave, a laugh, or a thumbs-up. He had fun, and it was infectious.

Security at Winfield House needed to be tight, but on occasions the Secret Service went too far. For Bush's visit they built a tent over the area through which the president's car entered. Puzzled, I asked why. The answer was they wanted to shield the vehicle from the view of high-rise apartments several blocks away. My guess was the agents posted at the gate didn't want to get wet if it rained. In any case, the tent cost the taxpayers about $2,200 to construct.

Indeed, security was so tight that Isa wasn't allowed to come home one night. She and a friend had been out to dinner and had taken a cab back to Winfield House. Stopped at the barricade, they alighted and began to explain the situation. "You can't come in this way," the policeman snapped. By then, their cab had left and they would have had to walk several blocks alone at night to get to the correct gate. The officer refused to radio the house. They were stymied. Fortunately, one of the house staff got word of the problem and woke me with the story. Donning slippers and robe, I stormed out into the street, trailing undiplomatic language, and got the young ladies in.

Trouble or not, presidential visits were useful to me—to anyone in government. Face-to-face time with the president is a valuable commodity. For example, during an afternoon run in a light rain, I brought up his relationship with the prime minister and learned his reaction to their first meeting at Camp David, when she had talked endlessly. I think he felt her verbal outpouring to be a bit condescending.

Dinner that night was black tie at 10 Downing and a gala occasion it was. Jessica and Bar, looking glamorous, wore Arnold Scassi dresses. There were celebrity guests such as John Cleese and Andrew Lloyd Webber, and major political figures such as Labour Party leader Neil Kinnock. John Cleese's fiancée, Alyce Faye Eichelberger, had bought a new gown for the event, but had not noticed a tag hanging down in the back. A Downing Street butler decorously asked her if he might remove it and then quietly did so.

After an excellent dinner, the speeches sparkled. Mrs. Thatcher may be the best extemporaneous speaker in the world. With no notes at all, she can hold forth for as long as necessary, speaking in parsable sentences, paragraphs, and whole concepts, her great beauty adding to the mesmerizing effect. That night she praised George immoderately. In his own way, he matched her; breezily informal, and articulate, he complimented even Neil Kinnock, in spite of intemperate remarks by the Labourite earlier that day on a radio show. The party broke up at a reasonably early hour, and afterward the four of us gossiped over cookies and milk in the Winfield House family room. There is no better company than Bar and George, and we loved their visit.

After the Bushes left the following morning, Jessica and I had a weekend to recover before our trip to Northern Ireland, a province fascinating for the variety of its personalities, the intensity of its hatreds, and the complexity of its history. Guided by our able consul in Belfast, Doug Archard, I called on Protestant extremist minister Ian Paisley, who revealed a stolid humorlessness. When I wondered why Protestant and Catholic city council members did not speak to one another, the young new lord mayor of Belfast explained, "You don't speak to people who are murdering your people."

We stayed at Hillsborough Castle, ancient and beautiful residence of the secretary of state for Northern Ireland (and site of the largest rhododendron tree in the world). Our host, Tom King (later to be defense secretary), told stories of old Joe Kennedy's tour as Franklin Roosevelt's ambassador to Britain. He claimed that on one occasion, the fanatically pro-Irish Kennedy sat in the front row at King George's opening of Parliament. During the king's speech, Kennedy chanted audibly, "Bullshit, bullshit," and finally stalked out of the hall. I asked a bit about the Irish Republican Army (IRA), and he explained that as the police feared going into certain Catholic neighborhoods, some police functions had devolved on the IRA. If you disturb your neighbor, he said, they will warn you not to do it again. If you disobey, they will shoot you in the ankles, shins, thighs, or elbows. Police fear is justified, for the militants put semtex, a particularly dangerous explosive, on gates and other places where a police "bobby" might venture.

Heavily guarded, we drove to Londonderry (the Irish call it Derry) to meet serene and brilliant John Hume, a member of the British Parliament and a moderate determined to bring peace to his troubled land. Jessica and I liked him enormously. Being placed between fanatical extremists is not easy, but Hume carried it off with skill.

It was as we left Northern Ireland that I held a press conference, saying, among other things, "It looks to me as if these people [the IRA] have their arms from the loonies of Libya and their inspiration from Don Corleone and the Mafia. It is not a happy combination." The results amazed me: the press assessments were uniformly favorable and total strangers expressed their thanks for my comments.

While Jessica returned to London, I flew to Scotland to participate in a memorial service for the victims of Pan Am Flight 103, destroyed by terrorist bombs the previous December. We visited the huge warehouse where volunteers were trying to clean up tables and tables of clothes, shoes, toys, and teddy bears, relics of the dead. At the service, a hysterical relative assaulted me with recriminations about the heartless American government. I could say nothing; what was there to say? It was a tragedy that brought tears to all our eyes.

That evening our able consul in Edinburgh, Doug Jones, and his wife had me to dinner. At each place was a wee bottle of Catto's Scotch, a nice touch by Mrs. Jones. Another guest was Sir Thomas Risk, head of the Bank of Scotland. I thought his name amusingly appropriate for a banker.

Shortly after my return from the Irish-Scottish trip, Bob Gilby came in with the welcome news that the government had decided to continue Scotland Yard protection, their previous decision notwithstanding. I thanked Bob for the information and chuckled to myself. I suspected that my denunciation of the IRA might have influenced the change of mind, though I certainly hadn't planned it that way.

A Procession of Dignitaries

RETURN FROM the brief spate of traveling made it clear that embassy life hadn't stopped — or even slowed — in my absence.

First of all, the Reagans arrived; no *Air Force One*, of course, just a plane borrowed from a friend. Former USIA director Charlie Wick and former attorney general William French Smith and wives accompanied the former president and first lady. I went to the airport to greet them, but, alas, they arrived an hour and a half late — fitting revenge for the slowness of our invitation for them to stay at Winfield House. Reagan's speech the next day at the ancient Guildhall proved he hadn't lost his touch in a set piece; I thought he looked a bit older up close, but all of the charm and humor was still there.

The Thatchers had a dinner in the Reagans' honor, a small black-tie affair at 10 Downing. The prime minister sat between the former president and me, and I overheard some of their conversation. He cracked jokes throughout, funny ones, I thought, but she never even feigned laughter. When toasting time came, she programmed him like a movie director: "Ron, I'll get up and offer you a welcoming toast. Then you'll get up and respond." Nancy beamed her approval from across the table, knowing her husband was in good hands, and sure enough, all went according to plan: she was brilliant, he was funny. Jessica and I had a glimpse of why the Reagan-Thatcher team worked so well.

The Bush-Thatcher alliance inevitably would be different. Indeed, the British press fretted (and I was often asked) if the much-treasured "special relationship" would suffer with the arrival of the new administration in Washington. The relationship didn't unravel, but it became a bit frayed at times.

Our friends Bob and Phyllis Oakley threw light on the matter. Both of them were career foreign service officers posted in Washington, and they had good access to what went on. During a London visit Bob told me that the president and Baker were concerned. They felt that the leadership of the Western alliance had slipped a bit during the flap over Iran-Contra and that Mrs. Thatcher had quickly picked up the slack. Bush set about changing the situation, deftly tightening the reins.

Not all of our dinners were at 10 Downing or "Buck House," as insiders flippantly called Buckingham Palace. Private homes could and did provide entertaining, gracious, and useful moments of insight into British life.

Shortly after my appointment as ambassador became known, we were in Aspen when I received a call from an old friend, James Hanson, head of the giant conglomerate Hanson Trust.

"Henry," said James, "Geraldine and I want to give a small dinner in your and Jessica's honor. Just a few friends. Maggie has said she could be there."

"Maggie?" I asked naively. "You mean the prime minister?"

"Of course, dear boy, who else?" he replied.

Delighted, I accepted, and on June 15 we arrived promptly at 8:00 P.M. at the Hansons' handsome home. Shortly thereafter, in came the Thatchers, and lively conversations ensued.

Jessica and I had discussed the evening a good bit. We assumed the dinner would proceed like a similar event in contemporary Washington: As dessert ended, the host would tap on a glass and offer a toast to the guest of honor. He or she would respond and all would adjourn for coffee or liqueurs.

Toasts could act as a way to send messages and with Mrs. Thatcher perforce a captive audience, I planned to do just that. I carefully crafted my remarks, memorized them, and rehearsed with Jessica as my audience and critic.

My message? The "special relationship" was alive and well. Bush admired her and planned to work with her, and the embassy under my direction would be a bastion of Anglo-American unity. The British, in short, were and would remain our core ally.

Sure enough, at the appropriate moment a spoon tapped a glass. It was not, however, the host; it was Geraldine Hanson, saying, "Come along, ladies, let's retire upstairs." The gents rose and *all* the ladies left, including the prime minister! For the next half hour I sat glumly enveloped in cigar smoke and banal business banter, remembering the Washington of twenty years before and regretting that London had not evolved as we had. The ladies-out rule prevailed at virtually every dinner I attended, and while having the men stay and talk business or politics did prove useful at times, I could never erase the picture of the prime minister gliding up the stairs; it was déjà vu, the Anne Armstrong scene of the early 1970s.

Mrs. Thatcher never seemed quite at ease, a problem she solved by compulsive talking. "I'm just a plain, straightforward provincial," she said, although she had expunged every trace of provincial accent. In meetings, she seemed to go on autopilot, as if a cassette switch had been thrown; out came entirely cogent prose, but I felt a lack of spontaneity. She always smiled but never laughed, even when the president was quite amusing, as he often was.

Over time, the president and the prime minister developed a good relationship, but even among speakers of the same language, problems arise. For example, in December 1989 Bush met with Soviet president Gorbachev, after which he briefed NATO colleagues in Brussels on the results. Quizzed by reporters afterward, the president commented that he urged the group to swift European integration.

Mrs. Thatcher had long been a skeptic about the pace and scope of cooperation among European countries, and when the British press, ever eager to find Anglo-American splits, played the story as a put-down of the prime minister, she naturally became alarmed. Aide Charles Powell called me and pointed out that the 7:00 P.M. news made it sound like a rebuke by Bush.

I reported all this to Brent Scowcroft by phone, as he and the president returned to the United States on *Air Force One*. Brent promised to alert White House press secretary Marlin Fitzwater so he could clear the matter up the next morning at his briefing.

The following day, as I went through the morning papers at breakfast, I was amazed. They played the matter as serious, even the responsible papers viewing it with alarm. I clipped a representative collection of headlines and when the working day at the White House had begun, I put in a call for George. When I read him how the press took his really rather offhand comment, he too was amazed. Shortly after we rang off, he called Mrs. Thatcher personally and assured her that he had no such thing in mind. He then rang me back to tell me what he had done.

His call in turn enabled the prime minister smartly to slap down rival

Neil Kinnock during parliamentary debate. Kinnock, gleefully anticipating an embarrassment for the prime minister, sarcastically accused her of poor leadership and depreciation of the U.S.-UK relationship. Waiting until Kinnock had walked all the way into the trap, Mrs. Thatcher snapped it shut, reporting that she and the president had spoken at length that very morning, with him assuring her that his comments were in no way aimed at Britain and certainly not at her.

The incident illustrated what a political ambassador in the Age of Communication can accomplish, especially one close to the president. Few, if any, career ambassadors would be likely to call the Oval Office to report such a matter; they would instead cable the State Department, with no assurance that the word would get through in a timely manner, or at all.

Dealing directly with a president can, on the other hand, ruffle feathers. George's attitude toward forced repatriation by the British in Hong Kong of Vietnamese boat people moved me at one point to fax him a letter making the case for a more understanding attitude, and I sent a copy to Deputy Secretary of State Larry Eagleburger. It clearly got under Larry's skin, and he went to Jim Baker in high dudgeon. Baker in turned called me, urging me to sin no more. I apologized and agreed to stick to channels in the future.

On substance, I felt quite at home with Mrs. Thatcher's positions. Early on, she dubbed Gorbachev "someone we can do business with." Nonetheless, I couldn't help recalling a line from T. S. Eliot that had struck me (and that I suggested to Charles Powell she use): "Do you think the faith has conquered the world / and that lions no longer need keepers?" But détente or no, her faith lay in dry powder, with regard not only to Russians but also to Germans.

Britain's "First Gent" was a different matter entirely. Denis Thatcher was easy to talk to. If he occasionally partook of too much of Scotland's national product, he nonetheless disarmed companions with frank and sometimes bawdy comments. Asked once if he had enjoyed the previous social evening, he quipped of the scantily clad wife of a prominent American columnist: "If looking at Mrs. X's cleavage can be considered enjoyable, I guess the answer is yes."

Tim Bell, a lively longtime Thatcher ally, repeated a story Denis tells. It seems he accompanied the prime minister on a visit to Malawi, and the ninety-year-old president-for-life, Hastings Banda, gave a dinner in the

Thatchers' honor. After the meal, Banda rose and announced that he would speak: "I will tell the story of my life, and go through it year by year." At about year forty, Denis looked at his wife, whose head had slumped. Charles Powell's chin lay on his chest. Denis thought, "My God, how am I going to stay awake for the next fifty years? I guess I'll use the old army trick. I'll put my index finger on the roof of my mouth. If I go to sleep and the finger slips, I'll either wake up or throw up."

Denis could be gallant. When the Bushes came in June 1989, he bent to kiss Bar's hand. She, full of fun and little given to European ways, quickly bent and kissed his hand in return. Fortunately, a photographer caught the exchange, to the amusement of the newspaper public; the first lady was never puffed up.

Jessica and I had a dinner honoring the prime minister in May 1990. It happened to be Denis's birthday, and we had a cake with his name written on it in icing. Alas, the name was spelled incorrectly, with two "n's" and I noticed to my amusement that during the after-dinner toasts, he took a knife and wiped the offending extra "n" away. In a remark recalling his wife's living above the family grocery in childhood, he quipped, "We live over the store." (The prime minister's quarters at 10 Downing Street are above the offices.) "But we have to pay thirty-five hundred pounds a year rent. Times eleven years, that's a lot. And she doesn't even take all her salary. Gives away ten thousand of it!"

At that same party, Jessica, Isa, and I did a bit of shuffling of seats during coffee, which was served at table. While Denis talked with the dinner partner to his right, Jessica slipped away and was replaced by Isa. Both blond and dressed in black, mother and daughter looked startlingly alike. Turning back to his left during a conversational pause, Denis found a younger version of his dinner partner and I suspect that for just a moment he thought of taking the pledge.

Our string of distinguished visitors included Vice President and Mrs. Quayle, who came in May 1990 and stayed with us. The prime minister had a dinner for them at Chequers, the beautiful official country residence of prime ministers, and the four of us rode out together in his car. Conversation was stiff at first, but as we got to know each other it eased considerably. The next day, while Jessica accompanied Marilyn Quayle on her schedule, I took Dan to see Mrs. Thatcher and the foreign minister, Douglas Hurd.

Quayle had had bad publicity from the day George named him candidate for vice president, and I wondered how he would comport himself. I could have saved myself any concern. He was totally in command of his brief at all meetings and left the British impressed. Later, he and I played tennis, with him winning both sets, to my surprise and chagrin. "You have a better game than I do," he said as we left the court. "It's just that I'm younger."

In July 1989, Supreme Court justices Sandra Day O'Connor and Anthony Kennedy came to London, and I took them to see the prime minister. The conversation was far-ranging and lively, particularly between the two women lawyers.

Mrs. Thatcher, emphasizing her respect for the rule of law, spoke of how anxious she had been to find legal justification for her support of the American air attack on Libya during the Reagan administration and her problems with the legality of our intervention in Grenada. The latter proved difficult since the governor-general's request that we intervene was entirely ex post facto. Justice O'Connor, asked about the prevalence of guns in the United States, explained that the right to bear arms, explicit in the Constitution, may refer to militias, not to individuals, and she predicted that one day, the Supreme Court will have to decide.

Turnover in the Ranks

THE COUNTRY team at the embassy consisted of nearly 100 percent newcomers. Normally, the rhythm of rotation is staggered, and old hands are available to give advice as new people arrive, an advantage that we did not enjoy. Raymond Seitz, the deputy chief of mission, had been vacuumed up by Jim Baker to become assistant secretary of state for European and Canadian affairs. His replacement, Ron Woods, did not arrive for several weeks, leaving Ann Berry, the newly arrived minister for economic affairs, as acting DCM, a job at which she proved to be a whiz. Bruce Burton took over the political section, John Condayan ran the administrative side, and Bert Kreig became consul general; all were excellent officers. Only CIA station chief Bert Dunn remained to provide us newcomers with a bit of perspective.

The newcomer whose talents affected me most personally was the USIS representative, Public Affairs Officer Charles Courtney. Part of his wide-ranging job lay in getting good publicity for the United States and for its number one representative, namely me. To help him, I had drafted an outsider, Michael Scully, to join my team as speechwriter — a wise move, as Mike proved to be first-rate and wonderful company.

Sam, as Courtney was known, scheduled my press exposures cautiously. He had no idea how adept I might prove in dealing with the notorious British journalism, and he wanted to take no chances.

One way of exposing us to the British and their press lay in interviews, several of which I had given without mishap before arriving. Another was in writing articles and letters, which both Jessica and I did frequently.

BBC Radio had a unique and amusing tool for arranging on-the-spot comments on breaking events, one that Sam had me do fairly often. An apparently ordinary London taxi, black and squat like thousands of others, would pull up in front of the embassy. I would climb in the backseat, but instead of the usual courteous and well-informed London cabbie, a BBC reporter, a driver, and copious transmitting equipment waited inside. The reporter could quickly get to the questions, my schedule suffered little interruption, and the resulting interview could be aired at once.

Occasionally I overruled Sam and, relying on my own instincts, made him nervous. One dark and cold winter afternoon, I looked out the window and saw a particularly forlorn group of pickets in Grosvenor Square across the street from the embassy. Protesters frequented the park; some fringe group or another always could be counted on to be present. The group in question carried signs reading, U.S. OUT OF EL SALVADOR and 70,000 DEAD.

I had a sudden thought: why not have them in, for tea and talk in my office? It would warm their bodies and conceivably even make them think better of Uncle Sam. I asked my able and patient assistant Susie Peake to go down and invite them in.

Sam viewed it all with alarm. The security people were quite concerned as well, saying they would have extra guards secreted behind potted palms, for fear that these dangerous radicals might bomb the embassy or assassinate the ambassador. I paid no attention and sent Susie on her way.

The four bedraggled young people who came diffidently into my office were not bomb-throwers. One was a Polish priest, the others were students. They earnestly explained their concerns and lamented the extent of U.S. imperialism. I suggested they consider picketing the Nicaraguan embassy as well as ours, since the Nicaraguans provided aid to the Salvadoran insurgents even as we helped the government. We took tea and, with thanks, they took their leave. I doubt I made any converts, but I at least gave them a good story to tell.

Sam could be a vigorous partisan. When the *New York Times*'s Elaine Sciolino, in a piece critical of Bush ambassadors, lumped me in with a number of very generous but wholly inexperienced appointees, he called her to complain. Her excuse was that her editor made her do it; my reaction was a Britishism: not bloody likely.

The Nicaraguan elections caused me another lapse into plain speaking. A British leftist group organized a protest, inundating my desk with postcards saying, "Support the results of the Nicaraguan elections." Their assumption was that the communist Sandinistas would win but the United States would try to subvert them. The surprising results showed the Nicaraguan people thoroughly tired of communism and Democrat Violeta Chamorro the easy victor. The only person I knew who was not surprised was John Sununu. At a White House luncheon a week or so before the election, I heard him flatly predict that the Sandinistas would lose. The day after the election, I riffled through the postcards and in the few instances where I found return addresses, I wrote the sender a card reading, "I will support the results. Will you?" Childish perhaps, but satisfying.

Sam's office did far more than press relations. USIS was the point of contact for the embassy with the cultural and intellectual elite, and it knew its business. One evening in early 1990, Sam had a dinner party for Jessica and me, to which came an extraordinary group of talented people, ranging from Irish novelist Edna O'Brien to feminist author Germaine Greer, Julian Barnes, and TV playwright Malcolm Bradbury, among others. A lively evening, it was typical of what USIS could do.

I came to realize that being just a bit contentious could be useful. The left-wing British playwright Harold Pinter loosed a vicious attack on the United States in the wake of the defeat of the left in the Nicaraguan election. It annoyed me. I wrote a letter to the newspaper *The Independent*, which had carried his latest screed. This triggered a letter of response from Pinter.

Rather than keep up the sterile exchange, I decided to ask the playwright to lunch. I called him with this suggestion and, somewhat to my surprise, he accepted. We went to Le Gavroche, my favorite restaurant. I made no dent in his view of my country, but I enjoyed his company and he apparently enjoyed my wine.

Good Company, Good Food, Good Entertainment

GUESTS CAME, not as single spies but in battalions, and fortunately, Winfield House was always ready for them. Nothing fazed Graham and his staff, though I suspect he may have blinked once or twice.

In October, our dear Washington friend Susan Mary Alsop arrived for an extended stay, to our delight. Susan Mary had many London friends and was always the easiest person imaginable to entertain. If we wanted company, she was always game; if we had duties, she took care of herself.

Jessica had to return home in late October, and no sooner had she left than the sensational daily *Today* headlined an article AUNT SUE MARCHES IN AS HEIRESS FLIES OUT. The piece quoted Susan Mary as saying, "It's terribly old fashioned, like the Aunt who comes to visit," but the implication was clear: the cat was away and I was playing. They even ran a picture of an attractively posed Susan Mary in her youth to add to the mischief. We were all amused and paid no attention. Susan Mary was great company, even accompanying me to the Marine Ball, an annual embassy event at which the lively conversation for which she was renowned was at a premium.

Family came. Jessica's brother Bill and his wife, Diana, visited, and their son Paul and daughter-in-law Janet as well. My aunt Liz Pritchett came from New York. Since she was a singer, I took her to the opera at Glyndebourne, always a treat. A long-lost cousin from Dallas, Fred Stradley, brought his new bride to visit, and cousin Martha Schenken and her husband, Rudy, popped in. Our children came when work and finances permitted. (Will, his wife, Kristina, and his sister, Isa, played tag one summer night on the second-story balcony and were abashed when I suggested the surveillance cameras might have recorded their frolics.)

A particularly gratifying visitor was Roxana Catto, widow of my uncle Jack Catto and the hostess of Mother, Dad, and me for all the summers of my childhood at her spectacularly beautiful West Texas ranch. At eighty-seven, amusing, interested, and lively, she, her daughter Roxie, and her son-in-law Jim Hayne (my business partner at Catto and Catto) hopped the supersonic British Airways Concorde and spent a week with us. (Grandchildren Walter and Nancy Hayne came too, on a slightly less posh flight.) Aunt Rox had been a Gage, and by coincidence I had gotten to know the scion of the British Gage family, Nicholas. Nick invited us to visit the beautiful family estate, Firle, and treated Aunt Rox as if she were the head of the clan. She loved it; we all did. It was her first visit to Britain in sixty years.

Friends came. Leonard Lauder and his stylish mother, Estée, had dinner. Business partners Bernard Lifshutz and Sheldon Gordon spent a few days with me. Our secretary and special friend Tina Sagris came, escaping from Washington.

They dropped in at the office. Billy Graham came, making a courtesy call. I asked him to offer a prayer, which he did — movingly. The enchanting Pamela Harriman came by, still as captivating as when I had last seen her years before.

The administration came. Housing Secretary Jack Kemp, his wife, Joanne, and their son Jim were our guests, as were Transportation Secretary Sam Skinner and his wife, Honey. Chief of Staff John Sununu and his wife, Nancy, amused us at dinner, and Bill Webster, director of the CIA, was always game for tennis.

The press came. George Will, columnist and old friend, spent several days. Susan Yerkes, a San Antonio newspaper columnist, dropped by for a chat.

Congress came. Senator Lloyd Bentsen and his wife, B.A., spent a night. Congressman Steve Solarz of New York came frequently and usually on short notice. He'd call and say, "Henry, I'll be there tomorrow. See if you can get this one and that one for dinner and appointments with . . ." I usually could and I was always glad, even when more warning would have been welcome, since I joined him on all his visits and he called only on the heavy hitters. Steve was active on the House Foreign Affairs Committee, and most British officials were willing to see him. That he was often mentioned as a possible secretary of state in some future Democratic administration didn't hurt.

Other members of Congress were not so lucky. Most wanted to see the legendary Mrs. Thatcher, but she husbanded her time carefully. She and aide Charles Powell had a code that they shared with me, and if, when I called for an appointment, I heard the "axe" word, I knew the Washington visitor was out of luck.

I insulted the congressional delegate from Guam. He came to a reception at Winfield House and didn't like what he saw: a Texas flag flying over the front door. (The U.S. flag flew on a much higher staff ten paces away.) On leaving our hospitality, he called a press conference to complain. "I didn't fight in World War II for the Texas flag; I fought for the American flag," he huffed.

There was never a shortage of junketeering congressional representatives, and since London was the gateway to Europe, we saw lots of them. Alas, a certain percentage were ignorant and self-impressed.

Some went beyond self-importance. The late Mickey Leland, Democrat of Houston, appreciated African art, and while in Addis Ababa he bought a fair amount of it. The American ambassador paid the bill and was paid in turn by Leland's check—a hot one—for $1,600. The ambassador had to threaten to go public before finally getting his money.

A word of financial explanation might be helpful here. All houseguests were my guests; my expense allowance was earmarked for entertainment of foreigners only. Everyone else, from the president to my family, was on me. At the end of every month I got a bill for all meals eaten and all drinks drunk by houseguests, and we paid a percentage of the staff costs as well.

One of the great things about Winfield House, in which it is similar to the White House, is its convening power. If a Briton receives an invitation, she is likely to accept, and for a reason: the company, the food, and the entertainment there are good.

The Fourth of July 1989 illustrates this power. American embassies frequently have functions on the Fourth, but I wanted something different. It turned out that the world-renowned conductor of the Chicago Symphony, Sir Georg Solti, was to be in town. When I suggested that he conduct a chamber concert before a dinner at Winfield House, he accepted. Fireworks on the lawn followed, and as they say in show business, we had a hit on our hands as the top layer of the British power structure flocked to join us.

Another event hit the bell as well. When the political section suggested a summer picnic for British labor leaders, I doubted how successful it would be, since union leaders tend to be skeptical of Republicans. Nonetheless, I agreed, and the result (both years, for we did it twice) was gratifying. Dress was Western, music was cowboy, food was Mexican, and everyone had a ball. Son John happened to be in town and became a great hit running rum to one group of the union leaders, and I cemented what became a real friendship with the head of the Trade Unions Congress (the British AFL-CIO), Norman Willis. Indeed, as a result of these contacts, embassy relations with the unions and the Labour Party became much more normal, reflected by a dinner we gave in honor of Labour Party leader Neil Kinnock.

Of course, the greatest volume of visitors to Winfield House came from receptions honoring groups, individuals, or causes. From the Winfield House staff at Christmas to British *Vogue,* from the Chicago Symphony to the board of the Prudential Insurance Company, from Ella Fitzgerald to Dave Brubeck, from the Anglo-American Legal Exchange Program to countless traveling members of Congress—we had them all. Jessica counted five thousand guests in one particularly busy week.

Clothing designer Calvin Klein and his wife, Kelly, donated $50,000 to our Fulbright Scholarship program. Such gifts were rare, and to show our appreciation we had a reception in honor of the Kleins. Haute couture not being exactly my bag, I recognized only a few of the guests as I wandered among the throng. At one point, a man came up and said, "Will you be exclusive with one store?" I'm sure that my face showed my total bafflement. At that very moment, we both realized what had happened: he thought I was Calvin Klein. With a look of genuine remorse, he blurted out, "Oh, shit!" and fled. Having done similar things myself, I felt for him.

Not all our social life took place at home, for the representatives of the American Republic are popular, not for themselves but for what they represent. Often, "official" evenings could be dull, but occasionally they were fun.

I remember one small dinner at the tiny home of the Hendersons, Sir Nicholas having been British ambassador to the United States and Mary being a talented author. The honoree was the "Queen Mum," Queen Elizabeth's mother. With only ten guests, the conversation tended to be general and often highly political. Her Majesty by custom is not supposed to talk politics, but that evening she clearly felt comfortable, and from time to time an opinion would slip out. This would cause her to clap her hand over her mouth in contrition, to the amusement of all. I marveled not only at her quick mind but also at her posture: her back never came close to the back of her chair.

Another small event honoring the senior queen was a luncheon given by Lord St. John of Fawsley at his elegant house not far from Clarence House, the Queen Mother's residence. As usual, she arrived last, in a handsome green Rolls-Royce, with royal flags on the fenders. I happened to be standing near the door as she came in, and I overheard the butler ask her drink preference. "Perhaps I'll have a Dubonnet," she chirped, and I thought, how nice; a mild drink for an older lady. Then, after a pregnant pause, she added, "With gin."

I once spent an evening with Princess Margaret, the queen's younger sister. The occasion was a supper for a corporate board on which she sat, and we chatted at some length; like her sister, she was easy to talk to and I liked her. I saw her again at a benefit performance of Stephen Sondheim's *Sunday in the Park with George*. At the interval I said to her, sotto voce, "Do you find it as tedious as I do?" Without a moment's hesitation, she quipped, "With a double 'e'!"

Over time, I came to know other members of the royal family. Sitting next to Prince Charles at a luncheon of the American Chamber of Commerce at which he spoke provided a chance in September 1989 to have a serious conversation with him. I asked about his well-known aversion to contemporary architecture and inferred that he sees it as a plot against his nation's history, almost an ideological attack. He is a stickler for good English grammar, a subject on which we saw eye to eye. I asked if he felt that Hong Kong Chinese should be admitted to the United Kingdom if they wanted to come after the colony reverted to China in 1997. While he felt that the country was already too crowded, he had no doubt that any who did migrate would become first-rate subjects. He talked of his favorite charity, the Prince's Trust, which provides seed capital for underprivileged entrepreneurs.

The speech, delivered from his own red ink notes, was well done, his thick hands moving back and forth to emphasize points and his self-deprecating humor winning the audience.

Each year the queen held a giant reception for the diplomatic corps. Each embassy was given a quota of lower-ranking people who could be invited, enabling not just the ambassador to go but also junior officers, secretaries — anyone the embassy wanted to honor.

Since our embassy is so large, we numbered perhaps a dozen on the great night. With typical Buckingham Palace planning, each group's proximity to the royal family's place of entry varied according to the ambassador's seniority.

The queen, Prince Philip, Prince Charles, Princess Diana, and the rest passed through the delegations, greeting each ambassador, to be sure, but chatting with people of lesser rank as well. The lively Princess Diana gave our group particular attention, spending several minutes with us. I have never seen a more attractive woman; tanned shoulders, perfect skin, bright-green gown, radiant smile, and an apparently genuine interest in each person with whom she spoke. Her popularity was no accident; she earned it.

I shared the dais with Prince Charles's sister, Princess Anne, at a white-tie event at the ancient Cutler's Hall in the steel center of Sheffield. There was very tight security. Since it took six motorcycle police to whisk my car from the hotel to the hall, I wondered if a motorized brigade had accompanied the princess. Bright and courteous, she wrote much of her talk in tiny handwriting during the meal, while managing to converse with me at the same time.

Small and informal dinners were particularly welcome. Evangeline Bruce, widow of former U.S. ambassador David Bruce, often gave salmon-and-champagne suppers on Sunday nights at her elegant flat in the Albany. Jill Ritblat, a friend from our Geneva days, and her husband, John, had frequent and excellent parties at home, where I met interesting people from the business and intellectual worlds. Such occasions provided a pleasant counterpoint to the large, formal affairs, and we participated in all of it with great enthusiasm.

The Beefsteak Club, the Middle Temple, and Me

AMBASSADORS GET invited to join things. For example, under the sponsorship of Sir James Spooner, I was bidden to join the Beefsteak Club, an eating and drinking organization with long history and distinguished membership. A story illustrates both.

It seems that in the 1890s, a policeman in central London saw an open door and a narrow stair going up. Given that the neighborhood was the theater district, where anything might happen, he ventured in and up. At the top, in a room by a fire, sat three elderly men. The "bobby," or policeman, thought them rather odd; the hour was late, and he demanded to know what they were up to.

"We're drinking," responded one.

"So I see," said the officer, "but who are you?"

Looking rather abashed, if not guilty, the first one replied, "I am the attorney general." Surprised but determined, the bobby asked, "And you, sir?" "I am the Archbishop of Canterbury," was the answer.

Beginning to be intimidated, the poor man turned to the third valetudinarian: "And you?"

"I am the prime minister," came the response.

Deciding the peace not to be endangered, the shaken bobby left them to their cups.

Another privilege of an American ambassador in London is to become a member of the Middle Temple, one of the four Inns of Court around which the British legal system is organized. Dating from the thirteenth century, these legal societies decide who will be admitted to the bar, teach the law, and test candidates.

Shortly after my arrival, Master Treasurer of the Middle Temple (as the head of the Inn of Court is called) phoned to set a date for my initiation and to explain what would happen. Named Peter Boydell, he was all business as he explained the hour I would arrive and the order of events. He warned me that after dinner I would be expected to give a ten-minute "account" of myself and that humor should not be neglected in so doing. I confess to having been a bit intimidated.

As the fateful day neared, I set to work in earnest, jotting down notes for my "account" and trying to recall amusing events in my life. I rehearsed with Jessica as a critical audience of one and when 6:30 P.M. on October 19, 1989 arrived, I felt ready.

John Bryant delivered me to the fourteenth-century building at exactly the appointed hour. Met at the curb, escorted into a small firelit room, and gowned in a black robe like the rest, I met Boydell and the others, all major movers in British law.

Geoffrey Howe, the deputy prime minister and foreign minister, greeted me warmly, as did Attorney General Sir Patrick Mayhew and all the other fifty or so who were to be seated at the head table. We sipped sherry and made polite conversation as I desperately rehearsed my talk with a part of my mind.

The sherry helped, and shortly the usher lined up the "masters" for the procession to the Great Hall. All left—save for me. Through a different door, the usher led me past hundreds of dining students seated at dozens of long tables in a huge room with hammer-arched ceilings of great beauty. The ancient building reflected the majesty of the law.

As we approached the high table, where by then all the masters were seated, the usher rapped for quiet with his staff and announced to Master Treasurer and all in attendance that "Master Junior" had arrived. Boydell nodded solemnly and the usher showed me to my seat at the foot of the table, where binoculars would have been useful to see Master Treasurer.

Dinner, served by serried ranks of waiters, began, the wine of excellent quality and endless quantity. Conversation flowed equally well at my end of the table, and I noted that there was only one woman (though many of the students were female).

At dinner's end, Master Treasurer rapped on his glass for order and asked my permission to adjourn. Recalling my instructions, I nodded and we all rose and formed a procession, Boydell first, me last.

Solemnly, we went past the now quiet students. The line stopped, and I approached the bust of an ancient barrister named Plowden, founder of the Temple. I reverently bowed my head to the bust and to the audience right and left, and we trooped out.

Shedding gowns, we went past paneled and portrait-lined walls to a small dining room called Parliament, Master Treasurer again at a high table, the rest at tables below.

At a signal from Master Treasurer, I reached behind my seat and found a rope, which when tugged vigorously rang a bell hung beneath a table. I pulled and brought forth a double bong, which was greeted with a ripple of "Hear, hear"; clearly I was still strong and sober enough to accomplish my first task.

The bell signaled readiness for coffee and liqueurs, which promptly arrived. Again, Boydell rang for order to propose a toast.

To my surprise, we stayed seated. Geoffrey Howe explained to me that a seated toast to the sovereign was a privilege of Middle Temple dating back centuries, a reward for services rendered. After the solemn "To the Queen," Boydell drank to "Domus," the ancient building in which we sat. Finally, a toast to "members absent"; our eyes watered as we drank to the dead.

As we sipped coffee and brandy, the talk—mostly politics—was lively. It was hot that evening, and someone rose to open a window, allowing cigar smoke to escape and fresh air to enter. I felt aglow, worries of my forthcoming ordeal repressed by wine, food, and conviviality.

After a half hour or so, Boydell rose to speak. I have a theory that the Brits have an extra gene that enables them to orate with an elegance and grace denied most Americans, and so it was with Peter. With nary a note, he touched on the British-American friendship; he recounted ties of the Middle Temple with American presidents (William Howard Taft was a member); he made gracious remarks about me. Gliding smoothly to his conclusion, he looked down on me and asked in dulcet tones: "Master Junior, would you give an account of yourself?"

Fortified by the dinner and Boydell's example, I rose, serene in the knowledge that I knew what I wanted to say and could do it without disgrace. Standing behind my chair, I began in clear voice.

About fifteen seconds into my oration, I heard an unpleasant noise. I had noticed that the elderly man seated to my right had become quieter as the evening proceeded and that he might be looking a bit gray, but I was not alarmed, assuming it was caused by the heat. As I looked down at my neighbor now, I saw what caused the noise: the poor fellow was throwing up. Not, mind you, a burp and a bubble, but a Niagara of vomit silently splashed over his generous stomach, down his lap, into his cuffs.

Here, thought I quickly, is a challenge. Should I break off my talk to help or soldier on? Since the man remained seated and made no fuss, few in the room knew what had happened, and at that moment, someone to the ill man's left appeared to see if he needed help. I made my choice. Drifting away to lessen the distraction, I carried on.

Chuckles greeted my humorous lines. An occasional "Hear, hear" burst forth, along with raps on the table. I finished in good time and was rewarded with very gratifying applause.

Master Treasurer rose with great good cheer and bade me join him at the high table for a final drink. Being a coward and not eager to return to my seat, I leapt to escape. The sick man, looking somewhat better, kept his seat. A few minutes later, one of my erstwhile lower-table companions came up and told Master Treasurer what had happened. Boydell then gave me the highest praise I ever received: "Quel sangfroid!" he said with a grin, and with that, we adjourned.

Covering the Territory

EMBASSY LIFE, seldom dull, can get downright frantic at times, often with an assist from the media.

There was a curious ritual in my native Texas. The men of a small West Texas community hold a rattlesnake hunt every year, in which thousands of the dread creatures are hunted, captured, skinned, and eaten. Hearing of the bloody business, BBC Radio sent a reporter to investigate, and in due course a program aired.

A flood of letters hit my desk. How, the writers wondered, could my country and especially my state be called civilized when we engaged in such primitive rituals? Having missed the program, I had no clue as to where the problem lay, but a call to the network brought a tape. I listened as the reporter poured it on with vivid descriptions of the blood-glee of the Texans. It was an embarrassing incident that I decided to handle via a letter thanking the writers for their concern, saying I had passed their comments on to the officer charged with environmental matters, yours very truly.

A few of the letters, however, went beyond the line of civility. (The British love animals, even reptiles, indiscriminately.) Those I also wrote, but I reminded them to check Genesis 3:15, in which we learn that the history of enmity between man and serpent goes back a bit and perhaps my fellow Texans weren't quite as bad as painted.

Helping U.S. businesses achieve a level playing field with local competitors always is a challenge for ambassadors. American Airlines and Pan American both felt that they were discriminated against in landing rights by the unseen but powerful hand of British Airways. I took up the cause with vigor and the U.S. airlines eventually won the day . . . more or less.

Tobacco presented me with problems. One day the head of U.S. Tobacco, Jack Afreck, came to call. An aggressive man, he quickly poured out three little piles of tobacco on the table in my office. One pile was chewing tobacco, one cigarette tobacco, and one snuff. "Chemically," he firmly announced, "they are exactly the same. Yet the British Health Ministry discriminates against our snuff, which by the way we manufacture here!"

It seems that the government had threatened to ban UST's snuff, called SKOL Bandits, as a health hazard. The American company claimed that since all tobacco was essentially the same, this amounted to unfair competition.

I duly called on Minister of Health Kenneth Clark and made the case. The British courts agreed with the American company, but for my efforts, a Massachusetts representative to Congress demanded that I be fired for defending tobacco of any kind; he may have had a point.

The great bane of all ambassadors abroad is visas. Human beings, I found, have three innate drives: money, sex, and a U.S. visa. So compelling is the attraction of our country that if we opened the gates, there would indeed be a "giant sucking sound" as virtually the whole world moved to the USA. As it is, entry is rationed and the embassies decide pretty much who gets to come to live or visit (subject to Congress's laws, of course).

I always tried to stay out of the business of the consular section, the issuers of visas; their job was hard enough without my meddling, as evidenced by the endless lines of applicants snaking around our building every day. Sometimes, however, circumstances indicated otherwise.

One day, for instance, I got a call from Senator William Roth of Delaware, a highly agreeable solon whom I knew slightly. After a brief chat he got down to business: an important constituent wanted a visa for an English friend. On another occasion, Mark Thatcher, the prime minister's peripatetic son who lived in Dallas, called with a request for a visa for his assistant. Even exiled King Constantine of Greece rang me one day, wanting visa help for his son at Georgetown University. In each case, I managed to assist.

Although from time to time I had seriously considered giving up my Scotland Yard protection, I didn't, and I was glad. For one thing, I liked Special Branch officers Bob Gilby and Rick Persich, but far more important was the ever-present threat of trouble.

I was not afraid of the IRA. Although I had blasted it publicly time and again, it was not likely to hit an American ambassador when so much of its funding depended on contributions from Irish Americans — even if the ambassador was obnoxious.

And I was. When New York mayor David Dinkins named a street corner in the city after an imprisoned murderer, I wrote him a letter saying he did not know what he was doing. (He probably did — there are lots of Irish voters in New York.) I released the letter to the press, and as luck would have it, shortly after that an IRA bomb went off in the heart of London, hurting two passersby, Americans from — where else — New York.[5]

There was once an incident at Winfield House, heavily fenced though it was. Taking my daily run on the grounds, I was startled by a guard dashing out breathlessly to warn me to avoid the east side of the house: "There's a bomb out by the fence!" It turned out to be an empty beer keg left by revelers in neighboring Regent's Park.

On another occasion the embassy loudspeaker, manned by the Marine guards, boomed out to all offices: "All personnel will evacuate the north side of the building at once." As people obeyed, streaming out of the building, I ran to the Marine office to find out what the problem was. A taxi, I learned, had delivered a wrapped package addressed to the ambassador at the north entrance and had driven off. To terror experts, that was about as dangerous an event as could be imagined, and so the police bomb squad was summoned.

Very quickly I heard the wail of sirens, then a few minutes of silence. Then a muffled "boom." Taking no chances, the bomb squad had detonated the package, first salvaging a rambling letter to me. Subsequently they determined the contents: a bottle of Scotch whisky. Oh, well . . .

Still, in spite of the false alarms our security people felt happier with Scotland Yard on duty — and so did I.

Travel within the country was a task that I enjoyed. Invitations to speak or take part in civic or business ceremonies were never in short supply. I spoke in or visited all the major cities in England and Scotland and always found a deep well of friendship for the Americans.

My third cousin Charles Little, president of a company in the Midlands, invited me to inaugurate a new plant. I hadn't seen him or his mother in thirty-eight years, and it was a treat to catch up with them.

Another gratifying occasion involved a trip to Aberdeen, Scotland, to receive an honorary degree from Aberdeen University. Ceremony in the best British tradition, great music, and colorful procession etched the event in my mind and provided me with a sheepskin assuring all the world (in Latin) that I was a Doctor of Laws.

As is well known, the British are sticklers for tradition. During one of my visits to the "shires," I paid a courtesy call on the mayor at the county seat. "He" turned out to be a black woman, but custom required her to be addressed as "Mr. Mayor." Though nonplussed, I complied.

In May 1990 I accepted an invitation to visit the construction site of the vast tunnel under the English Channel that would soon connect Britain to France. Recalling a trip into a huge dam in El Salvador, I wondered if I would again be struck with claustrophobia. I need not have worried. The underground work area was gigantic. Twelve thousand workers created a miasma of dust and dirt and noise while giant machines on railroad tracks clawed out the earth and extruded the detritus simultaneously, laying new tracks as they went. Trucks picked up the material and dumped it into the channel; old England literally grew. These were scenes from Dante's *Inferno*.

One evening I was guest of the head of U.S. naval forces in Europe, Admiral Jonathan Howe, at a "dining out." Mostly the guests were young and high-spirited officers not above surreptitiously hurling a broadside of bread at a fellow down the table. The toasts were numerous, but one stood out. A pink-cheeked ensign rose and proposed a toast not to U.S.-British solidarity or to the president or to the queen, but to Leonid Brezhnev. After a pregnant pause he explained: "At least when he ran Russia, we knew we had a job!" Everyone laughed, but the remark was poignant, for American military deployment abroad was to be sharply reduced in the future.

We also traveled for pleasure. For our first New Year's, I rented a place called Rottal Lodge on the estate of the Earl of Airlie in Scotland. While we had Christmas (including magnificent services at St. Martin-in-the-Fields and Westminster Abbey) with all the family at Winfield House and joined the Thatchers at their country retreat, Chequers, on Boxing Day, December 26, getting away during Christmas week attracted us. I invited Julia and Nigel Widdowson and their girls (he was British and she a close young friend from Texas), and Lewis and Stevie Tucker had come from San Antonio, so we made a considerable party.

The countryside, severe in its beauty, reminded us of Texas a bit. The lodge was perfect and the food superb. The Airlies asked us to join them on New Year's Eve for a rollicking party at their castle, where the young learned Scottish dancing and the old the further delights of Scotch whisky. Both learned the customs of "first footing," wherein the first person to cross a threshold in a new year can demand to have his or her whistle wetted.

Earlier in December, Frank Bennack, chief executive of the Hearst Corporation, had invited Will and me to join him and several others at Beaufort Castle, near Inverness in Scotland, for that most British of institutions, a driven bird shoot.

I had been shooting in Texas and in El Salvador, but nothing had prepared me for the way it is done in the United Kingdom. For one thing, everyone dresses smartly, in tie (or turtleneck at the least), tweeds, knickers with colorful garters, and sporty headgear. Two guns are de rigueur, one to shoot with and one for reloading by the man (equally well dressed) who accompanies the shooter to spot incoming birds, pick up kills, and generally be helpful.

The host of the shoot places the shooters at predetermined locations. They wait, and soon a din can be heard. It is the "beaters" (also well dressed) who walk through the woods with sticks, shouting and rapping trees to drive the birds (pheasant, chukar, etc.) toward the waiting shooters.

It works. At a given moment, the birds burst forth and the action begins. In a few minutes it is all over, downed birds are recovered, and shooters remount Range Rovers to move to another station. It is a fast sport, demanding quick reflexes. Will became quite good at it, in spite of little experience, getting a double at least once. The snow and frost of the early Scottish morning made it excruciatingly beautiful.

After three morning drives we returned to Beaufort, a huge, turreted rambling brick establishment, for lunch and, if one liked, a sip of wine or whisky. Thus fortified, three more drives came before the early darkness of the north closed things down. Then came a rest, a bath, and convivial dining.

In October 1990 Ed and Ann Hudson and Roger and Carolyn Horchow (of Fort Worth and Dallas) came to the United Kingdom, and we made a long-planned hike from village to village in the Cotswolds, an area of ancient dun-colored buildings and great beauty. Jessica and I had over the years done a lot of hiking holidays. A company in Oxford made all arrangements, provided transportation, picnic lunches at midday, and a guide. With various close friends, we had tripped through Provence, Tuscany, the Lake District, the Dordogne, and central Switzerland in a series of agreeable and sometimes strenuous tours. There is no better way to see a region, and our Cotswold trip had few peers in scenery or company. "Cotswold," incidentally, is a Celtic word, from "cot," for sheep, and "wold," a hill. We saw plenty of both and climbed over about a thousand stiles.

The Queen's English and Other Niceties

MANY AMERICANS think the British are pretty much like Americans, sort of Yanks with funny accents who drive on the wrong side of the street. Nothing could be further from the truth; we may be cousins, but we are different from each other. (The Brits would say "to each other.") Language differences can be puzzling. Most American travelers know the common ones, such as the British calling a car trunk a "boot" and the hood the "bonnet." There are, however, thousands of others, so many indeed that an American attorney and scholar, Norman W. Schur, gathered them all in a useful 475-page book called *British English from A to Zed.*

Living in the UK (or reading Schur), one learns quickly that one will chat "to," not "with"; will be nervous "of" doing something rather than nervous "about"; will be snowed "up," not snowed "in." "Knocking someone up" doesn't mean getting her pregnant, as American slang would have it; it simply means a rap on the door. A "moggy" is a scruffy cat; a "khasi" or a "loo" is a bathroom. (And by the way, don't expect to find one at many British filling stations, a disquieting discovery indeed.) A "yob" is a hooligan. It is "boy" spelled backward; "backward boy," get it? A "cock-up" is a mess; to "nick" is to steal; to "bonk" is to have carnal knowledge of. (I once got a fax from an amusing and irreverent British matron that read, "Hooray, hooray, it's the first of May / Outdoor bonking begins today.")

Brits do odd things with plurals. It is not rare to read that "Britain Sail Unto Fastnet" (a race) or "Jesus Row to Victory" (Jesus is a college at Oxford University). Teams, governments, and so forth are presumed to be groups in the UK, while in America they are single entities.

The British don't put return addresses on envelopes, implying great (and justified) faith in their postal service. If you mail a letter, the presumption is that it will be delivered; why bother with a return address? In the United States lazy postmen may well burn mail on the sly. British zip codes, by the way, include both letters and numbers and are much harder to memorize.

British advertising is generally more imaginative and amusing than advertising in the United States. British movie theaters have ads with most featured films, but the ads ("adverts," as they would call them) are so amusing that one doesn't resent it. Some ads are quaint; I once saw a billboard that said, "Nothing Sucks Like Electrolux" (a vacuum cleaner); I laughed out loud.

The list goes on. A business suit is a "lounge suit"; "knock-on effects" are long-term effects; to "fall off the perch" means to die; and a "lurgy" (pronounced with a hard "g") is a vague, undefined illness.

Once I was going somewhere with Bob Gilby and driver John Bryant, reading as we went. Coming across a word I did not know, I asked Bob what a "wanker" was. He was seated in front of me and I couldn't see his face, but the back of his neck turned bright red. "It's, er, an ineffective person," he stammered. I let it drop and checked in *British English* when we got home. It means what Bob said, but basically it means a masturbator.

British women could be startlingly frank. There was no hesitation among the upper class to use the word "pee," as there would be in the United States. And once at a very posh luncheon, my female luncheon partner, a biologist, caught even my attention. Describing her latest book, about the flea, she said, "It's quite interesting really, and the cover photo is beautiful; it's of a flea's vagina."

Pronunciation of British English, a major difference, kept me constantly muddled. Invited to Belvoir Castle, I pronounced it as one might expect, later learning to my chagrin the correct way is "Beever." The Oxford college Magdalen is "Mawdlin." Derby is "darby"; Pall Mall is either "Pell Mell" or "Pal Mal"; Beauchamp is "Beech'm"; and the Cholmondeley family answers to "Chumley." I always thought "et" was hillbilly for "ate." Wrong: a British toff (upper-class type) will say, "I ate an hour ago" but pronounce it "et" and go on to worry about its effect on his "figger" (figure).

Titles in the United Kingdom come in five or six flavors and mirror both the strengths and the weaknesses of the British system. The former stems from a title as recognition of distinction in the arts, science, education, or, most certainly, politics. The sovereign grants them, some on her own, some at the suggestion of the prime minister. The downside springs from titles' being the backbone of the class system, which many observers feel lies at the center of Britain's decline from world-class superpower in the nineteenth and early decades of the twentieth centuries to not even the front rank of secondary powers at the end of the twentieth. (Britain's gross national product, for instance, recently dropped below Italy's, to the dismay of proud Britons; it has long been below that of Germany and France.)

The British class system both vexes and fascinates Americans. Through our history, we have scoffed at its pretensions while hastening to seek to marry a title when our fortune grows large enough to warrant the zenith of conspicuous consumption.

For the rest of us, the differences among dukes, knights, earls, and barons present endless complexity. I finally got it straight—more or less.

At the top, and giving form and logic to the system, are the royals, the king or queen and a handful of their close kin. One calls the sovereign "Your Majesty" on being presented and "Sir" or "Ma'am" thereafter. The ancillaries (Princess Margaret or Princess Anne, for example) are "Your Royal Highness" at first and "Ma'am" afterward.

Below the royal family comes the nobility. In the murky mists of history, titles had to do with land ownership and feudal obligations, to which considerable clout attended. The top of this group is the duke, who is addressed as "Your Grace," as is his wife, the duchess. Scarcity breeds value and there being only a couple of dozen dukes and duchesses, they are much deferred to. They frequently own vast estates, such as Chatsworth, seat of the Duke and Duchess of Devonshire, an amusing and industrious pair who kindly invited me for a weekend not long after my arrival. The duchess, the former "Debo" Mitford, may be the world's best gardener, a talent that (along with the beauty of the house and grounds) attracts thousands of tourists every year.

Next comes the marquis (pronounced "markwiss") and his marchioness ("marshuness"), a title used during the Raj for former viceroys of India. He is "My Lord," she, "Madam."

Level three is saved for earls and their countesses. Former prime ministers often become earls. Once known as Anthony Eden, the onetime prime minister became the Earl of Avon, called Lord Avon.

Viscounts ("vyecounts"), with their viscountesses in tow, are next, while barons and baronesses occupy the bottom rung of nobles. Most barons are hereditary, but many are "life peers," people who may have been union leaders or corporate chieftains and whose title expires when they do. Lord Catto (Stephen), whose kindness and friendship I have enjoyed for close to fifty years, is a hereditary baron; he and his wife, Putt, are Lord and Lady Catto. He, along with all of the above and twenty-six Church of England officials, make up the House of Lords, which numbers more than 1,000, although only several hundred are active. Seven hundred sixty-three are hereditary and 314 are life peers and peeresses. Vintage hereditary peer Lord Carrington once told me there were so many new members of the House of Lords that "respectable old deadbeats like us have to sit on some Labour life peer's knee."

There are also titled commoners, baronets and knights (or "dames," if women). Knights cannot pass the title on; it has to be earned. But to the confusion of Americans, they are called by their first names. Sir Robin Renwick, the former British ambassador to the United States, is

Sir Robin (or Mr. Ambassador), never Sir Renwick. His wife, Annie, is Lady Renwick.

Another surprising difference lies in matters of ethics. A sitting member of Parliament would raise no eyebrow by lobbying the American ambassador on behalf of a private client, as happened to me. Members of Parliament are poorly paid and need to supplement their income as best they can.

Small things reminded me we weren't at home. Food, piled onto the back of the fork, is popped into the mouth via the left hand. An Englishman being introduced to a stranger will likely say, "How j'do?" but will seldom share his name; you have to ask him. The phone book also illustrated this passion for privacy, for full names are not given, just "J. Jones"—by the hundreds. Salt is put on the plate, not directly on the food. Showers are rare: tubs were good enough for Grandfather, why not for me? But towels are frequently hung on heated racks, making drying off a pleasure. Penmanship tends to the illegible; a letter from a Briton would stump a CIA cryptologist. The stripes on British neckties run upper left to lower right while on the American version, it is mostly the reverse. An Englishman once came up to me at Heathrow Airport and said snidely, "I see by your tie you were in my regiment; when was that?" I pointed out the different striping and suggested I was not an imposter after all. He slunk away. The British are polite, patient, and quiet; unlike drivers in New York City, London cabbies don't get their jollies from leaning on their horns. Finally, I suspect the British are made a bit uncomfortable that the accents of Americans, Australians, and so on, reveal nationality but not class. As I said, "Britain is different!"

Ties Between Nations

BRITAIN MAY not be like us, but despite all the trauma of shedding the world's largest empire with remarkable grace, it has nonetheless managed to play a major role and therefore is of vital importance to us.

There are several reasons for Britain's importance. First, it remains a key player in the financial world. As mentioned, the British are the largest foreign investors in the United States. They are a nuclear power, guaranteeing them a seat in any serious arms limitation talks, and their membership on the United Nations Security Council means they will be courted by any power seeking consensus in that forum. The Commonwealth, an organization of former colonies, gives Britain a worldwide sounding board. Our intertwining history, language, and traditions argue strongly for close U.S.-UK relations; as Mrs. Thatcher once said, "We don't seek to score off the other. We don't seek to involve the other in some commitment against his will." Perhaps Edmund Burke said it best: "Nothing is so strong a tie between nation and nation as correspondence in law, customs, manners and habits of life. They have more than the force of treaties in themselves. They are obligations written in the heart."

Not all Americans recognize the tie. Former vice president Walter Mondale, offered the jobs of ambassador to either London or Paris by President Bill Clinton, is reported to have said—rather undiplomatically, I thought—"No, I prefer to pay for my own vacations." (He accepted Tokyo.)

Rick Persich, one of my Scotland Yard Special Branch protective officers, once said to me, "We are a warlike people." At the time, I tended to dismiss the idea, but Rick was right, and that characteristic has benefited the United States on more than one occasion. Indeed, the British have in recent years been willing to use force when others shrank from it. Perhaps recalling the experience of Munich, they reacted in the Falklands and in the Gulf War in support of smartly slapping down tyrants before they could become real trouble.

Finally, the U.S.-UK tie in intelligence sharing is unique.[6] Since World War II, the two countries have kept each other closely informed on all manner of sensitive topics. The residue of empire and the British "diaspora" around the world have given them unique insights into local conditions in widespread areas, while our technological capability in satellites and other sensitive methods has been useful to "the cousins," as they were referred to at the CIA.

Thus it was that I felt my charge was to keep this important alliance, this "special relationship," on track. At times it was not easy. As I mentioned earlier in cases such as airlines and tobacco, specialness evaporated when competition arose. When a U.S. company faced a British company, my clients were my countrymen.

Early on I felt the need to know the prime minister better. She and my predecessor, Charles Price, had had a fine friendship, and I wanted the same. I therefore told Charles Powell of my concern at lunch one day, and he agreed that such a plan made sense. Toward that end, we gave a small dinner in the Thatchers' honor at Winfield House, as has been mentioned, and she asked us to her intimate Boxing Day party at Chequers. But how much good such social tra-la did was doubtful.

In January 1990 President Bush, fearing congressional pressure to cut back the American commitment to NATO, sent Deputy Secretary of State Larry Eagleburger to London on still another highly secret mission, this time to convince Mrs. Thatcher that a cut to 195,000 troops would not materially affect NATO's deterrent power. Larry arrived as I was entertaining the noted author Lord [Hugh] Thomas. I had to sneak Larry, Bob Gates of the National Security Council, and General Lee Butler in the back door because a London *Times* editor was present—a pity, since Larry and Lord Thomas were friends.

The following morning, off we marched to 10 Downing Street. Our reception left something to be desired, for the Iron Lady dripped venom.

"Now sit down and tell me what this letter means," she said of the missive he delivered. He sat, and opened his mouth, and that was it. Always a hard-liner regarding the Soviets, she knew what we were up to and she did not like it one bit.

"We know we have to swallow it," she said as Larry tried to insert a clarification here or an anodyne word there, to little avail. Phrases such as "we will support you, but . . . ," "we're not at peace yet," and "'peace divided' is a bad phrase" bubbled forth. "This is the second time we've gotten 'take it or leave it,' but we're an alliance," she complained. "It's perfectly obvious we'll do as we're told."

On she ran, telling how she and French president François Mitterand were both concerned that we were headed back to 1913. German reunification concerned them both, and the two would work together.

Perched on the edge of her chair, her back straight, and smiling all the while, she predicted grave danger with U.S. troops out of Europe, adding that it meant, of course, that the UK must keep its nuclear weapons. The proposal, she felt, should have gone to NATO before it was raised at the conventional weapons talks in Geneva. "Forward defense won't hold; we need a new strategy."

The Russians, she felt, would need their troops to solve ethnic troubles back home—a prescient comment; they would, she predicted, withdraw their men but not get rid of them. "This has been an earthquake under my feet, just like Reykjavík was in Ron Reagan's term." Germany was the only country that spoke of "ein Volk, ein Vaterland" (one people, one fatherland),[7] and we would enter the nineties in great fear unless we held firm. More than ever, Britain would need the flexibility of Trident missile submarines and dual-capable aircraft.

As the meeting drew to a close, she asked, "Will you be here in another six months, Larry? You have a rotten job, to have to face me." In a final soliloquy, she said that without the Vietnam War, communism would never have been stopped and we would not be where we were today. And by the way, the British would continue to ship refugees, the boat people, back to Vietnam from Hong Kong. "You're welcome back," she added, "but not on this kind of mission." All smiling.

If the "junior partner syndrome" plagued Mrs. Thatcher from time to time, it could clearly be diagnosed among lesser mortals within the government.

The most sensitive area, forcible repatriation of Vietnamese refugees, became a back-burner item not through compromise but through an agreement to disagree. When conditions at the camps became intolerable, the British would send them back whether George Bush liked it or not. In any case, British political nerves did not quiver over the issue.

Terminating military operations was a different thing. One day the Pentagon asked us to go in at the highest level and inform the Ministry of Defense that the Pentagon was looking at "closing" bases in Britain. I quickly asked for an appointment with Defense Secretary Tom King, telling him the bad news and that the announcement would be made the next day.

King, a crusty type, turned red. First he coldly told me that the United States does not "close" British bases; the British do that. "Perhaps you are vacating, but you are not closing," he snapped. (We leased the facilities from the Royal Air Force.)

His spleen vented, he urged me most strongly to postpone the announcement. A base closing is serious economic surgery, causing huge upset to the community in which it happens. King wanted time to lessen the economic and political effect. Furthermore, to the United States, the vacating of one of the bases depended on the results of talks then going on in Geneva on the reduction of conventional (non-nuclear) forces in Europe. King may have felt that the economic loss of a base, plus the possible junking of dozens of planes in the event that the talks proved successful, might alter the balance of British support for the Geneva effort. In short—the issues were complicated and he was in a tight spot. He needed time.

Returning to my office, I placed a call to Defense Secretary Dick Cheney, who was testifying at the time before Congress. Speaking to Deputy Secretary Donald Atwood instead, I tried earnestly to convey the politics, economics, and alliance aspects of the step and urged a postponement of the announcement. The following day Cheney reluctantly relented and postponed announcing the most sensitive of the closings. I told King, and the matter passed. But it showed astonishing lack of empathy on the part of the Pentagon and the State Department. It made me think of Shakespeare's comment: "Like flies to wanton children are we to the gods; they kill us for their sport." Such, sometimes, was the Anglo-American alliance.

At other times, of course, the administration could be very attentive to British sensibilities. At the April 1990 meeting between the president and the prime minister in Bermuda, our team consisted of the heavy hitters: Bush, Baker, Scowcroft, Chief of Staff John Sununu, and Ambassador Bob Blackwill, the National Security Council's European man. The British had only Thatcher, Ambassador to the United States Antony Acland, and Charles Powell. Perhaps the idea of a Bermuda golf game gave us extra incentive to go on the trip; we were there in strength. At one luncheon Jessica was seated next to the president. He quipped, "Jessica, we're almost through with the meal and you haven't told me what to do yet." (She was always frank with our old friend.) "George," she replied, "let me finish my wine and I'll take care of that." "Waiter," said Bush, "give this lady more wine." He could be smooth — and funny.

One sign of truly clear cooperation was that George had Maggie's phone number, and he didn't hesitate to use it. Therein lay a problem for me.

The British Foreign and Commonwealth Office (FCO), their version of the State Department, had a custom that the British ambassador from the country involved be informed at once of any "phone summits." (Note-takers listening in on "dead keys" record what the leaders for both sides say.) Unfortunately, the National Security Council had no such rule, and I had to learn as best I could. Phil Zelikow, who followed British affairs at the NSC, became a friend who would give me readouts after such conversations.

I took the problem to Bob Blackwill, who was sympathetic. As head of the U.S. delegation to some of the endless arms reduction talks, he had frequently suffered from information deprivation himself. To solve the problem, he inconspicuously rotated officers back to Washington on a regular basis to keep his flanks protected and learn what really was going on. He suggested that I call Zelikow regularly, or at least have my deputy chief of mission do so, perhaps on Tuesdays and Fridays on a secure phone. He further suggested that the members of the country team might regularly call their agencies to pick up background. "It's an imperfect system," he said, "but it's the future of diplomacy. Run your traps — and remember, part of your job is to keep *me* informed!"

Actually, it worked pretty well, thanks to Zelikow's talent and understanding. In June of 1990, for example, the prime minister met with Soviet president Gorbachev, and she shared her impressions with President Bush on the phone. Phil in turn informed me. The key issue at that moment concerned what would happen to NATO if the two Germanys, the Federal Republic and the communist Democratic Republic, merged. Would the Soviets insist on an all-German withdrawal from NATO as the price of reunification?

Mrs. Thatcher found Gorbachev remarkable, in command of events, even ebullient. She felt we had to give him credit, considering that his problems were worse than ours. She also noted that the Soviet leader liked George and Barbara.

On reunification, the Russian's thinking was evolving and had inconsistencies, but he took care not to rule out Germany in NATO, looking in the long term to an organization transcending NATO and the Warsaw Pact. The prime minister felt, therefore, that we should push to a conclusion of the matter before Soviet thinking crystallized; they would accept unification and we would not have to pay too high a price. She also noted that restless Lithuania was not high on the Russian's list of priorities; Gorbachev was sick of it.

In the struggle to stay current, such background was invaluable, especially as the deadline for Iraq to withdraw from Kuwait drew nearer.

Trouble in the Gulf

BRITISH-AMERICAN RELATIONS were excellent. The tone of close cooperation had been set at the summit between Thatcher and Bush in Colorado at our ranch, on the first day of the invasion. While the French and eventually many other countries played helpful roles, the core of the coalition was the "Anglo-Saxons," as the French liked to dub us. As Phil Zelikow told me one day, "Thatcher's stock is very high here since Woody Creek."

I took Secretary of State Jim Baker to see Mrs. Thatcher one day, and he asked her if the British army could send two more brigades to the Gulf to help with our buildup. Her assent was quick: "Yes, of course. I'll check with my military people, but I'm sure we can." When she was with you, it was all the way; it must have been like that between Churchill and Roosevelt.

The prime minister worried about delays caused by lining up jumpy UN members on our side. She said to Baker that our constant trips to the UN might tip Saddam to a forthcoming action.

Baker's response was revealing: "We need to be able to say to recalcitrant Democratic congressmen [the president wanted a congressional resolution in support of military action], 'Look, Ethiopia supports it; why can't you?'"

Thatcher asked, "What happens if you don't get UN support?" Baker replied, "Then George Bush has to make a hard decision." Mrs. Thatcher summed up her philosophy: "Great things in the world are always done by the few who don't falter."

Baker filled her in on his recent meeting with Gorbachev, knowing her interest in him. The Russian seemed relaxed, though he had many domestic worries; we might have to help, Baker said, with food aid. Always curious, she cut in and asked if it might be possible that the Russians were feeding information on coalition plans to Saddam. Baker thought that unlikely.

As I bade him farewell, the somber secretary said to me, "Enjoy your job. The whole administration is at stake."

My sailing was not always smooth. For example, British defense minister Tom King kept me out of a meeting between him and U.S. defense secretary Dick Cheney. "We'll be discussing deployments," he huffed pompously. In spite of such setbacks, I pressed always to be included, most of the time successfully.[8]

On another occasion, the queen's annual reception for the diplomatic corps, I got the verbal equivalent of a glove in the face. As I left the event, I happened to walk out with former prime minister Edward Heath. He had wanted to visit with Jim Baker on the latter's recent trip to Britain, but Jim's schedule did not permit it. When I expressed regret that we could not accommodate him, Heath showed his fangs. After my apology I commented on the troubles in Iraq, venturing an opinion on what might happen. "What do you know?" he snapped. "You're nothing but a businessman."

Middle Eastern issues and the "special relationship" took more and more of my time as we neared a climax in the Gulf. Foreign Secretary Douglas Hurd suggested we meet periodically, an idea that I readily accepted. Embassy Middle East specialist Desiree Milliken and I called on Charles Powell at 10 Downing, and to my surprise the prime minister and even Denis dropped in to say hello. (I wondered if it were a bit of a "thank you" greeting for our Colorado hospitality in August.) Mrs. Thatcher was mad at the Russians for taking so long to line up against the Iraqi aggression, and she was livid over Saddam's parading captive British children on Iraqi TV.

Allied refugees trapped in Iraq were a worry and getting them out a problem that Virgin Airways' Richard Branson helped solve by an offer of free transport. When the first planeload arrived at Heathrow airport, Ron Woods, the deputy chief of mission, was on hand with our embassy doctor. Two hundred British were allowed off, but some Iraqi thug gave Ron a hard time before letting the forty-four Americans debark. Jesse Jackson, that relentless self-promoter, was somehow there, managing to pick out and pick up the little British boy whom Saddam Hussein had singled out for a TV news shot. I made it a point to greet further refugee flights myself, trying to be of some comfort in a difficult time.

White House Chief of Staff and Mrs. John Sununu came by on the way home from a trip to Russia, accompanied by aides Roger Porter and Ed Rogers. We had a lively dinner and I took the former New Hampshire governor to call on the prime minister the next day.

The meeting lasted one hour and twenty minutes, longer than any I had attended save meetings with the president. They covered a lot of ground, Mrs. Thatcher voluble as always. She told of talking at lunch to King Hussein of Jordan, who had publicly sided with the Iraqis. She must have given him a "full handbagging," as British reporters called her lectures, explaining to the mild-mannered and probably startled king, "You're backing a loser."

The Governor, as Sununu was called, told how he foresaw the Russian transition to capitalism requiring three painful years, commenting that the Russian officials were amazingly open and frank about their problems.

Interestingly, the two got into a bit of an argument about the environment. Sununu thought environmental extremists and the Third World looked to capping growth as the solution to environmental threats. Mrs. Thatcher, to my surprise, came out vigorously for solutions to the challenge; she was far more concerned with environmental problems than the Governor was.

Paying for the costs of Operation Desert Shield (and the fighting that was to come, called Desert Storm) was very much on Washington's mind. President Bush was determined to have help, especially from countries like Japan, Germany, and Saudi Arabia, whose military contributions would be meager but whose stake in our success was major. Toward that end, he sent Secretary of the Treasury Nick Brady, Deputy Secretary of State Larry Eagleburger, Paul Wolfowitz of Defense, and Treasury official David Mulford on a mission abroad to broach this delicate topic.

I accompanied the group as they met with the prime minister, the chancellor of the exchequer, and other officials, and I wished I had been elsewhere. Brady acted as spokesman and was nervous to the point of inarticulateness. His concern showed physically: his leg under the meeting table jumped up and down like a pumping oil well. I thought of them as the Begging Bears (the name of a childhood book of mine), but they succeeded; the war cost us relatively little in money terms.

As combat neared, the stream of visitors increased, at least once with embarrassing results. General Colin Powell, chair of the Joint Chiefs of Staff, came to call on his counterpart, Air Marshal Sir David Craig. Craig had an engagement on December 4, the day of Colin's arrival, and he asked me if I would entertain Powell that night. Colin was a friend from my Defense Department days, so I jumped at the chance and put together an interesting small group for dinner.

Unfortunately, Colin's trip plans unexpectedly changed; he had to return a day early to testify before Congress. That left only the night of the fourth available, so Craig canceled his previous plans and called me on November 29 to say *he* wanted Colin on the fourth. "What about the party you asked me to put together?" I asked. He had no recall of that detail.

Thoroughly annoyed, I called Colin to ask his preference. Reluctantly, he said he should go with his counterpart, and I dis-invited my group.

Allied solidarity was not always what it might have been, as I learned on a speaking visit to the Royal Naval College at Greenwich. My host was the next chairman of the British Joint Defense Staff, General Sir Richard

Vincent. He told how the British, planning ahead for hostilities, had asked the Germans to give them ammunition as a contribution to the cause. (Thanks to NATO, the ammo used by the two countries was standardized.)

The Germans refused. Though taken aback, the Brits countered with an offer to buy what they needed. After a three-week wait, the Germans replied that wouldn't be possible either; their munitions had German markings. We'll file them off, replied the increasingly frustrated British, astonished at the spookiness of their ally. (I never learned the final outcome.) Sir Richard felt the matter illustrated why the United States had reason to be annoyed with its allies in time of crisis.

Changing of the Guard

DURING MY briefing at the CIA before coming to London, I asked about Mrs. Thatcher's political base. Was she vastly popular? The agency officer replied with a smile, "She's not hugely popular, but there's TINA." "Who's Tina?" I asked. "Oh, that stands for 'There is no alternative!'"

And so it seemed. Coming into office in 1979, she was reelected and then elected again, and by 1990 she quite openly discussed running for a fourth term. "I think I've become a bit of an institution," she told an interviewer. "And the place wouldn't be quite the same without this old institution. People seem to think 'She isn't so bad is she, this Maggie?'" [9]

Biographer Hugo Young felt that her success sprang from three factors that caused the very perception of Britain as a nation to be altered. First, he explained, was the Falklands War. "That Britain should have stood up for a principle so far from home, and returned victorious, gave her a special standing in the club of nations which the years did not erase." [10]

Second, Young said, was economic recovery and the end of the suffocating power of the trade unions.

Finally, the woman herself, the power of her intellect, and the strength of her personality gave her country clout. To Young, she "brought a sense of moral rectitude" and unlike "the grey men who preceded her," she gave the nation the "political equivalent of hormone replacement therapy." [11] And yet, as she moved through her eleventh year at 10 Downing Street, restlessness with her regime and with her personality became increasingly overt, and it became clear that she would be challenged as leader of the party and thus as prime minister, possibly to be toppled by her own people for her misjudgments. She had, for example, championed a head tax (called a "poll tax," though it had nothing to do with voting), which turned out to be highly unpopular. The other ministers in the cabinet seemed to many critics a bland lot; her giant shadow stifled growth in those around her. As Young put it, "All those around her were close to being pygmies." [12] Boredom doubtless played a role; a decade-plus of moral rectitude gets old. And the ambitions of younger men inevitably nibbled away at her power base.

The last time I had seen her was a few days earlier, when I took the head of the Council of Economic Advisors, Michael Boskin, by for a call. She seemed in total control, as usual. As Boskin came in, she said, "Ah, Mr. Boskin, I'm so glad to see you. It will be nice to talk about something concrete like economics instead of something artificial like politics. Of course, I'll have to fasten my seat belt for a few days!" She then launched into questions, giving total attention to his replies. I had never seen her equal for mental discipline.

On Thanksgiving Day I read the president's proclamation to a crowd of three thousand Americans in Saint Paul's Cathedral, the thrill of a lifetime for an old pol like me. Returning home to Winfield House, I took a call from Marylou Sheils, who breathlessly told me Mrs. Thatcher had just dropped out of the race. Under the British system, the majority party in Parliament elects a leader who becomes prime minister. A leadership election forced by members fearful of losing their seats in the next election saw her come within four votes of enough to remain party leader but not quite make it. She resigned.

Jessica and I could hardly believe our ears. She was a force so elemental, a power on the world scene so great, that the thought of Britain giving up this political nuclear weapon was unthinkable.

Discussing it, Jessica made a point I hadn't thought of. "There is a bit of male chauvinism at work here. Britain may have a female sovereign and a female prime minister, but it is a deeply male society." With that, she marched off to her computer and wrote an article on that theme that Meg Greenfield published in the *Washington Post*. In it, she said Mrs. Thatcher had suffered an "ordeal by a thousand undercuts" at the hands of her Tory colleagues. She made them mad, and "there is some not so subtle anti-feminism going on in the 'old boy system.'" Phil Zelikow, my friend on the National Security Council, called me after reading the article to compliment Jessica. "It was spot on," he said. I thought so too.

We spent a good bit of the afternoon watching the prime minister on TV, as she sang her swan song. She was feisty, tough, and smart, altogether wonderful. I wrote her a note that I hope helped.

She was, however, devastated. We had dinner Saturday two days after the Fall with Carla and Charles Powell, who had spent the day helping the Thatchers pack. They reported the depth of the prime minister's depression. British politics isn't for sissies: the tenants of 10 Downing had just a week to vacate the premises. Leisurely transitions are for Americans.

The succession struggle was close quarters with short swords. Michael Heseltine, Douglas Hurd, and John Major contended and in the final tally, Major got 185, Heseltine 132, and Hurd 65. Heseltine decided Major was too far ahead to be overtaken. He withdrew and Major called the movers.

A poll shortly thereafter was amazing. The Conservative Party just before the vote trailed Labour by 14 points. With Mrs. Thatcher gone, the Tories surged to an 18 percent lead.

ARCO, a California-based oil company, annually threw a black-tie dinner at Claridges' for Britain's movers and shakers. That year, former president Ronald Reagan and Margaret Thatcher were to be the two main speakers at a program obviously arranged before she was ousted, and I was to sum up afterward, with the traditional "appreciation."

Seated next to Mrs. Thatcher, I realized how shaken she had been. None of the verve and zest that always characterized her could be seen in her that night, no nonstop talk, no sparkle. She was lifeless.

Reagan spoke first. He was smooth, folksy, amusing, though when I had gone by his hotel to brief him earlier, he seemed to me a bit out of touch.

I thought, "Can she possibly pull it off?" But when her time came, she strode to the platform and in a flash, she was the old coruscant Maggie. It was as if a switch had been thrown, as she talked movingly for about twenty-five minutes, making it clear that while she was out, she was not history, not yet.

The rise of John Major, who succeeded Thatcher, pleased me. He had an easy informality that I had noticed first when three U.S. senators, led by Lloyd Bentsen, had called on him some months prior, and then again when Colin Powell, chair of the Joint Chiefs of Staff, and I went to see him.

As part of the run-up to the looming combat, Powell made a tour of key allied nations. He gave the new prime minister possible timing scenarios and said the plan called for hits on industrial and scientific targets. He added that we might destroy Saddam Hussein's ability to communicate with and propagandize his own people.

Major was totally unlike like his predecessor. The entire forty-five minutes he spent peppering the general with questions. Incidentally, in informal settings I had always called the prime minister "John"; while in meetings such as this, however, I called him "Prime Minister," though his elevation did not change our informality. Mrs. Thatcher was never anything but "Prime Minister." [13] I called on Major again on December 17, 1990, to brief him on his forthcoming visit to the United States, his first as prime minister. As always, he listened attentively, was interested, well informed, and just plain nice. Returning to my office, I wrote a paper for the president with my impressions of British concerns.

The trip to the United States began in frustration. The plan had been to go by helicopter to Camp David, the beautiful presidential retreat in Maryland's Catoctin Mountains, but a dense fog settled smotheringly over the Washington area, causing us to drive out instead. The trip took a couple of hours, leaving the two leaders more than enough time together to cover all issues. Only Charles Powell (who stayed on for a few months to help Major with the transition), and National Security Council head Brent Scowcroft rode in the president's limo, so British ambassador Acland and I and other aides missed the exchanges we otherwise would have heard. The business meeting once we arrived was pretty much limited to remaining peripheral issues such as South Africa and the plight of Pan American World Airways. The important topics of war and peace in the Middle East had already been covered.

The next morning at breakfast I mentioned to the president that I was headed to Aspen for Christmas the next day. He said, "Hey, call Bandar.[14] He's going to Aspen in his own plane. He might give you a ride."

Finishing a succulent pancake, I returned to my "cabin" (really a beautiful and very comfortable house) and asked White House communications to get me the Saudi ambassador in Washington. The young soldier acting as operator sounded a little confused but asked me no questions. Getting through took, I thought, an unconscionably long time, and on being told "Prince Bandar is on the line," I became even more puzzled.

The voice I heard sounded extremely faint, entirely confused, and much more distant than Washington. When I explained my mission, "Prince Bandar" politely suggested that perhaps I wanted his son, the ambassador, in Washington. It turned out that for some inexplicable reason I had been put through to Bandar's father, the minister of defense, in Riyadh. With profuse apologies, I rang off and finally got through to the younger Saudi. He did indeed have room, not only for me but also for Heather. Conversation with the ambassador during the flight gave me a good understanding of Saudi concerns.

John Major and his retinue, meanwhile, returned to Britain with a very comfortable feeling about George Bush and the "special relationship."

The Approach of War

ON JANUARY 5 I flew back to Washington from Christmas in Colorado to catch a ride to London with Jim Baker, traveling to brief our allies and visit with Iraqi foreign minister Tariq Aziz in Switzerland. He hoped passionately to convince the Iraqi that the coalition was serious, and his failure to do so bitterly disappointed him. TV pictures of President Bush after hearing of the session's failure made me think of those infinitely sad photos of Lincoln during the Civil War.

In Britain, the first stop, he met Foreign Secretary Douglas Hurd, and later I arranged a meeting with Labour Party leader Neil Kinnock and foreign secretary-in-waiting (if Labour won the next election) Gerald Kaufman. Baker, smooth as glass, reassured the two that every possible avenue to peace had been explored. I got the feeling that the Labourites would have depended on sanctions, forgoing force forever, but Jim wrung from them grudging support for the American and British government approach. His arguments were, I thought, unanswerable, and he presented them with the skill of a trained and brilliant polemicist. How, he asked, could Britons and other Westerners fail to support the cause when Syria's Hafez El-Assad and other self-proclaimed anti-imperialists were lined up with us?

Exposed to the proximity of war, I began to think what it might mean to the huge American community (some estimated it at 100,000 people) in Britain. Our intelligence agencies picked up information that Islamic militants might well try suicide attacks on U.S. installations. Scotland Yard began providing an additional security man, who followed my official car. In cooperation with the American Chamber of Commerce, I had groups of Americans come to the embassy for briefings on what to be alert to, the need to think of car bombs, and other unpleasant prospects. At embassy staff meetings, we even discussed searching employees, many of whom were foreign-born, an idea that I nixed.

The wartime atmosphere of January and February 1991 led to a spate of requests for me to appear on TV and radio. Staff meetings were moved to a secure room, safe from possible electronic probing (sophisticated devices set up in nearby buildings might actually hear through glass what was being said in my office).

Naturally, the IRA took advantage of the tense atmosphere by attempting to terrorize the British populace. A bomb set off in Victoria Station killed one. An audacious attack by mortars mounted on a nearby truck sent shells arching toward 10 Downing Street, fortunately missing the building, where a cabinet meeting was in progress. A crank sent me a written death threat.

Alarmists of all stripes proliferated. Even serious scientists such as Carl Sagan turned Jeremiahs. An opponent of the war, Sagan predicted (correctly) that Saddam Hussein would set fire to Kuwait's oil fields, that the sun would be dimmed, and that the apocalypse would be at hand. To me he sounded hysterical — and he proved to be wrong.

Amazingly enough, ordinary business got attended to as well. The great Pan American World Airways, the United States' most prominent airline, was in deep financial trouble. A creditor called me at home one night saying he was going to throw the airline into bankruptcy if debts were not paid the next day. I quickly called Pan Am's president and the end was postponed for a while. I called on British Transport Secretary Malcolm Rifkind for help in landing rights; though sympathetic, he could do nothing and we sadly watched the great old line die.[15] Jim Baker returned to Britain for a meeting January 13 with Prime Minister Major at Alconberry Royal Air Force Base, and I was on hand to meet him on arrival.

The meeting was a good one, giving Baker a chance to fill the prime minister in on his trip, the failure to convince Tariq Aziz that war loomed, and the plans for action. Charles Powell (soon to retire to a rewarding business career) took notes for Major, and I did the same for Baker. After the meeting, I hastened to London, a trip of two or so hours, woke Dorothy Baker, my secretary, and at midnight dictated, at Baker's request, details of the meeting for top secret dispatch to the State Department. Jim, meanwhile, left on the long flight to Washington.

A Bit of Celebration

A DIFFERENT kind of party did come off. I turned sixty in December 1990, and we celebrated with a grand dance at Winfield House. Gardener Stephen Crisp turned the house into a Scottish forest; Hans Kremer, the chef, and his team outdid themselves in the food department; and two bands, one dance and one Western, took turns providing music. Notables from Hollywood came. Melanie Griffith, our neighbor from Woody Creek, was in London making a movie with Michael Douglas, and they both came, as did Michael Caine, John Cleese, and our fellow Texan Alyce Faye Eichelberger, who later married John. (I liked Melanie, and feeling that she must be lonely, I asked Marylou Sheils to arrange a dinner some evening, since Jessica was in the States at the time. Negotiations with her secretary were protracted but unsuccessful. Was she reluctant to go out with a married man or afraid I might be blown up and she along with me? I never knew.)

The British government turned out in large numbers, as did our London friends. Many San Antonians made the trip. Family showed solidarity in the form of son John, daughter Isa, and Diana and Bill Hobby. It was, in short, a great evening, though my usual embassy staff meeting came awesomely early the next morning.

War

ON JANUARY 16, the air blitz against Iraq began, and at once, the entire American community became highly security-conscious. I had my fifteen minutes of fame as requests for radio and TV interviews continued to pour in. Most interviews were a piece of cake, but one caused public affairs adviser Sam Courtney to approach a coronary infarct.

David Frost asked me to be on his *First on Sunday* interview program. He and his wife, Carina, had become friends of ours, and I expected no traps. We had met the Frosts early in our tour and had found them attractive. They invited us to a dinner party; they set a good table and, not surprisingly, provoked good talk. The visit on TV went well, until toward the end when David asked my reaction to a recent anti-U.S. blast from Iran. I slipped the traces.

"The Iranians are practiced if not talented liars. I wouldn't trust them as far as I could throw them," I replied.

Sam Courtney was on the phone two minutes after the interview ended, disturbed by my undiplomatic remark. Sure enough, CNN picked up that segment and ran it hourly all day. No reaction from Washington was forthcoming and Sam's alarm proved unwarranted. And I had the satisfaction of being thoroughly undiplomatic . . . and right.

I did, however, worry about the war. What if the deck were reshuffled? What if Iran, against all expectation, came in on Iraq's side? Or if King Hussein were overthrown? Or if Israel tired of rockets raining on Tel Aviv and undertook to slap Saddam upside the head? When Iraqi troops took and held the Saudi town of Kafji, the press turned ominous. I thought of the president, who must have had similar concerns—multiplied a hundredfold.

Our country team met almost daily in the new secure "war room," as I dubbed it, as we tried to be sure every step to safeguard the embassy and alert U.S. citizens had been taken.

On February 22 I got a call on the secure phone that mostly gathered dust on the credenza behind my desk. In elliptical language, a man from the National Security Council warned me that the ground war was to begin almost immediately. To be told in advance was a pleasant change, and on the twenty-fourth General Schwarzkopf's long-planned ground attack began, with results successful far beyond our—or the press's—expectations.

A Compelling Offer

DURING THE considerable time I spent with Baker that January, he brought up a subject I had almost forgotten. In March 1990 I was playing tennis one Saturday with David Wallace, a talented young embassy officer who usually clobbered me. The phone rang at the court and when I answered I learned the caller was Chase Untermeyer, director of personnel at the White House.

Chase's message? Would I like to return to Washington to become director of the United States Information Agency? There was no pressure, he assured me, but the agency had problems and the president thought my communications background made me a good choice to solve them.

I was torn. I loved London and the job, but USIA, a worldwide foreign policy agency whose head reported directly to the president, was a much bigger challenge. I called Chase, an old friend from Texas, and told him sure, I'd be happy to do whatever the president wanted. He said to keep my mouth shut and await developments.

I did, but aside from an occasional comment from John Sununu that it was on hold, nothing more was said. Until, that is, Baker told me in January 1991 that the pieces were falling into place and to begin to get ready.

Shortly thereafter, it became official. Bruce Gelb, then USIA director, would leave and become ambassador to Belgium. Richard Carlson, director of the USIA's subsidiary Voice of America, would leave to become ambassador to the Seychelles. The two had not gotten along well; Gelb's firing of Carlson had been overturned by the White House, and having both of them depart seemed the tidiest way to resolve matters.

Sununu called me one day to discuss my successor. Having given the matter some thought, I told him that Ray Seitz would be ideal. Ray and I had become friends early in my London tenure when he was deputy chief of mission. He was well known and liked in Britain, he knew the country intimately, and he was tired of the endless stress and travel of his job as assistant secretary of state for European affairs.

"Can he afford it?" Sununu asked. I assured him Ray, a foreign service officer, could. The idea that the embassy in London required an extravagant financial commitment was incorrect. It had come from Walter Annenberg's having done so much to restore Winfield House. He had, indeed, given generously, but that done, further requirements from private purses were minimal and the expense allowance was adequate, if not lavish.

Later, the president, who liked Ray, called me to reassure himself. After hearing my comments he called Ray, who accepted and who became, to no one's surprise, a fine ambassador, the first career officer so to serve in decades.

A complication of our departure lay in what to do about a social event of major proportions. Jessica and I wanted to give a dinner in honor of the queen. In late 1990, word was quietly passed to Buckingham Palace of our interest, and Sir Robert Fellowes, an aide to Her Majesty, called to say she would be delighted. We set May 1991 as the time frame, exact date to be determined.

Planning began in earnest. Stephen Sondheim, the gifted American composer, frequently had musicals playing in London's West End theater district and he had once been our guest at dinner. (He also attended Williams College at the same time I did.) Jessica suggested I call Stephen and ask him to help us do an all-Sondheim program after the dinner; I did and he accepted. Meanwhile, Jessica and Graham Hartley began thinking about what to serve, and otherwise what decisions had to be made.

Suddenly, the likelihood of my being in Britain in May seemed remote, and I called Ray Seitz to get his thoughts. He feared he might not be there by May and that the whole thing had best be postponed. I agreed and so did the palace, though not without a bit of clucking: standing up the queen isn't often done. (Ray and Caroline did eventually entertain Her Majesty and Prince Philip, rescuing our honor.)

Plans for the great personnel swap, meanwhile, progressed apace. I called Bruce Gelb, soon to be named ambassador to Brussels, and learned at firsthand his view of the USIA and its problems. He thought the agency was shot through with right-wingers; he warned me that the *New York Times* would try to get me; he urged me to get "firing rights" in advance (recalling his unsuccessful attempt to fire Voice of America director Dick Carlson). "It is," Gelb warned, "a political cesspool. Put your own people in the key jobs." Turning to practicalities, we agreed that his last day would be March 23 and I would begin quietly going to the agency on March 25.

I also called Gelb's deputy, Gene Kopp. I knew that he and Bruce had not spoken to each other for months and that to say there was bad blood between them would be gross understatement. But I had known Gene slightly from the Nixon administration, when he served previously as deputy director; he knew the terrain and I needed advice. Supportive and forthcoming, he soon became a good friend and partner.

The days tumbled by, and I made preparations to leave. Graham and the Winfield House staff were, as always, knowledgeable, organized, and caring; we both felt they were genuinely sorry to see us go. Changing ambassadors is hard on the staff, for they must accustom themselves to the oddities of the new person and risk losing their jobs as well.

I learned that a farewell call on the queen was customary. It proved much less formal than my presentation of credentials. We sat, for one thing, and talked of all manner of things from the war to the grand old yacht *Britannia* and its service to the nation. She seemed mellow, and I thought it a pity she would never write down all she knew. Surely no one in Britain, probably no one in the world, could match her for knowledge of people, events, history. She was a walking encyclopedia of the postwar world, and her prime ministers were fortunate to have her available regularly to consult. I wondered if she found John Major more congenial than Mrs. Thatcher; he was assuredly less intense. I felt she reflected Britain's "melancholy long withdrawing roar," and I wished her well; life dealt her a difficult hand, but she played it exceedingly well.

Tradition called for a farewell reception, which we held at Winfield House. Jessica had come over for the closing days, and we stood for hours shaking hands as people came to wish us well. The next morning I had a farewell breakfast for the members of the country team. They had arranged to have a tree planted in the Winfield House garden in our honor and Ron Woods made a fine talk. I managed to avoid getting choked up, but it required an effort. The embassy officers and staff were first-rate, the job was important, and they did good work. I would miss them.

Our flight back to the States later in the day could have been sad,[16] but one of the onboard films was our friend John Cleese's achingly funny *A Fish Called Wanda,* and I laughed so hard (even though I had seen it before) that those seated nearby must have thought me daft.

I look back on my British days with great affection. For the grandson of a British subject to return as American ambassador seemed the quintessential American story. I made friends, lots of them, among British and Americans alike. The richness of London's intellectual life, the history so alive and close at hand, the physical beauty of the land and the architecture combined to make it the experience of a lifetime.

There had been, to be sure, disappointments. For one thing, Jessica's interests lay firmly rooted in Colorado, and she could ill afford to be gone for extended periods. She did, nonetheless, manage to be quite active during her times in Britain, writing for newspapers, becoming involved in conservation projects, and getting a reputation as a modern woman.

In spite of all this, her absence drew occasional criticism; the concept of the independent woman has not taken hold in that male-dominated country. One day CBS television did a half hour show on Winfield House, with the two of us as guides to its history and functions. To my surprise, the interviewer brought up Jessica's schedule in one of his questions. A good response came to me then, not later. I told him: "Jessica Catto half time is better than any other woman I know full time."

Part 6

U.S. Information Agency

"*Director of* What?"

M Y S O N Will's reaction to my new job was typical: "You are leaving London to be director of *what?*" He had got it right, for it was among the least-known government agencies.

Obscurity did not, however, diminish the scope of the work. The U S I A director was head of information and overseas cultural affairs, jobs that are often of Cabinet rank in other countries. He reported to the president, not the secretary of state, and in my day he spent more than $1 billion a year. Every American embassy abroad had a U S I A post, and we numbered just under 9,000 people. Counsellor of the agency McKinney Russell summed up U S I A's mission well with a quote: "When the cannons are silent, the Muses are heard." U S I A let the Muses be heard in an exciting variety of ways.

The best-known U S I A operation was the Voice of America (V O A), whose 2,700 employees broadcast more than a thousand hours a week on shortwave in forty-seven languages. (The choice of which languages was sometimes stripped from our control. If a powerful member of Congress or congressional staffer decided we should broadcast in, say, Kurdish, it was likely to happen.)

Voice of America programming consisted of news, interviews, music, and editorials. The news operations maintained the highest professional standards. V O A reporters had to have two confirmations of any story they broadcast. V O A's management and staff took pains to avoid letting any hint of propaganda taint their product. They knew that the British Broadcasting Company had achieved a worldwide reputation for accuracy, a reputation unsullied by ties to British foreign policy. The Voice was determined to match its older British cousin, and it succeeded.

The editorials, never numerous and always labeled as such, provided a practical argument for congressional support of V O A. They gave the vast listening audience brief explanations of why the United States did what it did and enabled the agency to argue that it was not a giveaway of taxpayer funds for the delectation of the unwashed. The most convincing reason for editorials lay, however, in the Voice's charter, which called for the service to be a source of accurate news, of American life and culture, and of the views of the U.S. government. No one I knew of came up with a better solution than editorials.[1]

VOA could, nonetheless, be used to support policy aims beyond the role of editorials, and the agency didn't hesitate to use it that way. For example, the normal eight and a half hours of Mandarin Chinese surged to twelve during the events at Tiananmen Square in Beijing. In the Gulf crisis of 1991, the Arabic service went from seven and a half to fifteen and a half hours. As refugees took to rafts to escape Haiti in 1994, the Haitian service in Creole sharply increased its pleas to Haitians to stay home. And during the attempted coup in the Soviet Union in 1990, Boris Yeltsin relied on VOA to spread the news of the coup's failure; President Mikhail Gorbachev later publicly thanked the Voice.

The Voice did not, of course, escape criticism. During the Persian Gulf crisis, VOA, always concerned with keeping the service's reputation for evenhandedness intact, had a reporter in Cairo interview a pro-Iraq Egyptian. The U.S. ambassador in Egypt erupted. He cabled the State Department that the United States was trying to build an anti–Saddam Hussein coalition with one hand while giving comfort to him by airing his views with the other. VOA officials hunkered down and weathered the storm.

At this point I should mention that VOA was not the only U.S. government broadcast service. During the Cold War, the CIA set up a service to the Soviet Union called Radio Liberty and one to Eastern Europe called Radio Free Europe. The idea was to provide for these countries news that their communist dictators suppressed, to offer a surrogate free press.

The paternity of these services became known, but so successful were they that the government transferred control from the CIA to an independent operator called the Board of International Broadcasting (BIB). I felt that the end of the Cold War made these entities superfluous and costly. Many conservatives, led by Steve Forbes, chairman of *Forbes* magazine and of the BIB, held to the contrary, arguing that a renascent communism or incipient fascism could once again draw the curtain over the east and we would be better off leaving the radios intact. I disagreed, feeling that should such disagreeable eventualities take place, VOA would be perfectly capable of filling the gap.

To make matters worse, the Voice and the BIB began to compete, abandoning shortwave and trying to place their programs directly with local Eastern European AM and FM stations.[2] I believed in competition, but only in the private sector. To me, the $200 million that BIB cost was wasted in a post–Cold War world.

My confidence in VOA's abilities in case of future need stemmed from the fact that USIA already did surrogate broadcasting. In 1985, during the Reagan administration, a radio service for Cuba was established. Called Radio Martí after a Cuban patriot, its authorizing legislation stipulated that it should parallel all VOA standards of objectivity, accuracy, and balanced, varied programming. Its daily fare consisted of 50 percent news (including local and neighborhood news, not just world events), 13 percent entertainment, 4 percent music, and about 30 percent talk—"magazine" format. Supervision was given to USIA, and broadcasting twenty-four hours a day on shortwave and AM, it became the most popular station in Cuba, with listenership estimated at 78 percent of the population.

Relations between USIA and BIB, never close, deteriorated when USIA's Advisory Commission, a congressionally mandated independent group that oversaw USIA's management, called in its annual report for the abolition of BIB. Chairman Forbes of BIB unleashed a vigorous campaign against the idea, and a compromise of sorts, merging the radios and the Voice, came to pass in the Clinton administration.

The Advisory Commission proved its evenhandedness by also calling for the abolition of a USIA operation called TV Martí. This sister service to radio, planning for which began during the Reagan administration, was inspired (as was Radio Martí) by Cuban Americans, mostly living in Florida. Organized with Prussian efficiency, they became a major force in Congress, and when they proved their clout at the ballot box, Congress listened. Seeing the success of Radio Martí, they decided television would be even more effective in toppling the Castro regime. Alas, it did not turn out that way, for by treaty our hours of broadcast were limited to 3:30 A.M. to 6:00 A.M., hardly prime time. And Castro jammed even that.

A far more successful TV endeavor was Worldnet, the brainchild of Reagan's USIA director, Charles Z. Wick. A satellite television delivery system, Worldnet beamed programs to more than two hundred USIA posts around the world. Seeing early in Reagan's administration that TV could be a useful way to tell America's story, Wick pushed it through Congress and it became a great success. News was presented in English, French, Spanish, and Arabic. *Science World,* the most popular program, featured the latest in medical, scientific, and technological advances. *Dialogue* provided teleconferencing to USIA posts; news conferences gave foreign reporters a chance to ask questions of U.S. officials thousands of miles away; and *Assignment Earth* covered the environment.

Programs did not go direct to foreign TV sets. They were first received via satellite and then distributed by USIA posts. They proved immensely popular, particularly in the developing world; cost-free programming finds a ready market.

The Voice's only rival for fame, the Fulbright scholarship program, began in 1946 to "increase mutual understanding between people of the United States and people of other countries." The inspiration of Arkansas senator J. William Fulbright, it was administered by the USIA with policy guidance and candidate selection by a board of twelve presidentially appointed citizens who serve for a three-year term.

Fulbright grants go to professors to study abroad, to U.S. and foreign graduate students, and to exchange teachers, usually from high schools. Pushed by Minnesota's late senator Hubert Humphrey, a category called Humphrey Fellows (senators are not shy about having their names attached to worthy endeavors) provides study in the United States for mid-career professionals from developing countries.

Finally, money is provided to U.S. and foreign universities to create partnerships for joint activities in various fields. In 1993, a typical year, 3,170 Americans and 4,915 foreigners received grants involving some 14 percent of the agency's budget. Another program, less well known but of great value, was the International Visitors (IV) program. It brought about 2,800 foreigners a year to the United States, visitors from all walks of life who came here for a taste of America as guests of the U.S. government. The visitors, picked by USIA posts abroad, outlined the program they would like and the agency put it all together, with the help of an army of volunteers stretching across America. The posts kept an eye out for future leaders as they selected the visitors, always on a nonpartisan basis. Their success has been startling: among the little-known up-and-comers of years past were future British prime minister Margaret Thatcher, future Japanese prime minister Toshiki Kaifu, South Africa's president-in-the-making F. W. de Klerk, Germany's Helmut Schmidt; Egypt's Anwar Sadat, India's Indira Gandhi, and dozens of others.

As USIA director, I readily acceded to a request for a visit by the young (thirty-seven) post–Cold War Bulgarian prime minister Philip Dmitrov. In Washington for an informal visit, he wanted to come by my office to thank the American people for having brought him under an IV grant to this country. Bulgaria was then under the apparently endless communist yoke; the firsthand experience of freedom changed his life and his story moved me.

As he left he paused at the door; clearly he had something else to say. "Would it be possible," he wondered, "to ask a favor? As a student, I was greatly influenced by the *Federalist Papers* of 1787–88.[3] Do you suppose USIA could have them translated into Bulgarian?" Swallowing the large lump in my throat, I said I would do my best. The project is now well under way.

Fulbright and IV proved that exchange programs are effective. Seeing this, congressional staffers were eager to immortalize their bosses, no less than the bosses themselves hastened to propose other programs. By my time, the USIA organization chart was cluttered with Pepper Scholarships (honoring the late Florida senator), Congress-Bundestag exchanges enabling German and American lawmakers to learn each other's problems, the World University Games and the World Scholar Athlete Games (everyone loves athletics), secondary student exchanges for high schoolers from the former Soviet Union, an Interparliamentary Exchange, and the Institute for Representative Government. There also was the Speaker's Parliamentary Exchange, the Nigeria Democracy Initiative, and the Central European Training Program. No Christmas tree in history was ever hung with more ornaments.

USIA Covers the World

THE BREADTH of agency operations was impressive. A research bureau collected and interpreted data on foreign attitudes about U.S. policies. The staff of forty-nine roamed the world, taking some ninety surveys a year that guided those who determined our foreign policy. They gauged foreign reaction to presidential summits or events such as the attempted coup in Russia or the Gulf War. They polled on listener levels for VOA and monitored public confidence in local mass media in Eastern Europe and the former Soviet Union. They tested Japanese and Korean attitudes on trade issues, South Africans on race, and Europeans on perceptions of the United States.

The U.S. government's oldest media product was called, rather quaintly, the Wireless File. Dating from 1935, it provided time-sensitive news and information for posts abroad and was extremely popular. It started as a "radio bulletin," sending radio teletype messages to U.S. Navy shortwave stations. By the late 1980s, five daily regional transmissions averaging 20,000 to 40,000 words each were beamed abroad by satellite in English, with shorter versions in French, Spanish, Russian, and Arabic. The file contained texts of government statements, speeches by officials, testimony before Congress, articles of interest, and staff-written analytical background. Our ambassador in Argentina, Terry Todman, regularly berated me because the file didn't reach him in what he considered a timely fashion. The president of newly free Estonia demanded a copy on his desk every morning. It was a very good product.

One of America's (and Britain's) secrets in dealing abroad was our hugely popular language, and as a result, both nations had extensive English-teaching operations, ours run by USIA. The English Language Programs Division provided curricula, teaching materials, television programs, and exchanges in some 130 countries, plus a magazine to aid instruction. An English-teaching corps worked with foreign universities, ministries of education, and teachers. In one hundred countries, Bi-National Centers run by local boards with help from USIS posts taught English, provided libraries, and promoted understanding of our culture. Is the popularity of English the result of imperialism? Undoubtedly. Is it a good thing? Undoubtedly, for it provides the world with its only lingua franca, spoken everywhere.

The richness and variety of American culture shine in the plastic and performing arts, and USIA spread the word. Fifteen to twenty performing artists or groups went abroad every year, selected in cooperation with the National Endowment for the Arts. While touring, the artists presented master classes and workshops and cooperated with foreign media. Fine arts exhibits such as "Continuing Traditions in American Folk Art" and "I Dream a World" (photographs of black women in America) toured for years.

A biennial show of art scheduled for Istanbul, Turkey, presented problems. A staff person came to me one day and suggested I might want to look at the works proposed by an independent commission as the U.S. contribution. I grabbed Gene Kopp and hurried to look at the slides.

We were appalled. One artist, for example, planned to show photos of Civil War generals with cartoonlike "balloons" that had them speaking homosexual obscenities. Another consisted of paintings perhaps two feet long but only a few inches wide. Each clearly depicted human skin with hair growing from it, but the viewer was never quite sure what he was seeing.

While not given to prudery, I found this art beyond the pale, especially since our authority to present shows sprang from an injunction to promote U.S. interests abroad. Gene and I felt such promotion would be, well, minimal in a Muslim country. We asked staff to check with two U.S. foundations that had cosponsored the project, with an eye to backing out, even though the outcry in the art world would probably be great. Fortunately, the foundations agreed, the artists were dropped, and the matter never became public (a minor miracle, considering this was Washington).

Books played vital roles, with 153 USIA libraries in ninety countries. Some were so popular that at times *all* the books were checked out, Bombay being a case in point. As budgets allowed, we placed computers in libraries as well, along with magazine subscriptions. Worldwide, there were 1.4 million books and 20,000 magazine subscriptions serving some 5.9 million users a year. The year 1992 marked the fiftieth anniversary of the United States' overseas libraries, the first having been the Benjamin Franklin Library in Mexico City; I visited it during the anniversary year. The Library/Book Fellows Program placed twelve to fifteen American librarians abroad, stressing projects designed to increase access to American information.

In a related activity, more than half a million copies of American trade books and textbooks were translated or reprinted every year. USIA underwrote translations by guaranteeing to buy a given number of books at a discounted price. The agency also distributed books (donated by U.S. publishers) on education, business, management, American literature, and social sciences, more than seven million titles since 1988.

The end of the Cold War enabled us to support programs to strengthen democratic institutions throughout Eastern Europe and the former Soviet Union. Grants to teach the precepts of free-market economics were awarded to numerous U.S. universities, and young faculty from Europe were given fellowships to study in our country.

Given the importance of a free press, USIA offered support to reporters from abroad. A media training center, established in 1983, offered training for foreign journalists (more than 2,400 of them in my time) in newswriting, reporting, broadcasting, media management, advertising, and technical skills.

Furthermore, there were foreign press centers located in New York, Los Angeles, and Washington, an idea born with the flood of journalists who came to New York in 1945 to cover the fledgling United Nations. The three centers assisted the 1,600 foreign journalists working here by piping in White House, State, and Defense Department briefings; by holding press conferences and backgrounders by American officials; and by conducting thematic tours of American cities.

Exhibits such as world's fairs, once a thriving USIA activity, had dwindled sharply by the time I arrived, but not soon enough to keep me out of trouble. Bruce Gelb, my predecessor, faced the task of putting together in a time of very scarce funding a U.S. pavilion at the 1992 Seville Expo, celebrating the 500th anniversary of Columbus's voyage. Our exhibit was to include an original copy of the Bill of Rights, which we thought would be popular. To get the cooperation of the steely-eyed Iowan who controlled funding, Representative Neal Smith, Bruce promised to raise any funds (beyond what Smith offered) from the private sector.

Stepping into this quagmire in 1991, I began soliciting help from corporations, with considerable success; of the $31 million budget, we raised $13 million privately. But in spite of a painful downsizing of the project, it soon became clear that if we didn't get additional government help, the world's only superpower would not be present at the celebration of its own discovery.

I scarcely knew Smith, but I had a strong feeling that he would not look on a request for more money with amusement. Arriving at his office, I was offered coffee by his receptionist and on seeing a well-stocked kitchenette, I asked her if I could borrow a knife and fork.

Used to odd ducks in government, she agreed, with a look that said, "You'd better hand 'em over when you leave." Tucking the utensils in my breast pocket, I entered the great man's lair with a deep breath. Waving me to a seat, he peered at me skeptically.

"Sir," I said, "I am here to eat crow." With that, I pulled out the knife and fork and laid them before me. It broke the ice, and though never enthusiastic, he understood our predicament and helped save us from a no-show.

Sending American speakers abroad played a key role in the agency. We picked them to speak on every imaginable topic: rule of law, democracy, economics, international trade, the environment, narcotics, science, and so on. Experts in confidence-building techniques traveled to India and Pakistan, helping to defuse the chronic enmity between these two nations; journalists held training workshops on the free press all over Africa, where that concept often found only barren ground; Justice Sandra Day O'Connor talked on an independent judiciary in Rwanda and Kenya.

We had telephonic conferences as well. John Updike spoke with a book reviewer in Brazil about his "Rabbit" series of novels; Senator John Glenn addressed people in Perth, Australia, on the thirtieth anniversary of his orbital flight (when he called Perth the City of Lights as he swept over it); the chief scientist at the National Oceanographic and Atmospheric Administration talked with scientists in Kuwait about that country's oil fires. In 1992, the number of teleconference talks was at 415.

USIA took on global issues. In 1990 a unit was formed to explain abroad our anti-narcotics programs and to organize conferences on international cooperation against the spread of drugs. A traveling environmental show proved popular.

Finally, USIA oversaw, at congressional insistence, the activities of the National Endowment for Democracy (NED), a joint effort for spreading democracy that was sponsored by the U.S. Chamber of Commerce, the AFL-CIO, the Republican National Committee, and the Democratic National Committee. (My first business luncheon as director was with Lane Kirkland, president of the AFL-CIO, who was unhappy with the way the agency supported his union's participation in the IV program. Lane basically wanted to pick program participants, a prerogative we could not, and did not, cede.) We also provided funding for the East-West and North-South centers in Honolulu and Miami. These "think tanks" studied Asian American and Latin American problems. Finding agency officials to inspect their programs was not difficult; I even managed to visit both myself.

Achieving Goals, Addressing Concerns

THE RUNNING of a huge government agency would be, I knew, challenging. I recalled Henry Kissinger's comment when he was secretary of state that no one above the level of assistant secretary had any time to think: just keeping the machinery moving precluded serious thought.

We did, nonetheless, develop five goals. The first was to bring the idea of "public diplomacy," that is, interpreting U.S. culture and dreams abroad and influencing the thinking of foreign publics, into the mainstream of the government's policymaking process.

Second was to recognize the vital nature of good relations with Congress. I intended to court key members vigorously and spread the word of our work.

Third, people often asked us what purpose we served after the end of the Cold War. I wanted, therefore, to be sure we knew our mission. Toward that end, I named study commissions within the agency to look ahead.

Fourth, I felt the need to toot our own bassoon. Post–World War II fears that USIA would become an internal propaganda agency had faded, and to the fullest possible extent I planned to make our work known to the public via a vigorous speaking schedule.

Finally, being unhappy with the fact that the agency was housed in five buildings scattered around Washington, I wanted to unite us all in a single headquarters.

As I surveyed my empire, two vexing problem areas stood out. The Seville Expo, mentioned earlier, was a mess. Our top priority was getting participation and money from the private sector. Luckily, companies such as USAA, American International Group, Philip Morris, and dozens of others rode to the rescue.

Yet for every inch forward, I learned of some new obstacle, one example being the U.S. Navy's plan to charge us more than $1 million to supervise the construction.

The media decided that we were going to do a bad job. A snide article in *New Republic* to that effect was picked up by the *New York Times* (embarrassingly close to verbatim, I thought), which proceeded in its usual haughty, imperious way to tut-tut everything we did. Fortunately, the U.S. pavilion turned out well, as measured by the only yardstick that counts: it was very popular with fairgoers.

The second worry concerned the inspector general, George Murphy. A large, gregarious man in his late sixties, Murphy, formerly with the Arms Control Agency, had been hired for this post by my predecessor, even though Murphy's peers in the inspector general's organization had questioned his qualifications.

Before my arrival, George had undertaken to investigate the Voice of America's activities during the Gulf War. Learning of this, I was uncomfortable. Although I liked George, I doubted that the inspector general's office was equipped for such a job; waste wasn't a factor, but political judgment was. I felt that the Voice's editors should not be second-guessed by people with no training or knowledge of journalism. Nonetheless, it was too late to turn back. The first results of the IG's report found little fault with the Voice's performance, but in the end, George rewrote the exculpatory report that his own inspectors had drafted, to the distress of many both in and out of the radio.

Murphy had worked as a staffer in Congress for years, and he knew his way around. That could have been valuable, but he began to threaten to run to Senator Helms, Congressman Berman, or others if crossed, an idea that drove me up the wall. An inspector general was not expected to be part of the "team," but there were within the trade ways of doing things, and that wasn't one of them.

In another case, the woman who ran the Press Center let her teenage son sell T-shirts at a center function. Murphy's men jumped on her with both feet, grilling her, causing her to hire an attorney, and generally showing what I thought was poor judgment and scant respect for due process. In the end, the case was dropped, but rules required that it be reported to the Justice Department nonetheless. Justice, of course, dropped the whole thing, but the innocent victim of Murphy's zeal paid a heavy price.

A visit from one of Murphy's senior people really disturbed me. Lynn Noah called on Gene and me and reported in harrowing detail the anomie within the inspector general's office itself. Numerous female employees found it a "hostile work environment," vacancies went unfilled, inspections of posts abroad sputtered to a halt. Noah's tale, detailed and dispassionately told, had the ring of truth.

Gene and I decided that we must consider a change. The trouble was, firing an inspector general was not a simple matter. It could easily appear that we bureaucrats were simply trying to be rid of a man asking vexatious questions—indeed, doing his job. We sought outside help, took affidavits from the inspector general's staff (many were bitter toward their boss), and generally tried to avoid the ultimate sanction. I kept my lines of communication with George open, hoping to guide him toward a less confrontational way of operating.

In the end, I decided to go see Constance Horner, head of White House personnel, for guidance. (Murphy, as a presidential appointee, could not be fired by me; my predecessor tested that theory by trying to fire Dick Carlson of VOA.) Connie was gratifyingly supportive. She read George the riot act, as did Frank Hodsel in the Office of Management and Budget. I urged him to retire, but it was all to no avail; we decided that after the election, George had to go. Murphy hired an attorney, resisting all the way, and he had, in the end, the satisfaction of outlasting me. Nothing in my nearly two years at USIA took more time or gave me more indigestion. The press views the system of having inspectors general in all departments as a safeguard against waste, fraud, and abuse. Unfortunately, it can easily produce its own abuse.

The problems that arose in day-to-day management were astonishingly diverse. At one point, Congressman Neal Smith's subcommittee abolished TV Marti funding; zap! a snap of the fingers and it was gone. (The full committee restored the funding.) Harris Wofford in the Senate did a similar trick with Worldnet. I called on him to explain the benefits of our TV service, but the only point that seemed to impress him was that we broadcast the *MacNeil-Lehrer News Hour*. The head of the VOA Amharic language service lost two brothers in the fighting in Somalia. His partisanship showed in his broadcasts, but we had no way of knowing until complaints began to flow in about prejudiced news reports.

Occasionally, amusing things happened. Someone in Iraq began to circulate counterfeit U.S. currency. The job they did was quite creditable save for just two details: they misspelled "treasury" and "department."

I began to have "brown bag" lunches in my conference room. Some were with groups of political appointees, whose work and support I valued. At others, I had as guests for a sandwich meal well-known news figures along with career officers. George Will, Tim Russert, Charles Krauthammer all came to discuss the news and how to handle it. These meetings did no harm to employee morale.

Another morale builder was to telephone people who served in hot spots. With an organization as sprawling as ours, trouble could be found somewhere at any time. Rebellions, earthquakes, floods, or war — there was never a shortage. McKinney Russell kept me advised of such situations, and I would place a call to the public affairs officer (as our heads of post were called) to see how things were going; these calls were, I felt, well received.

I called on the president in October to give a briefing on matters of concern: the uses of the agency, the value of courting the foreign media, the Seville Expo, our efforts in the former Soviet Union, and our search for a new headquarters. I hoped also to learn his opinion of the proposed Radio Free China. Steve Forbes, chairman of the board that ran Radio Free Europe and Radio Liberty, was pushing ever harder for a similar surrogate service in Asia, their European operations being increasingly outdated. As mentioned previously, I felt that voa could do the job. Bush, wisely no doubt, kept his counsel.

Freedom of the Press

IN THE SWIRLS and eddies of bureaucratic life at usia, broadcasting required particular attention. One day in May 1982, for example, *New York Times* columnist Bill Safire called me. We had been friends for years, so he started the conversation by saying, "Henry, this is an adversarial call."

Someone at the Voice had sent him a copy of a draft agreement between the United States and Kuwait for the construction of a shortwave radio transmitter. (I suspected that a couple of very conservative pro-Israel people in the editorial section at the Voice were responsible for the leak.)

The transmitter, to be used to cover weak spots in our reach to the Middle East, central Asia, and east Africa, had originally been scheduled to be located in Israel, but Israeli environmentalists had held up construction for an unconscionably long time. Eager to improve our "footprint" in Iraq, we began to look for an alternative site and found the Kuwaitis amenable to the idea.

What bothered Safire, whose ears always pricked up where issues of press freedom and Israel were concerned, was phrasing in the Kuwaiti draft. While it said there "shall be no restriction as to content," it went on to say the Voice would take into account the "customs and friendly ties" of Kuwait. "Didn't this amount to censorship?" Bill demanded. He wondered if we were to broadcast news of the Kurds or of the Palestinians, wouldn't VOA be subject to pressure from our landlords to temper our wind to Kuwait's foreign policy? Would I stand for this?

I explained the reasons for our souring on Israel and described the language in the agreement as standard; we always took local sensitivities into account as we prepared the news. I told the Voice's Joe Bruns of the problem, and he in turn called Bill, telling him the Kuwait contract read just like the one with, for instance, Botswana. He went on to say we had wanted an AM frequency in Israel but they wouldn't give us one, not wanting Arabic broadcast from their territory. When I called Bill again later in the day, I found his dudgeon lower and his mind turned to a different scoop.

In another instance, our editorial writers proposed to hit Syria and its leader Hafez el-Assad for sheltering terrorists. That the Syrians deserved censure could not be denied, but it happened at a time of sensitive negotiations with that stubborn foe of Israel, and we decided to put the editorial on hold. I held my breath for fear Safire's moles would tell him, but if they did, he chose not to make an issue of it. Either way, I was relieved.

Halfway across the world, broadcasting hatched ulcers. Our Office of Cuba Broadcasting, run by an urbane Cuban exile named Tony Navarro, churned with jealousy and conflict. Passions in the Cuban community always ran high, and when the methods and content of the message being sent to the homeland were involved, things got downright viperous. Tony always had to be alert to one or another of his people being too soft on Castro. Furthermore, with Miami-based Cuban American leader Jorge Mas Canosa always perched gargoyle-like on his shoulder, Tony clearly had an unenviable job.

Challenges arose at home and abroad. In the latter category, China loomed large. The USIS office in Beijing was woefully inadequate, so we searched for and found more satisfactory quarters. On applying to the appropriate Chinese ministry for permission, we learned that our choice was not suitable. By happy coincidence, the ministry had a "suitable" location in mind.

Our public affairs officer (PAO) took a look at the suggested substitute and found it totally inadequate — the location inconvenient, the parking nonexistent, and the rent too high. Furthermore, the possibility that we might be moving into a building heavily laden with listening devices lurked in our minds. Much to-ing and fro-ing with officials in Beijing brought no progress, so I determined to intervene: I would call on Chinese ambassador Zhu in Washington.

Normally, ambassadors are summoned to call on officials, not vice versa, but I decided to reverse the process by way of showing goodwill. Prickly from the beginning, Zhu became red-faced and agitated when I explained our view, an explanation that included a hint dropped that we might not renew our soon-to-expire cultural agreement with China unless a satisfactory solution could be found. At this, His Excellency went nuclear, reminding me that China was a sovereign nation, that it would not be intimidated, etc., etc. I left, inwardly pleased. Some weeks later, he called on me, bygones left behind, and in the end, we found adequate and secure quarters—my goal in the first place.

Domestic events can affect our image abroad, an example being the riots attendant to the Rodney King beating by Los Angeles police. Our people, especially the Africa bureau, worried that years of work would be lost as pictures of mindless rampage flashed around the world. I sent a telegram to all our posts, urging particular attention to the matter, with encouraging results. Our people at the embassy in Harare, Zimbabwe, proved particularly imaginative.

The PAO, Philix Aragon, showed great initiative. He culled American newscasts received on our Worldnet TV, taking clips of the rioting; he researched the history of race relations in the United States; and he amassed details of how the community and the country planned to cope. From these materials, he assembled a program and offered it to the national university. When presented, it drew a huge crowd, one large enough to justify a repeat performance. His quick and imaginative work lanced the boil; while he made no attempt to disguise reality, he did show Zimbabweans that we were capable of concern and not afraid to air our dirty laundry.

Events in the former Soviet Union had a profound effect on the USIA. For one thing, they prompted rethinking our overseas activities with an eye to quick expansion into the newly created republics. I lunched with financier-philanthropist George Soros to see if we could coordinate with his Eastern European activities. We couldn't; he had little desire even to be housed in the same building as USIS, a government entity.

These dramatic events energized Congress as well. Senator Bill Bradley of New Jersey and Congressman James Leach of Iowa decided we could best vaccinate the newly free Russians against a recurrence of the communist plague by bringing large numbers of them to the United States on fellowships. Bradley felt strongly that young Russians, especially, would benefit, even high schoolers. We blanched when the number 50,000 was bandied about. Our volunteer network would be swamped, the universities that normally accommodated us would rebel, and our budget would need a huge transfusion. Few people realized that the success of our exchange programs sprang from volunteer organizations all over the country, where hundreds of Americans gave time, money, and facilities to welcome USIA-sponsored visitors. I met with Bradley, trying to explain that while I agreed with his idea, practicalities intervened. He brushed them off, saying all I needed to do was convince President Bush, a project far easier said than done and one I chose not to undertake.

All our euphoria about Russia seemed in peril in mid-August of 1991. A coup rocked the nation, Gorbachev was taken prisoner (and later said that during his captivity he listened to VOA to learn what was happening), and fear spread that the communists had launched a counterrevolution.

I learned that Secretary Baker also was out west, at his Wyoming ranch, and I arranged to hitch a ride back to Washington on the Air Force plane sent to fetch him. Also hitching was Bob Strauss, ambassador nominee to Russia. On the flight, Baker emphasized that we must do nothing to imply recognition of a new regime in Moscow. Certainly, he warned us, Strauss (on his way to his new post) should not present his credentials to any usurper. And he expressed the hope that we would all return to our holidays, lest it be thought abroad that the American government was alarmed, an appealing idea. As it turned out, we need not have worried; the coup collapsed and Gorbachev returned to power—albeit briefly.

Public Diplomacy
and an Open Door Policy at USIA

MY RESOLVE to spread the word about public diplomacy burned bright. Someone once wrote that in the battle for men's minds, the United States often engaged in unilateral disarmament. Wanting to re-arm, I traveled and I talked: in San Francisco to the Commonwealth Club; in Los Angeles to the World Affairs Council; in Denver, San Antonio, Kansas City, New York, always stressing the need to tell the story of democracy and free enterprise abroad. Invariably, people were ignorant of what we did, and invariably they responded favorably when they learned about it.

A try at promoting rational government failed. The Department of Education, for some obscure reason, had a small Fulbright Scholarship program. I walked across the street one day in April 1992 and told Secretary of Education Lamar Alexander about it, suggesting that his program be consolidated with our vastly larger operation. Interested, he promised to look into it, but apparently the bureaucratic imperative triumphed: one agency seldom cedes turf to another without a fight. In this case the stakes were too small and the idea went nowhere.

Another try at rational government foreshadowed moves toward foreign policy unity during the Clinton administration. I regularly saw Dr. Ronald Roskins, director of the Agency for International Development (AID) at Jim Baker's staff meetings. Visiting after such a meeting, we hit upon an idea: why not meet regularly to discuss eliminating overlap between our two agencies? We did, expanding the program to include first Paul Coverdell and later his successor, Elaine Chou of the Peace Corps. All three agencies were involved, for instance, in English teaching. It proved a useful exercise; we moved to save money, discouraged interagency bickering, and headed off congressional criticism.

An example of bureaucratic struggles could be seen in ambassadorships. Our officers were every bit as much foreign service officers as were those at State. They suffered from a disadvantage, however, because decisions on who got what embassies lay mostly with our sister agency.

I made the matter the object of a bit of a crusade, lobbying as hard as I could with the director general of the Foreign Service to give our people a fair break. It apparently helped; during my tenure a record number of USIA officers headed embassies.

Among the pleasures of the new job, callers ranked high. I saw anyone who wanted to see me, from presidents to ambassadors, from employees to job seekers. Seldom did this "open door" policy prove a nuisance, though I'll admit that one or two would have had a hard time getting back in. Most ambassadors going out to a post dropped by for a courtesy call, as did incumbents with gripes, such as Terry Todman, ambassador to Argentina, and Vernon "Dick" Walters, ambassador to Germany. I had known Dick forever. A former Marine general, a superb linguist, former deputy director of the CIA, and the world's best teller of stories, he usually radiated ebullient good humor. The day he called on me, however, the blues had him. For one thing, we planned to cut our staff in East Germany, recently merged with our operation in West Germany. For another, he said he was too old to be cut out of meetings when Washington officials came to Germany and that he would resign in October (1991). I sympathized, recalling how Treasury Secretary Brady had finessed me in London.

Ambassador Bob Strauss came by at Gene's and my request to discuss the PAO in Moscow. Bob reported that he was doing well enough, a "B" performance. That taken care of, we turned to politics, a topic seldom far from the mind of that most amusing and entertaining man. Bob told us that Ross Perot had called, asking him to run his presidential campaign. Bob demurred, telling Perot, "I'm going to vote for Clinton and work for Bush." He reminisced about the time when he was chairman of the Democratic National Committee and George Bush was his Republican opposite number. Both of them were gregarious Texans, and they got on well, but Strauss said, "George learned more about politics from my secretary than Richard Nixon and all his Watergate burglars knew."

British friends came by. A brilliant and amusing Labour Party member of Parliament named John Gilbert popped in to catch me up on London doings. John was his party's expert on defense matters, and though that sounds like an oxymoron (Labour being heavily burdened with peace-at-any-price types), he was both realistic and effective in his role.

Albania, a small land squeezed between Greece and Yugoslavia, had long been plagued with the most virulently hard-line communist dictatorship in Europe. When the Reds were finally routed, the leaders of the newly elected democratic government wanted to come to the United States. Chase Untermeyer and I received President Sali Berisha at USIA's Voice of America. A big, good-looking man, he reminded me of actor Robin Williams, partially because of the air of good humor about him. His quite serviceable English had been learned, he explained, when he was a young shepherd listening to VOA: "The sheep wandered off while I studied verb forms."[4] VOA was the country's only contact with the world, since BBC had given up its Albanian service and Radio Free Europe never had one. The U.S. Agency for International Development had been a great help to his poverty-plagued country: "They sent us seven white Jeep Wagoneers; one is now the presidential limousine. They also sent us white paint to change red ballot boxes to white!" His gratitude was moving; America did make a difference.

A refugee from tyranny was a Chinese author resident in the United States, Nien Cheng, who called on me. In person she was a handsome woman in her sixties; in her book, she told of the unbelievable persecution of educated people during the Cultural Revolution of Mao Tse-Tung. The tales that she and so many others told made me wonder how they kept their serenity in the face of perhaps the most brutal dictatorship in history.

On the Road Again

RUNNING A worldwide foreign affairs agency would, I knew, require travel, a prospect that I greeted with pleasure. I knew Gene Kopp would mind the store ably while I was away, and I hoped Jessica could accompany me from time to time, though I realized her schedule and loathing of long plane trips made that unlikely. Most important, seeing our people abroad and learning what they faced could not be accomplished while seated at a desk in Washington. By the fall of 1991 travel planning began.

First, each of the area directors gave us reasons why their parts of the globe required my presence (and their own along with me). After much palaver, we decided on an Asian swing: Honolulu to visit the East-West Center, Tokyo, Hong Kong, Bangkok, Kuala Lumpur, and Singapore — all in seventeen days.

The trip, broken in Hawaii, began September 22. Having Marylou Sheils and area director David Hitchcock along made dull seem bright, and we arrived safely in Tokyo. Along the way we totally lost a Monday, which was all right since I don't much like Mondays anyway. I rose and ran at 6:00 A.M.; a run is the best cure I know for jet lag. We had a meeting and dinner with Ambassador Mike Armacost, visits with USIS people, Japanese prime minister Kaifu, members of Parliament, and cultural mavens. We even had music: at the ambassador's residence we heard a jazz concert (a good one) by Mike's son. The next day we had a crowded visit to our post in Nagoya after a two-hour trip on the superfast "bullet train." After forty-eight hours, PAO Rob Nevitt put us on the plane for Hong Kong, doubtless with relief.

Hong Kong was essentially a transit point over the weekend, so we ate, shopped, and gawked at a packed Chinese market. We did do a bit of business Monday morning, visiting USIS, signing a cultural agreement, and lunching at U.S. consul general Dick Williams's aerie high above the city.

In Thailand, we were met by U.S. ambassador David Lambertson and PAO Donna Oglesby. Throughout the visit I had a police escort, occasioned not by terrorists but by the appalling traffic. In booming Thailand, you can't get around without one. I was told that Bangkok added five hundred cars a day to streets already at gridlock—that, in a city without freeways.

The visit involved seeing USIS and AID people and operations. In discussions with staff, I learned a new, politically correct euphemism when we talked about Thailand's AIDS epidemic: prostitutes are called "commercial sex workers."

We called on Prime Minister Anand Pannyarachun, flew to the northern city of Udorn to visit a VOA transmitter, and called on the king. Our small motorcade, police siren wailing, turned into the spacious palace grounds at 4:30 P.M. on October 1. Once inside, we waited in a large portrait-filled room with petitioners and servitors. Eventually, an official escorted us to the receiving room, elaborately decorated and painted in gold, white, and what is called Siam ruby.

His Majesty King Bhumipol, the world's longest-serving monarch, bore no resemblance to Yul Brynner in *The King and I*. Perhaps sixty-five, dark hair, lean, straight, and dressed in a blue suit, he greeted us warmly and seated us in a circle around him. Tea was served by a man who entered the room on his knees, balancing a tray of cups precariously as he shuffled from person to person. As it turned out, his labor was in vain—the king didn't take a sip and therefore neither did we. Unlike his British counterpart, Bhumibol occasionally asserted authority, justifying his political intervention as the right of all Thai citizens. To the surprise of his 58 million subjects, who revere and trust him, he has publicly chastised a prime minister and has refereed political disputes.

Conversation proved easy—the king did all the talking. Seldom moving, he fixed us with his glass eye and for well over an hour, in faultless English and in a voice so soft that we had to strain forward to hear, told of his interests, birth control and artificial insemination leading the list. He also worried about radiation from broadcasting towers (which worried *me*, since we had one at Udorn).

An accomplished musician who played regularly in jam sessions, he told of listening to jazz while working out on his stationary bicycle. I had been told of his interest in music and had brought him a gift of CDs. When time to present it came, the hapless servant kneed his way across the floor, offering me an ornate tray called a *pann*. This was then presented to His Majesty; protocol forbids handing anything directly to the sovereign. I placed the gift on the *pann*, which in turn was offered to His Majesty. He didn't open it. Oh, well.

Protocol was elaborate. We had been warned to keep our feet flat on the floor; showing shoe soles wasn't de rigueur. When we addressed him, the opportunity for which was rare, protocol enjoined us never to say "you," always "Your Majesty," e.g., "How is Your Majesty?" It wasn't an easy habit to form. Rehashing the meeting later, we agreed that Thailand was lucky to have such a monarch.

The great German airline, Lufthansa, took us to our next stop, Kuala Lumpur in Malaysia. Normally government employees had to fly on U.S. carriers, but there were no U.S. flag flights from Bangkok to Kuala Lumpur. The customary program awaited us: met by Ambassador Paul Cleveland and PAO Jim Pollack, supper with foreign service nationals, and a dinner hosted by the ambassador. The minister of information received us in an office painted and furnished in blinding white, explaining to us his fear of too much television and too much democracy. Outside, smoke blown north from forest fires in Indonesia provided a dolorous backdrop for a disheartening interview.

Two days in Malaysia's neighbor, booming Singapore, left me feeling little better about the state of democracy in Southeast Asia. Ambassador Bob Orr and PAO Dennis Donahue explained how the government intimidated the media, including the Asian *Wall Street Journal*, which had been harassed for criticizing the country's judiciary. My call on the Ministry of Information drew neither light nor hope for improved behavior in the future. Our ideas of democracy are not Singapore's.

On the trip home we went via San Francisco, where a chat with the Immigration and Naturalization Service official proved something I had long feared: so obscure was our agency that not even our fellow government worker admitting people to America had ever heard of USIA or VOA.

In February I went with Chief of Staff Marylou Sheils and area director Ambassador Bill Rugh to India and Pakistan. These two populous, fractious, heavily armed countries of the Indian subcontinent were the focus of a USIA-sponsored exchange called the Neemrana Process. Under agency auspices, former government officials from each country met (in Neemrana, a New Delhi suburb) to talk about their endless and intractable enmity. The idea was for experienced people *not* in government to get to know one another and exchange ideas. Since they were not in office they could be frank, and having been of high rank, they could gain an audience with those in power and perhaps bring new ideas into play. All of this was done under USIS guidance, as we tried to bring conflict-resolution techniques learned across the world to bear in an area that some predicted could be the site of the next nuclear war. The officials I met were uniformly enthusiastic about the idea, one which is still ongoing today.

The U.S. representatives in India with whom we spent the most time, Ambassador Bill Clark and PAO Dr. Steve Dachi, were remarkable. Bill and his wife, Judith, were "pros" of the best sort. The ebullient and winning Dachi was trained as a dentist; indeed, on post in Brazil he helped identify the remains of deceased Nazi fugitive Josef Mengele by using the teeth as evidence.

We spent a day off in Agra visiting the Taj Mahal and the ruins at Fatipur Sikri. The Sheraton hotel was headquarters and, after a train trip (on which we noted that hundreds of people sleep every night in the train stations), a place to wash and relax briefly. After seeing the shimmering beauty of the Taj, we returned to the hotel. As I alit, a feathered hat was placed on my head, I was ushered into a horse-drawn cart, and away I went to the hotel garden, to be guest of honor at a surprise party—a festival no less—put together by the USIS staff.

While cameras clicked and I tried to keep a silly grin on my face, a camel carried me around the field, bobbing and nodding. A parrot told my fortune by picking out cards from a deck. Bears danced to Indian music and a snake (defanged) fought a mongoose (likewise). A cow picked out the shortest person in any crowd, and when all these miracles had been admired, we danced more enthusiastically than the bears. After the festival was over, I took a run around the hotel's extensive grounds. Noticing a group of tatterdemalions on a high garden wall, I waved as I loped by. Their return waves turned out to be rocks being tossed my way. I moved out of range and finished my run. It had been a great day.

Thinking about the circus as we rode back on the train, I ungraciously asked Steve who had paid. He said the entertainment fund of USIS but not to worry; the whole thing had cost only $300, though there must have been thirty people involved in the various acts. Embarrassed, I nonetheless insisted on reimbursing him, recalling all too clearly how the press would have loved such a story of wasting the taxpayers' money. As a wise man has said, "If you don't want it on the front page of the *Washington Post,* don't do it".

In New Delhi, I called on the foreign secretary, Mr. Solanki, for the usual "frank and useful" talks, addressed a regional PAO meeting, lunched with the Dachis, dined with the Clarks, and met carloads of government officials and businessmen. In Bombay, I lunched with a group of press people and ran along the Corniche, the beautiful road around the Bay of Bombay, called in Queen Victoria's time the "Queen's Necklace."

We hitched a ride from New Delhi on the U.S. Defense Attaché Office (DAO) plane with the ambassador to Pakistan, Nick Platt and his wife, Sheila, arriving in time for dinner with PAO Bill Lenderking and his wife, Susan. Islamabad, Pakistan's capital, is a new city whose parliament building looks much like Washington's Kennedy Center, not surprising since architect Edward Durrell Stone designed both (as well as the ambassador's residence in New Delhi).

A feature of Islamabad was "loadshedding." There is not enough power to supply the entire explosively growing city at once, so the electric authority divided it into segments, each subject to an unpredictable blackout at any time during the day. The residents, their candles and flashlights at the ready, took the whole thing with good humor; I thought they should privatize the power company.

I called on Pakistani president Ghulam Ishaq Khan ("G.I.K." to the press and people) at his Stone-designed office. He was pleasant but annoyed at the United States for cutting off military assistance and cooperation. I didn't really blame him. The U.S. government had been forced to take the step by Senator Larry Pressler of South Dakota, who disapproved of military aid to a developing country that was reputed to be building nuclear weapons. To me it seemed another congressional usurpation of foreign policymaking, supposedly the realm of the Executive Branch.

The DAO plane took us to Peshawar, site of the Khyber Pass, gateway to Afghanistan and at the time, home office of Islamic terrorists. Thousands of Afghan refugees, who had fled their nation's seemingly permanent chaos, lived there in mud huts, moving about by donkey cart. We fared better and were treated to a military parade complete with bagpipes (the Raj lives) and a visit to the fort overlooking the pass, where the wind roared out of the north with numbing force.

A trip to the former political and current economic capital, Karachi, completed the tour. We went to a Worldnet interactive press conference, had dinner with Consul General Dick Faulk, and returned to the U.S. via Frankfurt the following day.

The Seville Expo, celebrating the five hundred years since Columbus's trip to the New World, began the day after Easter. I attended, accompanied by Jessica, Isa, and Marylou Sheils, arriving the Thursday before the opening.

Seville at Easter, always crowded, was doubly so that year. There was a hotel employees' strike, and prices were high enough to make a Rockefeller blanch. Arriving hungry, I asked room service to send us four grilled ham-and-cheese sandwiches. They obliged in a dilatory way, presenting me with four inedible blobs and a bill for eighty-eight dollars.

The Good Friday parade made it all seem worthwhile, however. Snaking their way through the medieval streets, the participants were barefooted and dressed in costumes reminiscent of the Ku Klux Klan. Choirs of boys called "los Pasos" marched by solemnly, carrying long candles. Floats, carried by twenty-five men, portrayed scenes of Christ's passion carved in heavy plaster, while drums and brass instruments provided somber music for crowds too thick to move through. It was, in the true sense of the word, awesome.

We attended Easter mass at the cathedral in the morning; two somber hours of gothic gloom, seated on a dais, feet on the floor. Life brightened up afterward, thanks to a lunch of fried fish at a cave overlooking the River Guadalquivir and a walk through tiny plazas lined with fragrant orange trees. Dinner at the home of the U.S. commissioner to the fair, Fred Bush, was lively, and we fell into bed, replete.

The U.S. pavilion, subject of criticism among chic journalists and critics, bubbled with activity. It featured a large plaza where something (Indian dances, basketball games, singers, tumblers) was always happening. A tasteful and moving display of the Bill of Rights drew thousands. A typical American home had been built just off the plaza, and General Motors had provided not only cars but a fine short film that soundlessly summed up American life. So it wasn't an architectural prizewinner; thousands upon thousands of Expo visitors liked it, and I was one of them. Even Congressman Neal Smith, our reluctant financial lifeline, attended, calling it "well worthwhile." I would guess, nonetheless, that Seville will prove to be the last world's fair in which the U.S. government participates; from now on, we will have to depend on the private sector.

Opening day was lively. The ceremony included remarks by a genuine Indian chief named Two Moons. During his remarks there was a stir and some loud talk in the crowd. A young woman pushed her way forward, said she was Princess Pale Moon, and demanded a part in the proceedings lest she claim ethnic and sexist discrimination. We politely turned her down, in spite of dire threats. Investigation later revealed she was one Rose Ann Smith, origin unknown.

We closed out the trip with two days in Madrid, where PAO Jake Gillespie and I called on the Spanish minister of culture and met with the Fulbright Commission. Jessica, Isa, and I drove out to the Zarzuela Palace for a call on King Juan Carlos, who greeted us warmly, seemed serene, and looked very well; it was fun to see him and incidentally to see the John Safer sculpture that President Ford had presented to the king in 1976. Asked if he were well, he said he was, save for a knee problem. He had been skiing in Spain, when suddenly a young man slammed into him, knocking His Majesty into an unregal heap. The king knew he was hurt, but he told the offender to get out of there fast, knowing what trouble the youth would be in for if he stayed.

The View from the Great Wall

U.S. RELATIONS with China were then stable (as were mine with Ambassador Zhu), and I decided on a China trip for late July. The first stop was Detroit, the second Tokyo. There we (Marylou Sheils, area director George Beasley, and I) boarded an ancient Air China 747 for the last four-hour leg to Beijing. Assured via a lengthy form that we did not suffer from "HIV, AIDS, a rash, TB, a sore throat, or jaundice," the authorities admitted us to the Middle Kingdom, after twenty-three hours of travel. Chargé d'Affaires Scott Hallford and PAO Frank Scotton met and escorted their glassy-eyed guests to a very modern and comfortable hotel called Jing Guang, where we quickly collapsed.

Although the next day was Saturday, we had a full schedule. At 9:00 A.M. I called on Li Ruihuan, the number four man in the Communist Party hierarchy, at the Great Hall of the People. To him, and to all the Chinese officials, my approach was the same: don't jam the Chinese services of voa and do allow more flexibility in exchanges. (The Chinese government wanted to pick the U.S. travel and scholarship grantees, a demand we could not agree to.) Responding, Mr. Li warned us not to start a Radio Free China, a position to which I silently said, "Amen," having no interest in wasteful competition for voa.

Li, supposedly Deng Xiaoping's representative in the inner circle, spoke in long spurts with many gestures; he wore chic-looking Italian loafers on small feet. We sat in a huge room, in a semicircle of stuffed chairs with doilies on the arms. Li's defense of their jamming amused me. He said Americans claim the government of China doesn't want Chinese listening to the voa, but there may be something wrong: "Perhaps your radio is too loud, jarring to the Chinese ear. You shouldn't patronize your audiences; if the audience doesn't like you, don't blame it, like the doctor who isn't popular but blames his patients." The problem, he went on, was symbolic and doesn't matter much. China was developing and must have stability and good relations with the United States. "I am optimistic," he said. "Our grandchildren will laugh at our small disagreements."

At one point I caused an interpreter a problem. Discussing the jamming and tying it to better overall relations, I said, "Watch the donut, not the hole," a line from a Burl Ives folk song. The poor woman, whose understanding of English was excellent, nonetheless looked totally nonplussed, and I hastened to her rescue. At another point, Li Ruihuan, who drank beer throughout the meeting, questioned her meaning when she interpreted "jammed." With a smile, she explained it meant "the mike broke."

One day I lunched with Vice Minister of Foreign Affairs Liu Huagui and told him that we would view an end to radio jamming favorably, to which he replied with a grin, "Don't worry, our jamming is ineffective. My daughter is studying English on the voa!" Later, his interpreter announced, "Japanese love to eat ears." It took me a bit to catch on; he meant "eels."

The next day, Sunday, we toured the Great Wall. People packed every inch of space; we earned every view from the wall by imaginative and forceful use of elbows. George Beasley, a Chinese speaker and an old China hand, told us countless interesting things. For example, we learned that in China in 1975 the "three bigs," items everyone aspired to, were a bike, a watch, and a pen. Now the three were a color TV, a refrigerator, and a washing machine. Weather reports lied about high temperatures; the government didn't want fear of hot weather to discourage tourists. I could see why: it was hot, gray, and oppressive.

Graffiti, marring countless walls, urged BIRTH CONTROL, and DON'T SMOKE IN THE WOODS, and a sign directed at laborers said, HURRY AND FINISH BUILDING THE BRIDGE; THERE IS DANGER TO PEDESTRIANS.

Other facts: Hong Kong and Taiwan products frequently were shipped to the United States via the People's Republic to avoid tariffs. Foreign service nationals hired by the U.S. embassy were chosen by the Chinese Diplomatic Service Bureau, almost guaranteeing security risks. Chinese spending on military items was up 12 percent in the last year — disquieting information, although the basis of comparison was low.

Walking the streets was an adventure. As we returned from a restaurant one evening, an ancient man shook his cane at us, shouting angrily. We wondered who he thought we were — Russians perhaps? As we passed the city hall in Tianjin, a vigorously protesting pig was hung from a strut and slaughtered, blood pouring onto the street; no one save our group even noticed.

One night at our Jing Guan Hotel in Beijing, the most *luxe* in town, the phone in my room rang. I answered and a soft sexy female voice asked, "Are you feeling lonely?" I replied that I had quite enough company, thank you. I guessed she worked for Chinese intelligence, though she might have been a hotel employee or a freelancer. Credence to the first theory was lent as we checked out of the hotel the next day. The manager, a Westerner, waited by the door to bid us adieu, and I took advantage of the occasion to tell him of the phone call. He said that, yes, there were odd things that happened. For example, a group of rooms on the third floor was off-limits even to him.

We worked, hard. I met with a group of intellectuals for a roundtable discussion, had a supper at Frank and Sa Yun Scotton's flat (all Americans and other Westerners had to live in a high-rise ghetto) with U.S. reporters, signed a renewed cultural agreement, and ate with the embassy staff. In Tianjin, we dined at a restaurant called Goubeli, which I was told translated as "dog won't go near," not a name I would have picked, but it was said to ward off evil spirits.

To see the Chinese economic miracle firsthand, we flew to dusty, dynamic Guangzhou in the south, not far from Hong Kong. We called on the lieutenant governor and on local branches of such U.S. companies as

Nike and Avon. The frenzied activity in this exploding southern city reminded me of the beehive of construction at the tunnel under the English Channel.

The next day a train took us to Hong Kong and once again, getting there was *not* half the fun. A loudspeaker blaring propaganda and instruction in Chinese made thinking hard, and when the seemingly interminable chatter ceased, songs such as "Jingle Bells" and "Oh! Susanna" serenaded us.

In the Crown Colony, which awaited 1997 and reversion to Chinese control, I visited our beefed-up VOA operation and called on the British governor, Christopher Patten, a friend from my London days. Chris's residence, a large and beautiful mansion nestled in parklike grounds high above the city, reminded us of the glory of the Empire. The governor himself was a totally modern man, trying to cement democratic institutions in place so as to frustrate communist authoritarianism after the takeover.

I left China certain that it would play an increasingly important role in American foreign policy in the years ahead. Under Mao Tse-tung China had become a charnel house of murder, persecution, repression, and squalor. Americans and Chinese went to war in Korea. While President Nixon's opening of relations provided us with a brief moment of hope, illusions of genuine commonality of interest faded with the collapse of the Soviet Union, once a common threat, and the massacre at Tiananmen Square. China's partial conversion to free markets offered reason for optimism, but her stubborn resistance to Western ideas of human rights chilled the relationship, a chill made colder by foolish American efforts publicly to shame the proud Chinese into changing their errant ways. Perhaps the contagious virus of modern communications in the computer age would erode these refractory dictators, but I suspected it would be a slow process.

Next Stop, Eastern Europe

BEFORE AUGUST ended, we were off again, this time to Eastern Europe. As usual, Marylou Sheils accompanied me, as did wry and bright Len Baldyga, area director for Europe.

Monday, August 31, we flew from London via Balkan Air to Sofia and the long-planned acceptance of Prime Minister Dmitrov's invitation. Arriving at 9:00 P.M., we were whisked to the once-grand hotel run by Sheraton, fed supper, and sent to bed. I was glad to be there.

The next day at 8:00 A.M., we walked to the American embassy, met with Ambassador Ken Hill and PAO Mark Dillen, and drove through brown, rocky, rolling country that reminded me of Tuscany to Blagoev-grad, a medium-sized city south of Sofia that was the site of the new American University in Bulgaria.

AUBG, as the university is called, represented a bit of a miracle. Housed in the surprisingly handsome building that once served as Communist Party headquarters, it sprang to life in just six months after the fall of the dictatorship. Staffed and sponsored at the start by the University of Maine and financed in part by USIA, AID, and the Soros Foundation, it had quickly become a lively center of learning. Students had founded a radio station with USIA help, and I gave an interview — in English, to be sure — that doubtless sent the local folk rushing for their turn-off switches. The library boasted fewer than 10,000 books. On my return I tried to channel more volumes to AUBG through our programs, though with only meager results.

At 5:00 P.M. I visited the USIS-sponsored American Center to open an art show at the gallery there, and at 6:00 we called on the appealing Prime Minister Dmitrov. A soft-spoken intellectual, he was well versed in psychiatry, a useful discipline in the turmoil of Bulgarian democracy. Many believe, he said, that concern for the environment in Bulgaria had been a precursor of the democracy movement. Under the communists in Eastern Europe, no environmental depredation seemed to bother the rulers, whose lust for industrial development resulted in an ecological wasteland that made the moon seem like Jamaica. Concerned citizens eventually concluded that only with rule by the people would matters improve.

Sofia, a bustling and attractive city, tempts the visitor to walk to appointments, which we did, when feasible. A store in the ancient and handsome Russian Orthodox cathedral sold excellent copies of icons on aged wood, one of which I bought. Each bore a careful label of non-authenticity on the back, detailing the artist's name and the date of the original; no art forgers need apply.

On Wednesday I spoke to the Parliament, engaging in a lively question session afterward, and the vice president, a woman of considerable charm named Blaya Dimitrova, gave a luncheon in our honor. Told (correctly) that on arrival I debarked with a backpack strapped in place, she said in her toast that I must be the sort of person the hike-addicted Bulgarians would like. The signing of a Fulbright exchange agreement and a TV interview closed out the visit, and with an appreciative farewell to Ken and Yvonne Hill, we boarded a Hungarian Malev Air flight for the hour-and-a-half trip to Budapest.

I had never been to the Hungarian capital and when I threw back the curtains in the hotel room, the beauty of the city across the Danube was breathtaking. Not even Paris is more dramatically lighted.

Friday began with a talk to Fulbright scholars and a meeting with Foreign Minister Geza Jesensky, who passionately told us, "The hope of Europe lies not in changing frontiers but in uniting; frontiers do not matter." Meetings with Minister of Education Andros Falvy and Secretary of Education Elemer Bistersky followed. The number of Americans sitting in on these gatherings made me think of Henry Kissinger, who always fought to keep our numbers down; the U.S. team at any meeting with foreigners seems to be fissiparous, spawning Yankees by the carload.

It was hard not to think of Maggie Thatcher at the afternoon's meeting with Prime Minister Jozsef Antall. For more than two hours he told us of his problems, and when we groggily parted, I asked one of the embassy officers if his prolixity was standard. He explained that Antall was a former university professor and that he spoke only in B.L.U.'s. "What," I asked, "is that?" "Oh," he explained, "that's a basic lecture unit. Harking back to his professorial days, he can talk only in fifty-minute segments just as he did to his students. You got lucky and had two and a half B.L.U.'s."

The next day we drove with Ambassador Charles Thomas and his wife, Lorena, to the country home of President Arpad Goncz, a well-known and distinguished author. On the way through the lovely country, Charlie, seeing some pigs, told me an amusing story. For years, Hungarians had little choice in the cars they bought. They frequently drove Trabants, an East German make of doubtful reliability. With the end of communism they gained some choice and often abandoned their old Trabants, the bodies of which were made of plastic, in the countryside. Curious pigs tried eating the car carcasses, found them to their liking, and provided a novel form of recycling.

President and Mrs. Goncz welcomed and fed us. Charlie and I made our points, thanking our host for his country's constructive role in the ongoing Yugoslav crisis and urging him to help restrain a member of Parliament given to anti-Semitic remarks. Back in Budapest, we enjoyed a meal at the Gundel Restaurant, owned in part by American Ron Lauder and surely one of the most beautiful and best in the world.

The great gates of Kiev, threadbare but handsome capital of Ukraine, awaited us next. PAO Mary Kruger met us at the airport, and we spent our Sunday touring the eleventh-century cathedral, the attractive-looking but closed shops and galleries on St. Andrews Street, and the walkways along the Dnieper River. An auto tour in an old Russian-made Chaika limousine that had an oriental rug on the floor but reeked of gasoline revealed the changes and the unchanging: Statues of Lenin had disappeared and streets honoring communists had been renamed. A "speaker's corner" like that in London had become a symbol of Ukrainian freedom from Russia and of democracy.

We met press officials, the minister of education, and broadcasters. At 4:00 P.M. I called, along with our ambassador, Roman Popadiuk, on President Leonid Kravchuk. We gathered in a lavender meeting room at his office, sitting around a large and highly polished oval table. During the meeting, my foot somehow slipped, hitting the underside of the table with a sharp report, startling everyone and leaving me red in the face. Kravchuk, laughing, said, "I hope they're not shooting at us!"

The next day we visited the embassy, housed in a former Communist Party headquarters. An old familiar problem arises in Ukraine. "USIA," spoken in the Ukrainian language, comes out "UCIA," and our people often had to explain, "No, we are *NOT* the CIA."

We called on the minister of culture, a lively former actress named Larysa Khorolets and Foreign Minister Anatolyi Zlenko, a tall, handsome, well-groomed man who spoke perfect English. Khorolets made several things clear. "We don't want to be like other regimes," she said, meaning Russia. "If we decide to sell arms, we'll say so." Ukrainians "fear foreign suspicions," but "Russia is our partner — our equal partner. We may differ, but they are our neighbors and we are linked economically." Ukrainians walked the tightrope — and knew it.

Overnight robberies of passengers on Russian trains caused the prudent to take private and secure sleepers. Ours proved quite elegant, and since there was no dining car, we brought a picnic and ample Ukrainian wine to wash it down. Passing close to Chernobyl, site of the nuclear reactor meltdown, disturbed my sleep not at all.

At 9:15 Wednesday morning (September 9) we rolled into Moscow and checked into the German-owned Penta Hotel, modern, clean, efficient, and wildly different from my previous experience at the huge and depressing Rossiya Hotel. Before our luncheon appointment, we went to Lenin's tomb. There was virtually no queue, quite different from the Soviet years. We paid our respects to the waxy ex-icon and then toured the huge GUM department store across Red Square. Mostly dull and displaying shoddy goods, it had begun to sprout boutiques of Western stores that gave it more life and style.

Driving to lunch with Ministry of Education people, we passed the square where once stood the statue of the father of the KGB. Toppled by angry citizens, Comrade Derzhinsky had long since been hauled away. In his stead stood a wooden cross, inscribed "To the fallen."

After lunch, Mikhail Poltranin, deputy prime minister and minister of information, received us. He proved to be the most interesting government official we met. His ministry controlled hundreds of businesses, and he had one burning goal: get rid of them. No sunshine privatizer, he meant it. His reward for this reformist zeal was to be fired.

One of the reasons foreign service officers want to join USIA is that it gives them access to the most interesting, lively, and bright people in any given country, with the daunting challenge of making them understand America. On September 10, USIS Moscow gave me a taste of what it could produce. PAO Bob McCarthy and cultural affairs officer Cesar Beltran arranged for us to be invited to dinner at the apartment of a film producer named Yuli Gusman.

Though highly successful, Yuli lived in a small flat in one of the crumbling high-rise cement buildings that are the norm in the Russian capital. His wife, Valentina, and his mother-in-law prepared a large and traditional dinner, with a table set up in the living room to accommodate the fifteen or so guests.

Camaraderie developed quickly, as we were soon awash in a sea of vodka. Yuli, a strong-looking man in his early fifties, stood at the top of his profession. I asked him about the differences between life in Soviet Russia and life in post-Soviet Russia.

He replied that, of course, life for an artist had improved greatly; no longer did he need to worry about censors. But he added something arresting. "Maybe," he went on, "maybe we miss something exciting about living on the edge. A double entendre written into a play, its meaning clear to an audience but not so blatant as to bring the knock on the door, could be exciting. Today, we miss that; our creativity is challenged."

Another guest, an attorney and Yeltsin assistant named Andrei Makarov, had access to the files of the old Central Committee of the Communist Party, a treasury of insight into communist thinking. "It was not just grim," he said, "it was horrible," though he spared us details. This highest communist authority concerned itself with the most trivial matters of life. He found decisions on the ideological training of chess players and on whether to translate Guinean poetry into French. Communism was unquestionably brutal—and laughably inefficient as well. When we left—late—I knew we had met not only able but also good people. I hoped our paths would cross again.

The next day, the worse for wear, I got up early for breakfast with Bob Strauss at Spaso House, a historic building that served as the ambassador's residence. Bob and his wife, Helen, had replaced the huge abstract expressionist paintings that formerly hung at Spaso with representational art of high quality that suited them (and me) better. Bob had struck me as slow, even reluctant, to take up his post before he left the States, but once on the job he was a whirlwind of activity and hugely effective in dealing with the Russians. Our conversation dealt with less lofty themes than Russo-American relations; for two old pols like us, the forthcoming elections were irresistible, and Bob's predictions turned out a good bit better than mine.

A visit to the USIS cultural center and an interview with the paper *Izvestia* followed. A TV appearance with a reporter named Yuri Reshetnikov was startling. He told me that my hometown, San Antonio, site of several military installations, had been city number five on the Soviet hit list in case of war. I felt like the old frontiersman being run out of town on a rail, tarred and feathered: "If it weren't for the honor of the thing, I'd just as soon not."

After a lunch with U.S. journalists posted in Moscow (including old friends such as David Ensor, Margaret Shapiro, and Fred Hiatt), I raced across the city along twelve-lane boulevards smelling of traffic fumes to a meeting with Mikhail Gorbachev, the fallen president.

While polite enough, he seemed frustrated, a natural mood for one whose career path had taken him from president of the Soviet Union to president of a think tank. His message for the United States? Make up your mind what you want Russia to be. Is she a great power to be worked with or a candidate for breaking into even smaller pieces? And above all, don't tell us what to do. I assured him that I would deliver his message.

On our last evening we went to a performance by a small but brilliant American dance company called Pilobolus, on tour with partial funding by USIA. The young dancers were wonderfully talented, making me for the first time laugh aloud at a ballet performance. The theater was standing room only and while part of the reason doubtless was tickets that cost about twenty-five cents, the dancers were superb and a great hit; it pleased me deeply that USIA had helped make the tour possible.

The Berlin where we landed en route home had changed dramatically from the city I had visited years before. The wall had crumbled and one could move about freely. We saw the tattered East German checkpoint through which traffic from the West was filtered, the broken windows, graffiti — all the detritus of Red rule and failure.

One of the vexing problems the West Germans faced when the two Germanys were reunited concerned property rights. The mayor, on whom we called, told a wrenching story of a house that a young East Berlin couple had bought. At reunification, the elderly couple who owned it when the communists confiscated it after World War II reappeared, also claiming ownership. Such conflicts were common throughout the East.

I had stopped in Berlin to attend and address a meeting of European PAOS. U.S. ambassador Bob Kimmett came from Bonn to speak to us and gave a first-rate address. Speeches and meetings done, we returned to Washington.

The Changing Face of Africa

THOUGH MY last journey, with Isa coming along as my guest, began October 1 in Rome, the final destination was Africa. PAO Vic Olason and his wife, Dody, introduced us to the Rome operation and welcomed us to their apartment overlooking the Santa Andrea Church (famed site of the opening of the opera *Tosca*).

Housed on the embassy grounds in an ancient palace, USIS nonetheless had a thoroughly modern operation. I toured the spacious library, admired twenty-five-foot ceilings and crystal chandeliers, and checked out the bar-coded log of phone requests, a good guide to our activities. The calls we received were amazingly varied. People asked about Secretary of State Eagleburger (Jim Baker had resigned to run the president's reelection campaign), about abortion, congressional procedures, drugs, American architects — an endless number of topics.

We had lunch in the Forum Hotel roof garden with a journalist named Arrigo Levi, who shared his insight into Italian politics. Italy reeled from a kickback scandal that involved politicians at the highest level. The result, Arrigo said, was a topsy-turvy situation in which the two former leading parties, the Christian Democrats and the Communists, had virtually been wiped out. Noting that he sat on the board of the Aspen Institute of Italy, I asked how effective it was. His response was classically Italian, for he wondered if the Aspen idea of making Renaissance men out of businessmen could work in Italy: "They are already Renaissance men; we need to make them businessmen!"

The flight from Rome to Addis Ababa was long. Ambassador Mark Baas and PAO Dell Hood, with whom I had worked in London, greeted us, and after letting us rest a bit, took us to the home of an Ethiopian historian, publisher, and art collector, Getachew Paulos. (Like the Chinese, Ethiopians put the family name first.)

The guests included artists and intellectuals, all admiring of the Getachews' collection. I had a chance to visit with our handsome hostess, and I asked her about life during the regime of the fallen communist dictator, Mengistu, and his omnipresent Soviet advisers. "Did you see Russians socially?" I asked. "No," she snapped. "If I knew a Russian was going to be present, I wouldn't go to a function. They took away our pride and dignity." She told of the diaspora of Ethiopians during the long dictatorship, saying there were few intellectuals left in the country. We spoke of the late Emperor, Haile Selassie, a man of dignity overthrown by Mengistu. She said that since the dictator's fall, the authorities had discovered that the emperor had been murdered and his body buried three meters beneath his own toilet in the palace where he lived. His burial revealed more about the emperor's enemies than it did about the emperor.

Isa and I both admired the work of an artist named Zerihun Yetmgeta, who worked in carved wood and paint, and Dell took us to his studio. Much taken with his art, we later regretted that we had not bought an example, costly or not.

I made calls on government officials, all of whom were articulate and interesting. Acting foreign minister Tekeda, a handsome and gregarious man, made a comment I had heard before and would hear again. Referring to the fall of the Soviet Union, he said, "We in Ethiopia realize there is a new reality in the world." He added that Ethiopia was engaged in a dangerous experiment: abandoning one-man rule, embracing democracy, and accepting ethnic differences.

Dr. Negasso, the information minister, joined us for lunch at an excellent restaurant, as did former foreign minister Keflay, then in charge of the commission rewriting the constitution. From both we heard how most of the current government had been in the hills as exiles or rebels during the brutal Mengistu regime. Negasso, an agreeable and voluble man, said that the censorship department of his ministry would soon fade away, a happy but dubious prospect.

I liked President Melas Zenawi. Soft-spoken, young, and well educated, he said the country's chief challenge was the economy, and he made the point that rational decisions by a people depend on full stomachs. Given the nation's history of famine, it seemed a not-unreasonable position. I urged him to move toward a market economy, an independent judiciary, democracy, and a free press — Civics 101, which he showed no signs of resenting.

Ambassador and Mrs. Baas offered us dinner that evening at their handsome residence, whose whitewashed walls displayed a wide variety of art. They showed us their adopted Ethiopian twins, their first children, whom we admired extravagantly and justifiably. My dinner partner, the wife of the British ambassador, told me something I had not known. Any British ambassador who survives a visit by the queen to the country where he serves is knighted. Knowing what I did about royal visits, I said that seemed the very least that could be done. A thoroughly frank and engaging Scot, she nonetheless lamented that no visit to Addis was anticipated.

Desperately poor and strife-torn, with literacy at only 18 percent, Ethiopia might seem a likely case for the basket. Countless emaciated dogs wandered everywhere, howling their hunger through the night. Children, thin but handsome, begged at the windows of cars at every red light. Yet somehow the cultural vitality, talent, and energy of the people made me hope for their future.

At our next stop, Nairobi, PAO Fred Lasor met us and whisked us to the famed Norfolk Hotel. Later, Ambassador Smith Hempstone briefed us on the local scene. A smart, crusty journalist by trade, Smith was fun to be with, a great storyteller, a good tennis player, and an amazingly prescient observer of Africa. (A telegram he sent to the State Department when we intervened in neighboring Somalia predicted with uncanny accuracy how the venture would turn out.)

Smith broke the news that the president, Daniel arap Moi, would not be able to receive me, as he was too involved in campaigning for the forthcoming elections, an unalarming prospect, I would have thought, given Kenya's one-party status. Moi was a major presence in Kenya. "Moi Day," a celebration of his life, involved much preparation by all Nairobi each year. Civic, nongovernmental, and other organizations were led not by "presidents" but by people with other titles; Kenya had only one President.

Kenya had deteriorated since a visit the family had made in 1983. Roads, excellent when the British left in 1963, had turned pocked and rutted. Law and order had broken down; hoods made going out at night a chancy venture, and drivers regarded traffic lights as little more than suggestions. Rape was common, AIDS rampant. I admired the country and its people; its decline was sad, the result of poor leadership.

Air Zimbabwe put us gently down in the surprisingly beautiful city of Harare. A mile high, with clean streets and colonial buildings, the capital had more flower-laden jacaranda trees than I had ever seen. The water was potable and the police gave parking tickets, reminders that this country once had been a British colony called Rhodesia.

Zimbabwe's once-thriving democracy seemed a bit shopworn. Robert Mugabe, the president, treated opposition politicians high-handedly, but his popularity among the people was hard to deny, as even critics admit. In free elections, his party won 147 of 150 legislative seats. I asked to see him, but the embassy's request went unanswered; I was told that Vice President Bush had had a similar nonresponse on a visit some years before.

Ambassador Gib Lanpher and acting PAO Ray Orley greeted and entertained us, with the former giving a dinner for us and the country team, while Ray had a luncheon for press figures.

Monday, October 12, we reached our last stop, South Africa. Branch PAO Craig Stromme and his wife, Chris, had a garden party for the PAOS gathered for their annual meeting, and Ambassador Princeton Lyman invited me and Assistant Secretary of State for Africa Hank Cohen, who was in town for a meeting of U.S. ambassadors to Africa, for breakfast and a briefing the next morning. (Hank had somehow avoided the rule requiring government employees to travel only U.S. airlines whenever possible and had come direct to Johannesburg from New York. I had to return through London, which meant about six extra hours of travel.)

At 9:30 A.M. I called on Nelson Mandela. Tall, erect, gray of head, and elegantly tailored, he greeted me warmly. As we seated ourselves, I thanked him for receiving me. With a grin he said, "How could I do otherwise to a representative of the super power?" reflecting once again the profound change wrought by the Cold War's end.

We talked of the coming changes in his country. I suggested that the United States had had good luck with federalism, but Mandela remained doubtful, fearing federalism to be a trick of state president Frederik de Klerk. His opinion of his colleague in negotiations (and future vice president) was quite sour that morning, as he claimed that de Klerk had lost control of the security forces (some protesters had been killed) and that "he behaves like a petty political leader." He added, however, that de Klerk had reminded him, "When you share the government with me, you'll realize how hard it is to do things," a prediction doubtless come true. I urged that we and the African National Congress, which Mandela headed, engage in more exchanges, offering the ANC five fellowships to come to America and see how federalism works. I suggested as well more exchanges on market economics and conflict resolution and assured him of President Bush's continued interest in South Africa. I left feeling that Mandela was the most charismatic man I had ever met, but one capable of arrogance — though perhaps surviving twenty-seven years in a South African prison justified arrogance.

At noon we drove to the crowded black suburb of Soweto (an acronym for "Southwest Township") to see this troubled area, site of many protests and much repression, and to visit our USIS library, the only one around. The library was first-rate and much used, an intellectual oasis.

On October 14, a Wednesday, I met again with our people and drove in the afternoon to Pretoria to address the ambassadors' meeting, which had been broadened to include directors of African AID missions. A hard day was brightened by lunch with the irrepressible Helen Suzman at her home. Although as a member of Parliament she had fought apartheid, or segregation, for all of her career, she nonetheless deplored the sanctions that the United States and other nations had imposed on her country. Asked if she felt that, on balance, sanctions had helped, she stoutly denied it, saying the cost in lost jobs and trade outweighed any benefit.

PAO John Burns and branch PAO Rosemary Crockett offered dinner at our hotel that evening. The guests included such intellectuals as Don Mattera, a reformed gangster turned poet. He had written a book of myths, beautifully illustrated, in a copy of which he wrote a touching dedication to my grandchildren.

In the beautiful coastal city of Cape Town, we checked into the elegant pink stucco Mount Nelson Hotel, a colonial-style gem with Old World service and chintz-covered furniture. That evening, Consul David Halsted and his wife, June, had a reception for us. As we drove to their suburban home, I noted a bit of graffiti that made me laugh. It read, "I was an Anglican until I put tu and tu together," a reference to the controversial Anglican archbishop Desmond Tutu.[5] Supper was with an old friend and former member of Parliament, Colin Eglund and his wife, Joyce, both of whom were excellent company. Colin was optimistic about the new directions of his country. Of all the blacks and coloreds (mixed-race) he knew, none felt that he and his fellow whites (20 percent of the population) were outsiders.

Our last day in Cape Town we met with Deputy Foreign Minister R. S. Schoeman, called on press magnate Ton Vosloo, walked through the Parliament grounds and a nearby park, and lunched with a group of educators.

Afterward we drove through rich, rolling wine country to Steollon-bosch, an ancient university town, to spend our last night and stuff ourselves with a huge and delicious meal at the restaurant Volkskombuis. We were joined by a member of Parliament named Jannie Momberg, scion of an old Afrikaner family, who had done the unthinkable: he had joined the ANC—most unusual for a noncommunist white. Clearly, he was looking ahead, not without self-interest. "Quite frankly," he said, "I wouldn't mind being ambassador to Washington in the first ANC government." (He didn't make it.)

The day of our departure began in an unusual way. We toured the Simonsig Vineyard and graciously allowed the owner to give us samples of his craft. My thought: happy the day when South African wines again become available in the United States

At lunch we joined Christo Viljoen, head of the South African Broadcasting Corporation, at a handsome rural restaurant called the Lord Neetling House, on the way to the airport. I liked Viljoen. His was a difficult job, made more so by shortsighted Americans like Bill Cosby, who refused to allow his TV program to be shown on SABC. I felt the Cosby show was precisely what South Africa needed to see, and when I returned, I wrote Cosby, suggesting that he reconsider. I got no reply.

Waiting to board the eleven-hour flight to London, I thought about the beautiful, rich, troubled, and changing country we were leaving. One couldn't be optimistic. My security assistant, Jim Bowman, told us of being in the restaurant the previous night with a dark-skinned South African of Indian descent, provided by the government to beef up our security team. As they walked through the bar, two different whites grumbled, "Whites only, whites only." A USIS foreign service national whom I met had a similar experience. Officially she was "colored," of mixed race, though quite fair and assuredly beautiful. Going for dinner at a country inn, she was refused service by the proprietor, who somehow decided she was colored. She left, in tears. We alerted all embassy personnel of the incident and spread the word among the diplomatic corps.

Such stories made us realize how tricky the road ahead was. Still, leaders like Mandela and de Klerk might just guide the country through the shoals.

Arriving in Washington after a four-hour wait in London and an eight-hour flight, we fell exhausted off the plane and headed home. I was glad to be home but gladder still of Isa's coming along; she had made the trip unique for me and thanks in large part to the wonderful and amusing Marylou Sheils, with whom she roomed, I think she had a good time as well.

Meeting Notes

THE RELATIONSHIP between USIA and the State Department was a bit like that of stepsisters, with the former having the glass slipper but the latter having carriage, house, and mother. The USIA was created by taking responsibilities away from State, which in State's view made a tangle of the organization chart, created personnel problems, and generally caused mischief. The agency, meanwhile, felt dealt out of key decisions, cut off from the National Security Council, and unappreciated. It was, nonetheless, fiercely proud of the work its officers did with the informational and cultural aspects of foreign policy.

To minimize tension and ease communications, USIA directors traditionally attended the secretary of state's morning staff meeting. I did so enthusiastically, feeling that given the thirty-odd years I had known Jim Baker, any problems that might arise could be resolved between us. Furthermore, hearing the latest on the world's flash points every morning would enable me to keep USIA's senior officers informed.

As a result, I took notes (wondering all the while why shorthand wasn't mandatory in school), which I shared with my staff on arrival at the office. Most of the items I jotted down were of no lasting interest, just the stuff of the headlines for tomorrow or the day after. Some, however, such as the following, revealed glimpses of issues or personalities that might be of general interest. Mostly they reflect meetings at State, but a few come from USIA's own staff meetings.

May 14, 1991 [Deputy Secretary of State Lawrence Eagleburger, who often chaired the meetings, had not only keen insight but also a matching sense of humor.] "I would have been a great Foreign Service officer," he explained, "except for three things: I don't like travel, I can't stand parties, and I loathe foreigners."

May 22 U.S. Ambassador to Kuwait Skip Gnehm met with us, speculating that Saddam Hussein may last in Iraq for a long time.

May 24 Ethiopian disintegration diverted attention from a rescue effort by Israel and the U.S. to extract Ethiopian Jews known as Falashas and send them to Israel.

May 28 [Rebels in Ethiopia neared the capital of Addis Ababa in their effort to overthrow the brutal communist dictator Mengistu Haile Mariam.] Assistant Secretary for Africa Hank Cohen invited the rebels to enter Addis, hoping they could restore some semblance of order. They did. Counsellor Bob Zoelick worried that we might get egg on our face if the rebels failed and chaos worsened.

May 29 The U.S. spends proportionately less on foreign aid than any country in the world, save only Ireland. We do, however, keep our markets open to foreign imports more than any other country.

[The new U.S. embassy in Moscow had been honeycombed with listening devices during construction by Soviet contractors. Whether or not to tear down the nearly completed building, a hugely expensive undertaking, was the topic of hot debate.] Ivan Selin, Undersecretary for Administration, predicted Congress would let State do what it deemed best to solve the embassy conundrum. Hearing Selin's optimistic prediction, Baker asked with a grin, "Want to bet?"

May 30   Croatia is expected to declare its independence today from Yugoslavia. We will react negatively; our policy is to keep Yugoslavia's present borders.

The U.S. has asked Poland to represent us in Baghdad, where we have no diplomats. The designation received much attention in the Polish press, as a sign of post-communist Poland's new respectability.

I reported that the U.S. embassy in Addis Ababa regards the VOA's "inflammatory" Amharic language service as "the prime threat to Americans living in Ethiopia." [The service was seen as partisan by many Ethiopians, and the embassy feared retaliation by one or more of the factions.]

May 31   Larry Eagleburger reports that two Bulgarian nuclear power plants, of Soviet design, were stripped of their safety devices when the Soviets pulled out.

The Czech Foreign Minister says his country will not sign the planned bilateral trade treaty with the U.S., complaining it treats them like a banana republic. Larry's response: let's look at it and see if they are right.

A copy of a French arms control proposal was leaked to the U.S. In it the French called for a global approach, versus the U.S. preference for limiting matters to the Middle East. The British agreed with the French. Undersecretary Bob Kimmet fears if it goes beyond the Security Council's permanent five members, the Italians, Japanese, and others will want a say: "The more you globalize, the less gets done."

Someone asks, "I wonder who gets the $35 million the Israelis gave the Ethiopians?" [to help evacuate Ethiopian Jews to Israel].

June 3   Margaret Tutweiler, Assistant Secretary for Public Affairs, says VOA and Wireless File reporters accompanied Baker on his trip to Lisbon. They asked "off the wall," obscure questions and "drove him crazy."

France will join the Nuclear Nonproliferation Treaty, a move that could be important. With France on board, pressure would increase for

South Africa and China to join, and if they did, even Israel might follow.

Congressman Obey [D-Wisconsin] said he would try to force the Administration to certify that China does not engage in a policy of coercive abortions, as a price for support of giving China "most favored nation" trade status. Hearing this, Eagleburger hit the ceiling at how Congress nit-picks the Administration on foreign policy matters; he noted it is much worse than when he was last in government in 1977.

June 12   The House Appropriations Committee voted $130 million to solve the Moscow embassy problem, without detailed spending instructions. [Baker lost his bet.]

June 19   The ARA [American Republics Area] representative reported a captain in the Salvadoran army was murdered by the FMLN [the leftist rebels]. Their aim: to drive a wedge between President Cristiani, who is seeking peace, and the hard-liners in the military.

July 15   Secretary Baker visited Albania, newly free from history's most paranoid communist dictatorship. Speaking to a huge crowd in Tirana, the capital, he used our popular VOA Albanian service broadcaster, a man called Bibori, as his interpreter. Baker thus seemingly spoke with the best-known voice in Albania; the results were electric.

July 26   ARA Assistant Secretary Bernie Aronson met with his Soviet counterpart. In discussing Cuba, the Soviet assured us military aid to the island nation would be reduced to a level of "defensive sufficiency," sending nothing sophisticated.

July 31   Eagleburger reported Senator Paul Tsongas, a potential Democratic presidential candidate, wants a briefing on El Salvador prior to a trip there. Larry told the bureaus to study modes of briefing candidates; what we do for one, we have to do for all. Later, he called Assistant Secretary for Human Rights Richard Schifter the "Assistant Secretary for Hearts and Flowers."

A former ambassador to Yugoslavia, Larry said the troubles were spreading to Bosnia and "getting worse and worse." Larry often sounded like Cassandra, but he proved spot on with regard to that troubled Balkan area.

August 7   Texas Congressman Henry B. Gonzalez, in a show of congressional hubris, subpoenaed internal documents of the Bank of England. The British were not amused, pointing out how responsive the bank had been to our requests on prior occasions, for instance freezing Libyan accounts; they noted that congressional writ does not cross the Atlantic.

Kimmet, after the meeting, told me Baker and Tutweiler cared little about influencing what is said in the foreign press [a major goal of USIA], though interest in Israeli public opinion and its importance to the peace process in the Middle East may change that.

September 5   Someone reported that Israeli Prime Minister Shamir had defended terrorism under certain circumstances, i.e., if it were "personal" and conducted in one's own homeland. I wondered if that included the P.L.O.

Assistant Secretary of State Tom Niles said that German recognition of Slovenia and Croatia was "a setback" for the U.S. belief that a shattered Yugoslavia was dangerous. Baker said his instinct was to continue to stay out and let the Europeans handle Balkan peace-keeping.

September 6   Minor irony department: in its statement recognizing the independence of the Baltic states of Estonia, Latvia, and Lithuania, the Soviet Union demanded they join the Nuclear Nonproliferation Treaty and adhere to the International Convention on Human Rights.

September 11   The Japanese are being helpful in our base renewal negotiations with the Philippines. They have hinted to Manila that granting a much desired loan might hinge on approval of the U.S. offer. I wonder if they want to be sure we don't shift Philippine operations to a base in Japan.

One hundred fifty-seven countries are meeting in Geneva on the environment. Apparently the going is rough; one wag called it "the last international meeting of the '70s." The U.S. did, however, manage to get demographics on the agenda.

September 13   Hank Cohen reports that Boeing and Airbus Industries are competing for a nice order from Madagascar. Airbus, a consortium of European aircraft manufacturers, is subsidized by European governments in various subtle ways and Boeing quite correctly objects, having to make it on its own. Cohen reported that the French government had entered the game with both feet, telling the Madagascar government to go with Airbus or suffer the end of French economic assistance. Eagleburger went ballistic: "We must do something about this!"

September 16   Larry Eagleburger reported on the effort to repeal the UN resolution stating Zionism equals racism. Some Europeans voted for the resolution when it passed and we are determined this time to bring them around: "We are not going to lose this one," Larry fumed. "The President is the key and he feels strongly."

September 17   Ethnic politics rears its head. Senator Paul Sarbanes, of Greek heritage, wants to turn military loans to Greece into outright grants and got a bill to that effect passed. It will cost the U.S. government substantially; the question is: is it worth the political cost of a veto?

October 16   Chase Untermeyer, Director of VOA, told me the woman who runs his newsroom refuses to listen to a radio interview program he hosts. Reason? It might sully the integrity of her news operation. That, I thought, may be carrying Caesar's wife too far.

October 18   Trade problems with China persist. The Chinese refuse to prevent pirating of American intellectual property, e.g., Hollywood films, if you can call Hollywood intellectual. Someone suggests we release the means we will use to retaliate. "No," thunders Eagleburger.

October 25   Baker asks to see me after the meeting. A friendly chat? No, he wants USIA to cough up $2 million to help pay the cost of the press center at the Madrid conference on Middle East peace, the first direct talks between Arabs and Israelis in history. We are interrupted and conversation resumes on a political note: he worries about perceptions of the economy, that is, people think it worse than it is. It might be a problem in the election. I promise to see what we can do about Madrid.

October 28   Haiti's Prime Minister says his role is to prevent civil war over deposed President Jean Bertrand Aristide. All is in readiness to impose an embargo on Haiti.

October 30   Discussion on whether China is helping Iran build a nuclear weapon. Someone wonders if the Argentines are involved as well.

November 4   Gene Kopp and I meet with Counselor of USIA McKinney Russell, telling him, I hope diplomatically but firmly, that Foreign Service officers *must* take the views of political appointees into account. Apparently a Foreign Service officer pretty well told Chase Untermeyer to mind his own business. This simply won't do.

November 7   Senator George Mitchell, the majority leader of the Senate and a Democrat, has asked that the "150 account" [out of which come the budgets for State, USIA, AID, etc.] cough up $5.4 billion over the next five years so unemployment insurance can be expanded. Eagleburger, presiding, groans and says, "This is the beginning of a year of absolute agony."

November 14   Haiti is a mess. We fear street rioting or take-overs of our Coast Guard cutters. The issue is forced return to their homeland of jobless Haitians who flee in rickety boats toward the U.S. Human rights advocates in the U.S. are sure to be outraged. And it all arises from our desire to support elected governments!

November 15   Congressman Ben Gilman of New York, ranking Republican on the House Foreign Relations Committee, plans to tie aid to newly independent Lithuania to the availability of kosher chickens. He is under severe pressure from American rabbis: on such issues does American foreign policy turn.

November 22   Someone is drafting a paper outlining how forcible repatriation of refugees to Vietnam by the British is worse than forcible repatriation of refugees to Haiti by the Americans. Said a voice at the meeting [I didn't note who]: "It requires a great deal of imagination."

December 4   UN Secretary General Boutros Boutros-Ghali, in a speech to the UN General Assembly, said he was "proud to be elected Secretary General of the United Nations." A sleepy interpreter translating the original Arabic reported he was "proud to be elected secretary general of the United States." High hilarity resulted, Mr. Boutros-Ghali not being universally admired.

December 6   We are up to thirty-one co-sponsors to repeal the "Zionism equals racism" resolution in the UN. Japan is crucial and is leaning toward our position. Baker will call Soviet Foreign Minister Shevardnadze.

December 12   Undersecretary Arnie Kanter reports we're at sixty-one co-sponsors on Zionism. "The Latin American bureau gets the gold star for producing the most," he said. Egypt will abstain and the Saudis are keeping a low profile.

December 18   Former Ambassador to Yugoslavia Warren Zimmerman reported that the European Community is in effect pressuring the Yugoslav republics to declare independence; Kanter calls it a "perverse act" by the E.C.

December 19   Aid being sent to the constituent republics of the Soviet Union is routed through Moscow, a dubious procedure Baker fears, and one that must be stopped. Ambassador Strauss is also worried that goods will be stolen and diverted to the Russian black market. We may need to put U.S. officials on the ground to oversee distribution. Baker cautioned that the existence of debt can have implications for diplomatic recognition of new states, a presidential prerogative. Eagleburger predicted trouble with the European Community: "There's the E.C. and then there's the rest of the world."

The logistical problems of sending aid to the former Soviet Union are huge, Eagleburger said; perhaps we should enlist the aid of Aeroflot [the Soviet airline]. Don't bother came the reply. Most of its planes are grounded from lack of fuel. [This, in a country with oil reserves to rival Saudi Arabia.]

December 19 I talked to U.S. Ambassador to Saudi Arabia Charles Freeman, who said 104,000 Saudis have homes in the Washington area.

January 6, 1992 A Russian extremist named Vladimir Zhirinvoski wants to get Alaska back. A candidate in the elections, he got six million votes promising, among other things, to give away vodka.

January 7 McDonnell-Douglas, GE, and other defense contractors are mounting a major campaign on Capitol Hill, complete with brochures and videotapes. Purpose: to convince Congress to permit sale of F-15 aircraft to the Saudis.

Senior USIA officials, me included, are briefed on equal employment opportunity laws. The briefer warns us to leave a paper trail, as nothing is immune from scrutiny by the fairness police. Employee "A" has a desk near a window, and "B" doesn't? Be careful; it might be discrimination. Did you fail to hire a woman eight months pregnant because you need help now? Again, you can be liable. You're giving a reference on one of your former employees? Don't mention whether he has a record of discrimination claims; it's against the rules.

January 10 No Soviet ships [save for subs] are reported on patrol anywhere in the world! The news brought to mind the constant question during my Defense Department days: "How many Soviet ships in the Mediterranean today, Henry?" It's a new world out there.

Cape Verde's President won't make the Security Council Summit, even though his tiny West African nation is a member of that prestigious UN body. The reason? It takes five days to get to New York and he can't make it in time. So much for our "shrinking globe."

Baker worries about a new Estonian law barring those who can't speak Estonian from holding office; he feels we should weigh in heavily and "put down markers fairly and quickly."

February 26 Baker is fascinated with CNN; wonders if we could encourage its expansion into the Central Asian republics of the former Soviet Union. Their leaders, he says, would like to have it.

February 27 The cost of the peace-keeping mission in Cambodia will be formidable, almost two billion dollars. There will be sixteen thousand troops, three thousand civil servants, election watchers, etc.

March 3   Israel's former Prime Minister, Menachim Begin, is gravely ill. We should decide in advance whom to send to his funeral.

March 9   Strike the above worry: Begin's funeral will be private: no flowers, no diplomats.

March 18   Reality check: at my USIA staff meeting, it was reported that a man on Congressman David McCurdy's staff asked if USIA were part of the U.S. government.

March 20   Senator Strom Thurmond's office importunes me to see a constituent of his. The reason? To get a letter on USIA letterhead that she had met with me about a Japanese company with a nurse training program. I agree.

March 23   Congressman Henry Gonzalez is still putting classified information into the Congressional Record. Baker should talk to Brent Scowcroft to explore how to stop it.

March 24   Lunched with Congressman Dante Fascell of Florida, chairman of the subcommittee that oversees us. His mind is quick and he knows how government works. I explained to him USIA's fulsome letter of cooperation with AID and reached into my coat pocket. Said he: "And here are the unsigned facts!" He was right, and I handed him a background paper franker than the official letter. I like him and was sorry to learn he fears he will be re-districted into oblivion soon. Term limitations appeal to many people, but after working with members like Dante, I am not among them.

March 29   I learn the ballots used in the recent Albanian election were printed by the USIA printing office in Vienna.

March 30   Baker opens the meeting in a sour humor: "I see my letter to Savimbi [Angolan rebel leader] is all over the *Washington Post*. It's too bad; we were beginning to get a little business done in this meeting." Never one to trust anyone but his own tight circle of associates, he clearly feels leakers are at work among the attendees of these meetings, most of them Foreign Service officers.

April 13   Our USIA elevators are slow, stopping on most floors. It's a nuisance, but I note to Marylou that it does give me a chance to visit with employees, visits that can be important. For example, two women shared with me their concerns of a hostile work environment in the Inspector General's office as we moved slowly up; it was the first I had heard of it.

A telegram from our New Delhi office tells that even the Tibetan Ministry of Information, thought to be hostile to voa's new Tibetan service, feels [its] debut was ". . . the most significant event in the last two years." Sometimes having Congress force us into an action [as was the case of the Tibetan service] has good results.

April 15 Baker is on a tear about saving money, urging his colleagues and the independent agencies [usia, aid, acda] to shed consultants, cancel magazine and newspaper subscriptions, and discourage overtime. Only thus, he feels, can we open vital posts in the numerous new countries that have sprung from the ruins of the Soviet Union.

General Colin Powell, Chairman of the Joint Chiefs of Staff, feels the voa may be responsible for the flow of refugees from Haiti to the U.S. Its broadcasts paint a rosy picture of American life, says Assistant Secretary Bernie Aronson, thus encouraging the dangerous outflow. Strikes me as nonsense.

April 27 Columnist Charles Krauthammer came to "brown bag lunch" with usia officers. Left-wing isolationists, he said, feel the U.S. corrupts the rest of the world, while right-wing isolationists feel the rest of the world corrupts the U.S. He urged usia to look toward Islam, there being no reason for permanent mutual hostility. He cautioned us on the issues of the former Soviet Union, Islam, and nuclear proliferation, suggesting that some day an American city will disappear and only then will we wake up.

May 6 I ran into Congressman Dante Fascell. He warned me a "high Administration figure" wants to end usia's independence after the election. Baker, no doubt, probably Eagleburger as well.

May 8 Baker reports success in State's budget cutting, with $17 million saved to use for new posts in the former Soviet republics.

Yosi Ben Aron, an Israeli hard-liner, admitted to Baker that Israel now has a stake in the Mideast negotiations and that even Syria is easier to talk to. Bush and Baker must be doing something right.

May 21 Baker noted a new Chinese nuclear test, a "huge" one of 950 kilotons, the fall-out from which drifted over Japan — on the 20th anniversary of Japanese-Chinese diplomatic relations. Have a nice day.

The Saudis face problems paying their debts and the Department of Defense had sent a team to negotiate a refinancing. They have, however, paid their $16.4 billion share of the Gulf War.

May 22 Consular Affairs reported dolorous statistics. Three million people wait for visas to immigrate to the U.S. and one-third of all arrests in Los Angeles are illegal aliens.

Representative Jack Brooks of Texas told the President he wants a special investigator to look into the Reagan Administration policy toward Iraq. Cracked Eagleburger: "One of the joys of government service is thinking of special prosecutors two years later."

We learned of a classic VOA dust-up. Ms. X was named head of the Pushtu [Afghan language] service. Mr. Y protested: Afghan men don't like working for women, claiming, furthermore, that her relatives worked for Najbullah, the communist dictator. Y then goes off to Pakistan to run for the Afghan National Council. [He lost.] Jesse Helms's office, obviously tipped by Y, complains that there is a communist in the Pushtu service. Oi.

May 27 Undersecretary Arnie Kanter drew tough duty: a meeting with Rev. Jesse Jackson to discuss Haiti and refugees. Arnie reported him "almost seductive" in his well-rehearsed presentation. The meeting participants sat around a table, held hands, and prayed. This is not the way foreign policy decisions are normally made, but perhaps it merits a try.

May 28 Chinese arms shipments to rogue governments worry us, Reg Bartholomew reported. In an aside he lavishly praised Baker for his work on the nonproliferation treaty. Baker, with a wry grin, cracked, "Reg, I thought your appointment [as ambassador] was already accomplished."

June 12 An administrative officer reported on the advantages to the government of using CD-ROMs. One disc can hold the entire Congressional Record for 1991, and thus replace 125 pounds of paper. The cost benefits are "extraordinary," he said. Not to mention the forests saved.

June 17 Eagleburger reported two Mexican citizens were abducted by U.S. authorities and brought to Arizona, where they will stand trial. The Mexicans, predictably, are furious but the problem is that they won't sign an extradition treaty with us. Bernard Aronson, Assistant Secretary for Latin America, noted this creates real foreign policy problems; Baker mused that Bush would have to choose between wearing his foreign policy and law enforcement hats.

June 23 The Latin American bureau representative commented that Haiti's exiled President, Jean Bertrand Aristide, is literally insane, and yet our whole policy is dedicated to restoring him to office. However, if we don't support him, in spite of his increasingly shrill anti-American comments, violence may well result. This might in turn cause us to have to intervene, since perhaps half the population still wants his return.

July 13 Hank Cohen, Assistant Secretary for African affairs, reported that the Red Cross called the situation in Somalia "extremely bad." The contrast of our Bosnian concern with our Somalian indifference was "more and more apparent," Cohen said and he called for an airlift of assistance and perhaps UN observers.

I met with Jorge Mas and the Advisory Board of the Office of Cuban Broadcasting. OCB wanted to change the hours of our TV broadcasts to Cuba to attract a larger audience [3:30 A.M. to 6:00 A.M. are the current hours]. The State Department fears Cuban interference with U.S. commercial telecasting. Jorge pointed out that seven years before, State had the same objections, claiming policy can't be held hostage to what Cuba might do. I agreed with him but held my tongue; since our family company had a TV station in Orlando, I had agreed to recuse myself from any matter that might affect our properties.

July 17 Secretary Baker will be returning to Washington on a commercial flight instead of the customary [and costly] government flight. The idea? Dramatize efforts at economy in government. I doubt it will become a habit.

July 21 Beer wars! The Ontario government is charging a duty of about $8 a case on U.S. beer. We took it to GATT [the General Agreement on Trade and Tariffs] and won but the practice hasn't stopped. We may retaliate in kind. John Catto, a connoisseur of Canadian beer, will be heartsick.

I met with our USIA Resource Management Committee, discussing where we might cut costs. Ideas included the Los Angeles press center, magazines, the Wireless File, foreign exhibits, and more. Resistance was fierce and more study called for. I decided to end one of our oldest and best magazines, "Problems of Communism"; history and its own good work had rendered it obsolete.

July 22 We will have a new travel advisory system. Before the downing of Pan Am's flight over Lockerbie, Scotland, government employees had access to a special warning system. Embassy employees in Moscow had learned through that system of concern about terrorist bombings of U.S. airlines, information not available to the flying public. That will be changed so that everyone can be made aware of security concerns.

September 17 Russian ships heading toward the Middle East were reported to be foraging for goods along the way. The extent of the collapse of our former adversary amazes me.

September 25   Arnie Kanter, in the chair, complains strongly that briefing memos sent to Acting Secretary Eagleburger [Baker has taken over as campaign chairman], in New York for the UN General Assembly, have served him poorly. "They're just not very good," he told us. "We've missed an opportunity." The old cleavage between the Administration and the Foreign Service surfaces again.

The Russians plan to sell submarines to Iran. When Eagleburger objects, Foreign Minister Kozyrev, also in New York for the UN meeting, uses phrases the U.S. had often used on the Russians, such as, "We are carefully reviewing every sale." Eagleburger quipped, "I see you have the same people writing your briefing paper as I do." "No," retorts the Russian, "we just use yours."

I learned that Lane Kirkland and the AFL-CIO have checkmated me. Discouraged by gross inefficiency on the part of an AFL-CIO subsidiary that we worked with, we canceled the working arrangement. [It dealt with sponsoring international visitors.] Quietly, Kirkland and Co. went to Congress to overturn us and the next thing I knew, USIA was required to continue to work with them.

September 30   There is a rumor that Haiti's exiled President Aristide is encouraging Haitian-Americans to vote against Bush.

October 20   Election fever hits the foreign policy world. Candidate Ross Perot's charges that the Administration had sent special instructions to U.S. Ambassador to Iraq April Glaspie before the Gulf War broke out were not correct, Assistant Secretary Ed Djerejian reported; all documents on the topic had been released to Congress. "It's outrageous," Eagleburger snorted. "Don't be nice on this one."

There was a report on Libya's wily but erratic President, Mu'ammar Khadafi. Always keen to use his oil wealth to influence neighbors, he sent a check for $1 million in aid money to President Bongo of Gabon, drawn on Citibank. The bank in turned informed Bongo that it had a million for his account, but that since Libya's foreign assets were frozen as a response to that country's support for terrorism, the cash could not be delivered. The result? Bongo loves Khadafi and hates the U.S. And Khadafi isn't out a penny. Q.E.D.

October 28   Harry Porter reported on a constant headache. Vehicles of foreign embassies have diplomatic immunity and may, if they choose, blithely ignore parking regulations. The District of Columbia police, little concerned with foreign policy, nonetheless issue them tickets. Outraged, Congress ordered State not to give diplomatic license plates to embassies that have unpaid fines. If State complies, the Russian, Israeli, and Nigerian embassies would effectively be closed down, carless. We can't retaliate in Moscow, for example, as there are no parking meters.

November 6 Strobe Talbot, a columnist for *Time* magazine and currently on leave as an advisor to candidate Bill Clinton, called Undersecretary Frank Wisner. Who does he represent, we wondered, *Time* or Little Rock? [Talbot, a Clinton college roommate, became deputy secretary of state in Clinton's administration.]

November 10 Eagleburger, noting our loss of the election, said there are five areas of danger: Somalia, Angola, Yugoslavia, the Middle East peace process, and Cambodia. Saying that the Bush Administration's influence will steadily diminish, he urged we "take the public lead and try to contain them. We must be super-active, not just business as usual." He would like to turn over a tidier world to our successors. Good luck.

A Losing Campaign

I SHOULD have begun to worry on December 15, 1991. On that day, Jessica predicted George would lose. I didn't share her opinion; it was simply inconceivable to me that this superb man whose presidency seemed so surefooted and whose character so upright might be turned out.

One morning I stopped by Jim Baker's office to visit before his daily staff meeting. Talk turned to politics, and I asked if he was worried about the forthcoming election.

"Go look in my middle desk drawer," he said. (He was eating breakfast.) "You'll find a map, with the states where we lead in blue and states where we're behind in red." I found the map; it was a red sea, its findings based on the latest White House polling. Baker felt the Buchanan challenge and, even more important, the perception of a poor economy were causing voters to sour on Bush. Still, I couldn't believe George was in danger.

In October 1991 I went to see the president to report on my activities at USIA. While waiting to go into the Oval Office, I ran into press secretary Marlin Fitzwater, whom I (and the press) liked and trusted. I asked how the election looked and found him discerning just one cloud, "no bigger than a man's hand": the economy.

George showed no sign of worry. He bade me sit, put his feet on the

desk, and really listened to my report on our redoubled efforts in the
USSR; the Seville Expo and its problems; our USIA Vietnamese employees who had been abandoned unfairly in the 1976 evaluation of Saigon;
and my search for an office to bring all our employees under a single roof.
He looked very well and a decade younger than he was.

The following March I was invited to dinner and the theater at the
White House. Arriving alone at six-thirty (Jessica was in San Antonio), I
greeted retired Marine General P. X. Kelly and his wife, Barbara, Rose
and Tabb Moore, and Janet Steiger, and we were escorted to the family
quarters. Both Bushes were in high good humor and George read us the
jokes his speechwriters had proposed for his appearance two nights later
at the annual Gridiron Club dinner, a Washington institution at which
politicians make fun of one another. We commented on each joke, turning thumbs-down on several, including one referring to Ross Perot's
height. Most, however, were highly amusing and the president did a good
job at the event, with timing to rival Bob Hope's. If he had any doubts
about his political future, they were well hidden. We did talk at dinner of
the British election, due in June, and the president made no secret of his
hope that John Major and the Tories would win, which they did. Major
had fairly openly supported Bush, doing himself political harm when
Clinton won. The play, at the Kennedy Center, was a tour de force called
Solitary Confinement, in which Stacy Keach, unbeknownst to the audience until the end, played most of the characters.

By June, Ross Perot had roiled the political waters in his on-again, off-
again campaign for president. Vice President Dan Quayle, horrified by
Perot's apparent instability, said, "Think of him in charge of the FBI and
IRS." A July 18 poll showed Governor Bill Clinton with 55 percent to
Bush's 31 percent.

Even I, incurable optimist, began to worry. Quayle's disapproval ratings stood at 60 percent, and while I couldn't imagine Bush's dumping
him as a running mate (loyalty ranked high in George's book of virtues),
it surely must have been considered. Rumors abounded that Baker would
be dragooned from State and moved to head of the campaign. Clearly,
Jim didn't want any such move; he loved State and he saw looming defeat more clearly than I did. He did finally leave to take over the campaign, but it was too late.

Jessica and I debated where the weakness lay. She felt that letting
Bush's primary rival, the shrill Pat Buchanan, speak at the convention had

been a grievous error. She felt the likes of Pat should be "handled with a whip and a chair." George's flirting with flinty-eyed religious zealots, questions about Supreme Court appointments, and abandonment of his former pro-choice position on abortion affected her deeply. She was not alone. I recalled a dinner party I had in London. All the guests were Republican women; all were unhappy with the president's stand on choice. Had I paid more attention then, I might not have been such a Pollyanna about our chances.

As late as the campaign's final week, I believed George had a chance, though polls showed him behind by double digits. Perot's charges that Republicans had plotted to disrupt his daughter's wedding convinced me he was not sound and that surely few would vote for him. Wrong again.

Against this bleak background, Jessica and her brother Bill decided to sell the family television company, both having doubts about the industry's future and the best way of running things. I hated to see it happen. I loved the years spent working for H & C, and I had thought I might return to it if George lost and my government career ended. That, however, was not to be.

Six weeks after the election I jotted down what seemed to me the reasons for this devastating defeat.

First, I felt, Clinton ran a solid campaign. Snubbing Jesse Jackson, whose extremist rhetoric offended many voters, struck me as very smart; he managed to do it, furthermore, without alienating core constituency black Democrats.

Second, the Bush-engineered victory in the Cold War had a downside. While few Americans realized the full meaning of the Soviet collapse, the downsizing of the vast defense industry, with its widespread layoffs of workers, affected millions of voters and their families. Bush's defeat reminded me of Churchill's summary dismissal by the British electorate in 1945, on the very heels of victory in World War II.

Third, I heard many moderates, particularly women, comment on their revulsion at the extremist orgy at the nominating convention in Houston, a yahoo field day.

Fourth, Dan Quayle never succeeded in convincing voters he could, if called on, handle the presidency. That, combined with doubts about the Clarence Thomas appointment, with its attendant unpleasantness, turned many people off.

Finally, George struck a surprising number of observers as a listless campaigner. The memory of him surreptitiously glancing at his watch during a debate with Clinton seemed to Jessica a revealing moment. Furthermore, his focus on the future seemed blurred to critics, with no clear projection of where he wanted to lead us. I disagreed, especially in the field of foreign affairs, and the following incident illustrated the point.

Alfred Moses, my friend, attorney, and next-door neighbor, called one day in May. As president of the American Jewish Committee, Al had asked Bush to come by an AJC meeting to be held in Washington, but the White House turned him down. Both Clinton and Perot planned to attend; it would take only a few minutes and it would expose the president to six hundred politically active and aware citizens. I checked it out, explained the advantages of going, and learned that the reason for the refusal to attend lay in the forthcoming Israeli elections. The administration had worked diligently and successfully to move the Israeli-Arab peace process forward, and while Bush knew he might benefit from speaking to the AJC, it might be misinterpreted in Israel as detrimental to the peace process and to our role as honest broker. Bush stuck by his guns and let his opponents have the stage, and he doubtless paid a price for standing by his principles.

On a different front, I struck out in a good cause. Peggy Buchanan, Mrs. Hobby's longtime assistant, called me from Houston. The fiftieth anniversary of the founding of the Women's Army Corps would soon be celebrated and Peggy felt that if the Army would retroactively promote Oveta to general, a rank not available when she was a colonel and ran the WACs, it would be a fitting tribute to a gallant lady and a symbol of how far the military had come in recognizing women.

Agreeing enthusiastically, I wrote the president to explain the idea. To line up support on the other side of the aisle, I called Texas senator Lloyd Bentsen, a Democrat and old friend of the Hobby family. Lloyd said, "Stars would look good on her and would be much deserved," and he set about seeing what could be done.

I also called the chairman of the Joint Chiefs of Staff, Colin Powell. Colin was reserved in his response, fearing possible precedent being set, but he promised to check it out.

A few weeks later, Rose Zamaria, the president's key assistant, called and said a promotion would not be possible. The president had talked with Secretary of Defense Cheney and the secretary of the Army, and the problems were simply too great. A military delegation would, nonetheless, fly to Houston on the anniversary and present the colonel with a plaque. Though disappointed, I felt we had had a hearing at the highest levels.

Melancholy Denouement

MY MEMORIES of late 1992 are not happy ones. We flew to San Antonio on October 29 to prepare for a brief visit by Jane and Bob Geniesse and Marylou, and to vote. Bush aide Roger Porter sat next to me on the plane and while he had not given up hope, he had little encouraging to say.

Election day went by slowly. Jessica and I watched the returns with Lewis and Stevie Tucker and Will and Kristina. Desolate, I went to bed early. Clinton had won, with Bush receiving only 37 percent of the vote. I recalled George saying playfully to an aide who disagreed with him, "If you're so smart, why aren't you president?" and my heart went out to him.

Back in Washington, things seemed normal for a while. I attended staff meetings at State every day, saw to problems at USIA, received visitors. Nonetheless, our power leached slowly away and I was again reminded of poet Matthew Arnold's line referring to a "melancholy long withdrawing roar."

At the office I became a one-man placement bureau, as our political employees whose jobs would be lost came asking for letters of recommendation and advice. Glad to help, I put up a good front. But the truth was that I didn't know what I myself would do. I had assumed that a place would be found at H & C, that I would get offers of corporate directorships, and that I could find speaking engagements, but as I put out feelers, the response was not overwhelming. Old friend banker Tom Frost asked me to join his holding company board and I accepted with alacrity. But speakers were a dime a dozen and I knew few corporate moguls. H & C was being dismantled, closing that door.

One thing we did decide—to sell our beloved McLean property and move back to Texas but with time in Colorado. It would mean separation from the Crespin family, which I deeply regretted, but keeping up a large establishment that we would seldom use made no sense. Sadly, we put the house on the market.

I did not view the looming Clinton administration with much hope.

His plan to send a special envoy to Northern Ireland was a gratuitous insult to our closest ally, Great Britain. His comments on Haitian refugees seemed ill-advised. Speculation about increased taxes gave me indigestion. The arrival at USIA of Penn Kemble, advance scout for the new administration, brought the forthcoming end of the Bush administration and my government service into startlingly clear relief. Fortunately, Penn was a thoroughgoing gentleman, and we cooperated with him in every way we could. He later became Gene Kopp's replacement as deputy director.

Witch-hunt

THE PHONE rang at home on the night of December 16. I answered and a voice identified himself as Robert Barrett, an attorney from Special Counsel Lawrence Walsh's office. He said the investigation of wrongdoing by my former boss, Caspar Weinberger, was at a critical stage and they wanted to talk to me. Would I come by their office? I declined that honor; if they wanted to talk, they could come to me. My contempt for what was happening to Cap knew no bounds, and I let it show in my voice. We set a date for 4:00 P.M. the following day at my office.

At the center of this legal storm lay charges by Democrats that Reagan had lied about trading arms for hostages in the Iran-Contra affair. Weinberger, secretary of defense at the time of the alleged offense, had testified, but doubts remained and Lawrence Walsh was named to investigate.

I could not imagine how I could be helpful to Barrett. I had left government long before the incident and knew nothing about it whatsoever. My interest was nonetheless piqued, and I looked forward to the visit.

At 4:00 P.M. on the dot the next afternoon, in came one James Brosnahan accompanied by an FBI agent named Michael S. Foster. Brosnahan's presence surprised me, for I had expected yesterday's caller, Barrett, to be there. Instead, here was Walsh's newly appointed right-hand man, fresh from the West with the light of burning martyrs in his eyes. The FBI man's presence there puzzled me as well.

Wasting no time, Brosnahan whipped out a paper and handed it to me. "This," he said, "is a transcript of a press briefing you gave in October 1982." I looked at it and it seemed to be just what he said. The briefing had opened with a question about a British gossip columnist suggesting Cap was romantically interested in a British historian and writer named Janet Morgan; one of the Pentagon reporters wanted to know if there was anything to it. My response dismissed the idea as absurd, and the questioning moved to other topics.

I wondered what in the world was going on. Events from a decade ago, with zero relevance to Cap's current problems, were being unearthed. But why?

At that moment, the theretofore stolid Mr. Foster produced a subpoena for me to testify in the case of the *United States of America v. Caspar W. Weinberger,* Crim. #92-0235. I was assured I would be paid forty dollars for my services. My visitors rose and left.

Thoroughly puzzled, I called Cap, who suggested I call Robert Bennett, his attorney, which I did the following day.

By the time I reached Bennett, the mists in my mind had begun to lift. The Brosnahan visit portended an attack on Weinberger's character, using the flippant question from a long-forgotten press briefing as a starting point. I had to hand it to Walsh's team: they were thorough — and they cost the taxpayers $30 million.

Bennett confirmed my thesis. The investigators had found reference in Cap's notes of calls to Oxford, where Morgan lived at the time, and of flowers sent to her. They called the florist. They called Frank Carlucci, Cap's Pentagon deputy and longtime associate, to see if Weinberger had a drinking or a drug problem. They even sent two investigators to Scotland, where Morgan lived, to ask her if she and Weinberger had had an affair, which she flatly denied.

The prosecutors had offered Cap a plea bargain: If he would implicate Reagan in a conspiracy, they would charge him with only a misdemeanor with no jail term. If he refused, it would be an indictment on five felony charges. Frustrated, Walsh and company had apparently concluded their case was flimsy and the only recourse was to attack Weinberger's totally unimpeachable character.

That afternoon, Judge Bill Clark called me from San Francisco, where he lived. A former high-ranking Reagan aide, he was helping to formulate Cap's defense. I told him (as I had told Bennett and Weinberger) that I felt I should let Bush know what had occurred; it might be important as the president studied whether or not to pardon Weinberger. Clark said Bush was likely worried how a pardon would look in the press, since Walsh planned to call both him and Reagan as witnesses at Cap's trial.

He feared my talk with Bush might complicate matters, making it look as if a pardon would be construed as Bush dodging an unpleasant public testimony. I countered that Bush should know of Walsh's tactics, and I suspected his sense of decency would be deeply offended.

It happened that the evening of December 17 I was going to the White House for the Bushes' annual Christmas party, probably my last visit to that old and beautiful house I had come to know so well. I called Patty Presock, the president's secretary, told her I needed to see the man, and suggested I might come by before the party. She called back, suggesting that I come by half an hour before the six-thirty event.

The president greeted me, and we went into the beautiful yellow sitting room on the second floor. Though he seemed distracted, he showed me plans for their new house to be built in Houston after their return; it was the only time he showed any animation during our visit.

Seated, I told him as succinctly as possible what had happened. He asked few questions but requested that I write a memo summing it all up. I left and went down to the party. The next day I went to the office, wrote the memo, and asked my driver, James Rayford, to take it to the White House. That afternoon I flew to San Antonio for Christmas. On Christmas Eve, George pardoned Weinberger and several others who had been accused. Three years later, Weinberger was still paying off the huge sum spent defending himself from what surely was a modern Salem witch-hunt.

Moving On

MY LAST days in government went quickly but sadly. I loved USIA. Often people asked my favorite job, assuming it would be the Court of St. James's. Not so; USIA's scope and variety and the quality of its people made it totally beguiling.

Gene Kopp and I had a farewell ceremony in the courtyard behind our building; the crowd was gratifyingly large and we made brief talks. In mine, I touched on the accomplishments and shortcomings of my 665 days. My goals had been to bring public diplomacy into the policy-making process, to have good relations with Congress, to define our objectives in the post–Cold War world, to publicize our work to the American public, and to find a new headquarters.⁶ On the second, third, fourth, and fifth, I felt good, but on the first, we had not wholly succeeded. I did feel, nonetheless, that the divisions that rent the agency had been healed and pride had been restored.

In closing my comments I quoted from columnist Ellen Goodman:

> There is a trick to the Graceful Exit. It begins with the vision to recognize when a job, a life stage, a relationship is over — and let it go. It means leaving what's over without denying its validity or past importance to our lives. It involves a sense of future, a belief that every exit line is an entry, that we are moving on rather than out.

I got through the talk with a steady voice, and we adjourned to the eighth-floor offices for a reception to which hundreds came to squeeze Gene's and my hands or give us hugs.

Goodman's words comforted me as I looked back on fifteen years of government work as exciting and varied as could be imagined. I worried, nonetheless, about returning to Texas, for I knew I would miss the challenges, the friends, the excitement of being near the action and being involved in a field — foreign affairs — that had mesmerized me since childhood. I worried about what I would do about the strains on our marriage. Jessica had gotten used to having me gone much of the time: could she put up with having me "home for lunch"?

Our new life did prove to be a challenge. Jessica and the children (and grandchildren) nonetheless rallied 'round. I joined the faculty at the University of Texas San Antonio as adjunct professor, I became active again in my family firm, and I began to write this book. I moved on, not out.

In 1995, the San Antonio World Affairs Council honored me as International Citizen of the Year, and Jim Baker came over from Houston to deliver the keynote address. In my brief acceptance, I told the audience that forty years ago I had read Thomas Wolfe's novel *You Can't Go Home Again*. Its message of a man's unsuccessful attempt to return to the roots of his hometown after years of wandering far from home had haunted me. I concluded that Wolfe was wrong; you can go home again. I know. I did it.

Notes

Part 2

1. Washington fired many Soviet FSNs after the bugging and spy scandals of the 1980s, and the Soviets withdrew the rest. Replacing them was vastly expensive and made running the embassy almost impossible, for the Americans who took the place of the Soviets knew little of Russian life.

2. U.S. embassies do not, as a rule, provide political asylum, so we were spared troublesome guests.

3. Many in the Spanish world use three names. First comes their given name, then their father's name, and finally their mother's maiden name. Thus Fidel Chávez Mena is "Mr. Chávez" or "Mr. Chávez Mena," but never "Mr. Mena."

4. Technically, the intruders were not violating diplomatic usage. Only the embassy itself is safe haven, not the residences of embassy employees. The Venezuelans were nonetheless furious, threatening to break off relations. In the end, they did not do so, and the matter was forgotten.

5. In 1980 Duarte was named provisional president, and in 1984 he was elected by the people in the country's first free and fair election.

6. *Duarte: My Story,* by José Napoleon Duarte (New York: G. P. Putnam's Sons, 1986), p. 82.

Part 3

1. Homelike. Americans expecting to find Yiddish understood in Israel are in for a surprise: it isn't, save among immigrants from Eastern Europe.

2. During the intermission, Generals Haig and Scowcroft, suffering ruffled feathers, I suspect, were added to the select few.

3. Perhaps something of national character could be divined by the names of leaders' airplanes. Richard Nixon's was dubbed *Spirit of '76;* Leone's was called *Mirafiore* (Look at the flowers).

4. Many years later, when I was ambassador to Britain, Safer presented the U.S. embassy in London with a sculpture in honor of Jessica and me.

5. In the Bush administration, Don, long retired from the CIA, returned to Seoul as U.S. ambassador.

6. As the emperor arrived at John D. Rockefeller's home, I heard him present younger brother David to His Majesty thus: "This is my brother David; he is connected with one of our banks." David was the chief executive of Chase Manhattan, the second-largest bank in America.

7. Curiously, the phrase is very common in Japanese, and it means the same thing in both languages.

8. A perhaps apocryphal story circulated after the speech. Senator James Eastland of Mississippi, on being asked what he thought of the swarthy Egyptian, was reported to have said, "I think he's a nigger," thus winning simultaneously the prize for biggest non sequitur and smallest mind.

9. Jessica sympathized. Over the years, she was pushed, elbowed, and harassed by single-minded Secret Service agents, oblivious in crowds to all save their protectee. She finally concluded that directness was the only way to get their attention. Once confronted, they tended to treat her more courteously.

10. I called to congratulate her in 1981 on the announcement of her appointment and to tell her a bit about the job. When I commented that it offered good opportunities for reporting to the State Department, she asked what I meant. I explained that the chief of protocol is often with foreigners and can learn things useful to the U.S. government. She asked, "You mean I should tell what the British queen said in private to me?" I replied, "Of course, if it is relevant to American foreign policy" (a very unlikely event, to be sure). With an indignant huff, she said, "Never!" We had differing conceptions of the job.

Part 4

1. In France and the United States, having a private instructor entitles one to break the lift lines. Not so in democratic Switzerland. Mr. Welten's elbows, however, accomplished what custom did not allow.

2. Marylou eventually became Cap's advance person and stayed at Defense during the eight years of Reagan's administration.

3. After retiring in 1987, Weinberger had to get used to flying on commercial aircraft, a comedown after the luxury of military flights that left on his schedule, not on the airlines'. I asked him how he was adjusting to civilian life. In mock astonishment he replied, "Do you know the airlines seat you next to total strangers?"

4. Quoted in *New York Magazine,* June 20, 1983.

Part 5

1. Howard once told me a story typifying State's rigidities. Unable to find a memo he had written, he called the Departmental Secretariat to ask for a copy. The person he reached checked the computer and told him, "Sorry, we can't oblige. You don't have security clearance for that topic."

2. Americans are fond of using the phrase "Court of St. James's" (though they frequently drop the apostrophe and the second "s"). Indeed, the official seat of the British monarchy is St. James's Palace, not Buckingham, though most court functions are held at the latter.

3. The cow, done by San Antonio sculptor Patsy Sturts, did not just happen. I told questioners she reminded me of home and promoted Texas art. More important, she gave me a chance to complain to Brits about the European Community's refusal to allow hormone-fed American cattle into Europe, for health reasons. The idea was absurd; the real reason for excluding our beef was protection of European cattle raisers.

4. Henry would subscribe to former Dallas district attorney Henry Wade's dictum: "If you can say it, don't write it. If you can cough, don't say it. If you can wink, don't cough."

5. Three weeks after the matter became public I got a postcard, postmarked New York City and reading, "Dear Ambassador: You may kiss my black ass. Sincerely, Dinky Dave." Clearly some crank was at work. A month was to pass before the mayor replied, telling me politely to mind my own business.

6. At least I hope it still is. The Clinton administration is reported to have deprived the British of intelligence in Bosnia. If that is true, and the old ties become frayed, we shall both be the losers.

7. The Germans could be snide about their Western allies as well. John Korn-

bloom, a U.S. official in NATO, told my staff meeting one morning of German bitterness toward the French. After a meeting of Western ambassadors in Berlin, a German asked wryly, "What are the three victorious powers and France going to do about Berlin?"

8. U.S. ambassador to Germany and former Marine general Vernon "Dick" Walters suffered similar problems; he eventually resigned in disgust. Our ambassador in Italy, Peter Secchia, canceled a dinner party for Treasury Secretary Nicholas Brady when Brady kept Secchia from a meeting with Italian officials.

9. Quoted in Hugo Young, *One of Us* (New York: Macmillan 1989), p. 543.

10. Ibid., p. 540.

11. Ibid., p. 544.

12. Ibid., 543.

13. The British custom is to call prime ministers just that: "Prime Minister." Americans, accustomed to saying "Mr. President," invariably attached "Mr." or "Madam" to the British title. I tried to warn visitors of the correct form, but the U.S. habit died hard.

14. Saudia Arabia's Prince Bandar bin Sultan, ambassador to the United States, had a huge and handsome home in Aspen.

15. I liked the wry Rifkind. I once asked how things were going. His answer: "We're just trying to reconcile net income with gross habits."

16. Marylou Sheils said, "Those weren't contrails behind my plane as it flew me back home; they were me dragging my feet."

Part 6

1. State Department complaints led in 1992 to a procedure by which VOA submitted its editorials to State for clearance, with assurances of rapid (twenty-four-hour) turnaround to avoid having them become stale. VOA officials were not happy, but I thought it a reasonable action for us to take.

2. A post–Cold War irony developed in Volgograd, formerly Stalingrad. VOA found an AM station there that wanted our programming for broadcast. The equipment the Russian station used to send out our signal had once been used by the communists to jam VOA.

3. Essays urging the voters of New York to approve the fledgling U.S. Constitution.

4. VOA was the country's only contact with the world, since BBC had given up its Albanian service and Radio Free Europe never had one.

5. I once asked Jim Baker, recently returned from a trip to South Africa, how the famous clergyman was. "So-so," quipped the quick-witted secretary of state.

6. One concrete accomplishment: I managed to install a gym for USIA employees, the one amenity in an otherwise inhospitable physical plant.

Index